NUMBER TWO HUNDRED AND THIRTY-FOUR

THE OLD FARMER'S ALMANAC

CALCULATED ON A NEW AND IMPROVED PLAN FOR THE YEAR OF OUR LORD

Being the 2nd after Leap Year and (until July 4) 250th year of American Independence

FITTED FOR BOSTON AND THE NEW ENGLAND STATES, WITH SPECIAL CORRECTIONS AND CALCULATIONS TO ANSWER FOR ALL THE UNITED STATES.

Containing, besides the large number of Astronomical Calculations and the Farmer's Calendar for every month in the year, a variety of NEW, USEFUL, & ENTERTAINING MATTER.

**ESTABLISHED IN 1792
BY ROBERT B. THOMAS (1766–1846)**

The time is alwa[...]
–Martin Luther King Jr., American civil rights leader (1929–68)

Cover design registered U.S. Trademark Office

Copyright © 2025 by Yankee Publishing Incorporated, a 100% Employee-Owned Company
ISSN 0078-4516

Library of Congress Card No. 56-29681

Cover illustration by Steven Noble • Original wood engraving (above) by Randy Miller

The Old Farmer's Almanac • Almanac.com
P.O. Box 520, Dublin, NH 03444 • 603-563-8111

CONTENTS

2026 TRENDS
Fun facts and forecasts defining today and describing tomorrow 6

ABOUT THIS ALMANAC
Contact Us	1, 98, 100
To Patrons	4

ADVENTURE
Land Ladies	28

AMUSEMENT
The Fish Scales of Justice	178
Essay Contest Winners	248
Mind-Manglers	250
Anecdotes & Pleasantries	252

ASTROLOGY
The Man of the Signs	198, 224
Secrets of the Zodiac	224
Best Days for 2026	226

ASTRONOMY
A Crash Course on Space Trash: Journey to the Junkosphere	48
Eclipses	102
Bright Stars	104
The Twilight Zone/ Meteor Showers	106
The Visible Planets	108
Astronomical Glossary	110
The Planets of the Solar System	112

CALENDAR
Three-Year Calendar	114
How to Use This Almanac	115
Calendar Pages	120–147

Holidays and Observances	148
Glossary of Almanac Oddities	150
Save the Dates	152
Tides	235, 236
Time Corrections	238
Glossary of Time	243

FARMING
More Eggs in More Baskets	40
Well-Grounded	70

FISHING
Get Knotty	182
Best Fishing Days and Times	228

FOOD
Recipe Contest Winners	54
Unfinished Business	184

GARDENING
Gear Up, Gardeners!	26
Stop and Smell the Houseplants	78
Eat Your Skirrets	160
Planting by the Moon's Phase	230
Frosts and Growing Seasons	232
Phenology: Nature's Calendar	233

HISTORY
Sewing Patriotism	166

HOME REMEDIES
Sweet Sensation	60

HUSBANDRY
Gestation and Mating Tables	229

MISCELLANY
Table of Measures	234
Reference Compendium	257

SPECIAL REPORT
Secrets of the Sugar Bush	192

SPORTS
The Swingingest Summer of All Time	170

WEATHER
Winter/Summer Weather Maps	96
General Weather Forecast	97
Cool Truths About Pingos	154
The Wonders of Weather	158
How We Predict the Weather	202
How Accurate Was Our Forecast Last Winter?	204
Weather Regions Map	205
Forecasts by Region	206–223

TO PATRONS

WEATHERING

The bedrock of this humble publication is our long-range weather predictions—correct, or close to it, much of the time. Founder Robert B. Thomas studied astronomy, basing his formula on the Sun's magnetic storm cycles, believing in the predictive power of data.

Weather has bound together *Almanac* readers ever since. You tell us that you depend on these pages for an outlook for your farm or garden, or because you're a stargazer, a mail carrier, or emergency personnel—anyone for whom the weather matters.

To read 234 years of the *Almanac* is to witness that the human condition is about weathering storms—both literal and allegorical—about coming through, persisting. How we endure matters. The *Almanac* finds greatness in the deeds of daily life, in expressing gratitude for simple gifts. In this spirit, this year's essayists (page 248) remind us that the best gifts come from the heart.

The noun weather is from the Old English and Dutch *weder*, meaning air, sky, breeze, as well as storm, tempest. The verb weather is linked to Middle English *wederen*, to expose to open air, to dry by airing.

Whether weathering foul weather, personal challenges, or a public crisis, time is the only fix we can count on. With time, everything changes—including the weather.

That's likely why *kairos*, the Greek word for time, was used to mean weather in the Byzantine era. The Latin *tempestas* also originally meant time, and words for time came to mean weather in Irish, *aimsir*, and Polish, *czas*.

Though we can accurately predict the weather (to about 80%), we can't forecast how the costs of paper and distribution will rise and fall. Therefore, your greatest gift to us is your continued patronage; together, we can weather any storm.

–C. C., June 2025

May this year's *Almanac* be worthy of its predecessors.

It is by our works and not our words that we would be judged. These, we hope, will sustain us in the humble though proud station we have so long held in the name of

Your obedient servant,

Rob. B. Thomas.

Illustration: ChrisGorgio/Getty Images

2026 TRENDS

ON THE FARM

Farmers are using new approaches to engage visitors—from mobile applications to help them find and connect with farms to adventure-themed activities that engage people in the landscape, like zip-lining and trails for e-biking.

–Jason Entsminger, assistant professor of entrepreneurship and innovation, University of Maine

FARMER FACTS

- **1,011,715:** the number of early-career farmers (10 or fewer years)
- **51%:** amount of beginning farmers who work off-farm 200 days or more each year
- **1,900,487:** Farms in the U.S.
- **880.1 million:** Acres of land being farmed

47.1: AVERAGE AGE OF A BEGINNING FARMER*

- **568,972:** Farms specializing in cattle and dairy production
- **463:** Average farm size, in acres

–USDA 2022 Census of Agriculture

AG-UCATION

Farmers-as-educators teach about food production . . .

- **On-farm:** Customers pay to learn cheese-making, olive-curing, or maple sugaring.
- **Virtually:** "Farmers are collaborating with influencers as well as making use of short-form videos on social media,"

*USDA 2022 Census of Agriculture

FUN FACTS AND FASCINATING FORECASTS DEFINING TODAY AND DESCRIBING TOMORROW

Compiled by Stacey Kusterbeck

says Sarah Cornelisse, senior Extension program specialist at Penn State University.

- **In classrooms:** Older students follow a cow's life for a year; younger ones create informational booklets about farm animals, decorated with samples of wool, hay, or chicken feed.

GROWING HOPE

- **54%** of farmers are feeling more optimistic than the year before.

- **90%** of them would recommend their children enter the agricultural profession.

- Farmers' top three challenges are commodity/livestock prices, input costs, and government regulations.
–Missouri Farm Bureau

AG-VENTURE

Agritourism is a booming industry. It runs the gamut from pumpkin patches, corn mazes, farms that host bed and breakfasts, farmers' markets, roadside farm markets, U-pick orchards and berry farms, event barns for weddings and meetings, Christmas tree farms, fee hunting and fishing, and trail riding.
–Garrett Hawkins, president, Missouri Farm Bureau

FOLLOW THE DOLLARS

At 162 farms in Oregon's Willamette Valley region:

- **8** additional employees were hired, on average, to support agritourism activities.

- **34%** of farm visitors traveled over 50 miles.

$87,484: AVERAGE SALES PER FARM RELATED TO AGRITOURISM*

SHELLING OUT

- Of the 3,453 aquaculture farms in the U.S., oysters are raised on 900 of them, crawfish on 751, and catfish on 398.
–USDA 2023 Census of Aquaculture

Aquatourists dive in and learn about fish farming:

- **Oyster farms** offer kayak tours, with paddlers learning to shuck oysters before eating them.

- **Lobster farms** have tourists haul traps, measure catch, band

*Oregon's Willamette Valley region

2026 TRENDS

claws, and bait pots to return to the ocean.

■ **Oyster farmers** are using biosensors to monitor *oyster gape* (the space between the two sides of an oyster shell) to detect when oysters are stressed and intervening by moving oysters into deeper water during heat waves.

HEAT BEATERS

■ Researchers are engineering fruits and vegetables that survive and thrive in high temperatures and drought.

■ **In development:** potatoes that produce higher yields during heat stress; apples and pears that thrive in hot climates.

ALMOND TREES AND HONEYBEES

■ **2.6 million** is the number of honeybee hives needed to pollinate almond trees in California (2 hives per acre).

■ Almond growers are planting flowering cover crops that bloom before, during, and after the almond trees to provide added nutrition for honeybees.

LAND HO MY!

■ Top states for cropland value per acre:
California: **$17,330**
New Jersey: **$16,300**
Florida: **$10,170**

■ **$4,170:** the average price per acre of U.S. farm real estate (including all land and buildings)
–USDA 2024 Land Values Summary

MY LAND IS YOUR LAND

■ The British Columbia Land Matching Program has made 362 matches on 12,600 acres of land. Farmers who want land to start or expand agricultural operations are connected with landholders looking for someone to farm their land. The two parties agree on mutually beneficial terms.

FARMERS MARKETING

■ Farmers are differentiating themselves from competitors via social media platforms, value-added products with unique packaging, CSA boxes with recipe cards, and produce pop-up shops at retail stores.

"For small farms, most of the marketing and branding is being done by the farmers or farm employees themselves, since margins are narrow and hiring a marketing firm is likely cost prohibitive,"

Crafted for Beauty.
Built to Last.

Nature thrives when given the right space to flourish.

So does great design. At Outdoor Living Today, we blend expert craftsmanship with the natural beauty of sustainably sourced Western Red Cedar, creating structures that enhance your outdoor space for years to come. Whether it's a charming pergola, a robust garden shed, or a raised garden bed brimming with life, our handcrafted designs bring your vision to life with quality you can rely upon.

Trust the craftsmanship of Outdoor Living Today and (Re)discover your space™.

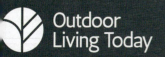

2026 TRENDS

says Shannon Rauter, small farms coordinator at Oregon State University Extension Service.

OLD APPLES, NEW TRICKS

■ **On farms:** Farmers are creating new orchards from old apple trees by grafting heirloom varieties to rootstock or by obtaining saplings of rare trees.

■ **In backyards:** Homeowners with apple trees are starting cider-making businesses.

WORKING OUT THE BUGS

■ Farmers are using ants in fruit orchards because the antimicrobial bacteria and fungi on the insects' feet are thought to improve crop health. To boost ant populations, companies are building rope bridges between trees to help ants get around and enticing them with sugar-water solutions in fields.

10,800 COMMERCIAL FARMS GREW FLOWERS AND GREENS FOR USE BY FLORISTS*

BUSINESS IS BLOOMING!

■ **Cut flowers:** "Farmers can set their flowers apart from mass-marketed imports by choosing varieties that do not ship well or by focusing on popular local trends and color palettes," says Rachel Painter, farm management specialist at the University of Tennessee Extension. She recommends:

LISIANTHUS

lisianthus; snapdragons; peonies; and specialty tulips in muted peach, deep burgundy, or orange tones.

■ **Custom floral arrangements:** "Cut flower farms can capture more of the consumer dollar by taking on the role of both the farmer and the florist, to meet the needs of the customer willing to pay for a particular flower, design, or service," says Painter.

■ **Flower festivals** are transforming farms into destinations. "Visitors can capture perfect social media moments among the blooms and experience the joy of handpicking their own beautiful bouquets," says Angie Day, spokesperson, International Agritourism Association.

(continued)

*USDA 2022 Census of Agriculture

It's Time to Fight the **Bites!**

Mosquito Dunks®
Kills mosquitoes *before* they're old enough to bite!®

CHEMICAL FREE!
Biological *BTI* Control
100% NATURAL
100% EFFECTIVE

- Kills mosquito larvae and nothing else —contains BTI.
- Use for *long term control*—30 days or more.
- Use in bird baths, rain barrels, ponds—or any standing water.

FOR ORGANIC PRODUCTION

Kills Mosquitoes that Transmit Viruses — ZIKA, WEST NILE & EEE

Mosquito Bits®

- **WORKS FAST** — *Quick Kill mosquito larvae* in any standing water.
- **Harmless to people, plants & pets.**
- **Small granules** — perfect for hard to treat areas like planter saucers.
- Use for *broad coverage* in low-lying swampy areas.

Summit®
Tick & Flea Spray

- *Quickly kills Ticks & Fleas* — including Deer Ticks (which carry Lyme Disease).
- **Spray tick and flea habitats** such as the yard perimeter and weedy, bushy areas.

Summit® ...*responsible solutions.*
800.227.8664   SummitResponsibleSolutions.com

MADE IN AMERICA

Summit ... *responsible solutions*®, Year Round® Spray Oil, Mosquito Dunks®, and Mosquito Bits® are registered trademarks of Summit Chemical Company.

2026 TRENDS

IN THE GARDEN

Gardeners are choosing garden practices that reflect their values. For some, it is an eye on sustainability, using fewer resources to garden, and growing their own fruits and vegetables. For others, it is a focus on the environment; gardening to provide food and shelter for wildlife and pollinators.

–Sharon Yiesla, plant knowledge specialist, The Morton Arboretum

WHAT WE DIG
- Plantings in the front yard to improve curb appeal
- Creating vegetable gardens
- Adding outdoor lighting

–Axiom Gardening Outlook Study

HOW WE DIG
- **41%** of gardeners say lack of time is the number one reason they don't garden more.
- Gardeners found the highest quality plants—and the most knowledgeable store associates—at independent garden centers.

–Axiom Gardening Outlook Study

56% OF GARDENERS PLAN TO EXPAND THEIR GARDENS IN THE COMING YEAR*

HOUSEPLANT HAPPY
- "The trend for houseplants has not slowed down a bit. Interior gardeners are not only embracing longtime favorites, like philodendrons, they are looking for newer types of houseplants," says Yiesla. In demand: different species and cultivars of figs, money plant, and cacti and succulents.

*Axiom Gardening Outlook Study

2026 TRENDS

EASY PICKINGS

Gardeners want fast-growing, pick-and-eat crops such as microgreens, cherry tomatoes, dwarf strawberries, and compact peppers. These new snack gardens aren't just for eating—they're for aesthetic enjoyment, wellness, and social sharing.
–Katie Dubow, president, Garden Media Group

PURPLE PASSION

- "We're seeing a lot of fun colors, especially purples—and great vegetables for snacking and salads," says Jaclyn Johnsen, spokesperson at Jung Seed Company.

Delectable edibles include:
- 'Rosa Bianca' eggplant: mild flavor; lavender and white color
- 'Purple Magic' broccoli: purple florets and stems; perfect for snacking

- 'El Camino' cucumber: high-yielding; holds well after harvest (allowing more time for canning)

ON-TREND GARDENERS:

- Tend to soil health by composting and planting cover crops (clover and buckwheat) between growing seasons
- Use every inch of available space, adding plants to windowsills, vertical trellises, and wall gardens
- Are heat savvy, choosing heat- and drought-resistant varieties (coneflowers, hesperaloes, and salvias)
- Create living fences, replacing traditional fencing with shrubs, vines, and evergreens

–Megan Proska, director of horticulture, Dallas Arboretum

YARD GUARDIANS

Gardeners are working hard to remove invasive species—burning bush, exotic honeysuckles, round leaf bittersweet, and Norway maple. They're battling buckthorn, introduced as an ornamental landscape plant but now considered a noxious weed, and replacing it with nannyberry and juneberry.
–Julie Weisenhorn, Extension educator, University of Minnesota Landscape Arboretum

WATER WORKS

- People are planting native perennials and ground covers and using river rock swales and permeable pavers that divert rainwater away from the house

2026 TRENDS

and filter it into the garden. In Ontario, Canada: "Gardeners are choosing native perennials and ground covers that can tolerate both wet and dry conditions: Butterflyweed, prairie smoke, black-eyed Susan, wild columbine, big bluestem, and little bluestem," reports Tara Nolan, co-founder of savvygardening.com.

PRAIRIE SMOKE

GOODBYE, GRASS!
■ **Homeowners** are eliminating lawns little by little, replacing narrow strips in full sun with a mix of perennials, leaving space for the odd tomato plant (with a fancy cage to make it look ornamental), or using herbs like lemon thyme as edging plants. "Don't eliminate all of your grass until you have a plan in place to fill that space immediately," says Nolan.

LEMON THYME

■ **Municipalities** are paying people to replace lawn with pollinator-friendly native plants (e.g., clover, honeysuckle, thistle). In Minnesota, a program emphasizes protection of its state bee, the rusty patched bumble bee.

LEAFING THEM ALONE
■ Gardeners have stopped bagging and removing leaves and are making good use of them instead. "Homeowners are increasingly opting to mulch leaves with lawn mowers and leave them on site to decompose, enriching the soil and reducing waste. Leaf composting is also gaining traction," says Ankit K. Singh, assistant Extension professor, APS Laboratory for Sustainable Agriculture, University of Maine.

YARD AU NATUREL
■ We're dedicating parts of our properties as "wild zones." This can be as simple as leaving a pile of leaves undisturbed in a back corner of the yard. Homeowners are using borders, plantings, or signage to make it clear that the wildness is intentional. "This is helping to shift the perception of 'neat' yards as more people embrace natural landscaping and appreciate the ecological benefits of less manicured spaces," says Singh.

(continued)

2026 TRENDS

GOOD EATS

Today's indulgent-minded consumer wants restaurant-quality meals at home. People don't want bland microwaved meals—they want sensory experiences that deliver gratification and pleasure, even in their own kitchens.
–Leana Salamah, spokesperson, Specialty Food Association

FLAVORS WE CRAVE
- syrup from beech, birch, sycamore, and walnut trees
- cucumber-flavored vinegar
- lavender-flavored cheese, honey, and tea
- black garlic

NORTHERN NOSHERS
- **57%** of Canadians eat breakfast every day.
- **6%** of Canadians never eat breakfast.
- **7** is the average number of trips Canadians make to the grocery store per month.

5% OF CANADIANS VISIT A GROCERY STORE DAILY*

- Canadians are using "food-rescuing" apps to buy discounted surplus food or food that's about to expire.
–Agri-Food Analytics Lab, Dalhousie University

PEOPLE ARE JAWING ABOUT:
- **Dining alone:** Solo restaurant reservations have risen 29% in the past 2 years in the U.S., according to OpenTable. Restaurants are offering communal tables and counter seats for parties of one.
- **Grocerants:** Grocery stores are offering in-store eating options and prepared foods as an affordable alternative to restaurants.

YES, YOU CAN CAN
- Libraries are loaning out equipment for food preservation, including steam juicers, pressure

*Agri-Food Analytics Lab, Dalhousie University

OW DOES YOUR GARDEN GROW?

USE CODE ALMANAC FOR 20% OFF AT SIMPLYGRO.COM

2026 TRENDS

canners, and dehydrators. Borrowers can learn how to use the equipment safely via free workshops.

AL FRESCO CHEFS

■ Many homeowners have a backyard grill. "We're seeing homeowners embrace other outdoor cooking methods as well," says Lindsey Reigel, spokesperson for Houzz. They're adding pizza ovens, smokers, deep fryers, ceramic kamado-style barbecues, and Argentinian-style gaucho grills that use wood or charcoal.

FLOWERY FLAVORS

■ People are incorporating calendula, nasturtiums, pansies, and violets into meals as garnishes, cocktail enhancers, and flavor boosters. "From petal-infused vinegars and floral ice cubes to edible bouquets and pressed flower cookies, the food-meets-flower movement is inspiring Instagram-worthy kitchen creativity," says Katie Dubow, president of Garden Media Group.

TO OUR HEALTH

We'll evolve beyond the find-it, fix-it, 'whack a mole' medicine that pays for treating more disease, with direct to primary care, an innovative business model that allows primary care physicians to focus on the context of a person through an ongoing, trusting relationship.

–David Rakel, MD, chair, Department of Family Medicine and Community Health, UW School of Medicine and Public Health

2026 TRENDS

WE EAT, WE FEEL
■ **90%** of Americans say what they eat and drink affects their emotional well-being.
–International Food Information Council, 2024 Food and Health Survey

HEALING ARTS
■ **Museum visits** are being prescribed by doctors who believe exposure to history, art, and culture will positively impact their patients' health.

■ **Quietcations** feature peace and quiet in natural settings, with the goal of improving travelers' health.

■ **Music** can affect the way we remember past events, specifically casting them in a more positive light.

LONG MAY WE LIVE
■ **Healthspan:** the number of years we spend in good health

■ "Advances in biomarkers, AI-powered diagnostics, and consumer wearables, and a growing emphasis on prevention, are reshaping how we approach aging. We're enabling earlier detection, personalized feedback, and, in some cases, delaying or preventing the onset of age-related conditions."
–Diane Ty, Managing Director, Milken Institute Future of Aging

SLEEP ON IT
■ **At-home sleep tests** offer an affordable way to evaluate sleep in a familiar environment.

■ **Smart mattresses** track sleep and vitals to automatically adjust temperature and firmness.

■ **Monitoring devices** discern our sleep patterns, heart rate, heart rate variability, and oxygen saturation to reveal overall sleep quality; some also offer meditation, breathing exercises, and coaching programs.
–The Media and Innovation Lab, University of Miami Miller School of Medicine

46: NUMBER OF MINUTES OF EXTRA SLEEP THAT CAN MAKE US FEEL MORE RESILIENT AND GRATEFUL*

HIGH-TECH HEALTH
■ **Bathmats** and **floor tiles** with pressure sensors that monitor our gait and posture

■ **Mouthguards** containing microrobots that form different shapes to brush and floss teeth

■ **Tooth gel** that regenerates enamel

■ **Bandages** that deliver a zap of electricity to speed healing or apply antibiotics stored in a small capsule

(continued)

*The Media and Innovation Lab, University of Miami Miller School of Medicine

2026 TRENDS

OUR ANIMAL FRIENDS

Consumers are looking for more ways to include their pets in their lives, whether it be while they travel, work, or play. We'll see more dogs and cats at workplaces, in hotels, and in outdoor dining and retail spaces.
–*Steve Feldman, president, Human Animal Bond Research Institute*

WHO LETS THE DOGS OUT

- **17,800:** number of self-employed workers in pet care services (e.g., dog walking, cat sitting)
–*U.S. Bureau of Labor Statistics*

- Of U.S. households:
46% own dogs
32% own cats
3% own fish
2% own birds
1% own rabbits
–*AVMA Pet Ownership and Demographics Survey*

CATS V. DOGS

- **$1,740:** yearly expenditures for dog-owning households

- **$1,311:** yearly expenditures for cat-owning households

- **$580:** average annual vet bill for dogs
–*AVMA Pet Ownership and Demographics Survey*

$433: AVERAGE ANNUAL VET BILL FOR CATS*

LEADING BREEDS

- **Dogs:** Labrador, Chihuahua, Golden Retriever

- **Cats:** Persian, British Shorthair, Siamese
–*Mars Global Pet Parent Study*

PETS ON HOLIDAY

- Pet owners are using apps to plan vacations around businesses that allow pets.

- Owner-and-dog cruises include dog

*AVMA Pet Ownership and Demographics Survey

RECLAIM YOUR YARD & GARDEN

Natural. Effective. Targeted.

Our patented strain of Bt is:
- Highly effective at controlling grub, beetle, weevil & borer invaders.
- Safe for kids, pets, bees, butterflies, ladybugs, birds, fish & earthworms.
- Used in organic farming; so use beetleGONE! in your fruit and vegetable garden, too!

grubGONE!® G OMRI LISTED
Spread Granule. Irrigate into Turf.

beetleGONE!® tlc
FOR ORGANIC GARDENING
Mix With Water. Apply to Foliage, Soil, or Turf.

Use grubGONE! during springtime to control grubs that have overwintered and are now feeding on the roots of your turf.

Apply beetleGONE! on foliage in order to control beetles feeding on fruits, vegetables, roses & other ornamental flowers, plants & trees.

Apply grubGONE! in midsummer or fall to control newly hatched grubs & prevent turf damage caused by secondary foragers while also reducing the grub population before next year.

grubGONE!.G	beetleGONE!.tlc	grubGONE!.G
Spring Through Late June	Late June to Mid-August	July to Mid-October

The New Standard for PERFORMANCE & SAFETY

- Target grubs with the High-Performing, Natural Protein BTG & kill grubs within days
- Adding to the power of BTG are 1000x more spores per pound than Milky Spore® Products.
- Does not contaminate soil or groundwater, nor put your children and pets at risk.
- Controls the grubs of all Scarab beetles & other listed turf insects, not just Japanese beetles.
- No need to sacrifice the high performance of leading chemicals for safety.
- Much higher performance than oils, nematodes & milky spore products.
- Better than GrubEx® (chlorantraniliprole) in the Summer and Fall.

Target the Pest . . . Not the Rest!®
APPLY EVEN WHEN BEES AND OTHER BENEFICIALS ARE ACTIVE

BUY NOW >>> beetleGONE.com

Growers, Landscapers & Arborists

Effectively target devastating insects such as: all Scarab Grubs & Beetles, Annual Bluegrass Weevils, Billbugs, Leaf & Darkling Beetles, Weevils Like Alfalfa & Rice Water, Borers like Emerald Ash & Oak and more!!

FOR PRICING CALL: 650-296-2574

made in USA

beetleGONE!® ag
FOR ORGANIC PRODUCTION
Kills a variety of agricultural crop insect pests.

2026 TRENDS

shows, costume contests, and parades.

- **34%** of dog owners took their dogs on three or more trips by car, and **22%** on three or more trips by plane.
- **31%** of cat owners own leashes, and **23%** own harnesses.

–American Pet Products Association's 2024 Dog and Cat Report

ANIMAL PHARM

- More companies will allow employees to take time off to care for a sick or new pet and will offer pet health insurance as a benefit.

–Feldman

CANADIAN PET PARENTS

- **70%** are single-animal homes
- **30%** have multiple pets

–2024 Pets Canada Survey

SMALLER IS BIGGER

There is a rise in ownership of small birds and rabbits. People are seeking companionship from pets that are manageable and fit well into a variety of living situations, including urban environments.

–Peter Scott, president, American Pet Products Association

CATS, ASCENDANT

Cats are now a defining presence in our homes and culture, and they're poised to become a focal point of the pet industry.

2,170,271: CATS ADOPTED FROM U.S. SHELTERS AND RESCUES IN 2024*

This shift is in large part driven by the Gen Z and Millennial generations, who gravitate toward pets that align with their lifestyles. Cats' independent, quirky, and loyal nature makes them a perfect fit. Many people are choosing to welcome multiple felines into their homes.

–Dr. Whitney Miller, chief veterinarian, Petco

PAMPERED PETS

We dote on our pet companions:

- **63%** of us designed a specific part of our homes for our pets.
- **51%** of us purchased a pet stroller or carrier.
- **53%** of us commissioned a custom portrait of our pet.

–The State of Pets: Unpacking America's Pet Preferences: The Harris Poll

*Shelter Animals Count

SAVE UP TO **80% off** your prescription drugs

NEW customers receive 25% off their first order, up to $250!

FEATURED PRODUCT
Apixaban (generic Eliquis)

Apixaban - 2.5mg - 60 tablets	$67.99
Apixaban - 5mg - 56 tablets	$62.99
Eliquis - 2.5mg - 56 tablets	$127.99
Eliquis - 5mg - 60 tablets	$156.99

Product may not be exactly as shown. Price subject to change without notice.

Drug	Dose	Quantity	Price
Xarelto	20mg	90 tablets	$104.99
Farxiga	10mg	100 tablets	$132.99
Ozempic*	0.25mg/0.5mg	2 pens	$863.99
Wegovy Flextouch*	0.25mg	1 pen	$765.99
Cialis	5mg	90 tablets	$46.99
Viagra	100mg	32 tablets	$48.99
Rybelsus*	14mg	90 tablets	$1,199.99
Jardiance	10mg	90 tablets	$143.99
Gemtesa*	75mg	90 tablets	$371.99

* Items marked with an Asterix are name-brands, all others are generic equivalents. Prices as of June 1, 2025, subject to change without notice.

Call or visit our website to start saving today!
1-800-267-2688 or buy online at
www.TotalCareMart.com

ADVERTISEMENT

Choose Life
Grow Young with HGH

From the landmark book *Grow Young with HGH* comes the most powerful, over-the-counter health supplement in the history of man. Human growth hormone was first discovered in 1920 and has long been thought by the medical community to be necessary only to stimulate the body to full adult size and, therefore, unnecessary past the age of 20. Recent studies, however, have overturned this notion completely, discovering instead that the natural decline of Human Growth Hormone (HGH) from ages 21 to 61 (the average age at which there is only a trace left in the body) is the main reason why the body ages and fails to regenerate itself to its 25-year-old biological age.

Like a picked flower cut from the source, we gradually wilt physically and mentally and become vulnerable to a host of degenerative diseases that we simply weren't susceptible to in our early adult years.

Modern medical science now regards aging as a disease that is treatable and preventable and that "aging", the disease, is actually a compilation of various diseases and pathologies: everything from a rise in blood glucose and pressure to diabetes, skin wrinkling, and so on. All of these aging symptoms can be stopped and rolled back by maintaining Growth Hormone levels in the blood at the same HGH levels we had when we were 25 years old.

There is a receptor site in almost every cell in the human body for HGH, so

New! Doctor Recommended
The Reverse Aging Miracle

RELEASE YOUR OWN GROWTH HORMONE AND ENJOY:

- Improved sleep & emotional stability
- Increased energy & exercise endurance
- Loss of body fat
- Increased bone density
- Improved memory & mental alertness
- Increased muscle strength & size
- Reverses baldness & restores color
- **Regenerates Immune System**

- Strengthened heart muscle
- Controlled cholesterol
- **Normalizes blood pressure**
- Controlled mood swings
- Wrinkle disappearance
- Reverses many degenerative disease symptoms
- Heightened five senses awareness
- Increased skin thickness & texture

All Natural Formula

This program will make a radical difference in your health, appearance, and outlook. In fact, we are so confident of the difference GHR can make in your life that we offer a 100% refund on unopened containers.

1-877-849-4777
www.biehealth.us
BIE Health Products
3840 East Robinson Rd.
Box 139
Amherst, NY 14228

A Product of Global Health Products

DIV 2037839 ON

ADVERTISEMENT

its regenerative and healing effects are very comprehensive.

Growth Hormone, first synthesized in 1985 under the Reagan Orphan Drug Act, to treat dwarfism, was quickly recognized to stop aging in its tracks and reverse it to a remarkable degree. Since then, only the lucky and the rich have had access to it at the cost of $10,000 US per year.

The next big breakthrough was to come in 1997 when a group of doctors and scientists, developed an all-natural source product that would cause your own natural HGH to be released again and do all the remarkable things it did for you in your 20s—now available to every adult for about the price of a coffee and donut a day.

GHR is now available in America, just in time for the aging Baby Boomers and everyone else from age 30 to 90 who doesn't want to age rapidly but would rather stay young, beautiful, and healthy all of the time.

The new HGH releasers are winning converts from the synthetic HGH users as well, since GHR is just as effective, is oral instead of self-injectable, and is very affordable.

GHR is a natural releaser, has no known side effects, unlike the synthetic version, and has no known drug interactions. Progressive doctors admit that this is the direction medicine is seeking to go; to get the body to heal itself instead of employing drugs. GHR is truly a revolutionary paradigm shift in medicine and, like any modern leapfrog advance, many others will be left in the dust holding their limited or useless drugs and remedies.

It is now thought that HGH is so comprehensive in its healing and regenerative powers that it is today where the computer industry was twenty years ago—that it will displace so many prescription and nonprescription drugs and health remedies is staggering to comprehend.

The president of BIE Health Products stated in a recent interview, "I've been waiting for these products since the 70s. We knew they would come if only we could stay healthy and live long enough to see them! If you want to stay on top of your game physically and mentally as you age, this product is a boon, especially for the highly skilled professionals who have made large investments in their education and experience. Also, with the failure of Congress to honor our seniors with a pharmaceutical coverage policy, it's more important than ever to take proactive steps to safeguard your health. Continued use of GHR will make a radical difference in your health. HGH is particularly helpful to the elderly who, given a choice, would rather stay independent in their own home, strong, healthy, and alert enough to manage their own affairs, exercise, and stay involved in their communities. Frank, age 85, walks two miles a day, plays golf, belongs to a dance club for seniors, has a girlfriend again and doesn't need Viagra, passed his driver's test, and is hardly ever home when we call—GHR delivers."

HGH is known to relieve symptoms of Asthma, Angina, Chronic Fatigue, Constipation, Lower back pain and Sciatica, Cataracts and Macular Degeneration, Menopause, Fibromyalgia, Regular and Diabetic Neuropathy, Hepatitis, and helps Kidney Dialysis and Heart and Stroke recovery.

**For more information or to order call
877-849-4777
www.biehealth.us**

These statements have not been evaluated by the FDA. Copyright © 2000. Code OFA.

GARDEN ESSENTIALS

Gear Up, Gardeners!

GET SHARP, HOE DOWN, AND WASH UP

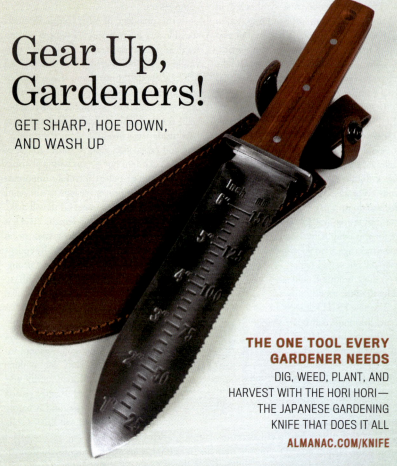

THE ONE TOOL EVERY GARDENER NEEDS
DIG, WEED, PLANT, AND HARVEST WITH THE HORI HORI— THE JAPANESE GARDENING KNIFE THAT DOES IT ALL
ALMANAC.COM/KNIFE

If you're like us, you love spending time in the garden admiring your flowers, herbs, and veggies, and maybe even doing a few "garden patrols" to check on daily progress.

On your rounds, the handiest tool to keep by your side is the Hori Hori Knife. This Japanese-inspired multi-tool makes quick work of all sorts of everyday garden tasks. Deadhead a coneflower. Relocate a volunteer. Pop out a dandelion. Scrape away shallow-rooted weeds. Saw off a dead branch. Plant a bulb.

It's sturdy, sharp, and surprisingly versatile—once you start using it, you'll wonder how you ever gardened without it.

Photo: Nicole Melanson

SMART DESIGN. SERIOUS WEEDING POWER.

THE BRIDGETOWN HANDY HOE

- Modern, angled head slices through soil and tough weeds
- Sharp edges dig, weed, and uproot with ease
- Compact size is perfect for tight spots and raised beds

ALMANAC.COM/HOE

SCRUB AWAY THE DIRT—KEEP THE GREEN THUMB!
THE OLD FARMER'S ALMANAC GARDENER'S SCRUB
- Cleans deep with the natural exfoliating power of apricot seeds and coffee grounds
- Softens skin with rich, nourishing shea butter
- Awakens the senses with a bright citrus-lavender scent

ALMANAC.COM/SCRUB

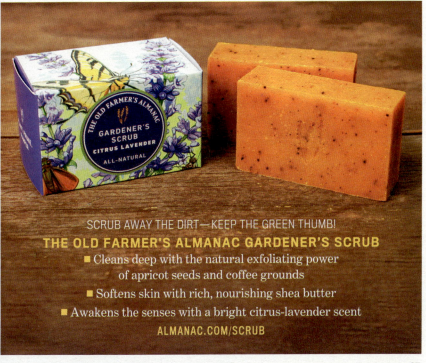

Photos, from top: Nicole Melanson; Lori Pedrick

ADVENTURE-WORTHY GARDENS AND THE WOMEN WHO MADE THEM

ADVENTURE

LAND LADIES

Landscape design history is dominated by the stories of men, yet these long-established gardens were, and still are, the provenance of pioneering women.

BY SUSAN PEERY

LISTENING TO LIGHT

The terraced gardens of Dumbarton Oaks in Washington, D.C., are the legacy of landscape architect Beatrix Farrand and Mildred Bliss. Farrand and Bliss formed a friendship and professional relationship that lasted 3 decades as they developed the property. Oakdom, as Farrand nicknamed the site, has blazes of forsythia and wisteria as well as forest glades in subdued palettes. The duo created a garden distinguished by vistas—with Bliss writing about Farrand's direction, "She 'listened' to the light and wind and grade of each area." Bliss, with her husband, Robert, purchased the property in Georgetown in 1920. It was transferred to Harvard University in 1940 and is now a research center dedicated to Byzantine and pre-Columbian studies and the history of landscape architecture.

Women continue to lead in the care and development of the garden. Thaïsa Way, director of garden and landscape studies, brings a deep knowledge of Dumbarton Oaks and its importance to her field. Farrand and the garden were a focus

Photos, opposite from top: Dumbarton Oaks; KidFriendly DC; KidFriendly DC. Above: National Park Service

ADVENTURE

FARRAND UNDERSTOOD THAT "THE LANDSCAPE WAS A LIVING WORK OF ART. . . . SHE MADE CLEAR THAT AS THE GARDENS MATURED, THE DESIGN INTENTIONS WOULD NEED TO BE TENDED AND STEWARDED."

of Way's first book, *Unbounded Practice: Women and Landscape Architecture in the Early Twentieth Century* (2009). In her introduction to *Garden as Art: Beatrix Farrand at Dumbarton Oaks* (2022), she writes that Farrand understood that "the landscape was a living work of art. In her guide to the stewardship of the property . . . she made clear that as the gardens matured, the design intentions would need to be tended and stewarded."

VISIT: *Open afternoons, Tuesday through Sunday, year-round; admission is free November 1 through the end of February. Doaks.org*

EAST MEETS WEST

Flight was in its infancy when Marion Beck took to the skies to find her perfect garden plot. From a cockpit, she spotted the land surrounding Tyrrel Lake in Millbrook, New York. It would become Innisfree, a dreamy, peaceful, strolling garden with 185 acres of native plants, mature trees, water lilies, and boulders surrounding the glacial lake.

Beck, an avid gardener with a vast knowledge of botany, purchased the property in the 1920s. Soon after, she and her husband, Walter, began developing a design inspired by an 8th-century scroll painting depicting the garden of poet and painter Wang Wei. In the late 1930s, the Becks started working with Lester

30

Photo: KidFriendly DC

CELEBRATING 100 years
OF LAND & LIFESTYLE REAL ESTATE EXPERTISE

Since 1925, United Country has led the way in country and lifestyle real estate, specializing in land, farms, ranches, horse properties, certified organic properties, recreational land, country homes and the most sought-after lifestyle real estate across the nation.

800.999.1020
UnitedCountry.com

Discover What A Century's Worth Of Expertise & Knowledge Can Do For You

ADVENTURE

Collins, who would later chair Harvard's landscape architecture program. Together, they developed this romantic landscape's stonework, waterfalls, and small vistas. After the Becks' deaths in the late 1950s, Collins transformed Innisfree into a public garden.

A modern-day horticultural pioneer continues the legacy: Kate Kerin has been Innisfree's landscape curator since 2013, having spent her career studying, preserving, teaching about, and designing landscapes, especially historical ones. Kerin describes Innisfree as cinematic —a space that is very much about our bodies in motion, experiencing the garden's narrative. "Taking two steps can completely change what something looks like, and that's on purpose."

VISIT: *Open late April through mid-November; special programs highlight celestial events, such as full Moons, meteor showers, and equinoxes. Innisfreegarden.org*
(continued)

Photos, from top: Innisfree; Innisfree; National Park Service

ADVENTURE

OPENING DOORS

Sarah Pearson Duke had a reputation for her gardening and her generosity. The spouse of tobacco tycoon Benjamin N. Duke, she helped design the campus of Durham, North Carolina's Duke University. After her husband's death, Duke donated $20,000 to establish her eponymous garden, begun in a debris-filled ravine. It took the design vision of Ellen Biddle Shipman, a foremost garden architect of the early 20th century, to realize the site's full potential.

Dedicated in 1939, the botanical garden fills a broad range of educational and cultural purposes. Five miles of allées, paths, and walkways wind among gardens devoted to roses, native plants, historic collections, East Asian plants, and other specialties. In one of her garden notebooks, now

Photos, from top: Jonathan Fredin/Cary Magazine; Find a Grave; Jonathan Fredin/Cary Magazine

GOD'S REMEDY for a World GONE *MAD*

With powerful nations fighting within while threatening to destroy one another, many believe we are nearing the prophecy of Matthew 24 when, *"There will be a **great tribulation**, such as has not occurred since the beginning of the world ... and if those days had not been cut short, no life would be saved."* Will peace ever come, or will we destroy each other? There **is** hope. Read about the promise which says *"... those days **will** be cut short."*

See what the Bible says in:

"God's Remedy for a World Gone Mad"

Request your FREE 24-page booklet

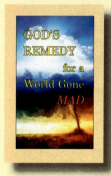

DAWN PUBLISHING
PO BOX 521167
LONGWOOD, FL 32752
800-234-3296
dawnbible@aol.com

Read online at
www.DawnBible.com

ADVENTURE

"GARDENING OPENS A WIDER DOOR THAN ANY OTHER OF THE ARTS. . . . IT HAS NO DISTINCTIONS; ALL ARE WELCOME."

housed in the Cornell University archives, Shipman wrote, "Gardening opens a wider door than any other of the arts. [All] can walk through, rich or poor, high or low, talented or untalented. It has no distinctions; all are welcome."

This inclusive spirit continues today with programs for all, from botany classes for toddlers to year-round learning opportunities for every age group. Many take place at the Blomquist Garden of Native Plants, where curator Annabel Renwick and horticulturist Maegan Luckett are revolutionizing low-maintenance public plantings through their championing of "Piedmont prairie" grassland ecosystems and biodiverse planting beds.

VISIT: *Open every day from 8 A.M. to dusk. The gardens are free, but there is a fee for parking. Gardens.duke.edu*

AMONG THE WILDFLOWERS

"Wherever I go in America," said Lady Bird Johnson, wife of President Lyndon B. Johnson, "I like it when the land speaks its own language in its own regional accent . . . native plants give us a sense of where we are in this great land of ours." The plants at the Lady Bird Johnson Wildflower Center may be local, but the vision is as wide as the Texas sky.

Under the auspices of the University of Texas at Austin, the center's 284 acres are a mix of cultivated gardens, an arboretum, and managed natural areas. Nearly 900 species of native plants from most of the ecoregions of Texas are on display. (Visit Texas Hill Country during bluebonnet time—end of March through mid- to late April—and you'll know why these wildflowers are so beloved.)

(continued)

Photo: Sarah P. Duke Gardens

ATTENTION SEPTIC SYSTEM OWNERS!

That Septic Additive You've Been Flushing...
...*Is Like Spitting On a Fire!* It's Not Enough!

Consider "The Gallon Analogy":
Imagine you filter all the bacteria out of your septic tank and you get one gallon of pure bacteria -- a milk jug of bacteria.

Now imagine that tiny packet or scoop of bacteria additive next to that jug. It's not nearly enough to matter but it has always been the only option (until now).

Accelerator by Dr. Pooper® is a true innovation in septic treatments...

It's a commercial-strength bio-accelerator that **multiplies the reproduction of septic bacteria by up to 40 times!**

That means **that 1-gallon jug of bacteria becomes 40 gallons -- plenty to eat the organic solids in your system fast to get it clean and flowing properly.**

This innovation is changing the industry and can save you big money. Plus, it's easy. Just flush a tablet. Discover more below.

Get Your Septic Tank & Drain Field *Flowing & Flushing Smoothly Again.* Rejuvenate Failing Drain Fields!

Commercial-Strength Septic System Cleaner

- Clears Tanks & Drain Fields
- Cleans Tough Organic Clogs
- Eliminates Odors
- Gets Your Tank & Drain Field Flowing Smoothly Again
- Stay-Clean Septic Maintenance

It's NOT just another bacteria or enzyme.
It's a BIO-ACCELERATOR, based on our commercial products for clearing organic sludge, clogs, and odors in municipal wastewater system and livestock lagoons.

✓ Aerobic & Anaerobic Systems
✓ Totally Safe & Non-Toxic
✓ Safe For Old Systems
✓ Easy to Use: Just Flush a Tablet!

100% Money-Back Guarantee
No Risk. Accelerator by Dr Pooper® is Guaranteed to Work or Your Money Back.

Easy to Use! Just Flush a Tablet!

⭐⭐⭐⭐⭐
Real Customer Testimonials
"I can complete laundry & take showers on the same day now. No water in yard. YEAH!" -- Jessica Bowen, Homeowner

"Was skeptical at first as our septic system is 53 years old, has a huge 1500 gallon tank and 4 leech lines, drains very slowly, not now, drains good, and still have some more to add, highly recommended." -- Steven Williams

"I can't believe it. We were about to order the $468 pump service and canceled it. It was full of built-up [stuff]. We poured the Accelerator in the toilet and BOOM! A week later no more problems. Flowin' smooth! This stuff is crazy."
-- Robert Voss

Buy Today at
DoctorPooper.com

PLUS! Save 10% with Coupon Code ALMANAC26

ADVENTURE

Conservation, plant research, and respect for native plants are paramount. The Native Plants of North America database on the website is a treasure. Don't miss the open-air Pollinator Habitat Garden, home to 350 species in 10 different plant communities designed to support butterflies and other invertebrates throughout their life cycles.

Director of Horticulture Andrea DeLong-Amaya carries on the mission, overseeing the Center's gardens and nursery programs, teaching, and writing. She's been a staff member since 1998, and has nearly 30 years of experience with native plants in horticulture, ecology, and garden design. "One of my goals," says DeLong-Amaya, "is to expand people's understanding and vision of how to work with native plants."

VISIT: *Open year-round; admission is free for members of other gardens through a reciprocal program. Wildflower.org*

"NATIVE PLANTS GIVE US A SENSE OF WHERE WE ARE IN THIS GREAT LAND OF OURS."

Photos, from top: Lady Bird Johnson Wildflower Center; Wikimedia; Lady Bird Johnson Wildflower Center

ROCK STAR

In 1904, Jennie Butchart, wife of a pioneering cement manufacturer on Vancouver Island, looked out upon the limestone quarry in her backyard and envisioned turning the eyesore into a garden. She spent almost 10 years pouring her energy and money into reclaiming the quarry and the rest of the property. The plantings grew, one cartload of topsoil at a time, into a dazzling destination with stunning garden beds and landscaping.

Of special note, the Mediterranean Garden, called a "testament to the temperate climate of Vancouver Island," features an array of drought-resistant and exotic plants from across the globe—from electric-blue delphiniums to massive-leafed banana plants and an awe-inspiring agave plant.

Still in family hands, The Butchart Gardens is run by Jennie's great-granddaughter, Robin-Lee Clarke. Now a National Historic Site, the gardens host concerts, fireworks, and children's activities.

VISIT: *Open year-round; in summer at dusk, Wednesday through Sunday, thousands of lights gleam during Night Illumination, open for viewing until 11 P.M. Butchartgardens.com* ■

Susan Peery is the "land lady" of her garden in Nelson, New Hampshire.

Photos, from left: Shiplap and Shells; Butchart Gardens; Destinationless Travels

FARMING

More Eggs in More Baskets

MODERN FARMERS HATCH NEW SOURCES OF REVENUE

by Stacey Kusterbeck

For farmers today, the old advice—*don't put all your eggs in one basket*—is apt indeed. Farmers receive less than 16 cents of every dollar Americans spend on food, according to the U.S. Department of Agriculture's Economic Research Service. "Input costs have gone up dramatically, and production challenges remain," says Christa Hartsook, small farms program manager at Iowa State University Extension and Outreach. "It is more important than ever to think of opportunities to capture additional revenue through a wide variety of methods."

Farmers are diversifying their income streams by adding new crops and livestock, floriculture, farm experiences, and value-added food products, and they are expanding sales through aggregation hubs and online channels. In 2022, 116,617 farms sold directly to consumers, with sales of $3.3 billion—a 16% increase from 2017.

"Farmers and ranchers work every day in response to the marketplace," says Gary Joiner, spokesperson for the Texas Farm Bureau. "Some diversify their operations to add value to their product and to meet specific market opportunities."

BEEFING UP THE BOTTOM LINE

At Basinger's Beef in Pretty Prairie, Kansas, all of the farm's income once depended on the whims of the commodities market, where prices fluctuate rapidly. "My paycheck, so to speak, for the whole year was earned in a 5- to 15-minute window, with buyers paying as low a price as possible," says Chad Basinger. It seemed to him there was money being left on the table. "We wanted to be a price maker instead of a price taker," he explains.

Adding direct-to-consumer sales

BRING DIVERSITY BACK TO AGRICULTURE. THAT'S WHAT MADE IT WORK IN THE FIRST PLACE.
–David R. Brower, American environmentalist (1912–2000)

A curious onlooker eyes Chad Basinger and two of his children.

"ONCE THEY START EATING THIS MEAT, THEY CAN'T GO BACK TO THE GROCERY STORE."

accomplished this—and resulted in ranchers needing to play a broader role in promoting their products and themselves. "Most farmers are humble and don't want to toot their own horns," says Basinger. Farmers now travel to arts and crafts shows to offer samples of specialty products like beef jerky and snack sticks. "It gets our foot in the door with the customer, then we can offer to ship them hamburger or steaks," says Basinger. Some customers want front-door delivery, while others make a point of traveling to the farm to pick up orders. A small number are willing to pay whatever the cost (for one out-of-state customer, $700) to have meat shipped.

STRENGTH IN NUMBERS

Two Tennessee farm families found a new source of steady revenue after joining forces to create Garrison Valley Farms. The families raise mainly Angus cattle on 2,700 acres and had been jointly marketing cattle to buyers through video sales. Together, the farm families changed their business model and opened a farm store to sell directly to consumers. It took years to build up a reliable, repeat clientele, all through word of mouth.

"It gives us more control over price. We are not at the mercy of the buyers and beef traders and can market our products based on actual costs of production rather than on market speculation," says Claudia Curl. Locally, their reputation is so well established that a new customer wanted to buy a whole processed steer, which costs about $3,500, without ever having tasted it. Steak prices are about 20% more than in grocery stores, but customers are willing to pay a bit extra for the flavor. Says Curl, "Once they start eating this meat, they can't go back to the grocery store."

BUSINESSES ARE BOOMING

At Big Maple Family Farm in Ridgway, Pennsylvania, new revenue sources have become an integral part of operations. The

Photo: Garrison Valley Farms

ATHENA PHEROM♡NES™ INCREASE AFFECTION YOU GET FROM OTHERS

Dr. Winnifred Cutler co-discovered human pheromones in 1986
(Time 12/1/86; Newsweek 1/12/87)

Athena Pheromones increase your attractiveness.
Effective in 3 published scientific studies.
Add to your fragrance. Should last up to 6 months used daily or use straight. Athena Pheromone 10:13™ for women $98.50. Athena Pheromone 10X™ for men $99.50.

Not guaranteed to work for <u>all</u>; will work for <u>most</u>.
Cosmetics – not aphrodisiacs.

unscented cosmetics

♥ **Erin (PA)** "There are weird things that I can only attribute to this pheromone. I am decently attractive, in good shape. Single for 8 years, really interested in a new relationship, nothing changed. **Since I started wearing the 10:13, 2 months ago, I have literally had men noticing me, paying attention to me, acting attentive.**"

♥ **Karl (GA)** "My wife and I don't normally keep secrets. I have not said anything about using the 10X because I did not want to influence her reaction. **But I do notice a difference in her responsiveness to me.**"

♥ **Liz (IL)** "My husband of 30 years is **friendlier and more affectionate** toward me. He's not demanding, **just..nicer.**"

ATHENA PHEROM♡NES: The Gold Standard since 1993™

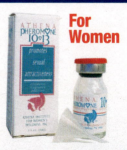
For Women

SAVE $100: 6-Pak special
2+ vials ship free to US

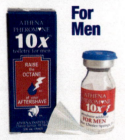
For Men

To order, call: **(610) 827-2200**   www.**athenainstitute**.com
Or mail to: **Athena Institute, Dept FA, 1211 Braefield Rd., Chester Spgs, PA 19425**
Not in stores. We ship abroad—See website for rates and options.   FA

FARMING

100-year-old farm started as a dairy farm but switched to produce, sheep, and wool in the 1980s. The 80 acres functioned as a hobby farm for years, and about a decade ago, Amanda Balon set out to change that. "I wanted to make the farm sustainable and a source of the family's income so that we wouldn't have to work outside the farm like I had to growing up," explains Balon. "I also wanted a place where people could find help on the farm."

The first of many new businesses was a nonprofit that offered equine interactions to children and adults with physical, mental, or emotional challenges. Next, the farm added a store to sell chicken and eggs; then came value-added products and beef production, as well as home delivery and online options.

With steady growth, each of the new businesses has allowed the farm to survive. "We have grown from 12 subscribers to more than 40," says Balon. Subscribers receive two bundles each month of items such as eggs, maple syrup, microgreens, and produce ($75 if picked up at the farm, $85 for delivery). The number of home deliveries is surging. "We see a huge shift towards that model instead of people visiting the farm store. It's convenient, which is what people are looking for," she notes. The farm uses unsold produce to make canned goods. Sales have increased from a few hundred jars to more than 1,000 of apple butter, applesauce, pasta sauce, and tomato basil soup. "These are becoming more expensive to produce," says Balon, "but the consumers enjoy purchasing them,

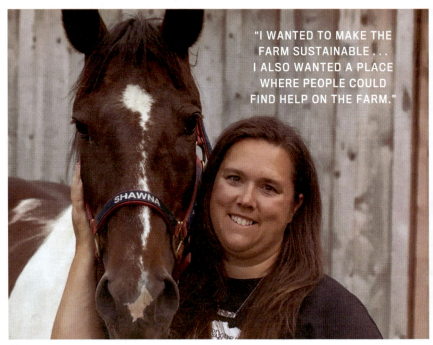

"I WANTED TO MAKE THE FARM SUSTAINABLE... I ALSO WANTED A PLACE WHERE PEOPLE COULD FIND HELP ON THE FARM."

Photo: Big Maple Farms Natural Therapies, Inc.

THE OLD FARMER'S GUIDE TO
SEEDS, PLANTS, AND BULBS

Botanical Interests
Discover rare seeds and unique varieties. For 30+ years, delivering organic, heirloom, and non-GMO seeds. Because your garden is art!
**BotanicalInterests.com
720-782 2506**

Filaree Farm
As stewards of the largest collection of garlic in N. America, we offer more than 100 strains, as well as shallot sets, seed potatoes, asparagus crowns, and sweet potato slips. We look forward to helping you grow!
**FilareeFarm.com
509-422-6940**

Grow Better with Plantco
Nourish your plants with our premium fertilizers and biostimulants. Use coupon code ALMANAC to get 10% off. Free Shipping!
**PlantcoGarden.com
979-353-2474**

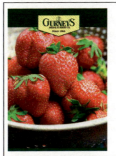

Gurney's Seed & Nursery Co.
Since 1866, gardeners have come to respect our selection of better-tasting varieties backed by our no-risk guarantee.
Gurneys.com

K. van Bourgondien
Quality Bulbs & Perennials at Wholesale Prices
Our money-saving landscape quantities and exceptional customer service keep landscapers and serious gardeners coming back.
**DutchBulbs.com
800-552-9996**

Southern Exposure Seed Exchange
Heirloom • Organic • Non-GMO
You'll find our farm in the rolling hills of Virginia and our network of small farm growers throughout the U.S.
540-894-1470
Southern Exposure.com

Jung Seed
Seeds • Plants Bulbs • Supplies
From our garden to yours for 119 years.
Take 15% Off with code: ALMANAC26
**JungSeed.com
800-247-5864**

Breck's
Direct to you from Holland since 1818
Gardeners have trusted Breck's for more than two centuries. We offer affordable, top-quality Dutch bulbs, perennials, and more.
Brecks.com

FARMING

"AGRITOURISM ACCIDENTALLY FOUND ITS WAY INTO MY LIFE."

so we want to make sure they are available. We want to create a place where people can get the items they need and trust what is on their plate."

CARVING A PUMPKIN NICHE

At Red Barn Ranch Farm in Harrisonville, Missouri, a crop of unsold pumpkins inspired a lucrative side business. Matt Moreland, a fourth-generation dairy farmer, had purchased an additional 102 acres and planted pumpkins on one of them. The crop was successful, but Moreland had no luck with sales at harvesttime since local grocers had already contracted to buy from other growers.

About 1,000 unsold pumpkins, 15,000 pounds, were hauled back to the patch, and Moreland put up a "U-Pick Pumpkins" sign. One picker, a teacher, asked if she could bring her class to the farm for a field trip, and Moreland, who was in the habit of talking with customers about food production, found a new calling. Tens of thousands of schoolchildren have since visited the farm—on a typical October weekday, the farm may host 150 students before lunchtime.

Once started, Red Barn Ranch Farm's diversification movement gained momentum. "Agritourism accidentally found its way into my life. That accident, or experiment, if you will, turned into a life-changer for a whole bunch of people," says Moreland. The school trips, weddings, and corporate events now support 46 seasonal employees, attracting enough visitors to require a new parking lot. "We are still reliant on the Sun and the rain to some extent," says Moreland. "But if we have a drought or a flood that cuts off our production, this is another way to bring in money and keep our heads above water." ∎

Stacey Kusterbeck stocks her pantry, refrigerator, and freezer with local farm goods, which she finds are healthier and more flavorful.

Train at home to
Work at Home
Be a Medical Coding & Billing Specialist

WORK AT HOME!
- ✓ Be home for your family
- ✓ Be your own boss
- ✓ Choose your own hours

SAVE MONEY!
- ✓ No day care, commute, or office wardrobe/lunches
- ✓ Possible tax breaks
- ✓ Tuition discount for eligible military and their spouses
- ✓ Military education benefits & MyCAA approved

Train at home in as little as 5 months to earn up to $48,780 a year!*

Now you can train in the comfort of your own home to work in a medical office, or from home as your experience and skills increase. Make great money…up to $48,780 a year with experience! It's no secret, healthcare providers need Medical Coding & Billing Specialists. In fact, the U.S. Department of Labor projects 9% growth by 2033, for specialists doing coding and billing.

No previous medical experience required. Compare the money you can make!

Coders earn great money because they make a lot of money for the people they work for. Entering the correct codes on medical claims can mean the difference in thousands of dollars in profits for doctors, hospitals and clinics. Since each and every medical procedure must be coded and billed, there's plenty of work available for well-trained Medical Coding & Billing Specialists.

Get FREE Facts. Contact Us Today!

 U.S. Career Institute®
2001 Lowe St., Dept. FMAB2A95
Fort Collins, CO 80525

1-800-388-8765
Dept. FMAB2A95
www.uscieducation.com/FMA95

YES! Rush me my free Medical Coding & Billing information package.

Name _____ Age _____
Address _____ Apt _____
City, State, Zip _____
E-mail _____ Phone _____

DEAC Accredited • Affordable • Approved
Celebrating over 40 years of education excellence!

*W/experience, https://www.bls.gov/ooh/healthcare/medical-records-and-health-information-technicians.htm, 9/4/24

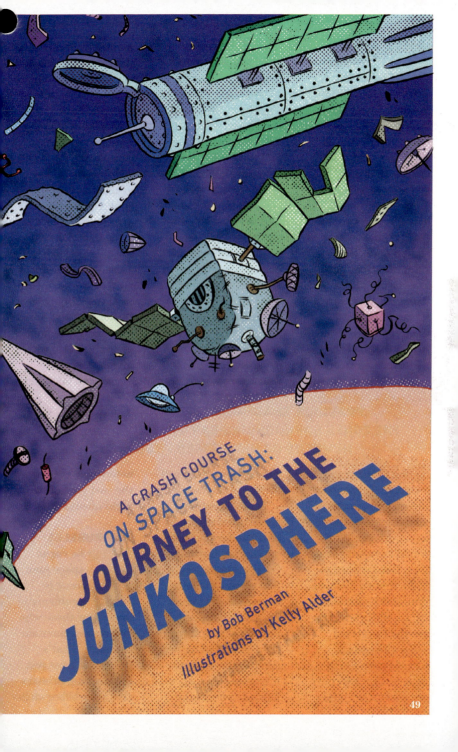

ASTRONOMY

Old-timers remember October 4, 1957, when the first Soviet satellite—*Sputnik 1*—went into orbit. People all over the world stood on street corners and watched the sky during its predicted passage, unaware that the 22.8-inch sphere of aluminum, magnesium, and titanium alloy was not visible and that what they were seeing instead was the third stage of the rocket that had thrust the satellite into orbit.

Despite the confusion, lites, characterized by size, orbit, and distance from Earth. Man-made satellites are categorized by what they do, such as navigation, like GPS; military, like the sharp-eyed KH-11 reconnaissance satellites (which, incidentally, cannot identify individuals even though they can indeed see people's heads); weather and climate monitors; and communications services, like the thousands of newly-launched or proposed cell phone satellites designed to work for users everywhere, even mountains, regret that the constellations and sense of infinitude are punctured by moving points of light.

Members of both groups have the consolation that orbiting objects are made visible by reflecting sunlight and thus are invisible when in Earth's shadow. The satellite-free sky lasts a few hours in summer, centered on 1 A.M. local time. September through March, satellites and space junk are only visible within 90 minutes after sunset and 90 minutes

> **PREVIOUS SPACE COLLISIONS HAVE FILLED THE ZONES SURROUNDING EARTH WITH ASTONISHING NUMBERS OF HIGH-SPEED FRAGMENTS.**

on that October day, everything changed. Before then, nothing man-made littered the sky overhead. Who would have imagined that, fast-forward to 2026, there'd be more than 11,000 functioning satellites whizzing around the globe?

For the record, natural near-Earth objects, like asteroids, are also called satel- when there are no cell towers in the vicinity.

These intentional space invaders are no problem for the vast majority of Earthlings. Sure, astronomers find many of their astrophotos bombed by glittering space junk streaking through the frame, and nature lovers, who dislike intrusions such as lighted towers atop before sunrise, leaving the vast part of the night unsullied.

TINY RUBBLES

The rogue space junk issue is problematic mainly for those who launch and maintain satellites. That's because it's not just the working orbiters that your billion-dollar

AN ESTIMATED 29,000 OBJECTS LARGER THAN 4 INCHES ARE MOVING FAR FASTER THAN HIGH-VELOCITY BULLETS.

machine could slam into. Previous space collisions, and even stuff like globs of frozen urine released during manned missions, have filled the zones surrounding Earth with astonishing numbers of high-speed fragments. NASA operates an Orbital Debris Program Office that, along with other sections of its operations, attempts to track everything in orbit and provide timely warnings when operating satellites or the International Space Station (ISS) are threatened with a likely collision.

It isn't easy. NASA estimates there are 29,000 orbiting objects larger than 4 inches, each moving far faster than high-velocity bullets, yet much smaller objects can cause catastrophic effects. Space agencies put the number of orbiting objects in the ½- to 4-inch size at more than 1 million. As for pieces smaller than peas, we're talking 130 million. NASA's ongoing efforts to continually calculate orbits for everything it can detect and track—some 45,000 objects as of 2025—has been surpassed by what's being created.

DEBRIS SPREE

Though several collisions have happened, the most notorious wasn't accidental. In January 2007, the China National Space Administration tested its ability to terminate

ASTRONOMY

enemy orbiters by sending up a ballistic missile that destroyed its old non-operational *Fengyun-1C* weather satellite. This created an ever-widening cloud of more than 3,000 pieces of orbiting debris, most of which still pose hazards today. One of them so closely approached the ISS that ground controllers warned the astronauts, who made an evasive maneuver. On another occasion, the ISS was hit by a piece of space junk that created a 5-millimeter hole in a boom segment of the Canadian-built robot arm, Canadarm2.

SCRAPPY ACCIDENTS

Accidents, it turns out, do happen, including in space. In 2009, the commercial *Iridium 33* communication satellite collided with a non-functioning Russian *Cosmos 2251* satellite. The 26,000-mph impact created more than 2,000 pieces of debris over 4 inches wide, which continue orbit-

ing in a widening cloud.

Gravity, a 2013 fictional movie in which a series of satellite collisions rapidly produce exponential amounts of junk until most communications satellites are destroyed, created public awareness of Kessler Syndrome. It was named for the now-retired NASA scientist Donald Kessler,

RESEARCHERS ARE WORKING GALACTIC GARBAGE, BUT THE IDEAS, ARE EXPENSIVE

who published a 1978 paper on the "Collision Frequency of Artificial Satellites: The Creation of a Debris Belt." Kessler's paper still has experts debating the likelihood of an escalating profusion of junk sizable enough to make future space missions overly risky, and whether it would unfold over years,

ASTRONOMY

ON WAYS TO MITIGATE SUCH AS MESH-LIKE SCOOPERS, AND UNPROVEN.

decades, or centuries.

Some regions around Earth are riskier than others. Low Earth Orbit, meaning below around 300 miles where the recent profusion of cell phone satellites have been sent, is the least hazardous because such orbiters, when their useful service lives are completed, will naturally be slowed by the friction of that region's thin air and will re-enter the atmosphere to self-destruct (within a few years) on their own.

ADDRESS THIS MESS

Researchers are working on ways to mitigate galactic garbage, but the ideas, such as mesh-like scoopers, are expensive and unproven. The consensus is that greater publicity may embarrass spacefaring countries into being more vigilant about creating debris in the first place.

One possibility is a total ban on any future anti-satellite exercises, like the 2019 and 2021 events, when India and Russia respectively destroyed satellites, together creating more than 1,500 pieces of space junk. A European Space Agency computer analysis predicted that even if everyone discontinued launching satellites now, space junk will keep increasing for the next 200 years.

So the next time you're distressed by your cluttered closets, step outside and find refuge in the kindred starry heavens! ■

Bob Berman is *The Old Farmer's Almanac* astronomy editor and prefers his night sky free of passing space junk.

FOOD

2025 TOMATO RECIPE CONTEST WINNERS

We asked you to send us your terrific tomato recipes, and you delivered. Sincere thanks go out to all of you who took the time to share them with us!

**STYLING AND PHOTOGRAPHY:
SAMANTHA JONES/VAUGHAN COMMUNICATIONS**

FIRST PRIZE: $300
FRESH TOMATO BACON JAM
(recipe on page 190)

FOOD

SECOND PRIZE: $200
GRAMPS' TOMATO TURKEY BURGERS
(recipe on page 190)

(continued)

FOOD

THIRD PRIZE: $100
ZESTY TOMATO-BASIL ICE CREAM
(recipe on page 191)

ENTER THE 2026 RECIPE CONTEST: BERRIES

Got a great recipe using berries that is loved by family and friends? Send it in and you could win! See contest rules on page 251.

HONORABLE MENTION
TRIPLE TOMATO SALAD WITH CREAMY BALSAMIC DRESSING
(recipe on page 191)

(continued on page 190)

$1 Marketing Giveaway for Our Readers Who Love Olive Oil

As a reader of the *Old Farmer's Almanac,* you qualify to receive a free $39 bottle of rare, fresh-pressed extra virgin olive oil direct from the new harvest at one of the world's top artisanal farms. Pay $1 shipping and it's yours free as your introduction to the Fresh-Pressed Olive Oil Club, with no commitment to buy anything, now or ever.

T. J. Robinson, aka The Olive Oil Hunter®, is one of the world's most respected authorities on all matters of olive oil. Known for his "platinum palate," he is one of the few Americans invited to serve as a judge in Italian olive oil tasting competitions.

If you've never tasted extra virgin olive oil fresh from the farm, get ready for a revelation...

As the culinary experts at America's Test Kitchen have said, when it comes to olive oil, *"the fresher, the better."*

Freshness endows olive oil with extraordinary flavor because the olive is a fruit and olive oil is a fruit juice. Just like other fruit juices such as orange juice, olive oil is at its zenith of robust flavor and nutritional goodness when fresh-pressed.

Your first taste of fresh-pressed olive oil will be a revelation. Just born of earth and tree, farm-fresh olive oil is bright, vivid, and grassy, like a garden in a bottle.

Problem is, you can't find farm-fresh olive oil in supermarkets. That's because most olive oils are sent here by slow cargo ships, perhaps months or even a year after the harvest in their native country. Then these oils sit on store shelves for more months, even years, growing dull, lifeless, stale, and finally rancid.

Never again tolerate stale oil!

Of course, we all insist on fresh milk, fresh eggs, fresh fish, fresh meat, fresh fruit, and fresh vegetables. In every case, freshness makes a big difference in flavor and nutrition, right?

Don't we deserve fresh olive oil? *Of course!* But you'll never find it in supermarkets. However, now you can have it delivered to your door direct from the latest harvests at top-rated, gold medal-winning artisanal farms.

At last, a farm-to-table solution

My name is T. J. Robinson. As a food writer and former chef, I've launched an exclusive club for those who, like me, demand nothing less than the freshest, most flavorful, and purest artisanal olive oils in the world. Our group is called the Fresh-Pressed Olive Oil Club.

How the club works

Four times a year, I travel to the latest olive harvests around the world. From scores of the finest extra virgin olive oils at award-winning artisanal farms, I choose the three best oils of the harvest. Then I rush a three-bottle set to each of my eagerly awaiting club members. Conveniently, this works out to one bottle per month.

Members can choose either the larger set (three 16.9 oz. bottles) for $139 per quarter… or the smaller set (three 8.45 oz. bottles) for $99 per quarter. These prices include all shipping and handling.

For this reasonably modest sum, you'll enjoy three months of outrageously flavorful farm-fresh olive oil rushed to you direct from the harvest. Members say these best-of-the-best fresh oils are well worth the cost, since each bottle elevates dozens of meals to new heights of dining pleasure.

Every oil is independently lab certified to be 100% extra virgin olive oil. Every oil also comes with a 100% money-back guarantee. You don't even have to return the oil to receive your 100% refund.

Every oil arrives with a Pressing Report that helps you cultivate your palate, quickly turning you into a connoisseur of the finest extra virgin olive oils in the world. I also include lots of delicious kitchen-tested recipes from each oil's native land, plus profiles of the proud artisans who produced each oil.

The club is truly an adventure in olive oil appreciation. Your family and guests will love these oils.

Available nowhere else in America, these oils have caused quite a sensation in the food world.

TV Chef Chris Kimball says:

"When we tasted T. J.'s harvest-fresh olive oils here at Milk Street, we fell in love with their vibrant, grassy flavors."

Food journalist Larry Olmsted writes in his best-selling book Real Food/Fake Food, "I now get most of my oil from T. J. Robinson's Fresh-Pressed Olive Oil Club, and every time I open a bottle, my kitchen literally fills up with the smell of fresh-crushed olives—the scent explodes out of the bottle. Just breaking the seal transports me to Italy or Spain or Chile."

"I have died and gone to Italy!!!"

Jennifer of Newport, RI, says in her review, "I have died and gone to Italy!!! I love these oils."

Joy of Salem, OR, writes, "Words cannot describe this! Pssst—since no one else was around, I even licked my plate clean—yummy!"

Try a free full-size bottle and then decide

All I ask is that you try one of my full-size bottles—on the house—and then decide. There's no commitment to buy anything, ever.

The only reason we can make such a generous free sample offer is because the vast majority of those who try our olive oil want more of it. I believe you will, too, once you try this divine harvest-fresh olive oil on your crisp salads, delicate fish, grilled steaks, fresh veggies, or luscious pastas, or simply on a hunk of warm, crusty bread or with a slice of tangy cheese. *Mmm—so delish!*

Happy drizzling!

T. J. Robinson

My prove-it-to-yourself offer:
Try a full-size bottle (a $39 retail value) **FREE**. Pay just $1 shipping. No obligation to buy anything, now or ever. Supplies are limited.

Claim yours now at:
HarvestFresh333.com or by calling:
1-800-390-6688.

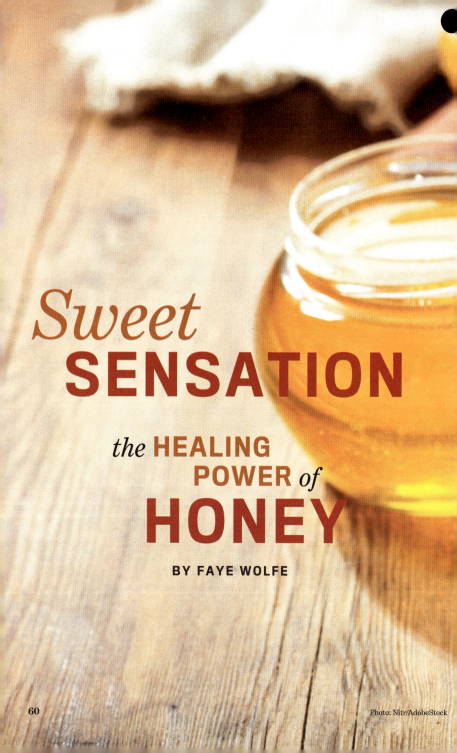

Sweet SENSATION

the HEALING POWER of HONEY

BY FAYE WOLFE

HOME REMEDIES

HONEY WILL AT ALL TIMES CURE THE GRAVEL, AND AS CERTAINLY PREVENT THE STONE.
–Sir John Hill, English botanist (c. 1714–75)

HOME REMEDIES

THE ONLY REASON FOR BEING A BEE THAT I KNOW OF IS MAKING HONEY.

–Winnie the Pooh, character in *Winnie the Pooh* by A. A. Milne, English writer (1882–1956)

Winnie the Pooh loved it. The Beatles sang about it. After he died, Alexander the Great was preserved in it. As one of the oldest foods, honey can be eaten raw, from the comb, creamed, or whipped. You can choose from several colors—white, light, or a shade of amber—and 300 or so varietals, including acacia, alfalfa, clover, lavender, macadamia, orange blossom, and tupelo. Honey is produced around the world, from New Zealand to Ukraine. In the U.S., North Dakota produces the most: 38.3 million pounds in 2023.

As depicted in 15,000-year-old cave paintings, people have been harvesting honey for millennia. Serious honey production probably began about 3,500 years ago. According to a study published in *Nature*, honey may have helped *Homo sapiens* evolve: "Honey is energetically dense and easy to consume and digest and thus may

AS ONE OF THE OLDEST FOODS, HONEY CAN BE EATEN RAW, FROM THE COMB, CREAMED, OR WHIPPED.

The Vermont Bun Baker!
Wood Cook-Stoves

Vermont Bun Baker N-350

Vermont Bun Baker 750

Vermont Bun Baker XL 2500

Vermont Bun Baker XL N-500

- Bake Oven
- Cook Top • Broiler • Cook-Stove
- Soapstone Veneer Packages

New! Bigfoot Barbecue
Wood-Fired Soapstone Grilling Surface

- 100% Pure Soapstone Searing and Cooking Deck
- Raised Stainless Steel Rack for Direct Flame Cooking
- Rolled Steel Wood Burning Cone
- Charcoal Grate Pan Inside
- Sturdy Angle Iron Legs
- Easy Disconnect Ash Pan
- Sturdy Lockable Casters

Everything Soapstone...

"...Even the Kitchen Sink"

Visit our New Flagship Showroom!
10014 US State Route 4
Whitehall, New York
802.468.8800
VermontMarbleandGranite.com

VERMONT MARBLE GRANITE
SLATE & SOAPSTONE CO.

HOME REMEDIES

HONEY IN THE OVEN
Try substituting honey for sugar when baking your favorite recipes.

- For every cup of sugar, use ¾ cup of honey.
- For every cup of honey used, reduce other liquids by ¼ cup. In recipes without other liquids or recipes that call for eggs, increase the amount of flour by 2 tablespoons for each cup of honey used.
- A tiny bit of acidity can help balance honey's sweetness. Add a squeeze of lemon juice or a dash of vinegar to round out the flavors, especially in sweeter desserts.
- Reduce the oven temperature by 25°F. Honey caramelizes more quickly than granulated sugar, so turning down the heat prevents baked goods from browning too fast. Keep an eye on baking times in case they need adjustment, too.

have contributed to potential links between nutrition and neural expansion of the enlarging hominin brain."

Rightly or wrongly, for centuries, honey has been said to cure earaches, gout, hair loss, snake bites, and sore eyes and—according to the Reverend Charles Butler in his *Feminine Monarchy, or the History of Bees* (1609)—can be used as an aphrodisiac. John Hill's *The Virtues of Honey in Preventing Many of the Worst Disorders; and in the Certain Cure of Several Others* (1759) was the first book in English to focus on its healing properties.

Long before that, Hippocrates, aka the father of medicine, recommended it as a cure for carbuncles. In China and India, people started using honey to treat ailments and diseases thousands of years ago. According to archaeologist and beekeeper Gil Stein, "Honey was considered an almost magical substance in the ancient Near East. People used it for everything: as a food and as a raw material to make alcoholic beverages like mead and honey wine." Stein says it was the most common ingredient in ancient medicine in Mesopotamia and Egypt, and "they even used it for mummification."

BEE HEALED

Honey's medicinal powers are not just the stuff of folklore. In recent decades, scientists have explored its potential to treat antibiotic-resistant infections, herpes, and COVID-19. It's being studied as a treatment for major health problems—breast cancer, heart disease, osteoporosis—and less life-threatening ones, too, like conjunctivitis, heartburn, menopause symptoms, allergies, and even gingivitis. Before antibiotics, honey was commonly used to dress wounds, and recent research indicates that New Zealand's manuka honey, processed as "medical-grade," seems to be effective for that purpose.

"Honey is well known for its health benefits, having antibacterial, antioxidant, anti-inflammatory, antimutagenic, anticarcinogenic, and bacteriostatic qualities," stated a 2024 *Food Chemistry* article, a review of numerous studies. Honey, it stated, "can be utilized in new

A LEGACY IN EVERY BUILD

HOMES BY COUNTRY CARPENTERS, INC.
EARLYNEWENGLANDHOMES.COM   (860) 643-1148

Model on Display  Shipped Nationwide

HOME REMEDIES

HONEY LOVE
The word honey seeped into the language of love long ago, first appearing in print as a term of endearment in 1375, according to *The Oxford English Dictionary*. We'll never know why some medieval wooer decided to whisper that sweet nothing into a beloved's ear, but the obvious explanation is that honey is sweet. Six centuries later, it popped up in movie titles and songs, such as *Honey, I Shrunk the Kids* and "Sugar, Sugar," the Archies' 1968 bubblegum pop masterpiece with the immortal lyrics, "Ah, sugar, ah, honey, honey. You are my candy girl. And you've got me wanting you."

treatments without causing the side effects that frequently go along with the use of synthetic chemical drugs."

Before swapping out amoxicillin for the sweet stuff, bear in mind that much about honey's medical potential remains to be determined. Because it may contain bacteria that cause infant botulism, honey should never be given to children younger than a year old.

TASTY AS CAN BEE

When you slip a spoonful of honey into your tea, you're reaping the bounty of 5,000 apian visits to flowers. On those visits, the bee collects nectar and carries it in its crop (honey stomach) to the hive. There, the bee expels the nectar into the mouth of another bee, a process that is repeated from one bee to the next until the nectar has thickened enough to be transferred to the honeycomb's storage cells. As part of the complex honey-making process, bees collectively fan their wings to evaporate the nectar's water content.

Of around 30,000 species of bees worldwide (about 5,000 in North America), less than 4 percent are honey producers. The one we rely on for honey (and for pollinating commercial crops), *Apis mellifera*, originated in the Middle East or Northeastern Africa and is now found everywhere except Antarctica. Honeybees are among the 3 percent of bees that live in colonies—most bees are ground-dwellers and build solitary nests. (Another distinguishing characteristic, according to apian authority Eric Mussen: "hairy eyes.") *(continued)*

Photo: ElementalImaging/Getty Images

HOME REMEDIES

HOT TODDY

This age-old remedy can help you fall asleep, especially if you've got a cold or the flu. To make a child's toddy, replace whiskey with 1 teaspoon of lemon juice.

2/3 cup boiling water
2 teaspoons honey
2 tablespoons whiskey or bourbon
1 lemon slice
1 cinnamon stick
ground nutmeg, for topping (optional)

■ In a mug, combine water and honey. Stir until honey is dissolved. Add whiskey, lemon, and cinnamon stick. Let sit for 2 to 3 minutes, then remove lemon and cinnamon stick. Sprinkle with nutmeg, if using, and serve.

Makes 1 serving.

Panacea or not, honey is an indisputable staple in pantries everywhere, esteemed for its ability to add flavor to a cup of tea, bowl of yogurt, or stack of pancakes. Apples dipped in honey are front-and-center at Rosh Hashanah seders, as is honey-glazed ham at Easter dinners. During Ramadan, many a Muslim's evening meal ends with honey-drenched baklava.

A century ago in Madison, Wisconsin, Malitta D. Fischer promoted her approach to cooking with honey in her restaurant, the Honey Tea Room, and in *Honey Way Menus*. The 1926 book gave recipes for Honey Hospitality Salad, Honey Way Halibut, and a Honey Peanut Butter Lettuce Sandwich "suitable for evening card parties, missionary society gatherings, [and] sewing clubs." At about the same time, Honey Maid graham crackers appeared in grocery stores and went on to dominate the market.

Less than 100 years later, hot honey, made from honey, chilies, and vinegar, became all the rage. In 2024, Julia Moskin wrote in *The New York Times*, "In a world gone mad for condiments, hot honey is king."

Apparently, honey itself is virtually immortal, discovered unspoiled in pots in ancient Egyptian tombs. According to scientist Amina Harris, "As long as the lid stays on it and no water is added to it, honey will not go bad."

Honey—truly a food for posterity. ■

Faye Wolfe wouldn't be without a jar of honey in her kitchen.

ACORN STAIRLIFTS

Enjoy all of the home you love, inside and out.

Acorn Stairlifts are the perfect solution for **people with arthritis, COPD sufferers, those with mobility issues,** or **anyone who struggles with the stairs.**

America's NUMBER ONE selling stairlift.

✓ The only stairlift with the **Ease of Use Commendation** from the **Arthritis Foundation**

✓ **Installed quickly with no structural changes**; designed for comfort, reliability, and peace of mind

✓ **Our stairlifts fit almost any indoor or outdoor staircase**

 FOLDS *of* HONOR   BBB ACCREDITED BUSINESS A+ Rating   Trustpilot

SPECIAL OFFER

$250.00
TOWARD A BRAND NEW ACORN STAIRLIFT!*

Call today to receive your **FREE STAIRLIFT BUYING GUIDE** and your **FREE** in-home consultation!

1-800-340-4875

Scan to learn more!

*Not valid on previous purchases. Not valid with any other offers or discounts. Not valid on refurbished models. Only valid towards purchase of a NEW Acorn Stairlift directly from the manufacturer. $250 discount will be applied to new orders. Please mention this ad when calling. AZ ROC 278722, CA 942619, MN LC670698, OK 50110, OR CCB 198506, RI 88, WA ACORNSI894OB, WV WV049654, MA HIC169936, NJ 13VH07752300, PA PA101967, CT ELV 0425003-R5, AK 134057, HIC.0656293.

FARMING

CANADIAN FARMERS TALK DIRT(Y) ABOUT TENDING THE SOIL

BY KAREN DAVIDSON

WELL-GROUNDED

For geographers, the Earth's outer skin is known as the pedosphere. The stuff that's underfoot—an ever-evolving layer of decaying organic matter and living creatures—plays a critical role in mitigating climate change, contributing to biodiversity, and putting food on tables, says Senator Rob Black, chair of Canada's Senate Committee on Agriculture and Forestry, which published a landmark report in 2024: *Critical Ground: Why Soil is Essential to Canada's Economic, Environmental, Human, and Social Health.*

The report outlines 25 strategies for saving the soil, including designating dirt as a national asset. For Canadian farmers, stewarding those precious inches of topsoil is an odyssey. While no single formula fits all situations, Canadian farmers are employing strategies to improve long-term soil resilience.

ROOTS OF THE MATTER

The seedy underworld of soil biology has always intrigued Charles Emre. A year before sowing potatoes, the Ontario farmer plants cover crops so that their roots interact with the bacteria and fungi in the ecosystem underfoot.

His goal is tricky in sandy soils. Nitrogen-fixing clovers, for example, burn in droughty weather. He has fine-tuned a mixture of cover crops for his Windham Centre location, choosing specific species to perform particular tasks. Forage peas and pearl millet build organic matter in the soil while the taproots of tillage radish loosen it, increasing rain-absorbing capacity. The fibrous roots of the oilseed radish (no relation) exude a substance that suppresses nematodes, growing in a mix with yellow mustard, also a biofumigant. *(continued)*

Photo: Emre Farms

LIFE BEGINS WITH THE SOIL. SOIL FEEDS PLANTS, ANIMALS, AND PEOPLE.
–Senator Rob Black,
Canadian politician (b. 1962)

Charles Emre (right) and son-in-law Nick Bell

FARMING

Seeded together in the spring, the resulting amalgam of plants is also attractive to pollinators before it's tilled under in late summer.

Understanding growth habits and seasonal variations is key to thriving in extreme weather. Too much heat or too much rain demands that farmers employ strategies to make their crops and soils more resilient. "Improvement in soil organic matter is glacial, but there are other metrics of success," says Emre. "Yields are satisfactory, and the quality of the shiny, smooth potato skins is noteworthy."

FRUITFUL INTERCROPPING

Most cover crops are plowed under as green manure to enhance soil tilth in annual cropping systems. The challenge is different for perennial fruit trees like apples, cherries, peaches, and plums. For Angelique and Jesse Slade Shantz near Lake Country, British Columbia, cover planting serves several purposes in the grassy strips between their 10 acres of trees where preventing erosion of the sandy soil is paramount.

In collaboration with the Living Laboratories Initiative, or Livings Labs for short, a national program that's working with growers on innovative cover crop mixes, these farmers are using bird's-foot trefoil, winter rye, cicer milkvetch, and sainfoin, the latter a legume thought to deter hole-digging gophers, an endemic nuisance in the region. Sainfoin is also lauded for its non-bloating properties, an advantage for the grazing of sheep and horses.

Asparagus is another experimental cover crop, employed since 2023 as a perennial planted underneath young cider apple trees to keep soil in place. Not only can asparagus take advantage of existing drip irrigation, but it also drives its roots deep into the soil. *(continued)*

COVER PLANTING SERVES SEVERAL PURPOSES IN THE GRASSY STRIPS BETWEEN TREES WHERE PREVENTING EROSION OF THE SANDY SOIL IS PARAMOUNT.

Photo: Angelique Slade Shantz

THE GARDENER'S GUIDE TO CANNABIS

AN OLD CROP MAKES A COMEBACK
GROWING CANNABIS IN YOUR SEASONAL GARDEN

For generations, thoughtful gardeners have cultivated plants that serve multiple needs. Cannabis, one of humanity's oldest domesticated crops, is making a well-deserved return to home gardens, offering remarkable versatility for today's holistic gardener.

IF YOU'VE GROWN TOMATOES, YOU CAN GROW CANNABIS

Cannabis thrives under the same conditions as summer vegetables. It requires well-draining soil, full sun, and consistent watering and benefits from organic feeding. Like tomatoes, it responds beautifully to compost tea and mineral-rich amendments.

A BENEFICIAL GARDEN ALLY

Cannabis contributes to your garden's ecosystem by attracting beneficial pollinators, including bees and helpful predator insects. Its deep taproot helps break up compacted soil, improving growing conditions for neighboring plants.

GROWING WITH THE SEASONS

Follow your *Almanac*'s planting calendar: start seeds indoors in early spring, transplant after last frost when soil reaches 60°F, and harvest in early autumn alongside your other garden crops.

NATURAL GARDEN HARMONY

Surround cannabis with fragrant thyme to attract pollinators and vibrant marigolds to naturally repel pests. This trio enhances biodiversity, improves soil health, and creates a thriving ecosystem.

FROM GARDEN TO HOME
Your homegrown harvest can be transformed into a variety of practical preparations:

 Infused oils for topical applications

 Extracts for your home apothecary

 Ingredients for your culinary creations

SPECIAL OFFER FOR ALMANAC READERS

25% OFF GROW KITS AND SUPPLIES
USE CODE: ALMANAC25

- Germination Guarantee
- Grown in the USA
- 24/7 Customer Service
- Fast, Discreet Shipping Nationwide

Visit: *homegrowncannabis.com/almanac25*
Call: 760-313-7455

For adults 21+ only. Check local laws and regulations before growing.
Offers valid for a limited time; terms and conditions apply: homegrowncannabis.com/terms-and-conditions

FARMING

"I'M SURPRISED HOW QUICKLY OUR SOIL HAS IMPROVED."

"Glyphosate products aren't used to control weeds under our trees," explains Angelique. "This intercropping method is beneficial for both trees and asparagus while providing more income in our U-pick operation."

DO NOT DISTURB

For some Western Canadian farmers, not plowing the land after harvest and leaving the crop stubble in place to trap moisture helps to preserve soil integrity. Jocelyn Velestuk and her husband, Jesse, don't disturb the soil when they use specialized equipment to plant 3,500 acres of canola, oats, and wheat near Broadview, Saskatchewan.

"We grow a lot of roots," says Jocelyn, who holds a master's degree in soil science. "When you keep soil in place, the root channels create pores in the soil. The idea is to have [it behave like] a sponge."

The relationship between chernozemic soils—black soils rich in humus—and their water-holding capacity is key in a region that's prone to drought. On average, eastern Saskatchewan receives 7 to 8 inches of precipitation annually. In prairie parlance, this scant rainfall is called "moisture."

Every fall for the last decade, Jocelyn has returned to test sites to measure the physical properties of the soil, such as color, porosity, texture, and aggregate stability. These contribute to the soil's capacity to prevent erosion, support nutrient cycling, and aid in biological activity for species such as earthworms. She gives a thumbs-up when the soil crumbles easily into small clumps.

"Based on our analysis, we determine the balance of nutrients to add with fertilizer, which we apply to the soil when we direct seed our crops," says Jocelyn. "I'm surprised how quickly our soil has improved." *(continued)*

Photo: Jocelyn Velestuk

REMEDIES.NET

The Essiac Herbal Remedy Handbook

OLDEST MANUFACTURED IN USA

Learn about the Famous Ojibway Herbal Healing Remedy

Help Fight the War on Cancer • Detoxify Liver
Vet-Owned • Made with Love & Prayers from Pure
Rocky Mtn. Water in Small Batches • Safe for Pets Too!

For Your **FREE** *Copy:*
Call: 1-719-256-4876 *or Write:* PO Box 278 | Crestone, CO 81131

8 Free Ebooks on Healing

STEEL FARM STORAGE

100% MADE IN USA

25 YEAR WARRANTY

100% USABLE SPACE
No Posts • No Beams • No Trusses

IDEAL FOR:
- Hay & Grain
- Equipment
- Workshops

CLEARANCE MODELS

25 x 40	45 x 80
30 x 50	50 x 100
40 x 60	60 x 140

1-800-480-2458
EASY TO ERECT
NO HEAVY EQUIPMENT NEEDED

AgriBilt
BUILDING SYSTEMS

FARMING

SHADES OF GRAZE

Near Byemoor, Alberta, ranchers Terri and Brad Mappin rotationally graze their Hereford-Angus cross cattle on 3,500 acres. Having experienced extreme drought—3 inches of rain fell in 2023 and about twice that in 2024—they have transitioned away from traditional prairie crops, such as canola and wheat, to tame grass pasture (non-native grasses and legumes cultivated for grazing livestock). They started the Palliser Grazing Club around a kitchen table in 2022 to build knowledge with other farmers. Members share pasture recipes for "relay blends" that protect the soil and keep pasture in reserve for spring grazing.

The Mappins' blend now contains chicory, forage peas, forage rape, Italian ryegrass, turnips, and winter wheat. It's planted in spring and can be grazed the first summer with the expectation that some of the crop will emerge the following year. The concept is to extend grazing seasons under adverse conditions with minimal disturbance of the soil.

"We utilize cover crops, such as winter cereals, and ensure we maintain cover on our grasslands by not overgrazing," explains Terri. Keeping soil covered with plants reduces temperature and loss of moisture and prevents bare soil from acting like a solar panel.

"My goal is to stockpile grass where possible," she says. Fearing repeated drought, these farmers practice not haying or grazing a pasture for a year. Says Terri, "It's a grass bank account." ∎

Karen Davidson treads every type of soil across Canada as editor of *The Grower*.

THE CONCEPT IS TO EXTEND GRAZING SEASONS UNDER ADVERSE CONDITIONS.

Photo: Terri Mappin

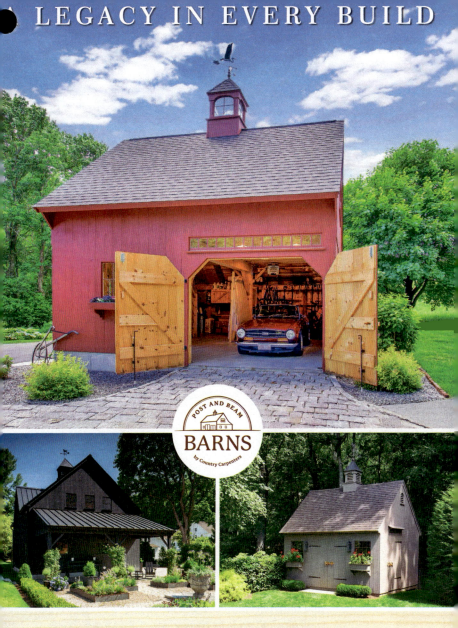

LEGACY IN EVERY BUILD

BARNS BY COUNTRY CARPENTERS, INC.
POSTANDBEAMBARNS.COM (860) 228-2276

Models on Display   Shipped Nationwide

Winter-blooming jasmine

Look after the root of the tree, and the fragrant flower and luscious fruits will grow by themselves. Look after the health of the body, and the fragrance of the mind and richness of the spirit will follow.
–B.K.S. IYENGAR, INDIAN WRITER AND EDUCATOR (1918–2014)

GARDENING

STOP and SMELL the HOUSEPLANTS

IN NEED OF AROMATHERAPY?
FRAGRANT FRIENDS TO THE RESCUE!

BY TOVAH MARTIN

What if the most wonderful perfume imaginable bombarded your nose when you walked through your front door? What if you awoke to the mingled essence of citrus and jasmine waltzing in your bathroom? Imagine if those heady encounters had nothing to do with scented candles or air fresheners. Fragrant flowers tend to have more subtle, ethereal scents than man-made perfumes.

Your nose deserves better. In general, we use it to troubleshoot—to make sure fish fillets haven't gone bad and dinner isn't burning. Instead, your olfactory friend could be enjoying wonderful wafts from a menagerie of potted plants—wouldn't that be nirvana for your nose?

Some flowers send aromas into the air to lure pollinators to do their duties. Other fragrances are hidden in the flower petals and are only discovered when you sample blossoms up close and personal.

Reactions to scents vary according to individual perception. One person's *ahhh* might be someone else's *yuck*, although some scents tend to be universally two thumbs up—like citrus. And fragrance isn't the sole domain of flowers. Some herbs boast aromatic leaves. Their essential oils are held in tiny flasks on a leaf's surface. Tickle the leaf and release the scent into the air. But note: Some fragrant plants may be poisonous—keep away from children or nibbling pets.

Grow one or more of these fragrant houseplants, and aromas (and aromatherapy) will be floating all around: Studies have found that floral scents can improve our mood, putting us in our happy place. *(continued)*

Photo: Bozena Piotrowska/GAP Photos

GARDENING

JASMINE

If French perfume is your ideal, veer straight for the poet's jasmine *(Jasminum officinale)*. The good news is that this loose vine will easily produce its modest star-shaped white flowers in a bright window—a south-facing sill is your best bet. Visually, you won't be thunderstruck by these flowers, but your nose will notice appreciatively. If you want something soapier in scent, go for the bushier angelwing jasmine *(J. nitidum)* with shiny green leaves, a tidy growth habit, and loads of pointed-petal white blossoms, wholesomely perfumed. If you don't mind a muskier montage, the winter-blooming jasmine *(J. polyanthum)* is the beauty queen in the family, forming plump clusters of white-tinged-pink flowers in the dead of winter. Most jasmines do fine in east- or west-facing windows and are easy to grow.

Every fragrant flower wants to be likened to a jasmine, or so it would seem, judging from nicknames. And truly, star jasmine *(Trachelospermum jasminoides)* does mimic jasmine in every sense except family ties. They form meandering vines and produce starry white or cream-colored flowers that spew a scent even more lovely than the namesake they are often mistaken for. We're talking sugary aromas with hints of vanilla or honey. Like jasmines, they're easy to grow, thriving on windowsills facing south, east, or west. They tend to bloom in spring and autumn, forming little nosegays of pinwheel-like blossoms on wiry stems that grow best when supported on mini-trellises. Water them regularly to remain on their good side—and spark a "heaven-scent" host of stars. *(continued)*

Longlight
Beeswax Candles

Think GREEN - Think BEESWAX
- *Environmentally friendly*
- *No Toxins or Carcinogens*
- *Produces Negative Ions to Help Purify the Air*
- *Smokeless & Dripless*

100 Hour Coiled Beeswax Candle
- Beautiful Unique Brass Base
- Self-Extinguishing Holder
- 100+ Hour Burn Time
- Refills Available

100 Hour Candle — $130
30, 60 & 75 hour available

Our candles make great gifts... place your order today!

50 Hour Decorator Candle
- Unique Cast Brass Base
- Self-Extinguishing Holder
- 50+ Hour Burn Time
- Refills Available

50 Hour Candle — $75
30, 60 & 75 hour available

Made in USA. All orders plus shipping & handling.

Longlight Candles
1-866-583-3400
longlightcandles.com

81

GARDENING

STEPHANOTIS

If you like your blossoms buxom, set your sights on stephanotis. With clusters of large, waxy, tubular flowers, stephanotis is such a visual crowd-pleaser that it was once a florist mainstay for wedding bouquets. In keeping with the nuptial theme, the flowers are pearly white, and they're held on vining stems amidst large oval matte-green leaves. The whole presentation is glam, especially when stephanotis is trained into a wreath form. Part of the good news is this acrobat performs its flower-producing stunts in the middle of winter, given a bright south, east, or west window. No special treatment is needed besides regular fertilizing. Stephanotis is a notoriously hungry plant whose appetite should be fed nonstop throughout the year to maintain those deep green leaves and produce its cherry cobbler–scented flowers. Similarly, don't forget to give it pot promotions regularly. *(continued)*

Photo: Visions/GAP Photos

MAXIMUM®
WEATHER INSTRUMENTS

A weather watcher's dream come true.

Get accurate, real-time weather information and enjoy heirloom-quality craftsmanship with our fine weather instruments, handcrafted in the USA. From temperature, wind speed, humidity, and rainfall to interior conditions, there's a Maximum Weather Instrument to measure them all. Many models are Wi-Fi compatible.

**Shop All Styles at Maximum-Inc.com
Or Call to Learn More 508-995-2200**

SAVE 20% WITH CODE "WEATHER26"

Call for free info/pricing!

Shuttercraft
QUALITY WOOD SHUTTERS
INTERIOR & EXTERIOR
EST. 1986

Authentic wood shutters in all types & sizes!
(203) 245-2608 – shuttercraft.com – Madison, CT

GARDENING

CITRUS

Talk about a houseplant with perks—citrus comes with dividends on all levels, and amazingly, you can reap the rewards on a sunny windowsill. A bright south-facing window is sufficient to produce flowers that are plentiful as well as deeply perfumed with a scent that is universally adored. We're talking a clean, effervescent, and sweet (but not cloying) perfume that will float into every nook of your domain. Plus, the blossom bounty hits a crescendo during autumn and winter when your nose needs a little extra love. This can all be yours in the space it takes to host a 12-inch pot. Then, when your little citrus matures, fruit is a potential.

How long it takes to create a crop depends on the type of citrus, the amount of light, and whether you started the plant from a pip or a cutting. Patience and discipline are imperative because fruit must be removed from immature branches until they grow sufficiently strong to support a crop. In addition, steady drinks of water and generous fertilizer (at least once a month, year-round) are the secrets to securing all the good things that citrus can provide. *(continued)*

Photo: New Africa/Shutterstock

AccuWeather
The Most Trusted Weather App

Get real-time, hyperlocal weather updates powered by proven Superior Accuracy™, helping you plan, prepare, and stay better informed.

Download on the **App Store** | GET IT ON **Google Play**

Cellular Service on the Nation's Most Dependable Network.

SWITCH TODAY AND RECEIVE $50

All the latest iPhones and Androids at **Discount Prices!**

That's right a FREE Phone, FREE Shipping and $50

Talk and Text	STARTING AT $10 PER MONTH
Talk, Text and Data	STARTING AT $20 PER MONTH

FREE Flip Phone or Smartphone

Affinity® CELLULAR
AffinityCellular.com

855-893-2893

$50 will be credited to your Affinity account at time of purchase to be used for air time charges, Credit balances from promo are not refundable and are applied to your Affinity charges. Credits may be used over multiple months.

GARDENING

HOYA

In the same family as stephanotis (and also milkweeds), porcelain flowers (aka hoyas) are almost too easy. If your hoya isn't producing abundant clusters of star-within-a-star blossoms, you've probably been killing it with kindness. Fussing over hoyas results in flowerless foliage. Instead, don't repot, don't fertilize, don't overwater, and don't expose the plant to direct light. Lean and mean is what this heirloom plant prefers. For your benign neglect, your reward will be basking in blossoms from spring through late autumn that give off a scent dangerously identical to hot cocoa—chocoholics, beware. Because the leaves sunburn swiftly if exposed to direct sun, you'd be wise to keep your hoya indoors over the summer. Besides that, remember to check the plant periodically for flowers. Hoyas are plants that grow on autopilot—with benefits. *(continued)*

Photo: Visions/GAP Photos

GROW YOUR KNOWLEDGE— AND YOUR BEST GARDENS!

Never touched a trowel in your life? Been gardening at home for decades? Gardeners of every skill level always benefit from having trusted knowledge at their fingertips.

The Old Farmer's Almanac's Gardener's Handbooks are loaded with advice and inspiration to guarantee success for every gardener.

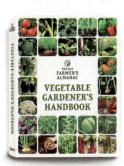 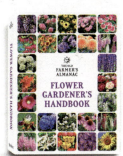 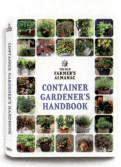

EACH HANDBOOK INCLUDES . . .

- step-by-step guidance on growing more than 30 vegetables or flowering plants
- advice to minimize maintenance and maximize harvests, color, and fragrance
- pages for notes and records
- tips for seed-starting
- the lowdown on disease and pest prevention
- charts and tables for ready reference
- and much more to help you achieve the gardens of your dreams!

COLLECT THEM ALL! GET YOUR COPIES TODAY!
GO TO ALMANAC.COM/SHOP OR AMAZON

GARDENING

HERBS

If you are the touchy-feely type, you've probably already nurtured a few herbs. Plants with fragrant foliage provide positive reinforcement every time you reach out and touch a leaf to release its essential oil. Not all herbs are easy to host indoors, but marjoram, mints, oregano, scented-leaf geraniums, and thyme are a snap. Lavender isn't difficult, but only 'Goodwin Creek Gray' will produce aromatic foliage throughout the winter in a home environment. All herbs require a bright south-facing window, basil being the most demanding in its light requirements. (Then again, you could keep a constant supply of basil—started from seed—growing on the sill in order to harvest the leaves continually.)

On the difficulty scale, rosemary can be a frustration. In addition to bright light, it requires cool temperatures, good air circulation (to prevent mildew), and good luck. Achievers win rights to walk around with their noses in the air. ∎

Writer, lecturer, gardener, and photographer **Tovah Martin** tends more than 200 houseplants in her home, a hobby that makes good scents.

JOIN THE CLUB THAT GROWS WITH YOU

Members receive three seasonal deliveries—packed with Almanac favorites and trusted gardening advice—and save 30% or more compared to buying each item separately!

CLUB-ONLY EXTRAS
• Always save 10% in our online store!
• Exclusive access to our digital archives—more than 200 years of planting wisdom, tips, lore, and more!

Learn more: Go to Almanac.com/Garden2026 or call 1-800-ALMANAC (800-256-2622) and select Option 2.

Just $39.97 + $9.95 shipping

Membership renews annually • Cancel anytime • U.S. shipping only

The World's Most Popular Garden Planning Tool

Go From This . . .

. . . To This!

QUESTIONS? Live chat with gardening experts, available 7 days a week!

7-Day Free Trial, No Credit Card Required!

- Free plot plans and plant pairing recommendations
- Planting calendar, customized for your local climate
- Helps you grow 400+ vegetables, herbs, and flowers!
- Works on any device—no download required

Perfect for beginners and experienced gardeners alike!
GO TO ALMANAC.COM/PLANNER

ALMANAC MARKETPLACE

H₂O Scams Exposed
FREE Report — $15.00 Value

Learn the truth about distilled, mineral, tap, spring, filtered, bottled, well, alkalized, reverse osmosis... Which one is best for you?

Call for FREE Report & Catalog

drinkingwaterhoax.com

Waterwise Inc PO Box 494000 Leesburg FL 34749

800-874-9028 Ext 675

CANADIAN RIVER CRUISING VACATIONS

Experience the beauty and history of Canada's rivers. 4, 5, 6, 7 nights of small ship river cruising with departures from Kingston, Ottawa, and Quebec City.
Call to request our free travel brochure.

1-800-267-7868
www.StLawrenceCruiseLines.com

253 Ontario St., Suite 200 Kingston, ON K7L 2Z4

NEW! LX30 PORTABLE SAWMILL ONLY $2,495*

SAW YOUR OWN LOGS INTO LUMBER

FREE Brochure

Wood-Mizer
from forest to final form

800.553.0182 | woodmizer.com
© 2025 Wood-Mizer LLC   *Price subject to change.

SANDWICH LANTERN

ONION LIGHTS • SCONCES
ANCHOR LIGHTS

made in USA Since 1988

HANDMADE on Cape Cod

Available in:
SOLID COPPER or SOLID BRASS
17 Jan Sebastian Dr., Unit #1, Sandwich, MA 02563
508-833-0515
www.sandwichlantern.com

ALMANAC MARKETPLACE

Cape Cod Cupola, Ltd.

View our quality, one-of-a-kind Azek (PVC) cupolas & handcrafted copper weathervanes & finials at:

www.capecodcupola.com

78 State Rd, Dept. OFA25 • N. Dartmouth, MA 02747

Phone: 508-994-2119

Dallas Pridgen Jewelry
-one at a time, by hand-

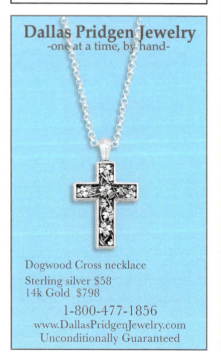

Dogwood Cross necklace
Sterling silver $58
14k Gold $798

1-800-477-1856
www.DallasPridgenJewelry.com
Unconditionally Guaranteed

Family Owned – Gloucester, MA
ORGANIC FERTILIZER FOR EVERYTHING YOU GROW

Neptune's Harvest

Products from the ocean, to set your plants in motion!

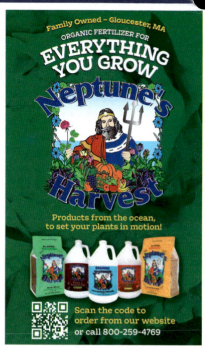

Scan the code to order from our website or call 800-259-4769

ADOPT A COW

Your recipient will be "udderly" delighted to pick their own Vermont cow and get the finest cheddar cheese sent from the dairy. Includes a beautifully illustrated, personalized certificate and a photo of their cow!

We offer 18 unique farm-to-you gifts including Maple Syrup!

Visit RentMotherNature.com

RENT MOTHER NATURE
(617)871-0123

ALMANAC MARKETPLACE

SAVE 10%
USE CODE **OFA25**
@WIDESHOES.COM

SCAN ME

Hitchcock
WIDESHOES.COM
Men's & Women's

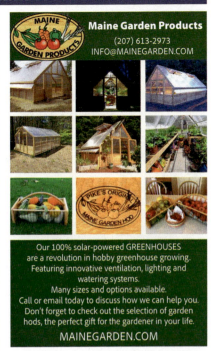

Maine Garden Products
(207) 613-2973
INFO@MAINEGARDEN.COM

Our 100% solar-powered GREENHOUSES are a revolution in hobby greenhouse growing. Featuring innovative ventilation, lighting and watering systems.
Many sizes and options available.
Call or email today to discuss how we can help you.
Don't forget to check out the selection of garden hods, the perfect gift for the gardener in your life.

MAINEGARDEN.COM

Finally, a civilized way to polish your silver!
... and your brass, copper, & nickel, too!

CAPE COD METAL POLISHING CLOTHS

before — after

Economy-Size Tin
contains
12 Polishing Cloths
1 Buffing Cloth
1 Pair of Gloves

www.**capecodpolish**.com

Charming cedar shutters
All types/sizes

Shuttercraft
QUALITY WOOD SHUTTERS
INTERIOR & EXTERIOR
EST. 1986

Shuttercraft.com
Madison, CT
(203) 245-2608

ALMANAC MARKETPLACE

We'Moon 2026

Inspiring astrological moon phase calendar brimming with women's creative art & writing.

Use code **Almanac26** for 15% off!

mothertongue@wemoon.ws
1.877.693.6666 • wemoon.ws

Hernia Brief

10-DAY MONEY-BACK GUARANTEE
Use Code **OFA25** for 20% Off!

MAY AVOID OPERATION

Looks like regular undergarment. 50,000+ satisfied customers! Super comfortable. Invented & made in Europe. Wear 24 hrs.
CALL 1-866-888-1331
www.HerniaBrief.com

HAIR FOR MEN
www.nobocorp.com
1 800 732 4359
Human or Synthetic Hair.
12,000+ Systems in Stock!
50+ Years in Business.
30-DAY MONEY-BACK!

Use code **OFA25** for 10% Off!

Starting at $389+

TRULY UNDETECTABLE!

CREATEK WELL COVERS & SEPTIC COVERS

The most realistic artificial rock covers

BEFORE AFTER

BEFORE AFTER

(413) 455-5511 • createkrocks.com
6 Chambers Road • Palmer, MA

Mohican Wind Harps

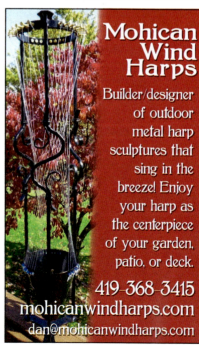

Builder/designer of outdoor metal harp sculptures that sing in the breeze! Enjoy your harp as the centerpiece of your garden, patio, or deck.

419-368-3415
mohicanwindharps.com
dan@mohicanwindharps.com

ALMANAC MARKETPLACE

Mrs. Nelson's
CANDY HOUSE
"Your house for all occasions"

Candies! For over 50 years we have used only the finest ingredients in our candies—cream, butter, honey, and special blends of chocolates. Call for a FREE brochure. Long famous for quality candies mailed all over the world. Treat yourself or someone special today.

Come visit us today!
292 Chelmsford St. • Chelmsford, MA 01824

For Free Brochure Call:
978-256-4061
Visit Our Website:
mrsnelsonscandyhouse.com

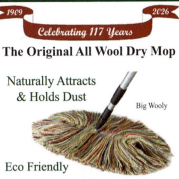

1909 — Celebrating 117 Years — 2026

The Original All Wool Dry Mop

Naturally Attracts & Holds Dust

Big Wooly

Eco Friendly

Handmade in Vermont, this pure Wool Dust Mop is the ecological alternative to disposable, chemically-laced pads. The natural lanolin in the wool attracts and holds the dust. The Velcro backing allows for quick & easy removal of the dust head from its 12" frame for laundering. Handle included. Dusting area measures 11" x 18". Starting at $49.98 FREE S&H.

Shop online: sladust.com
Sladust - 217-4 Maxham Meadow Way
Woodstock, VT 05091
802-779-2541
Online Coupon for 6% off - Code: FA6

Restoration Motors
Restomods • Street Rods • Hot Rods
Muscle Cars • Customs • Pickup Trucks

OUR SERVICES

Mechanical Work • Body • Paint
Restorations • Sheet Metal Fab
Chassis Suspension • Custom Fabrication
LS Swaps • EFI Installs

603-465-7270
RESTORATIONMOTORS.COM
Email: info@restorationmotors.com

269 Proctor Hill Road • Hollis NH 03049

*FORMERLY KNOWN AS RMR RESTORATION

Millie's PIEROGI

are HANDMADE using the finest quality ingredients, and are fully cooked before packaging. One dozen delicious pierogi are nestled in a tray, making a one pound package of pure enjoyment!

Try any of our popular fillings:
Cabbage • Potato & Cheese • Cheese
Prune • Kielbasa w/Potato & Cheese
•Blueberry • Potato & Onion

Box of 3 Trays - $34
Box of 6 Trays - $53
Box of 10 Trays - $79
Polish Picnic - $53
Polish Party Pack - $79
Kapusta & 5 Trays - $56

Call Toll free or visit our website:
800-743-7641 - milliespierogi.com

PERISHABLE
Open Me Up and Store in Fridge or Freezer

Here comes another RUSH

WEATHER

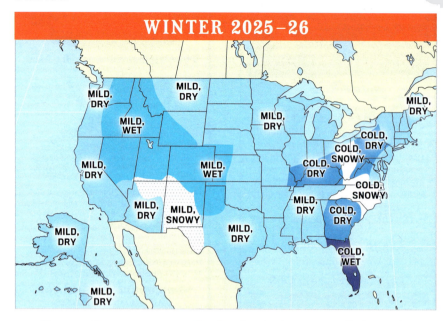

These weather maps correspond to the winter and summer predictions in the General Weather Forecast (opposite) and on the regional forecast pages, 206–223. For maps corresponding to the spring and fall predictions, visit Almanac.com/2026.

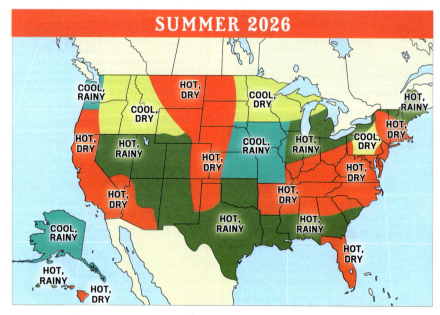

Maps: AccuWeather, Inc.

THE GENERAL WEATHER REPORT AND FORECAST

FOR REGIONAL FORECASTS, SEE PAGES 206-223

What's shaping the weather? Solar Cycle 25 is peaking, with its peak already exceeding that of Solar Cycle 24. Historically, solar cycles have been linked to temperature trends, on average, across Earth, but this relationship has become weaker in recent decades. The transition of La Niña from weak to neutral is another important factor. Oscillations are linked to ocean-atmosphere weather patterns recurring over long periods. We expect the warm phase of the Atlantic Multidecadal Oscillation and the cool phase of the Pacific Decadal Oscillation to continue. We're also monitoring the stratospheric winds near the equator, the Quasi-Biennial Oscillation. Some or all of these factors may cause the polar vortex to displace southward this winter, sending cold air from across Canada south into the United States.

WINTER will be colder than normal from the Appalachians southward through the Southeast and Florida and westward across the Ohio Valley and near normal or milder elsewhere. Precipitation will be below normal for most areas, except for near- to above-normal amounts across Florida and from the southern High Plains through the Intermountain region and the eastern Desert Southwest. Snowfall will be above normal for much of the Carolinas and throughout the southern Appalachians, into the eastern Ohio Valley, and across the southern Rockies and eastern Desert Southwest. Snowfall will be near to below normal everywhere else.

SPRING temps will be warmer than normal for most places, but near normal or cooler across parts of the eastern Upper Midwest and from the northern Rockies through much of the northern Pacific Northwest. Rainfall will be above normal from the southern Appalachians through the eastern Ohio Valley, from the western Lower Lakes through much of the Upper Midwest, the Tennessee Valley through the southern Plains and New Mexico, northward along the front range of the Rockies into the northern Intermountain region, and across northern Alaska and central and western Hawaii.

SUMMER will be hotter than normal, except for near- to below-normal temps across the northern Appalachians, from the Heartland through the Upper Midwest, from the northern Rockies to the Washington and northern Oregon coasts, and throughout Alaska. Rainfall will be above normal across the northern Northeast and the Lower Lakes through the Heartland, from the South Carolina coast through the Gulf Coastal Plain into Texas and Oklahoma, across the lower Rockies through the Great Basin, over western Washington and northwest Oregon, and across Alaska and central and western Hawaii; it will be near to below normal elsewhere.

Watch for a **TROPICAL DEPRESSION** in Florida in early November and in the northern Appalachians in late June. The best chances for **TROPICAL STORMS** will be in Texas in late May, the Deep South in early June, Florida through the Atlantic Corridor in late June, the Atlantic Corridor in mid-August, across the Deep South and Texas in late August, and Hawaii in mid-September. Watch for a **HURRICANE** across Florida and the Southeast in mid-August.

AUTUMN will be cooler than normal, except for near normal or warmer temps from the Deep South through most of Texas and the Heartland, from the High Plains through the central Rockies and the Desert Southwest, and across southern Alaska. Rainfall will be above normal in the Northeast, across southern Florida, from Oklahoma into Texas, from the central and northern Rockies through much of the West Coast, and across Hawaii. It will be near to below normal everywhere else.

TO GET A SUMMARY OF THE RESULTS OF OUR FORECAST FOR LAST WINTER, TURN TO PAGE 204.

THE OLD FARMER'S ALMANAC

YANKEE PUBLISHING INC.
EDITORIAL AND PUBLISHING OFFICES
P.O. Box 520, 1121 Main Street, Dublin, NH 03444
Phone: 603-563-8111 • Fax: 603-563-8252

EDITOR *(14th since 1792)*: Carol Connare
CREATIVE DIRECTOR: Colleen Quinnell
MANAGING EDITOR: Sarah Perreault
EXECUTIVE EDITOR: Heidi Stonehill
COPY EDITOR: Cate Hewitt
ASSOCIATE EDITORS: Joe Bills, Tim Goodwin
WEATHER GRAPHICS AND CONSULTATION:
AccuWeather, Inc.

V.P., NEW MEDIA AND PRODUCTION: Paul Belliveau
PRODUCTION DIRECTOR: David Ziarnowski
PRODUCTION MANAGER: Brian Johnson
SENIOR PRODUCTION ARTISTS:
Jennifer Freeman, Rachel Kipka, Janet Selle

ALMANAC.COM
EXECUTIVE DIGITAL EDITOR: Catherine Boeckmann
DIGITAL EDITOR: Jennifer Keating
SENIOR WEB DESIGNER: Amy O'Brien
DIGITAL MANAGER: Holly Sanderson
EMAIL MARKETING MANAGER: Eric Bailey
DIGITAL MARKETING SPECIALIST: Jessica Garcia
E-COMMERCE DIRECTOR: Alan Henning
E-COMMERCE SPECIALIST: Nicole Melanson
CUSTOMER RETENTION: Kalibb Vaillancourt
SENIOR DRUPAL DEVELOPER: Mark Gordon

CONTACT US
We welcome your questions and comments about articles in and topics for this almanac. Mail all editorial correspondence to Editor, The Old Farmer's Almanac, P.O. Box 520, Dublin, NH 03444-0520; fax us at 603-563-8252; or contact us through Almanac.com/Contact. *The Old Farmer's Almanac* cannot accept responsibility for unsolicited manuscripts and will not acknowledge any hard-copy queries or manuscripts that do not include a stamped and addressed return envelope.

All printing inks used in this edition of *The Old Farmer's Almanac* are soy-based. This product is recyclable. Consult local recycling regulations for the right way to do it.

Thank you for buying this almanac! We hope that you find it "useful, with a pleasant degree of humor." Thanks, too, to everyone who had a hand in it, including advertisers, distributors, printers, and sales and delivery people.

No part of this almanac may be reproduced in whole or in part, or stored in a retrieval system, or transmitted in any form or by any means (electronic, mechanical, photocopying, recording, or other) without written permission of the publisher.

OUR CONTRIBUTORS

DAVID BARTONE writes the Farmer's Calendars from his multi-acre permaculture homestead in the western Massachusetts foothills. A faculty member at UMass Amherst's University Without Walls, he teaches courses in writing, sustainability, and other subjects. His poetry books include *Spring Logic* (H_NGM_N, 2010) and *Practice on Mountains* (Ahsahta Press, 2014).

BOB BERMAN, our astronomy editor, leads annual tours to Chilean observatories as well as to view solar eclipses and the northern lights. He is the author of 12 books, including *Zoom* (2014) and *Earth-Shattering: Violent Supernovas, Galactic Explosions, Biological Mayhem, Nuclear Meltdowns, and Other Hazards to Life in Our Universe* (2019), both published by Little, Brown and Company.

DAN CLARK writes the weather doggerel verse that runs down the center of the Right-Hand Calendar Pages. His late father, Tim Clark, wrote the weather doggerel for more than 40 years.

BETHANY E. COBB, our astronomer, is an Associate Professor of Honors and Physics at George Washington University. In addition to conducting research on gamma-ray bursts and teaching astronomy and physics courses to non–science majors, she enjoys rock climbing, figure skating, and reading science fiction.

CELESTE LONGACRE, our astrologer, often refers to astrology as "a study of timing, and timing is everything." A New Hampshire native, she has been a practicing astrologer for more than 40 years. Her book, *Celeste's Garden Delights* (2015), is available on her website, CelesteLongacre.com.

BOB SMERBECK and **BRIAN THOMPSON,** our meteorologists, bring more than 50 years of forecasting expertise to the task, as well as some unique early accomplishments: a portable, wood-and-PVC-pipe tornado machine built by Bob and prescient 5-day forecasts made by Brian—in fourth grade.

ADVERTISEMENT

Popular CoQ10 Pills Leave Millions Suffering

Could this newly-discovered brain fuel solve America's worsening memory crisis?

PALM BEACH, FLORIDA — Millions of Americans take the supplement known as CoQ10. It's the coenzyme that supercharges the "energy factories" in your cells known as mitochondria. But there's a serious flaw that's leaving millions unsatisfied.

As you age, your mitochondria break down and fail to produce energy. In a revealing study, a team of researchers showed that 95 percent of the mitochondria in a 90-year-old man were damaged, compared to almost no damage in the mitochondria of a 5-year-old.

Taking CoQ10 alone is not enough to solve this problem. Because as powerful as CoQ10 is, there's one critical thing it fails to do: it can't create new mitochondria to replace the ones you lost.

And that's bad news for Americans all over the country. The loss of cellular energy is a problem for the memory concerns people face as they get older.

"We had no way of replacing lost mitochondria until a recent discovery changed everything," says Dr. Al Sears, founder and medical director of the Sears Institute for Anti-Aging Medicine in Palm Beach, Florida. "Researchers discovered the only nutrient known to modern science that has the power to trigger the growth of new mitochondria."

Why Taking CoQ10 is Not Enough

Dr. Sears explains, "This new discovery is so powerful, it can multiply your mitochondria by 55 percent in just a few weeks. That's the equivalent of restoring decades of lost brain power."

This exciting nutrient — called PQQ (pyrroloquinoline quinone) — is the driving force behind a revolution in aging. When paired with CoQ10, this dynamic duo has the power to reverse the age-related memory losses you may have thought were beyond your control.

Dr. Sears pioneered a new formula — called **Ultra Accel Q** — that combines both CoQ10 and PQQ to support maximum cellular energy and the normal growth of new mitochondria. **Ultra Accel Q** is the first of its kind to address both problems and is already creating huge demand.

In fact, demand has been so overwhelming that inventories repeatedly sell out. But a closer look at **Ultra Accel Q** reveals there are good reasons why sales are booming.

Science Confirms the Many Benefits of PQQ

The medical journal *Biochemical Pharmacology* reports that PQQ is up to 5,000 times more efficient in sustaining energy production than common antioxidants. With the ability to keep every cell in your body operating at full strength, **Ultra Accel Q** delivers more than just added brain power and a faster memory.

People feel more energetic, more alert, and don't need naps in the afternoon. The boost in cellular energy generates more power to your heart, lungs, muscles, and more.

"With the PQQ in Ultra Accel, I have energy I never thought possible at my age," says Colleen R., one of Dr. Sears's patients. "I'm in my 70s but feel 40 again. I think clearly, move with real energy and sleep like a baby."

The response has been overwhelmingly positive, and Dr. Sears receives countless emails from his patients and readers. "My patients tell me they feel better than they have in years. This is ideal for people who are feeling old and run down, or for those who feel more forgetful. It surprises many that you can add healthy and productive years to your life simply by taking **Ultra Accel Q** every day."

You may have seen Dr. Sears on television or read one of his 12 best-selling books. Or you may have seen him speak at the 2016 WPBF 25 Health and Wellness Festival in South Florida, featuring Dr. Oz and special guest Suzanne Somers. Thousands of people attended Dr. Sears's lecture on anti-aging breakthroughs and waited in line for hours during his book signing at the event.

Will Ultra Accel Q Multiply Your Energy?

Ultra Accel Q is turning everything we thought we knew about youthful energy on its head. Especially for people over age 50. In less than 30 seconds every morning, you can harness the power of this breakthrough discovery to restore peak energy and your "spark for life."

So, if you've noticed less energy as you've gotten older, and you want an easy way to reclaim your youthful edge, this new opportunity will feel like blessed relief.

The secret is the "energy multiplying" molecule that activates a dormant gene in your body that declines with age, which then instructs

MEMORY-BUILDING SENSATION: Top doctors are now recommending new *Ultra Accel Q* because it restores decades of lost brain power without a doctor's visit.

your cells to pump out fresh energy from the inside-out. This growth of new "energy factories" in your cells is called mitochondrial biogenesis.

Instead of falling victim to that afternoon slump, you enjoy sharp-as-a-tack focus, memory, and concentration from sunup to sundown. And you get more done in a day than most do in a week. Regardless of how exhausting the world is now.

Dr. Sears reports, "The most rewarding aspect of practicing medicine is watching my patients get the joy back in their lives. **Ultra Accel Q** sends a wake-up call to every cell in their bodies... And they actually feel young again."

And his patients agree. "I noticed a difference within a few days," says Jerry from Ft. Pierce, Florida. "My endurance has almost doubled, and I feel it mentally, too. There's a clarity and sense of well-being in my life that I've never experienced before."

How To Get Ultra Accel Q

This is the official nationwide release of **Ultra Accel Q** in the United States. And so, the company is offering a special discount supply to anyone who calls during the official launch.

An Order Hotline has been set up for local readers to call. This gives everyone an equal chance to try **Ultra Accel Q**. And your order is backed up by a no-hassle, 90-day money back guarantee. No questions asked.

Starting at 7:00 AM today, the discount offer will be available for a limited time only. All you have to do is call TOLL FREE 1-888-358-9716 right now and use promo code OFAUAQ825 to secure your own supply.

Important: Due to **Ultra Accel Q** recent media exposure, phone lines are often busy. If you call and do not immediately get through, please be patient and call back.

THESE STATEMENTS HAVE NOT BEEN EVALUATED BY THE FOOD AND DRUG ADMINISTRATION. THIS PRODUCT IS NOT INTENDED TO DIAGNOSE, TREAT, CURE OR PREVENT ANY DISEASE. RESULTS MAY VARY. 15.

EnergAire

CLEARS THE AIR OF SMOKE, POLLEN, and POLLUTION

- Purifies up to 4,000 cubic feet (a large room)
- No noisy fan or costly filter
- Requires no maintenance
- Uses less than 2 watts
- 9" high, 3" diameter
- Weighs less than 1 pound
  $69.95

RODAR® II ULTRASOUND GETS RID OF RATS, MICE, BATS, ROACHES, and OTHER PESTS

- Super-powerful professional ultrasonic pest repeller
- RODAR ultrasound equals a jet engine— a noise unbearable to pests
- Handsome simulated walnut cabinet 5-5/8" high
- Uses less than 5 watts
- Weighs 1½ pounds **$99.95**

Made in the U.S.A.

―――――― **To Order** ――――――

Send cost for unit(s) plus $12.00 each for S&H (in Mass. add 6.25% tax) by check, money order, or credit card number and expiration date to:

MICRON CORPORATION
Dept. 937, 89 Access Road
Norwood, MA 02162

CALL TOLL-FREE 1-800-456-0734
www.MicronCorp.com/ofa

THE OLD
FARMER'S ALMANAC

Established in 1792 and published every year thereafter
ROBERT B. THOMAS, *founder* (1766–1846)

YANKEE PUBLISHING INC.
P.O. Box 520, 1121 Main Street, Dublin, NH 03444
Phone: 603-563-8111 • Fax: 603-563-8252
PUBLISHER *(23rd since 1792)*: Sherin Pierce

FOR DISPLAY ADVERTISING RATES
Go to Almanac.com/AdvertisingInfo or
call 800-895-9265, ext. 109

Stephanie Bernbach-Crowe • 914-827-0015
Steve Hall • 800-736-1100, ext. 320

FOR CLASSIFIED ADVERTISING
Cindy Levine, RJ Media • 212-986-0016

SENIOR AD PRODUCTION COORDINATOR:
Janet Selle • 800-895-9265, ext. 168

PUBLIC RELATIONS
Vaughan Communications • 360-620-9107
Ginger Vaughan • ginger@vaughancomm.com

CONSUMER ORDERS & INFO
Call 800-ALMANAC (800-256-2622), ext. 1
or go to Almanac.com/Shop

RETAIL SALES
Stacey Korpi • 800-895-9265, ext. 160
Janice Edson, ext. 126

DISTRIBUTORS
NATIONAL: Comag Marketing Group
BOOKSTORE: HarperCollins Publishers
New York, NY
NEWSSTAND CONSULTANT: PSCS Consulting
Linda Ruth • 603-924-4407

Our publications are available for sales promotions
or premiums. Contact Beacon Promotions,
info@beaconpromotions.com.

YANKEE PUBLISHING INCORPORATED
A 100% EMPLOYEE-OWNED COMPANY

Jamie Trowbridge, *President*
Paul Belliveau, Ernesto Burden, Judson D. Hale Jr.,
Brook Holmberg, Jennie Meister, Sherin Pierce,
Vice Presidents
Judson D. Hale Sr., *Editor Emeritus*

Yankee Publishing Inc. assumes no responsibility for claims made by advertisers or failure by its advertisers to deliver any goods or services advertised herein. Publication of any advertisement by *The Old Farmer's Almanac* is not an endorsement of the product or service advertised therein.

PRINTED IN U.S.A.

ASTRONOMY
ECLIPSES

There will be four eclipses in 2026, two of the Sun and two of the Moon. Solar eclipses are visible only in certain areas and require eye protection to be viewed safely. Lunar eclipses are technically visible from the entire night side of Earth, but during a penumbral eclipse, the dimming of the Moon's illumination is slight. See the **Astronomical Glossary, page 110,** for explanations of the different types of eclipses.

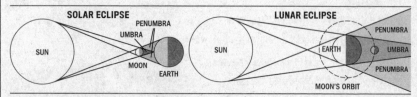

FEBRUARY 17: ANNULAR ECLIPSE OF THE SUN. This eclipse is not visible from North America. (The annular solar eclipse is visible from regions in East Antarctica, although most of Antarctica will experience only a partial solar eclipse. The partial eclipse will also be visible from southern regions in Argentina and Chile, and southern Africa.)

MARCH 3: TOTAL ECLIPSE OF THE MOON. This eclipse is visible from North America, although it is best observed from central or western North America, because the Moon will set during the umbral phase when observed from eastern North America. The Moon will enter the penumbra at 3:44 A.M. EST (12:44 A.M. PST) and umbra at 4:50 A.M. EST (1:50 A.M. PST). It will leave the umbra at 8:17 A.M. EST (5:17 A.M. PST) and penumbra at 9:23 A.M. EST (6:23 A.M. PST).

AUGUST 12: TOTAL ECLIPSE OF THE SUN. This eclipse is visible only as a partial solar eclipse from Canada and some northern U.S. states. (The total eclipse will be visible from the Arctic, Greenland, Iceland, and Spain.) The eclipse begins at 11:34 A.M. EDT (8:34 A.M. PDT) and ends at 3:57 P.M. EDT (12:57 P.M. PDT), with local visibility dependent on location. As with all partial eclipses, this event is safe to observe only when using proper eye protection, such as eclipse glasses or viewers.

AUGUST 27–28: PARTIAL ECLIPSE OF THE MOON. This eclipse is visible from North America. In western regions, the Moon will be rising during the eclipse, so the Moon may be very low on the horizon while entering the umbra. The Moon will enter the penumbra at 9:22 P.M. EDT (6:22 P.M. PDT) on August 27 and umbra at 10:33 P.M. EDT (7:33 P.M. PDT). It will leave the umbra at 1:52 A.M. EDT on August 28 (10:52 P.M. PDT, August 27) and penumbra at 3:03 A.M. EDT (12:03 A.M. PDT).

THE MOON'S PATH

The Moon's path across the sky changes with the seasons. Full Moons are very high in the sky (at midnight) between November and February and very low in the sky between May and July.

FULL-MOON DATES (ET)

	2026	2027	2028	2029	2030
JAN.	3	22	11	30	19
FEB.	1	20	10	28	18
MAR.	3	22	10	29	19
APR.	1	20	9	28	17
MAY	1 & 31	20	8	27	17
JUNE	29	18	7	25	15
JULY	29	18	6	25	14
AUG.	28	17	5	23	13
SEPT.	26	15	3	22	11
OCT.	26	15	3	22	11
NOV.	24	13	2	20	9
DEC.	23	13	1 & 31	20	9

ADVERTISEMENT

New Blood Flow Breakthrough Helps Men Enjoy Strong, Long-Lasting Intimacy – At Any Age

A new discovery that supports nitric oxide production and healthy blood flow gives men across the country new hope for a satisfying bedroom performance

After age 40, it's common knowledge that performance begins to decline in many men. However, a new potency formula is showing that any healthy man can now enjoy strong, long-lasting, and frequent performance at any age.

This doctor-designed protocol, created by leading anti-aging expert Dr. Al Sears, is celebrating its highly effective 5th generation formula, which is already helping men support a healthy performance and libido.

When Dr. Sears released the first pill — Primal Max Black — it quickly became a trusted men's performance helper, promoting bedroom fun across America.

It worked by supporting healthy testosterone levels. However, Dr. Sears knows from almost 30 years in private practice that testosterone isn't the only performance challenge men face. That's why his dual strategy includes attention to blood flow because no amount of testosterone will replace the need for healthy blood flow for successful intimacy.

And this second formula became Primal Max Red.

SUPPORTING THE MECHANICS IS AS IMPORTANT AS SUPPORTING THE HORMONES

While Primal Max Black helped maintain optimal testosterone, Primal Max Red tackles a lesser-known challenge.

Truth is, we ignore the importance of blood flow and circulation for supporting a man's sex life. Because without blood flow, nothing happens.

Luckily, a Nobel prize-winning scientist discovered a means to help support performance, strength, and confidence by supporting vital blood flow, which is essential for a satisfying performance.

Using this landmark Nobel Prize as its basis, Primal Max Red supports healthy blood flow by using a key ingredient to support nitric oxide production. Nitric oxide is the molecule that allows blood vessels to relax and expand, thereby increasing blood flow.

Al Sears MD, who has authored over 500 scientific papers and has appeared on more than 50 media outlets including ABC News, CNN, ESPN, and many more says, "Supporting optimal blood flow is an essential component of maintaining sexual health as men age. Then, once we optimized it and had a great deal of success, we set out to see if we could do even better."

Conventional nitric oxide supplements are limited to smaller doses of key ingredients because everything must fit into small capsules. But Dr. Sears followed the science and introduced a revolutionary new powder version of his Primal Max Red formula.

This new powder formulation enabled him to include bigger doses of the key nutrients, which matched the doses used in published clinical studies. Not only is the formula more effective because it uses proven doses, it also means you get a delicious drink instead of more and more pills.

HEALTHY BLOOD FLOW DELIVERS SATISFYING RESULTS

IMMEDIATE GAME CHANGER FOR AMERICAN MEN: Doctors are now recommending Primal Max Red for its ability to support the vital but overlooked need for healthy blood flow during intimacy.

Primal Max Red is the best way to maintain an active life. It works by supporting blood flow and the production of nitric oxide.

This critical support is the reason men across the country are enjoying a full and satisfying performance at any age. Because testosterone is not the only factor men need to consider.

Primal Max Red effectively promotes healthy blood flow that men can use to support intimacy in the bedroom. The unique and powerful blend of ingredients in Primal Max Red supports the kind of sexual health and performance men are looking for.

"There was a time when supporting healthy blood flow for men was impossible," Dr. Sears said. "But science and technology have come a long way in recent years. And now, with the creation of nitric oxide-supporting Primal Max Red, men can feel more confident and more in control while they enjoy intimacy at any age."

Now for men across America, it's much easier to support peak performance as they get older.

HOW TO GET PRIMAL MAX RED ALONG WITH COMPLEMENTARY BOTTLES OF PRIMAL MAX BLACK

To secure the new Primal Max Red formula, readers should contact the Primal Max Red Health Hotline at **1-888-358-8923** and use promo code **OFAPMAX825** within 48 hours. And to cut down on the cost for customers, it can only be purchased directly from the company.

READERS ALSO GET AN EXTRA BONUS SUPPLY OF PRIMAL MAX BLACK

Every order of Primal Max Red gets a matching supply of Dr. Sears' testosterone formula Primal Max Black for no additional charge.

All orders are backed by a 100% money-back guarantee. If any user is not satisfied, just send back the bottle(s) or any unused product within 90 days from the purchase date, and you'll get all your money back.

ASTRONOMY
BRIGHT STARS

TRANSIT TIMES

This table shows the time (ET) and altitude of a star as it transits the meridian (i.e., reaches its highest elevation while passing over the horizon's south point) at Boston on the dates shown. The transit time on any other date differs from that of the nearest date listed by approximately 4 minutes per day. To find the time of a star's transit for your location, convert its time at Boston using Key Letter C **(see Time Corrections, page 238).**

STAR	CONSTELLATION	MAGNITUDE	JAN. 1	MAR. 1	MAY 1	JULY 1	SEPT. 1	NOV. 1	ALTITUDE (DEGREES)
Altair	Aquila	0.8	**12:51**	8:59	5:59	1:59	**9:51**	**4:51**	56.3
Deneb	Cygnus	1.3	**1:41**	9:49	6:49	2:49	**10:41**	**5:42**	92.8
Fomalhaut	Psc. Aus.	1.2	**3:57**	**12:05**	9:05	5:06	1:02	**7:58**	17.8
Algol	Perseus	2.2	**8:07**	**4:15**	**1:15**	9:16	5:12	1:12	88.5
Aldebaran	Taurus	0.9	**9:35**	**5:43**	**2:43**	10:43	6:39	1:39	64.1
Rigel	Orion	0.1	**10:13**	**6:21**	**3:21**	11:21	7:17	2:18	39.4
Capella	Auriga	0.1	**10:16**	**6:24**	**3:24**	11:24	7:20	2:21	93.6
Bellatrix	Orion	1.6	**10:24**	**6:32**	**3:32**	11:32	7:28	2:28	54.0
Betelgeuse	Orion	var. 0.4	**10:54**	**7:02**	**4:02**	**12:02**	7:58	2:58	55.0
Sirius	Can. Maj.	-1.4	**11:43**	**7:51**	**4:51**	**12:52**	8:48	3:48	31.0
Procyon	Can. Min.	0.4	12:41	**8:45**	**5:46**	**1:46**	9:42	4:42	52.9
Pollux	Gemini	1.2	12:48	**8:52**	**5:52**	**1:52**	9:48	4:48	75.7
Regulus	Leo	1.4	3:10	**11:14**	**8:14**	**4:14**	**12:11**	7:11	59.7
Spica	Virgo	var. 1.0	6:26	2:34	**11:31**	**7:31**	**3:27**	10:27	36.6
Arcturus	Boötes	-0.1	7:16	3:24	12:25	**8:21**	**4:17**	11:17	66.9
Antares	Scorpius	var. 0.9	9:30	5:38	2:38	**10:35**	**6:31**	**1:31**	21.3
Vega	Lyra	0	11:37	7:45	4:45	12:45	**8:37**	**3:37**	86.4

RISE AND SET TIMES

To find the time of a star's rising at Boston on any date, subtract the interval shown at right from the star's transit time on that date; add the interval to find the star's setting time. To find the rising and setting times for your city, convert the Boston transit times above using the Key Letter shown at right before applying the interval **(see Time Corrections, page 238).** Deneb, Algol, Capella, and Vega are circumpolar stars—they never set but appear to circle the celestial north pole.

STAR	INTERVAL (H.M.)	RISING KEY	DIR.*	SETTING KEY	DIR.*
Altair	6 36	B	EbN	E	WbN
Fomalhaut	3 59	E	SE	D	SW
Aldebaran	7 06	B	ENE	D	WNW
Rigel	5 33	D	EbS	B	WbS
Bellatrix	6 27	B	EbN	D	WbN
Betelgeuse	6 31	B	EbN	D	WbN
Sirius	5 00	D	ESE	B	WSW
Procyon	6 23	B	EbN	D	WbN
Pollux	8 01	A	NE	E	NW
Regulus	6 49	B	EbN	D	WbN
Spica	5 23	D	EbS	B	WbS
Arcturus	7 19	A	ENE	E	WNW
Antares	4 17	E	SEbE	A	SWbW

*b = "by"

Fast-disappearing classics...

1935-1937 Set of Buffalo Nickels!

SAVE OVER 75%!

Get 3 Buffalo nickels from 1935—1937 for only $3.95! Struck over 85 years ago, these classic coins feature the most uniquely American design ever minted! The Indian/buffalo motif was a major change from traditional Liberty designs, and these coins have been cherished since their introduction in 1913. Produced in limited quantities, most Buffalo nickels wore out, were lost in circulation, or have disappeared into permanent collections. And those that remain in existence today are scarce and in great demand!

SAVE OVER 75% plus FREE GIFT!
Get a consecutive 3-year set of 1935-1937 Buffalo nickels now for ONLY $3.95 – **SAVE OVER 75%** off the regular price of $17.25, and get **Free Shipping**.

You'll also receive a handpicked trial selection **of fascinating coins from our No-Obligation Coins-on-Approval Service**, from which you may purchase any or none of the coins—return balance in 15 days—with option to cancel at any time. **Order now and *SAVE!***

45-Day Money Back Guarantee of Satisfaction

Mail Coupon Today! For Faster Service Visit:
LittletonCoin.com/Respond

Offer Code: 44T400

©2025 LCC, Inc.

Special Offer for New Customers Only

☑ YES! Please send me the following:

QTY	DESCRIPTION	PRICE	TOTAL
	3-Coin Buffalo Nickel Set Consecutive Dates (*limit 5 sets*)	$3.95	
	Display Folder Made in USA	$5.95	
	Lincoln "Wheat" Cent	**FREE!**	
	Sales Tax	**FREE!**	
	Shipping	**FREE!**	
	TOTAL $		

Mail to: **Littleton Coin Company®** *Serving Collectors Since 1945*
Offer Code: 44T400
1309 Mt. Eustis Road
Littleton NH 03561-3737

ORDER DEADLINE: 12:00 MIDNIGHT JULY 31, 2026

☐ Check payable to Littleton Coin Company

Charge my: ☐ VISA ☐ MC ☐ AMEX ☐ DISC

Card #: _____ Exp. Date __/__

Name _____
Please print clearly
Address _____ Apt# ____
City _____ State ____ Zip ____
E-Mail _____

ASTRONOMY
THE TWILIGHT ZONE/METEOR SHOWERS

Twilight is the time when the sky is partially illuminated preceding sunrise and again following sunset. The ranges of twilight are defined according to the Sun's position below the horizon. **Civil twilight** occurs when the Sun's center is between the horizon and 6 degrees below the horizon (visually, the horizon is clearly defined). **Nautical twilight** occurs when the center is between 6 and 12 degrees below the horizon (the horizon is distinct). **Astronomical twilight** occurs when the center is between 12 and 18 degrees below the horizon (sky illumination is imperceptible). When the center is at 18 degrees (**dawn** or **dark**) or below, there is no illumination.

LENGTH OF ASTRONOMICAL TWILIGHT (HOURS AND MINUTES)

LATITUDE	JAN. 1–APR. 10	APR. 11–MAY 2	MAY 3–MAY 14	MAY 15–MAY 25	MAY 26–JULY 22	JULY 23–AUG. 3	AUG. 4–AUG. 14	AUG. 15–SEPT. 5	SEPT. 6–DEC. 31
25°N to 30°N	1 20	1 23	1 26	1 29	1 32	1 29	1 26	1 23	1 20
31°N to 36°N	1 26	1 28	1 34	1 38	1 43	1 38	1 34	1 28	1 26
37°N to 42°N	1 33	1 39	1 47	1 52	1 59	1 52	1 47	1 39	1 33
43°N to 47°N	1 42	1 51	2 02	2 13	2 27	2 13	2 02	1 51	1 42
48°N to 49°N	1 50	2 04	2 22	2 42	–	2 42	2 22	2 04	1 50

TO DETERMINE THE LENGTH OF TWILIGHT: The length of twilight changes with latitude and the time of year. See the **Time Corrections, page 238,** to find the latitude of your city or the city nearest you. Use that figure in the chart above with the appropriate date to calculate the length of twilight in your area.

TO DETERMINE ARRIVAL OF DAWN OR DARK: Calculate the sunrise/sunset times for your locality using the instructions in **How to Use This Almanac, page 116.** Subtract the length of twilight from the time of sunrise to determine when dawn breaks. Add the length of twilight to the time of sunset to determine when dark descends.

EXAMPLE:
BOSTON, MASS. (LATITUDE 42°22')

Sunrise, August 1	5:37 A.M. ET
Length of twilight	– 1 52
Dawn breaks	3:45 A.M.
Sunset, August 1	8:04 P.M. ET
Length of twilight	+ 1 52
Dark descends	9:56 P.M.

PRINCIPAL METEOR SHOWERS

SHOWER	BEST VIEWING	POINT OF ORIGIN	DATE OF MAXIMUM*	NO. PER HOUR**	ASSOCIATED COMET
Quadrantid	**Predawn**	**N**	**Jan. 4**	**25**	**–**
Lyrid	Predawn	S	Apr. 22	10	Thatcher
Eta Aquarid	Predawn	SE	May 4	10	Halley
Delta Aquarid	Predawn	S	July 30	10	–
Perseid	**Predawn**	**NE**	**Aug. 11–13**	**50**	**Swift-Tuttle**
Draconid	Late evening	NW	Oct. 9	6	Giacobini-Zinner
Orionid	Predawn	S	Oct. 21–22	15	Halley
Northern Taurid	Late evening	S	Nov. 9	3	Encke
Leonid	Predawn	S	Nov. 17–18	10	Tempel-Tuttle
Andromedid	Late evening	S	Nov. 25–27	5	Biela
Geminid	**All night**	**NE**	**Dec. 13–14**	**75**	**–**
Ursid	Predawn	N	Dec. 22	5	Tuttle

*May vary by 1 or 2 days   **In a moonless, rural sky   **Bold** = most prominent

ASTRONOMY
THE VISIBLE PLANETS

Listed here for Boston are viewing suggestions for and the rise and set times (ET) of Venus, Mars, Jupiter, and Saturn on specific days each month, as well as when it is best to view Mercury. Approximate rise and set times for other days can be found by interpolation. Use the Key Letters at the right of each listing to convert the times for other localities **(see pages 116 and 238)**.

GET ALL PLANET RISE AND SET TIMES BY ZIP CODE VIA ALMANAC.COM/2026.

VENUS

The sky's brightest starlike object, Venus, begins a long evening apparition at the end of February, when it stands 7 degrees high in the west at 6:00 P.M. In mid-May, Venus and Jupiter, the night's two brightest "stars," gradually get visibly closer each evening, culminating in a brilliant conjunction from June 7 to 10. Venus reaches maximum brilliance from July through September, but in August, at its brightest, it hangs lower in the sky each evening and becomes too hard to see by early October. Venus makes its return as a morning "star" in November, standing next to the crescent Moon on November 7. As it ascends in the sky, the planet is spectacular throughout December, dominating the east at 6:00 A.M.

Jan. 1	rise 7:13 E	Apr. 1	set 8:54 D	July 1	set 10:45 E	Oct. 1	set 6:57 A
Jan. 11	set **4:34** A	Apr. 11	set 9:20 E	July 11	set 10:32 D	Oct. 11	set 6:12 A
Jan. 21	set **4:58** A	Apr. 21	set 9:45 E	July 21	set 10:15 D	Oct. 21	set 5:24 B
Feb. 1	set **5:26** B	May 1	set 10:09 E	Aug. 1	set 9:53 C	Nov. 1	rise 5:22 D
Feb. 11	set **5:52** B	May 11	set 10:30 E	Aug. 11	set 9:32 C	Nov. 11	rise 4:22 D
Feb. 21	set **6:17** C	May 21	set 10:46 E	Aug. 21	set 9:08 B	Nov. 21	rise 3:43 D
Mar. 1	set **6:37** C	June 1	set 10:56 E	Sept. 1	set 8:39 B	Dec. 1	rise 3:22 D
Mar. 11	set **8:02** C	June 11	set 10:59 E	Sept. 11	set 8:10 B	Dec. 11	rise 3:15 D
Mar. 21	set **8:27** D	June 21	set 10:55 E	Sept. 21	set 7:37 A	Dec. 21	rise 3:17 D
						Dec. 31	rise 3:25 D

MARS

Mars's once-every-26-month opposition means that it has alternating good and bad years for viewing—2026 being one of the latter. The Red Planet first appears low in the east before dawn in mid-May. It's easily found on May 14, when the thin crescent Moon stands above it at 5:00 A.M. At around 4:30 A.M. on July 4, a close conjunction of Mars and dim green Uranus is best seen through binoculars. Mars is to the right of the crescent Moon on August 9 at 4:30 A.M. It's just below the Moon at 5:45 A.M. on September 6, and, reaching a bright magnitude 0.7, forms a tight conjunction with Jupiter and Leo's main star, Regulus, on November 16. Mars, at a magnitude 0, rises around 10:00 P.M. in mid-December to the left of Jupiter.

Jan. 1	set **4:26** A	Apr. 1	rise 5:53 C	July 1	rise 2:44 A	Oct. 1	rise 12:57 A
Jan. 11	rise 7:17 E	Apr. 11	rise 5:30 C	July 11	rise 2:28 A	Oct. 11	rise 12:47 A
Jan. 21	rise 7:05 E	Apr. 21	rise 5:08 C	July 21	rise 2:13 A	Oct. 21	rise 12:36 B
Feb. 1	rise 6:49 E	May 1	rise 4:46 C	Aug. 1	rise 1:59 A	Nov. 1	rise **11:21** B
Feb. 11	rise 6:32 E	May 11	rise 4:24 B	Aug. 11	rise 1:47 A	Nov. 11	rise **11:06** B
Feb. 21	rise 6:14 D	May 21	rise 4:02 B	Aug. 21	rise 1:36 A	Nov. 21	rise **10:49** B
Mar. 1	rise 5:58 D	June 1	rise 3:39 B	Sept. 1	rise 1:26 A	Dec. 1	rise **10:30** B
Mar. 11	rise 6:38 D	June 11	rise 3:20 B	Sept. 11	rise 1:16 A	Dec. 11	rise **10:07** B
Mar. 21	rise 6:17 D	June 21	rise 3:01 B	Sept. 21	rise 1:07 A	Dec. 21	rise 9:41 B
						Dec. 31	rise 9:09 B

BOLD = P.M. LIGHT = A.M.

JUPITER

♃ The largest planet has its opposition on January 10, making it the night's most brilliant "star" during the first 2 months. Low in the east at nightfall, Jupiter hovers next to the Moon on January 3 and again on January 30, and March 25 and 26. The gas giant dominates the night through early spring, then gloriously meets Venus from June 7 to 10. Jupiter returns as a morning "star" in August, closely meeting Mercury at mid-month. On October 6 at 4:22 A.M., Jupiter is eclipsed by the Moon in an event called an occultation. Jupiter will reappear about an hour later.

Jan. 1	rise	5:00	A	Apr. 1	set	2:49	E	July 1	set	9:38	E	Oct. 1	rise	2:31	B
Jan. 11	set	7:18	E	Apr. 11	set	2:12	E	July 11	set	9:05	E	Oct. 11	rise	2:01	B
Jan. 21	set	6:34	E	Apr. 21	set	1:37	E	July 21	set	8:33	E	Oct. 21	rise	1:29	B
Feb. 1	set	5:46	E	May 1	set	1:02	E	Aug. 1	rise	5:26	B	Nov. 1	rise	11:50	B
Feb. 11	set	5:03	E	May 11	set	12:28	E	Aug. 11	rise	4:58	B	Nov. 11	rise	11:16	B
Feb. 21	set	4:21	E	May 21	set	11:52	E	Aug. 21	rise	4:30	B	Nov. 21	rise	10:41	B
Mar. 1	set	3:48	E	June 1	set	11:15	E	Sept. 1	rise	3:59	B	Dec. 1	rise	10:04	B
Mar. 11	set	4:08	E	June 11	set	10:43	E	Sept. 11	rise	3:30	B	Dec. 11	rise	9:26	B
Mar. 21	set	3:30	E	June 21	set	10:10	E	Sept. 21	rise	3:01	B	Dec. 21	rise	8:46	B
												Dec. 31	rise	8:04	B

SATURN

The Ringed Planet is the only bright "star" in the south at nightfall in January. In February, it sinks lower in the southwest each evening and will be a challenge to observe when it meets Venus in the west at 7:15 P.M. on March 7 and 8—but telescope users may want to try since Saturn's rings are nearly edgewise, which only happens every 15 years. Also, its many moons are in a row and imitate Jupiter's satellites. After being lost in the solar glare in March and April, Saturn returns as a morning "star" and can be seen to the right of the Moon on May 14 at 5:00 A.M. Saturn reaches opposition on October 4. The Ringed Planet is near the Moon on November 20 and December 17, when it's seen best through a telescope earlier in the night.

Jan. 1	set	10:37	C	Apr. 1	rise	6:25	C	July 1	rise	12:48	C	Oct. 1	rise	6:37	C
Jan. 11	set	10:01	C	Apr. 11	rise	5:48	C	July 11	rise	12:09	C	Oct. 11	set	6:17	C
Jan. 21	set	9:26	C	Apr. 21	rise	5:12	C	July 21	rise	11:27	C	Oct. 21	set	5:34	C
Feb. 1	set	8:48	C	May 1	rise	4:35	C	Aug. 1	rise	10:44	C	Nov. 1	set	3:47	C
Feb. 11	set	8:14	C	May 11	rise	3:58	C	Aug. 11	rise	10:04	C	Nov. 11	set	3:05	C
Feb. 21	set	7:40	C	May 21	rise	3:21	C	Aug. 21	rise	9:24	C	Nov. 21	set	2:24	C
Mar. 1	set	7:14	C	June 1	rise	2:41	C	Sept. 1	rise	8:40	C	Dec. 1	set	1:43	C
Mar. 11	set	7:41	C	June 11	rise	2:03	C	Sept. 11	rise	7:59	C	Dec. 11	set	1:03	C
Mar. 21	set	7:08	C	June 21	rise	1:26	C	Sept. 21	rise	7:18	C	Dec. 21	set	12:25	C
												Dec. 31	set	11:43	C

MERCURY

Due to its close proximity to the Sun, the smallest planet presents observational challenges. To avoid being overwhelmed by sunlight, observers must look for the innermost planet when it's near the edges of its orbit and angled most vertically from the horizon. In 2026, Mercury is best seen in the western evening sky from February 8 to 18. Look for its striking conjunction with the crescent Moon at 6:00 P.M. on February 18. For morning observers, Mercury is best seen during the first week of August and especially from November 14 to 27, when it's below Venus.

DO NOT CONFUSE: *Jupiter with Venus*, when both are in the west at nightfall, during May and June. While they outshine everything else in the sky, Venus is brighter. • *Mars with Leo's main star, Regulus*, on November 16 and 30. Mars is brighter and appears orange. • *Uranus with the faint stars in Taurus* when it dangles beneath the Moon on October 27. Seen through binoculars, Uranus is the only green "star" below the famous Pleiades star cluster.

ASTRONOMY
ASTRONOMICAL GLOSSARY

APHELION (APH.): The point in a planet's orbit that is farthest from the Sun.

APOGEE (APO.): The point in the Moon's orbit that is farthest from Earth.

CELESTIAL EQUATOR (EQ.): The imaginary circle around the celestial sphere that can be thought of as the plane of Earth's equator projected out onto the sphere.

CELESTIAL SPHERE: An imaginary sphere projected into space that represents the entire sky, with an observer on Earth at its center. All celestial bodies other than Earth are imagined as being on its inside surface.

CIRCUMPOLAR: Always visible above the horizon, such as a circumpolar star.

CONJUNCTION: The time at which two or more celestial bodies appear closest in the sky. **Inferior (Inf.):** Mercury or Venus is between the Sun and Earth. **Superior (Sup.):** The Sun is between a planet and Earth. Actual dates for conjunctions are given on the **Right-Hand Calendar Pages, 121–147**; the best times for viewing the closely aligned bodies are given in **Sky Watch** on the **Left-Hand Calendar Pages, 120–146**.

DECLINATION: The celestial latitude of an object in the sky, measured in degrees north or south of the celestial equator; comparable to latitude on Earth. This almanac gives the Sun's declination at noon.

ECLIPSE, LUNAR: The full Moon enters the shadow of Earth, which cuts off all or part of the sunlight reflected off the Moon. **Total:** The Moon passes completely through the umbra (central dark part) of Earth's shadow. **Partial:** Only part of the Moon passes through the umbra. **Penumbral:** The Moon passes through only the penumbra (area of partial darkness surrounding the umbra). See **page 102** for more information about eclipses.

ECLIPSE, SOLAR: Earth enters the shadow of the new Moon, which cuts off all or part of the Sun's light. **Total:** Earth passes through the umbra (central dark part) of the Moon's shadow, resulting in totality for observers within a narrow band on Earth. **Annular:** The Moon appears silhouetted against the Sun, with a ring of sunlight showing around it. **Partial:** The Moon blocks only part of the Sun.

ECLIPTIC: The apparent annual path of the Sun around the celestial sphere. The plane of the ecliptic is tipped 23½° from the celestial equator.

ELONGATION: The difference in degrees between the celestial longitudes of a planet and the Sun. **Greatest Elongation (Gr. Elong.):** The greatest apparent distance of a planet from the Sun, as seen from Earth.

EPACT: A number from 1 to 30 that indicates the Moon's age on January 1 at Greenwich, England; used in determining the date of Easter.

EQUINOX: When the Sun crosses the celestial equator. This event occurs two times each year: **Vernal** is around March 20 and **Autumnal** is around September 22.

EVENING STAR: A planet that is above the western horizon at sunset and less than 180° east of the Sun in right ascension.

GOLDEN NUMBER: A number in the 19-year Metonic cycle of the Moon, used in determining the date of Easter. See **page 149** for this year's Golden Number.

MAGNITUDE: A measure of a celestial object's brightness. **Apparent magnitude** measures the brightness of an object as seen from Earth. Objects with an apparent magnitude of 6 or less are observable to the naked eye. The lower the magnitude, the greater the brightness; an object with a magnitude of –1, e.g., is brighter than one with a magnitude of +1.

MIDNIGHT: Astronomically, the time when the Sun is opposite its highest point in the sky. Both 12 hours before and after noon (so, technically, both A.M. and P.M.), midnight in civil time is usually treated as the beginning of the day. It is displayed as 12:00 A.M. on 12-hour digital clocks. On a 24-hour cycle, 00:00, not 24:00, usually indicates midnight.

MOON ON EQUATOR: The Moon is on the celestial equator.

MOON RIDES HIGH/RUNS LOW: The Moon is highest above or farthest below the celestial equator.

MOONRISE/MOONSET: When the Moon rises above or sets below the horizon.

MOON'S PHASES: The changing appearance of the Moon, caused by the different angles at which it is illuminated by the Sun. **First Quarter:** Right half of the Moon is illuminated. **Full:** The Sun and the Moon are in opposition; the entire disk of the Moon is illuminated. **Last Quarter:** Left half of the Moon is illuminated. **New:** The Sun and the Moon are in conjunction; the Moon is darkened because it lines up between Earth and the Sun.

MOON'S PLACE, Astronomical: The position of the Moon within the constellations on the celestial sphere at midnight. **Astrological:** The position of the Moon within the tropical zodiac, whose twelve 30° segments (signs) along the ecliptic were named more than 2,000 years ago after constellations within each area. Because of precession and other factors, the zodiac signs no longer match actual constellation positions.

MORNING STAR: A planet that is above the eastern horizon at sunrise and less than 180° west of the Sun in right ascension.

NODE: Either of the two points where a celestial body's orbit intersects the ecliptic. **Ascending:** When the body is moving from south to north of the ecliptic. **Descending:** When the body is moving from north to south of the ecliptic.

OCCULTATION (OCCN.): When the Moon or a planet eclipses a star or planet.

OPPOSITION: The Moon or a planet appears on the opposite side of the sky from the Sun (elongation 180°).

PERIGEE (PERIG.): The point in the Moon's orbit that is closest to Earth.

PERIHELION (PERIH.): The point in a planet's orbit that is closest to the Sun.

PRECESSION: The slowly changing position of the stars and equinoxes in the sky caused by a slight wobble as Earth rotates around its axis.

RIGHT ASCENSION (R.A.): The celestial longitude of an object in the sky, measured eastward along the celestial equator in hours of time from the vernal equinox; comparable to longitude on Earth.

SOLSTICE, Summer: When the Sun reaches its greatest declination (23½°) north of the celestial equator, around June 21. **Winter:** When the Sun reaches its greatest declination (23½°) south of the celestial equator, around December 21.

STATIONARY (STAT.): The brief period of apparent halted movement of a planet against the background of the stars shortly before it appears to move backward/westward (retrograde motion) or forward/eastward (direct motion).

SUN FAST/SLOW: When a sundial is ahead of (fast) or behind (slow) clock time.

SUNRISE/SUNSET: The visible rising/setting of the upper edge of the Sun's disk across the unobstructed horizon of an observer whose eyes are 15 feet above ground level.

TWILIGHT: See **page 106.** ■

Note: These definitions apply to the Northern Hemisphere; some do not hold true for locations in the Southern Hemisphere.

ASTRONOMY
THE PLANETS OF THE SOLAR SYSTEM

Our solar system is made up of eight planets (including Earth), each unique in its own way. Five of these—Mercury, Venus, Mars, Jupiter, and Saturn—are visible to the naked eye, but to truly see all of the planets and their remarkable features, you should use a telescope if possible. (In 2006, the International Astronomical Union reclassified Pluto—once considered our solar system's ninth planet—as a dwarf planet.)

The best times to view each planet, including its conjunctions and brightest moments, can be found in **Visible Planets (pages 108–109)** and **Sky Watch (pages 120–146)**. (Note: Only objects with an orbit whose path takes it farther from the Sun than Earth can be in opposition—when the Moon or a planet is on the opposite side of the sky from the Sun and appears at its brightest.)

How do planets in our solar system compare? Read on to learn more.

MERCURY
Facts: smallest planet and closest to the Sun; temperature can go to as low as –290°F at night; second densest planet
Mean temperature: 333°F
Radius: 1,516 miles
Distance from Sun (avg.): 36 million miles
Closest distance to Earth: 48 million miles
Length of day: 59 Earth days
Structure: solid, metallic inner core with molten outer core; rocky mantle; solid crust
Length of year: 88 Earth days
Moons: None

VENUS
Facts: 1 day on Venus is longer than 1 Venus year; 36,000-foot-tall Maxwell Montes (mountain) is taller than Mount Everest; thousands of volcanoes
Mean temperature: 867°F
Radius: 3,760 miles
Distance from Sun (avg.): 67 million miles
Closest distance to Earth: 24 million miles
Length of day: 243 Earth days
Structure: iron core (similar to Earth's) enveloped by a hot rock mantle; rocky, exterior crust
Length of year: 224.7 Earth days
Moons: None

EARTH
Facts: 70 percent ocean; surface includes volcanoes, mountains, valleys, rivers, lakes, trees, plants; densest planet in solar system; only planet to sustain life
Mean temperature: 59°F
Radius: 3,963 miles
Distance from Sun (avg.): 93 million miles
Length of Day: 23.9 hours
Structure: iron and nickel metals (core), iron and nickel fluids; molten rock; oceanic and continental crust
Length of year: 365.25 days
Moons: 1

MARS
Facts: reddish surface due to oxidation; Valles Marineris canyon system is 10 times the size of Grand Canyon; Olympus Mons is largest volcano in solar system
Mean temperature: –85°F
Radius: 2,106 miles
Distance from Sun (avg.): 142 million miles
Closest distance to Earth: 34.6 million miles
Length of day: 24.6 hours
Structure: core made of iron, nickel, and sulfur; rocky mantle; crust made of iron, magnesium, aluminum, calcium, and potassium
Length of year: 687 Earth days
Opposition: every 26 months—next: February 19, 2027
Moons: 2—Phobos and Deimos

JUPITER
Facts: largest planet in solar system; four rings; largest ocean in solar system—made of hydrogen
Mean temperature: –166°F
Radius: 43,441 miles
Distance from Sun (avg.): 484 million miles
Closest distance to Earth: 367 million miles
Length of day: 10 hours
Structure: hydrogen and helium
Length of year: 4,333 Earth days (about 12 Earth years)
Opposition: every 13 months—next: January 10, 2026
Moons: 95, including Callisto and Ganymede (largest in solar system)

SATURN
Facts: rings composed of ice, dust, and rock; winds in upper atmosphere reach 1,090 mph—more than four times faster than the strongest hurricane-force winds on Earth
Mean temperature: –220°F
Radius: 36,183 miles
Distance from Sun (avg.): 886 million miles
Closest distance to Earth: 746 million miles
Length of day: 10.7 hours
Structure: core of iron and nickel; hydrogen and helium
Length of year: 10,756 Earth days (about 29.4 Earth years)
Opposition: every 378 days—next: September 21, 2025; October 4, 2026
Moons: 146, including Titan—second largest in solar system

URANUS
Facts: two sets of rings (13 total); blue-green color comes from methane gas in atmosphere; near core, temperature can reach 9,000°F
Mean temperature: –320°F
Radius: 15,759 miles
Distance from Sun (avg.): 1.8 billion miles
Closest distance to Earth: 1.6 billion miles
Length of day: 17.4 hours
Structure: small, rocky core; one of two ice giants in solar system; most of mass made up of swirling fluids—water, methane, and ammonia
Length of year: 30,687 Earth days (about 84 Earth years)
Opposition: every 369 days—next: November 21, 2025; November 25, 2026
Moons: 28—named for characters in works by William Shakespeare and Alexander Pope

NEPTUNE
Facts: has the only large moon (Triton) in the solar system that orbits in the opposite direction of its planet's rotation; 5 rings, 4 ring arcs; windiest planet with surface speeds of more than 1,200 mph
Mean temperature: –330°F
Radius: 15,299 miles
Distance from Sun (avg.): 2.8 billion miles
Closest distance to Earth: 2.7 billion miles
Length of day: 16 hours
Structure: small, rocky core; one of two ice giants in solar system; most of mass made up of swirling fluids—water, methane, and ammonia
Length of year: 60,190 Earth days (about 165 Earth years)
Opposition: every 367 days—next: September 23, 2025; September 25, 2026
Moons: 16, including Triton

CALENDAR

2025

JANUARY
S	M	T	W	T	F	S
			1	2	3	4
5	6	7	8	9	10	11
12	13	14	15	16	17	18
19	20	21	22	23	24	25
26	27	28	29	30	31	

FEBRUARY
S	M	T	W	T	F	S
						1
2	3	4	5	6	7	8
9	10	11	12	13	14	15
16	17	18	19	20	21	22
23	24	25	26	27	28	

MARCH
S	M	T	W	T	F	S
						1
2	3	4	5	6	7	8
9	10	11	12	13	14	15
16	17	18	19	20	21	22
23	24	25	26	27	28	29
30	31					

APRIL
S	M	T	W	T	F	S
		1	2	3	4	5
6	7	8	9	10	11	12
13	14	15	16	17	18	19
20	21	22	23	24	25	26
27	28	29	30			

MAY
S	M	T	W	T	F	S
				1	2	3
4	5	6	7	8	9	10
11	12	13	14	15	16	17
18	19	20	21	22	23	24
25	26	27	28	29	30	31

JUNE
S	M	T	W	T	F	S
1	2	3	4	5	6	7
8	9	10	11	12	13	14
15	16	17	18	19	20	21
22	23	24	25	26	27	28
29	30					

JULY
S	M	T	W	T	F	S
		1	2	3	4	5
6	7	8	9	10	11	12
13	14	15	16	17	18	19
20	21	22	23	24	25	26
27	28	29	30	31		

AUGUST
S	M	T	W	T	F	S
					1	2
3	4	5	6	7	8	9
10	11	12	13	14	15	16
17	18	19	20	21	22	23
24	25	26	27	28	29	30
31						

SEPTEMBER
S	M	T	W	T	F	S
	1	2	3	4	5	6
7	8	9	10	11	12	13
14	15	16	17	18	19	20
21	22	23	24	25	26	27
28	29	30				

OCTOBER
S	M	T	W	T	F	S
			1	2	3	4
5	6	7	8	9	10	11
12	13	14	15	16	17	18
19	20	21	22	23	24	25
26	27	28	29	30	31	

NOVEMBER
S	M	T	W	T	F	S
						1
2	3	4	5	6	7	8
9	10	11	12	13	14	15
16	17	18	19	20	21	22
23	24	25	26	27	28	29
30						

DECEMBER
S	M	T	W	T	F	S
	1	2	3	4	5	6
7	8	9	10	11	12	13
14	15	16	17	18	19	20
21	22	23	24	25	26	27
28	29	30	31			

2026

JANUARY
S	M	T	W	T	F	S
				1	2	3
4	5	6	7	8	9	10
11	12	13	14	15	16	17
18	19	20	21	22	23	24
25	26	27	28	29	30	31

FEBRUARY
S	M	T	W	T	F	S
1	2	3	4	5	6	7
8	9	10	11	12	13	14
15	16	17	18	19	20	21
22	23	24	25	26	27	28

MARCH
S	M	T	W	T	F	S
1	2	3	4	5	6	7
8	9	10	11	12	13	14
15	16	17	18	19	20	21
22	23	24	25	26	27	28
29	30	31				

APRIL
S	M	T	W	T	F	S
			1	2	3	4
5	6	7	8	9	10	11
12	13	14	15	16	17	18
19	20	21	22	23	24	25
26	27	28	29	30		

MAY
S	M	T	W	T	F	S
					1	2
3	4	5	6	7	8	9
10	11	12	13	14	15	16
17	18	19	20	21	22	23
24	25	26	27	28	29	30
31						

JUNE
S	M	T	W	T	F	S
	1	2	3	4	5	6
7	8	9	10	11	12	13
14	15	16	17	18	19	20
21	22	23	24	25	26	27
28	29	30				

JULY
S	M	T	W	T	F	S
			1	2	3	4
5	6	7	8	9	10	11
12	13	14	15	16	17	18
19	20	21	22	23	24	25
26	27	28	29	30	31	

AUGUST
S	M	T	W	T	F	S
						1
2	3	4	5	6	7	8
9	10	11	12	13	14	15
16	17	18	19	20	21	22
23	24	25	26	27	28	29
30	31					

SEPTEMBER
S	M	T	W	T	F	S
		1	2	3	4	5
6	7	8	9	10	11	12
13	14	15	16	17	18	19
20	21	22	23	24	25	26
27	28	29	30			

OCTOBER
S	M	T	W	T	F	S
				1	2	3
4	5	6	7	8	9	10
11	12	13	14	15	16	17
18	19	20	21	22	23	24
25	26	27	28	29	30	31

NOVEMBER
S	M	T	W	T	F	S
1	2	3	4	5	6	7
8	9	10	11	12	13	14
15	16	17	18	19	20	21
22	23	24	25	26	27	28
29	30					

DECEMBER
S	M	T	W	T	F	S
		1	2	3	4	5
6	7	8	9	10	11	12
13	14	15	16	17	18	19
20	21	22	23	24	25	26
27	28	29	30	31		

2027

JANUARY
S	M	T	W	T	F	S
					1	2
3	4	5	6	7	8	9
10	11	12	13	14	15	16
17	18	19	20	21	22	23
24	25	26	27	28	29	30
31						

FEBRUARY
S	M	T	W	T	F	S
	1	2	3	4	5	6
7	8	9	10	11	12	13
14	15	16	17	18	19	20
21	22	23	24	25	26	27
28						

MARCH
S	M	T	W	T	F	S
	1	2	3	4	5	6
7	8	9	10	11	12	13
14	15	16	17	18	19	20
21	22	23	24	25	26	27
28	29	30	31			

APRIL
S	M	T	W	T	F	S
				1	2	3
4	5	6	7	8	9	10
11	12	13	14	15	16	17
18	19	20	21	22	23	24
25	26	27	28	29	30	

MAY
S	M	T	W	T	F	S
						1
2	3	4	5	6	7	8
9	10	11	12	13	14	15
16	17	18	19	20	21	22
23	24	25	26	27	28	29
30	31					

JUNE
S	M	T	W	T	F	S
		1	2	3	4	5
6	7	8	9	10	11	12
13	14	15	16	17	18	19
20	21	22	23	24	25	26
27	28	29	30			

JULY
S	M	T	W	T	F	S
				1	2	3
4	5	6	7	8	9	10
11	12	13	14	15	16	17
18	19	20	21	22	23	24
25	26	27	28	29	30	31

AUGUST
S	M	T	W	T	F	S
1	2	3	4	5	6	7
8	9	10	11	12	13	14
15	16	17	18	19	20	21
22	23	24	25	26	27	28
29	30	31				

SEPTEMBER
S	M	T	W	T	F	S
			1	2	3	4
5	6	7	8	9	10	11
12	13	14	15	16	17	18
19	20	21	22	23	24	25
26	27	28	29	30		

OCTOBER
S	M	T	W	T	F	S
					1	2
3	4	5	6	7	8	9
10	11	12	13	14	15	16
17	18	19	20	21	22	23
24	25	26	27	28	29	30
31						

NOVEMBER
S	M	T	W	T	F	S
	1	2	3	4	5	6
7	8	9	10	11	12	13
14	15	16	17	18	19	20
21	22	23	24	25	26	27
28	29	30				

DECEMBER
S	M	T	W	T	F	S
			1	2	3	4
5	6	7	8	9	10	11
12	13	14	15	16	17	18
19	20	21	22	23	24	25
26	27	28	29	30	31	

Love calendar lore? Find more via Almanac.com/2026.

HOW TO USE
A CALENDAR OF THE HEAVENS FOR 2026

The **Calendar Pages** are the heart of *The Old Farmer's Almanac*. They present sky sightings and astronomical data for the entire year and are what make this book a true almanac, a "calendar of the heavens." In essence, these pages are unchanged since 1792, when Robert B. Thomas published his first edition. The long columns of numbers and symbols reveal all of nature's precision, rhythm, and glory, providing an astronomical look at the year 2026.

HOW TO USE THE CALENDAR PAGES

The astronomical data on the **Calendar Pages (120–147)** are calculated for Boston (where Robert B. Thomas learned to calculate the data for his first almanac). Guidance for calculating the times of these events for your locale appears on **pages 116–117**. Note that the results will be *approximate*. Find the *exact* time of any astronomical event at your locale via **Almanac.com/2026**. You can also go to **Almanac.com/SkyMap** to print each month's "Sky Map," which may be useful for viewing with "Sky Watch" in the Calendar Pages.

For a list of 2026 holidays and observances, see **pages 148–149**. Also check out the **Glossary of Almanac Oddities** on **pages 150–151**, which describes some of the more obscure entries traditionally found on the **Right-Hand Calendar Pages (121–147)**.

ABOUT THE TIMES: All times are given in ET (Eastern Time), except where otherwise noted as AT (Atlantic Time, +1 hour), CT (Central Time, -1), MT (Mountain Time, -2), PT (Pacific Time, -3), AKT (Alaska Time, -4), or HAT (Hawaii-Aleutian Time, -5). Between 2:00 A.M., March 8, and 2:00 A.M., November 1, Daylight Saving Time is assumed in those locales where it is observed.

ABOUT THE TIDES: Tide times for Boston appear on **pages 120–146;** for Boston tide heights, see **pages 121–147**. Tide Corrections for East Coast locations appear on **pages 236–237**. Tide heights and times for locations across the United States and Canada are available via **Almanac.com/2026**.

HOW TO USE

The Left-Hand Calendar Pages, 120 to 146

On these pages are the year's astronomical predictions for Boston (42°22' N, 71°3' W). Learn how to calculate the times of these events for your locale here. For more tools, go to **Almanac.com/2026**.

A SAMPLE MONTH

SKY WATCH: The paragraph at the top of each Left-Hand Calendar Page describes the best times to view conjunctions, meteor showers, planets, and more. (Also see **How to Use the Right-Hand Calendar Pages, page 118**.)

	1		2		3	4	5		6		7	8
DAY OF YEAR	DAY OF MONTH	DAY OF WEEK	☀ RISES H.M.	RISE KEY	☀ SETS H.M.	SET KEY	LENGTH OF DAY H.M.	SUN FAST M.	SUN DECLINATION ° '	HIGH TIDE TIMES BOSTON	☾ RISES H.M.	RISE KEY	☾ SETS H.M.	SET KEY	☾ ASTRON. PLACE	☾ AGE
60	1	Fr.	6:20	D	5:34	C	11 14	4	7 s. 30	7¼ 8	3:30	E	12:58	B	SAG	25
61	2	Sa.	6:18	D	5:35	C	11 17	4	7 s. 07	8¼ 9	4:16	E	1:51	B	SAG	26
62	3	**F**	6:17	D	5:36	C	11 19	4	6 s. 44	9¼ 9¾	4:56	E	2:47	B	CAP	27
63	4	M.	6:15	D	5:37	C	11 22	4	6 s. 21	10 10½	5:31	E	3:45	C	CAP	28

1. To calculate the sunrise time in your locale: Choose a day. Note its Sunrise Key Letter. Find your (nearest) city on **page 238**. Add or subtract the minutes that correspond to the Sunrise Key Letter to/from the sunrise time for Boston.†

EXAMPLE:
To calculate the sunrise time in Denver, Colorado, on day 1:

Sunrise, Boston, with Key Letter D (above)	6:20 A.M. ET
Value of Key Letter D for Denver (p. 238)	+ 11 minutes
Sunrise, Denver	6:31 A.M. MT

To calculate your sunset time, repeat, using Boston's sunset time and its Sunset Key Letter value.

2. To calculate the length of day: Choose a day. Note the Sunrise and Sunset Key Letters. Find your (nearest) city on **page 238**. Add or subtract the minutes that correspond to the Sunset Key Letter to/from Boston's length of day. *Reverse* the sign (e.g., minus to plus) of the Sunrise Key Letter minutes. Add or subtract it to/from the first result.

EXAMPLE:
To calculate the length of day in Richmond, Virginia, on day 1:

Length of day, Boston (above)	11h.14m.
Sunset Key Letter C for Richmond (p. 242)	+ 25m.
	11h.39m.
Reverse Sunrise Key Letter D for Richmond (p. 242, +17 to −17)	− 17m.
Length of day, Richmond	11h.22m.

3. Use Sun Fast to change sundial time to clock time. A sundial reads natural (Sun) time, which is neither Standard nor Daylight time. To calculate clock time on a sundial in Boston, subtract the minutes given in this column; add the minutes when preceded by an asterisk [*].

†For locations where Daylight Saving Time is never observed, subtract 1 hour from results between the second Sunday of March and first Sunday of November.

To convert the time to your (nearest) city, use Key Letter C on **page 238**.

EXAMPLE:

To change sundial to clock time in Boston or Salem, Oregon, on day 1:

Sundial reading (Boston or Salem)	12:00 noon
Subtract Sun Fast (p. 116)	− 4 minutes
Clock time, Boston	11:56 A.M. ET**
Use Key Letter C for Salem (p. 241)	+ 27 minutes
Clock time, Salem	12:23 P.M. PT**

**Note: Add 1 hour to the results in locations where Daylight Saving Time is currently observed.

4. This column gives the degrees and minutes of the Sun from the celestial equator at noon ET.

5. This column gives the approximate times of high tide in Boston. For example, the first high tide occurs at 7:15 A.M. and the second occurs at 8:00 P.M. the same day. (A dash indicates that high tide occurs on or after midnight and is recorded on the next day.) Figures for calculating approximate high tide times for localities other than Boston are given in the **Tide Corrections** table on **page 236**.

6. To calculate the moonrise time in your locale: Choose a day. Note the Moonrise Key Letter. Find your (nearest) city on **page 238**. Add or subtract the minutes that correspond to the Moonrise Key Letter to/from the moonrise time given for Boston.

LONGITUDE OF CITY	CORRECTION MINUTES	LONGITUDE OF CITY	CORRECTION MINUTES
58°–76°	0	116°–127°	+4
77°–89°	+1	128°–141°	+5
90°–102°	+2	142°–155°	+6
103°–115°	+3		

(A dash indicates that the moonrise occurs on/after midnight and is recorded on the next day.) Find the longitude of your (nearest) city on **page 238**. Add a correction in minutes for your city's longitude (see table, bottom left). Use the same procedure with Boston's moonset time and the Moonset Key Letter value to calculate the time of moonset in your locale.†

EXAMPLE:

To calculate the time of moonset in Lansing, Michigan, on day 1:

Moonset, Boston, with Key Letter B (p. 116)	12:58 P.M. ET
Value of Key Letter B for Lansing (p. 240)	+ 53 minutes
Correction for Lansing longitude, 84° 33'	+ 1 minute
Moonset, Lansing	1:52 P.M. ET

7. This column gives the Moon's *astronomical* position among the constellations (not zodiac) at midnight. For *astrological* data, see **pages 224–227**.

Constellations have irregular borders; on successive nights, the midnight Moon may enter one, cross into another, and then move to a new area of the previous. It visits the 12 zodiacal constellations, as well as Auriga **(AUR),** a northern constellation between Perseus and Gemini; Cetus **(CET),** which lies south of the zodiac, just south of Pisces and Aries; Ophiuchus **(OPH),** primarily north of the zodiac but with a small corner between Scorpius and Sagittarius; Orion **(ORI),** whose northern limit first reaches the zodiac between Taurus and Gemini; and Sextans **(SEX),** which lies south of the zodiac except for a corner that just touches it near Leo.

8. This column gives the Moon's age: the number of days since the previous new Moon. (The average length of the lunar month is 29.53 days.) *(cont.)*

HOW TO USE

The Right-Hand Calendar Pages, 121 to 147

The Right-Hand Calendar Pages contain celestial events; religious observances; proverbs and poems; civil holidays; historical events; folklore; tide heights; weather prediction rhymes; Farmer's Calendar essays; and more.

A SAMPLE MONTH

1	2	3	4	5	6	7	8	9	10
1	Fr.	ALL FOOLS' •		*If you want to make a fool of yourself, you'll find a lot of people ready to help you.*				*Flakes*	an inch long, who v
2	Sa.			Tap dancer Charles "Honi" Coles born, 1911	• Tides {9.5 / 9.0}			*alive!*	in fresh water, pro pond across the
3	**B**	2nd S. of Easter	•		Writer F. Scott Fitzgerald married Zelda Sayre, 1920			*Spring's*	emerged a month (
4	M.	Annunciation[T]	• ♂♆☾ •		*Ben Hur* won 11 Academy Awards, 1960			*arrived!*	to spend the next 3
5	Tu.		☾ AT ☋ •		Blizzard left 27.2" snow, St. John's, Nfld., 1999	• Tides {10.8 / 10.8}		*Or is this*	on land before ret their wet world.
6	W.		☾ ON EQ. • ♂♀☾ •		Twin mongoose lemurs born, Busch Gardens, Tampa, Fla., 2012			*warmth*	You can't mis

1. The bold letter is the Dominical Letter (from A to G), a traditional ecclesiastical designation for Sunday determined by the date on which the year's first Sunday falls. For 2026, the Dominical Letter is **D**.

2. Civil holidays and astronomical events.

3. Religious feasts: A[T] indicates a major feast that the church has this year temporarily transferred to a date other than its usual one.

4. Sundays and special holy days.

5. Symbols for notable celestial events. For example, ♂♆☾ on the 4th day means that a conjunction (♂) of Neptune (♆) and the Moon (☾) occurs.

6. Proverbs, poems, and adages.

7. Noteworthy historical events, folklore, and legends.

8. High tide heights, in feet, Boston, Massachusetts.

9. Weather prediction rhyme.

10. Farmer's Calendar essay.

Celestial Symbols

☉ Sun	⊕ Earth	♅ Uranus	♂ Conjunction	☋ Descending node
○ ● ☾ Moon	♂ Mars	♆ Neptune	(on the same celestial longitude)	☍ Opposition
☿ Mercury	♃ Jupiter	♇ Pluto		(180 degrees
♀ Venus	♄ Saturn		☊ Ascending node	from Sun)

PREDICTING EARTHQUAKES

Note the dates in the Right-Hand Calendar Pages when the Moon rides high or runs low. The date of the high begins the most likely 5-day period of earthquakes in the Northern Hemisphere; the date of the low indicates a similar 5-day period in the Southern Hemisphere. Also noted are the 2 days each month when the Moon is on the celestial equator, indicating the most likely time for earthquakes in either hemisphere.

EARTH AT PERIHELION AND APHELION

Perihelion: January 3, 2026 (EST). Earth will be 91,403,637 miles from the Sun. **Aphelion:** July 6, 2026 (EDT). Earth will be 94,502,962 miles from the Sun.

Why We Have Seasons

The seasons occur because as Earth revolves around the Sun, its axis remains tilted at 23.5 degrees from the perpendicular. This tilt causes different latitudes on Earth to receive varying amounts of sunlight throughout the year.

In the Northern Hemisphere, the summer solstice marks the beginning of summer and occurs when the North Pole is tilted toward the Sun. The winter solstice marks the beginning of winter and occurs when the North Pole is tilted away from the Sun.

The equinoxes occur when the hemispheres equally face the Sun. At this time, the Sun rises due east and sets due west. The vernal equinox marks the beginning of spring; the autumnal equinox marks the beginning of autumn.

In the Southern Hemisphere, the seasons are the reverse of those in the Northern Hemisphere.

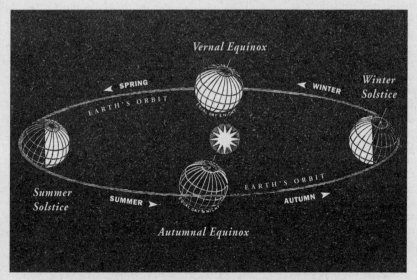

THE FIRST DAYS OF THE 2026 SEASONS

VERNAL (SPRING) EQUINOX:	March 20, 10:46 A.M. EDT
SUMMER SOLSTICE:	June 21, 4:24 A.M. EDT
AUTUMNAL (FALL) EQUINOX:	Sept. 22, 8:05 P.M. EDT
WINTER SOLSTICE:	Dec. 21, 3:50 P.M. EST

NOVEMBER 2025

SKY WATCH: On the 1st, brilliant Venus is low in the east, next to Virgo's main star, blue Spica. The morning star is gone after midmonth, with Mercury taking its place in November's final days. The Moon's closest approach of 2025 is on the 5th, at a distance of 221,725 miles. On the 15th, Jupiter rises before 9:00 P.M. to begin its optimum viewing season. Uranus reaches opposition on the 21st; below the Pleiades star cluster in Taurus at midnight, the Green Planet appears very dim to the naked eye, even from pristine rural sites. Binoculars will make for easier viewing of Uranus's brightest appearance since the 1990s. Saturn stands to the left of the Moon on the 28th and to its lower right on the 29th.

○ **FULL MOON** 5th day 8:19 A.M. ● **NEW MOON** 20th day 1:47 A.M.
◐ **LAST QUARTER** 12th day 12:28 A.M. ◑ **FIRST QUARTER** 28th day 1:59 A.M.

After 2:00 A.M. on November 2, Eastern Standard Time is given.

GET LOCAL RISE, SET, AND TIDE TIMES VIA ALMANAC.COM/2026.

Day of Year	Day of Month	Day of Week	☼ Rises H.M.	Rise Key	☼ Sets H.M.	Set Key	Length of Day H.M.	Sun Fast M.	Sun Declination ° '	High Tide Times Boston	☾ Rises H.M.	Rise Key	☾ Sets H.M.	Set Key	☾ Astron. Place	☾ Age
305	1	Sa.	7:18	D	5:37	B	10 19	32	14 s. 39	8	8¼	3:33	D	2:19	D	AQU	11
306	2	E	6:19	D	4:36	B	10 17	32	14 s. 58	7¾	8¼	2:55	C	2:33	D	PSC	12
307	3	M.	6:20	D	4:35	B	10 15	32	15 s. 17	8¾	9¼	3:18	C	3:49	E	PSC	13
308	4	Tu.	6:22	D	4:33	B	10 11	32	15 s. 35	9½	10	3:45	B	5:09	E	PSC	14
309	5	W.	6:23	E	4:32	B	10 09	32	15 s. 54	10¼	10¾	4:18	B	6:33	E	ARI	15
310	6	Th.	6:24	E	4:31	B	10 07	32	16 s. 11	11	11¾	5:00	A	7:58	E	ARI	16
311	7	Fr.	6:25	E	4:30	B	10 05	32	16 s. 29	12	—	5:54	A	9:19	E	TAU	17
312	8	Sa.	6:27	E	4:29	B	10 02	32	16 s. 46	12½	12¾	6:59	A	10:30	E	TAU	18
313	9	E	6:28	E	4:28	B	10 00	32	17 s. 04	1½	1¾	8:13	B	11:26	E	GEM	19
314	10	M.	6:29	E	4:27	B	9 58	32	17 s. 20	2½	2¾	9:29	B	**12:09**	E	GEM	20
315	11	Tu.	6:30	E	4:26	B	9 56	32	17 s. 37	3½	3¾	10:42	C	**12:41**	E	CAN	21
316	12	W.	6:32	E	4:25	B	9 53	32	17 s. 53	4½	4¾	11:51	C	**1:07**	E	LEO	22
317	13	Th.	6:33	E	4:24	B	9 51	31	18 s. 09	5¾	6	—	-	**1:28**	D	LEO	23
318	14	Fr.	6:34	E	4:23	B	9 49	31	18 s. 24	6¾	7	12:57	D	**1:48**	D	LEO	24
319	15	Sa.	6:35	E	4:22	B	9 47	31	18 s. 40	7½	8	2:01	D	**2:06**	C	VIR	25
320	16	E	6:37	E	4:21	B	9 44	31	18 s. 55	8¼	8¾	3:04	E	**2:24**	C	VIR	26
321	17	M.	6:38	E	4:20	B	9 42	31	19 s. 09	9	9½	4:06	E	**2:44**	B	VIR	27
322	18	Tu.	6:39	E	4:19	B	9 40	31	19 s. 23	9¾	10¼	5:09	E	**3:07**	B	VIR	28
323	19	W.	6:40	E	4:19	B	9 39	30	19 s. 37	10¼	11	6:14	E	**3:34**	A	LIB	29
324	20	Th.	6:41	E	4:18	B	9 37	30	19 s. 51	11	11½	7:17	E	**4:07**	A	LIB	0
325	21	Fr.	6:43	E	4:17	B	9 34	30	20 s. 04	11½	—	8:19	E	**4:48**	A	SCO	1
326	22	Sa.	6:44	E	4:17	A	9 33	30	20 s. 17	12¼	12¼	9:16	E	**5:37**	A	OPH	2
327	23	E	6:45	E	4:16	A	9 31	29	20 s. 29	12¾	12¾	10:05	E	**6:34**	A	SAG	3
328	24	M.	6:46	E	4:15	A	9 29	29	20 s. 41	1½	1½	10:46	E	**7:38**	B	SAG	4
329	25	Tu.	6:47	E	4:15	A	9 28	29	20 s. 53	2¼	2¼	11:20	E	**8:45**	B	SAG	5
330	26	W.	6:48	E	4:14	A	9 26	28	21 s. 04	3	3	11:48	E	**9:53**	C	CAP	6
331	27	Th.	6:50	E	4:14	A	9 24	28	21 s. 15	3¾	4	**12:12**	E	**11:02**	C	CAP	7
332	28	Fr.	6:51	E	4:14	A	9 23	28	21 s. 25	4¾	4¾	**12:34**	D	—	-	AQU	8
333	29	Sa.	6:52	E	4:13	A	9 21	27	21 s. 35	5½	5¾	**12:55**	D	12:13	D	AQU	9
334	30	E	6:53	E	4:13	A	9 20	27	21 s. 45	6½	6¾	**1:17**	C	1:25	E	PSC	10

120 To use this page, see p. 116; for Key Letters, see p. 238. LIGHT = A.M. **BOLD = P.M.** 2026

NOVEMBER

THE ELEVENTH MONTH · 2025 — NOVEMBER HATH 30 DAYS

*For the year of peace and plenty / And for blessings without end,
Let the voices of the people / In Thanksgiving praises blend.*
—George Carlton Rhoderick Jr.

DAY OF MONTH	DAY OF WEEK	DATES, FEASTS, FASTS, ASPECTS, TIDE HEIGHTS, AND WEATHER
1	Sa.	All Saints' • Sadie Hawkins Day • ☾ AT ☍ • Tides {9.3/9.7} — *Clock hands*
2	E	21st S. af. P. • DST ENDS, 2:00 A.M. • ☾ ON EQ. • ☉♄☾ • ☉♅☾ — *spin,*
3	M.	All Souls' • 1st major auto show in U.S., Madison Sq. Garden, N.Y.C., 1900 • {10.7/10.4} *let's sleep in!*
4	Tu.	ELECTION DAY • Artist Guido Reni born, 1575 • Tides {11.4/10.7} — *Snowfalls*
5	W.	FULL BEAVER ○ • ☾ AT PERIG. • Franklin D. Roosevelt elected to 3rd term as U.S. president, 1940 — *begin*
6	Th.	♂☉☾ • 1st national Canadian Thanksgiving as annual event after Confederation, 1879 — *and*
7	Fr.	*If horses stretch out their necks and sniff the air, rain will ensue.* • Tides {12.2/—} — *frost*
8	Sa.	☾ RIDES HIGH • Game show host Alex Trebek died, 2020 • Tides {10.4/12.0} — *nips*
9	E	22nd S. af. P. • ☿ STAT. • Great Northeast Blackout, 1965 • {10.0/11.5} — *your*
10	M.	♂♃☾ • U.S. Marine Corps established (as Continental Marines), 1775 • {9.6/10.9} — *skin.*
11	Tu.	St. Martin of Tours • VETERANS DAY • ♃ STAT. • Tides {9.3/10.3} — *Veterans*
12	W.	♂♀☉ • Suffragette Elizabeth C. Stanton born, 1815 — *deserve*
13	Th.	World Kindness Day • Writer Robert Louis Stevenson born, 1850 • {9.1/9.4} — *thanks*
14	Fr.	☾ AT ☍ • Last use of manned maneuvering unit (MMU) in space, 1984 • {9.2/9.2} — *from*
15	Sa.	☾ ON EQ. • Arthur Dorrington 1st Black to sign professional hockey contract, 1950 • {9.4/9.1} — *us all*
16	E	23rd S. af. P. • UNESCO established, 1945 • Tides {9.6/9.1} — *and maybe*
17	M.	St. Hugh of Lincoln • 1st time U.S. Congress met in Capitol Bldg., D.C., 1800 • {9.8/9.0} — *some*
18	Tu.	St. Hilda of Whitby • *New dishes beget new appetites.* • Tides {9.9/9.0} — *help*
19	W.	☾ AT APO. • ♂♀☾ • Frederick Blaisdell granted 1st U.S. patent for paper pencil, 1895 — *when*
20	Th.	NEW ● • ♂☉☾ • ☾ IN INF. ♂ • Tides {10.0/8.8} — *shovelin'*
21	Fr.	♂☉☾ • ♄ AT ☍ • W. Berger (76 yrs., 128 days) oldest to summit tallest mtns. on 7 continents, 2013
22	Sa.	☾ RUNS LOW • *First weigh, then venture.* • Tides {8.7/9.9} — *calls!*
23	E	24th S. af. P. • Quarterback Doug Flutie completed "Hail Mary" pass in Boston College win over Miami, 1984
24	M.	♂♀♃ • Tribal leader/activist Lucy Covington born, 1910 • Tides {8.5/9.7} — *Annual*
25	Tu.	♂♃☽ • Robert S. Ledley granted patent for CT scanner, 1975 • Tides {8.4/9.5} — *feasts now*
26	W.	Movie *Casablanca* premiered, 1942 • Tides {8.4/9.4} — *are fixed,*
27	Th.	THANKSGIVING DAY • Martial artist/actor Bruce Lee born, 1940 • {8.5/9.3} — *amidst*
28	Fr.	☾ AT ☍ • ♄ STAT. • *WSM Barn Dance* (later, *Grand Ole Opry*) debuted on radio, 1925 — *a*
29	Sa.	☾ ON EQ. • ☉♄☾ • ☉♅☾ • ☿ STAT. • {9.2/9.3} — *bone-chilling*
30	E	1st S. of Advent • Writer Oscar Wilde died, 1900 • {9.8/9.5} — *wintry mix.*

Farmer's Calendar

Pop, this one looks like a bear paw! Long drawn to treetops that rattle every which way on windy days, my daughter leads me on a saunter among the yellow stalks of time. The mammoth sunflowers have been ransacked by squirrels and jays. Most of the corn is hinged at the waist, fallen over. The scarecrow is so roughed up, it's practically a comedy. She starts tracking prints pressed into the top inch of soil: deer, turkey, and Bram, our Bernese mountain dog.

I'm thinking ahead to next year's crop, but mostly I'm taking a break from my labor. It's all leaves and aches around here. I swear that you could tell the time of year by which chore-based muscles are doing the throbbing. Over time, we've retired the fancy power tools—mulching mowers and leaf blowers—for a rake and a tarp. The stand of 100-year grandfather oak lets out a cackle. There are weeks of leaves still up in the limbs. Most will go where they please. The rest get dragged to the leaf mold pile or the chicken run, but there's still a gnaw to hauling at such scale. Next year, we ought to bribe the wind to blow in one convenient direction for a change.

DECEMBER 2025

SKY WATCH: Saturn is highest from the 1st to the 15th and best seen around early evening; after midmonth, it sets by midnight. Brilliant Jupiter is below the Moon on the 6th and above it on the 7th. The year's best meteor shower occurs on the 13th and 14th. The Moon will not interfere with these Geminids, which produce a meteor a minute for observers watching any wide expanse of rural sky before 1:00 A.M. On the 31st, Jupiter is at its biggest and brightest of the year. It has no opposition in 2025—a rare occurrence—but the gas giant is now nearing its closest approach to Earth in 13 months, on January 9, 2026. Winter begins with the solstice on the 21st at 10:03 A.M. EST.

○ **FULL MOON** 4th day 6:14 P.M.
☾ **LAST QUARTER** 11th day 3:52 P.M.
● **NEW MOON** 19th day 8:43 P.M.
☽ **FIRST QUARTER** 27th day 2:10 P.M.

All times are given in Eastern Standard Time.

GET LOCAL RISE, SET, AND TIDE TIMES VIA ALMANAC.COM/2026.

DAY OF YEAR	DAY OF MONTH	DAY OF WEEK	☀ RISES H.M.	RISE KEY	☀ SETS H.M.	SET KEY	LENGTH OF DAY H.M.	SUN FAST M.	SUN DECLINATION ° '	HIGH TIDE TIMES BOSTON	☾ RISES H.M.	RISE KEY	☾ SETS H.M.	SET KEY	☾ ASTRON. PLACE	☾ AGE
335	1	M.	6:54	E	**4:12**	A	9 18	27	21 s. 54	7¼ / 7¾	**1:41**	B	2:40	E	PSC	11
336	2	Tu.	6:55	E	**4:12**	A	9 17	26	22 s. 03	8 / 8¾	**2:10**	B	3:59	E	ARI	12
337	3	W.	6:56	E	**4:12**	A	9 16	26	22 s. 11	9 / 9¾	**2:47**	B	5:23	E	ARI	13
338	4	Th.	6:57	E	**4:12**	A	9 15	25	22 s. 19	9¾ / 10½	**3:35**	B	6:47	E	TAU	14
339	5	Fr.	6:58	E	**4:12**	A	9 14	25	22 s. 27	10¾ / 11½	**4:36**	B	8:05	E	TAU	15
340	6	Sa.	6:59	E	**4:12**	A	9 13	25	22 s. 34	11½ / —	**5:48**	B	9:10	E	AUR	16
341	7	**E**	7:00	E	**4:11**	A	9 11	24	22 s. 41	12¼ / 12½	**7:07**	B	10:01	E	GEM	17
342	8	M.	7:01	E	**4:11**	A	9 10	24	22 s. 47	1¼ / 1½	**8:24**	C	10:39	E	CAN	18
343	9	Tu.	7:02	E	**4:11**	A	9 09	23	22 s. 53	2¼ / 2¼	**9:38**	C	11:08	E	CAN	19
344	10	W.	7:03	E	**4:12**	A	9 09	23	22 s. 58	3¼ / 3¼	**10:47**	D	11:32	E	LEO	20
345	11	Th.	7:03	E	**4:12**	A	9 09	22	23 s. 03	4 / 4¼	**11:52**	D	11:52	D	LEO	21
346	12	Fr.	7:04	E	**4:12**	A	9 08	22	23 s. 07	5 / 5¼	—	-	**12:11**	C	VIR	22
347	13	Sa.	7:05	E	**4:12**	A	9 07	21	23 s. 11	6 / 6¼	12:56	E	**12:29**	C	VIR	23
348	14	**E**	7:06	E	**4:12**	A	9 06	21	23 s. 15	6¾ / 7¼	1:58	E	**12:49**	B	VIR	24
349	15	M.	7:06	E	**4:12**	A	9 06	20	23 s. 18	7¾ / 8¼	3:01	E	**1:11**	B	VIR	25
350	16	Tu.	7:07	E	**4:13**	A	9 06	20	23 s. 20	8½ / 9	4:05	E	**1:36**	B	LIB	26
351	17	W.	7:08	E	**4:13**	A	9 05	19	23 s. 22	9¼ / 9¾	5:09	E	**2:07**	A	LIB	27
352	18	Th.	7:08	E	**4:13**	A	9 05	19	23 s. 24	9¾ / 10½	6:12	E	**2:46**	A	SCO	28
353	19	Fr.	7:09	E	**4:14**	A	9 05	18	23 s. 25	10½ / 11¼	7:10	E	**3:33**	A	OPH	0
354	20	Sa.	7:10	E	**4:14**	A	9 04	18	23 s. 26	11¼ / 11¾	8:02	E	**4:28**	A	SAG	1
355	21	**E**	7:10	E	**4:14**	A	9 04	18	23 s. 26	11¾ / —	8:46	E	**5:31**	B	SAG	2
356	22	M.	7:11	E	**4:15**	A	9 04	17	23 s. 26	12½ / 12½	9:22	E	**6:37**	B	SAG	3
357	23	Tu.	7:11	E	**4:16**	A	9 05	17	23 s. 26	1¼ / 1¼	9:51	E	**7:46**	B	CAP	4
358	24	W.	7:11	E	**4:16**	A	9 05	16	23 s. 24	1¾ / 1¾	10:16	E	**8:54**	C	CAP	5
359	25	Th.	7:12	E	**4:17**	A	9 05	16	23 s. 22	2½ / 2¾	10:38	D	**10:02**	D	AQU	6
360	26	Fr.	7:12	E	**4:17**	A	9 05	15	23 s. 20	3¼ / 3½	10:59	D	**11:11**	D	AQU	7
361	27	Sa.	7:13	E	**4:18**	A	9 05	15	23 s. 17	4 / 4¼	11:20	C	—	-	PSC	8
362	28	**E**	7:13	E	**4:19**	A	9 06	14	23 s. 14	5 / 5¼	11:42	C	**12:23**	E	PSC	9
363	29	M.	7:13	E	**4:20**	A	9 07	14	23 s. 10	5¾ / 6¼	**12:07**	B	1:37	E	PSC	10
364	30	Tu.	7:13	E	**4:21**	A	9 08	13	23 s. 06	6¾ / 7¼	**12:39**	B	2:56	E	ARI	11
365	31	W.	7:13	E	**4:22**	A	9 09	13	23 s. 02	7¾ / 8½	**1:20**	A	4:17	E	ARI	12

THE TWELFTH MONTH · 2025

DECEMBER

DECEMBER HATH 31 DAYS

He seems as 'twere to prompt our merriest days,
And bid the dance and joke be long and loud.
–Barry Cornwall, of winter

DAY OF MONTH	DAY OF WEEK	DATES, FEASTS, FASTS, ASPECTS, TIDE HEIGHTS, AND WEATHER	
1	M.	St. Andrew[T] • Electronic engineer/video game pioneer Gerald "Jerry" Lawson born, 1940	*All the*
2	Tu.	St. Viviana • Babe Ruth's bat used to hit 1st Yankee Stadium home run sold for $1,265,000, in 2004	*cars*
3	W.	☌⛢☾ • G. Gershwin presented "Concerto in F," 1st jazz concerto for piano and orchestra, at Carnegie Hall, N.Y.C., 1925	*are*
4	Th.	FULL COLD ○ • ☾ AT PERIG. • Astronaut Roberta L. Bondar born, 1945 • {12.0 / 10.2}	*are*
5	Fr.	☾ RIDES HIGH • Montgomery Bus Boycott began, Ala., 1955 • Tides {12.2 / 10.2}	*going*
6	Sa.	St. Nicholas • U.S. Naval Observatory established (as Depot of Charts and Instruments), 1830	*slow*
7	**E**	2nd S. of Advent • NAT'L PEARL HARBOR REMEMBRANCE DAY • ☌♃☾ • ☿ GR. ELONG. (21° WEST)	*but*
8	M.	*Knowledge in youth is wisdom in age.* • Tides {9.9 / 11.4}	*can't*
9	Tu.	1st U.S. stamp (10-cent Special Delivery) to depict bicycle issued, 1902 • Tides {9.7 / 10.8}	*get far*
10	W.	St. Eulalia • ♆ STAT. • Mathematician Ada Lovelace born, 1815 • {9.5 / 10.2}	*in blowing*
11	Th.	☾ AT ☋ • End of overnight tornado outbreak, southern U.S./Ohio Valley, 2021 • {9.3 / 9.5}	*snow!*
12	Fr.	OUR LADY OF GUADALUPE • ☾ ON EQ. • Singer Dionne Warwick born, 1940	*Windchill*
13	Sa.	St. Lucia • Actor Dick Van Dyke born, 1925 • Tides {9.1 / 8.6}	*grating,*
14	**E**	3rd S. of Advent • Chanukah begins at sundown • Halcyon Days begin.	*not*
15	M.	Beware the Pogonip. • 1st rendezvous of two manned spacecraft, *Gemini 6A* and *Gemini 7*, 1965	*abating.*
16	Tu.	Writer Jane Austen born, 1775 • Tides {9.4 / 8.4}	*Plunging temps*
17	W.	Ember Day • ☾ AT APO. • Aztec Calendar Stone rediscovered, Mexico City, Mexico, 1790	*getting*
18	Th.	☌☿☾ • Ratification of 13th Amendment, prohibiting enslavement in the U.S., announced, 1865	*coldest*
19	Fr.	Ember Day • NEW ● • ☾ RUNS LOW • ☌♀☾ • {9.9 / 8.5}	*right*
20	Sa.	Ember Day • ☌♂☾ • Surgeon Ambroise Paré died, 1590 • {10.0 / 8.6}	*around the*
21	**E**	4th S. of Advent • WINTER SOLSTICE • Tides {10.0 / —}	*winter solstice.*
22	M.	St. Thomas[T] • ☌♇☾ • Edward Johnson employed the 1st electric Christmas tree lights, 1882	
23	Tu.	Pianist Victor Borge died, 2000 • Tides {8.7 / 10.0}	*Holiday*
24	W.	Family moved into world's 1st fully solar-heated home, Dover, Mass., 1948 • Tides {8.8 / 9.9}	*season now*
25	Th.	Christmas • ☾ AT ☊ • *Cheerful company shortens the miles.* • {8.9 / 9.7}	*freezin'*
26	Fr.	St. Stephen • BOXING DAY (CANADA) • KWANZAA BEGINS • ☾ ON EQ. • ☌♄☾	*for*
27	Sa.	St. John • ☌♆☾ • ALH 84001 Mars meteorite found in Antarctica, 1984	*most . . .*
28	**E**	1st S. af. Ch. • –42.1°C (–44°F), Edmonton, Alta., 2021 • {9.7 / 9.1}	*warm up*
29	M.	Holy Innocents[T] • Inventor Charles Goodyear born, 1800 • Texas statehood, 1845	*with a '26*
30	Tu.	*It takes three cloudy days to bring a heavy snow.* • Tides {10.5 / 9.1}	*New Year's*
31	W.	St. Sylvester • Make Up Your Mind Day • ☌⛢☾ • {10.9 / 9.2}	*toast!*

Farmer's Calendar

Last offer: three buttercreams for two pizzelles

Last year, I set to keep the laundry from piling sky-high on the chair. Ha! Let's bring our resolutions down to Earth: • Ring an old friend; ask for their best recipe. Ask for their mother's, their grandmother's. • Give loved ones a single, elevated ingredient. Homemade extracts or toasted sugar. Brown a large block of butter for Dyane's ambitious baking schedule, then get out of the way. • Try not to guilt everyone over the generosity of your recent gifts when it comes to horse-trading cookies later in the month. • But then again, do whatever it takes to get your hands on some extra buttercreams. • Pass out the leftover Halloween candy to the neighborhood kids to use on gingerbread houses. • Toss the hens some of the good mealworms. • Tell a knock-knock joke at dinner, a soldier's joke at dessert. • Turn your dignity over to Victorian parlor games. It's not a party until you get people playing "Are You There, Moriarty?" (Remember to have enough newspaper and blindfolds on hand.) • Sing your lover a song, especially since you can't sing. • Give yourself whole. Everything to everyone.

JANUARY

SKY WATCH: The year begins with Saturn, in Pisces, halfway up the southern sky at nightfall; through a telescope, the Ringed Planet's famous rings can barely be seen, as they are just weeks from angling nearly edgewise toward Earth and the Sun. After 8:30 P.M., brilliant Jupiter rises in the east and is visible all night. In the daytime sky, the Sun appears bigger because Earth arrives at perihelion on the 3rd. The 10th brings Jupiter's opposition, its nearest and brightest moment of the year. On the 27th, the Moon hovers to the left of the famous "Seven Sisters" (Pleiades) star cluster, a stunning scene visible through binoculars. The 30th presents an eye-catching, all-night conjunction when the nearly full Moon hovers above Jupiter.

CALENDAR

○ FULL MOON	3rd day 5:03 A.M.	● NEW MOON	18th day 2:52 P.M.
◑ LAST QUARTER	10th day 10:48 A.M.	◐ FIRST QUARTER	25th day 11:47 P.M.

All times are given in Eastern Standard Time.

GET LOCAL RISE, SET, AND TIDE TIMES VIA ALMANAC.COM/2026.

DAY OF YEAR	DAY OF MONTH	DAY OF WEEK	☼ RISES	RISE KEY	☼ SETS	SET KEY	LENGTH OF DAY	SUN FAST	SUN DECLINATION		HIGH TIDE TIMES BOSTON		☾ RISES	RISE KEY	☾ SETS	SET KEY	☾ ASTRON. PLACE	☾ AGE
			H. M.		H. M.		H. M.	M.	°	'			H. M.		H. M.			
1	1	Th.	7:13	E	**4:22**	A	9 09	12	22 s.	57	8½	**9½**	**2:13**	A	5:37	E	TAU	13
2	2	Fr.	7:13	E	**4:23**	A	9 10	12	22 s.	52	9½	**10¼**	**3:20**	A	6:48	E	TAU	14
3	3	Sa.	7:13	E	**4:24**	A	9 11	11	22 s.	46	10½	**11¼**	**4:36**	B	7:46	E	GEM	15
4	4	**D**	7:13	E	**4:25**	A	9 12	11	22 s.	39	11½	—	**5:56**	B	8:31	E	GEM	16
5	5	M.	7:13	E	**4:26**	A	9 13	10	22 s.	33	12¼	**12¼**	**7:14**	C	9:05	E	CAN	17
6	6	Tu.	7:13	E	**4:27**	A	9 14	10	22 s.	25	1	**1¼**	**8:28**	C	9:32	E	LEO	18
7	7	W.	7:13	E	**4:28**	A	9 15	10	22 s.	18	1¾	**2**	**9:37**	D	9:54	D	LEO	19
8	8	Th.	7:13	E	**4:29**	A	9 16	9	22 s.	10	2½	**2¾**	**10:43**	D	10:14	C	LEO	20
9	9	Fr.	7:13	E	**4:30**	A	9 17	9	22 s.	01	3½	**3¾**	**11:47**	E	10:33	C	VIR	21
10	10	Sa.	7:13	E	**4:31**	A	9 18	8	21 s.	52	4¼	**4¾**	—	-	10:52	C	VIR	22
11	11	**D**	7:12	E	**4:32**	A	9 20	8	21 s.	43	5¼	**5¾**	12:51	E	11:13	B	VIR	23
12	12	M.	7:12	E	**4:34**	A	9 22	7	21 s.	33	6	**6½**	1:55	E	11:38	B	LIB	24
13	13	Tu.	7:12	E	**4:35**	A	9 23	7	21 s.	23	7	**7½**	2:59	E	**12:07**	A	LIB	25
14	14	W.	7:11	E	**4:36**	A	9 25	7	21 s.	12	7¾	**8½**	4:02	E	**12:42**	A	SCO	26
15	15	Th.	7:11	E	**4:37**	A	9 26	6	21 s.	01	8½	**9¼**	5:02	E	**1:26**	A	SCO	27
16	16	Fr.	7:10	E	**4:38**	B	9 28	6	20 s.	50	9¼	**10**	5:57	E	**2:19**	A	SAG	28
17	17	Sa.	7:10	E	**4:39**	B	9 29	6	20 s.	38	10	**10¾**	6:44	E	**3:20**	B	SAG	29
18	18	**D**	7:09	E	**4:41**	B	9 32	5	20 s.	26	10¾	**11½**	7:22	E	**4:27**	B	SAG	0
19	19	M.	7:08	E	**4:42**	B	9 34	5	20 s.	13	11½	—	7:54	E	**5:36**	B	CAP	1
20	20	Tu.	7:08	E	**4:43**	B	9 35	5	20 s.	00	12	**12**	8:21	E	**6:45**	C	CAP	2
21	21	W.	7:07	E	**4:44**	B	9 37	5	19 s.	47	12¾	**12¾**	8:44	D	**7:54**	D	AQU	3
22	22	Th.	7:06	E	**4:46**	B	9 40	4	19 s.	33	1¼	**1½**	9:05	D	**9:04**	D	AQU	4
23	23	Fr.	7:06	E	**4:47**	B	9 41	4	19 s.	19	2	**2¼**	9:25	C	**10:14**	E	PSC	5
24	24	Sa.	7:05	E	**4:48**	B	9 43	4	19 s.	05	2¾	**3**	9:46	C	**11:26**	E	PSC	6
25	25	**D**	7:04	E	**4:49**	B	9 45	4	18 s.	50	3½	**4**	10:10	B	—	-	PSC	7
26	26	M.	7:03	E	**4:51**	B	9 48	3	18 s.	35	4¼	**5**	10:38	B	12:41	E	ARI	8
27	27	Tu.	7:02	E	**4:52**	B	9 50	3	18 s.	19	5¼	**6**	11:14	A	1:59	E	ARI	9
28	28	W.	7:02	E	**4:53**	B	9 51	3	18 s.	03	6¼	**7**	**12:00**	A	3:17	E	TAU	10
29	29	Th.	7:01	E	**4:54**	B	9 53	3	17 s.	47	7¼	**8¼**	**12:59**	A	4:30	E	TAU	11
30	30	Fr.	7:00	E	**4:56**	B	9 56	3	17 s.	31	8½	**9¼**	**2:10**	B	5:32	E	AUR	12
31	31	Sa.	6:59	E	**4:57**	B	9 58	2	17 s.	14	9½	**10¼**	**3:28**	B	6:22	E	GEM	13

To use this page, see p. 116; for Key Letters, see p. 238. LIGHT = A.M. **BOLD = P.M.**

THE FIRST MONTH · 2026 — JANUARY — JANUARY HATH 31 DAYS

Upon the year's first day / My grateful wishes I to you would pay;
May gladness be around your path alway.
—Georgiana Bennet

DAY OF MONTH	DAY OF WEEK	DATES, FEASTS, FASTS, ASPECTS, TIDE HEIGHTS, AND WEATHER		
1	Th.	Holy Name • NEW YEAR'S DAY • ☾AT PERIG. • Tides {11.2 / 9.4}		New year
2	Fr.	☾RIDES HIGH • Record low of 14°F, Haleakalā summit, Maui, Hawaii, 1961 • {11.5 / 9.7}		swoons for
3	Sa.	FULL WOLF ○ • ☌♃☽ • ⊕ AT PERIHELION • {11.7 / 9.9}		a super-moon!
4	D	2nd S. af. Ch. • Great hopes make great men. • {11.7 / —}		Snowy
5	M.	Twelfth Night • In 1 min., Marissa Waldrum made 51 cartwheels w/o hands, setting record, 2023		surge
6	Tu.	Epiphany • ♀IN SUP. ☌ • Tides {10.0 / 11.1}		makes shoveling
7	W.	Orthodox Christmas (Julian) • Distaff Day • ☾ AT ☊ • ☌♀♂		
8	Th.	☾ON EQ. • L. Foucault's pendulum proved Earth's rotation, 1851 • Singer Elvis Presley born, 1935		slower,
9	Fr.	☌♂☉ • U.N. headquarters opened, N.Y.C., 1951 • Tides {9.6 / 9.3}		time
10	Sa.	♃AT ☍ • 23rd consecutive day of rain, Vancouver, B.C., 2006 • Tides {9.3 / 8.7}		to
11	D	1st S. af. Ep. • 1st Canadian prime minister Sir John A. Macdonald born, 1815		splurge
12	M.	Plough Monday • Writer Agatha Christie died, 1976 • {9.0 / 7.9}		on
13	Tu.	St. Hilary • National Rubber Ducky Day (U.S.) • ☾AT APO. • Tides {9.0 / 7.8}		a
14	W.	*If you see grass in January, Lock your grain in your granary.* • Tides {9.1 / 7.9}		new
15	Th.	Online encyclopedia Wikipedia launched, 2001 • {9.3 / 8.0}		snow-
16	Fr.	☾RUNS LOW • 1st flower (zinnia) to be grown in space debuted, International Space Station, 2016		blower!
17	Sa.	☌♂♀ • U.S. statesman Benjamin Franklin born, 1706 • 30" snow, St. John's, N.L., 2020		Milder,
18	D	2nd S. af. Ep. • NEW ● • ☌♂☾ • ☌♀☾ • ☌♂☾ • ☌♆☾		
19	M.	MARTIN LUTHER KING JR.'S BIRTHDAY, OBSERVED • Singer Dolly Parton born, 1946 • {10.3 / —}		then
20	Tu.	☌♂♇ • Actress Patricia Neal born, 1926 • Tides {9.0 / 10.4}		wilder:
21	W.	☾AT ☊ • ♀IN SUP. ☌ • Lincoln Alexander, 1st Black member of Canadian Parliament, born, 1922		sun,
22	Th.	St. Vincent • ☌♂♇ • Key West Extension of Florida East Coast Railway completed, 1912		rain,
23	Fr.	☾ON EQ. • ☌♄☾ • ☌♅☾ • ☌♆☉ • Tides {9.7 / 10.0}		and
24	Sa.	*One peace is better than ten victories.* • Tides {9.9 / 9.6}		flurries
25	D	3rd S. af. Ep. • January thaw traditionally begins about now. • {10.0 / 9.3}		float,
26	M.	Conversion of Paul[T] • U.S. first lady Julia Grant born, 1826 • {10.1 / 8.9}		ending
27	Tu.	☌♂☾ • Ornithologist John James Audubon died, 1851 • Tides {10.2 / 8.6}		the
28	W.	St. Thomas Aquinas • ☌♂♀ • ☌♂♇ • Tides {10.3 / 8.6}		month
29	Th.	☾RIDES HIGH • ☾AT PERIG. • Writer Philippe de Gaspé died, 1871 • {10.5 / 8.7}		on a
30	Fr.	☌♃☾ • Raccoons mate now. • Musician Phil Collins born, 1951 • {10.8 / 9.1}		chilly
31	Sa.	Barometric pressure rose to 31.85 inches in Northway, Alaska, setting record for continental N.Am., 1989		note.

Farmer's Calendar
Mores and Lesses

"Listen, I grew up in the Northeast Kingdom of Vermont," Keller, our guest, tells us, "so kitchen talk about sourdough feels like home." It's his first time over, and we're throwing pizzas on the stone. I had just apologized for going on about fermented sourdough crust as pre-digested grain—yum! Keller peruses our disarray of fridge magnets. Kitchen ephemera is, after all, a time-tested way to learn something about a new friend. He studies our "Mores and Lesses"—our version of resolutions. We make drawings of how we want 2026 to go. Here's our method. After a deep winter's brunch of fried eggs, arugula, and *pain au levain,* we take a New Year's walk, chock full of the whining and euphoria that color most of our family hikes. My grandpa used to say, "Cold cheeks make clear thoughts." That's our aim. When we get home, we put on a fire and get to drawing what we want to grow and what we want to shed. My sketches are messier than my gardens. "What's this one?" Keller asks, politely pointing to a scribble on the "More" side. "That's a jar of sourdough starter. See the microbial colony?" "Oh, I see," he says, even more politely. "Yum!"

Find more facts and fun every day at Almanac.com.

FEBRUARY

SKY WATCH: Saturn appears as early as 6:00 P.M. as the only bright "star" in the southwest. It is lower each evening, making this its final full month of visibility. On the 8th, Mercury begins an evening star apparition, best seen at 6:00 P.M. Though low in the sky, it conspicuously floats above Venus at midmonth. On the 18th, Mercury is next to the thin crescent Moon with Saturn to their upper left. At 6:00 P.M. on the 20th, a rare vertical line appears in the west, including, from bottom, Venus, Mercury, Saturn, and the Moon. By the 28th, Mercury has dimmed and dropped lower in the west, while dazzling Venus now appears 7 degrees high at 6:00 P.M., as it begins its long 2026 apparition as an evening star.

○ **FULL MOON** 1st day 5:09 P.M.   ● **NEW MOON** 17th day 7:01 A.M.
☽ **LAST QUARTER** 9th day 7:43 A.M.   ☾ **FIRST QUARTER** 24th day 7:27 A.M.

All times are given in Eastern Standard Time.

GET LOCAL RISE, SET, AND TIDE TIMES VIA ALMANAC.COM/2026.

Day of Year	Day of Month	Day of Week	Rises H.M.	Rise Key	Sets H.M.	Set Key	Length of Day H.M.	Sun Fast M.	Sun Declination ° '	High Tide Times Boston	Rises H.M.	Rise Key	Sets H.M.	Set Key	Astron. Place	Age
32	1	D	6:58	E	4:58	B	10 00	2	16 s. 57	10¼ 11	4:47	B	7:00	E	CAN	14
33	2	M.	6:57	E	5:00	B	10 03	2	16 s. 40	11¼ 11¾	6:03	C	7:30	E	LEO	15
34	3	Tu.	6:55	E	5:01	B	10 06	2	16 s. 22	12 —	7:15	D	7:54	D	LEO	16
35	4	W.	6:54	E	5:02	B	10 08	2	16 s. 04	12½ 12¾	8:24	D	8:16	D	LEO	17
36	5	Th.	6:53	E	5:04	B	10 11	2	15 s. 46	1¼ 1½	9:31	E	8:35	C	VIR	18
37	6	Fr.	6:52	D	5:05	B	10 13	2	15 s. 27	2 2¼	10:36	E	8:55	C	VIR	19
38	7	Sa.	6:51	D	5:06	B	10 15	2	15 s. 09	2¾ 3¼	11:41	E	9:15	B	VIR	20
39	8	D	6:50	D	5:08	B	10 18	2	14 s. 49	3½ 4	—	-	9:39	B	VIR	21
40	9	M.	6:48	D	5:09	B	10 21	2	14 s. 30	4¼ 5	12:46	E	10:06	A	LIB	22
41	10	Tu.	6:47	D	5:10	B	10 23	2	14 s. 11	5¼ 5¾	1:50	E	10:39	A	LIB	23
42	11	W.	6:46	D	5:11	B	10 25	2	13 s. 51	6 6¾	2:52	E	11:19	A	SCO	24
43	12	Th.	6:45	D	5:13	B	10 28	2	13 s. 31	7 7¾	3:48	E	12:09	A	OPH	25
44	13	Fr.	6:43	D	5:14	B	10 31	2	13 s. 11	8 8¾	4:38	E	1:07	A	SAG	26
45	14	Sa.	6:42	D	5:15	B	10 33	2	12 s. 50	8¾ 9½	5:20	E	2:11	B	SAG	27
46	15	D	6:40	D	5:17	B	10 37	2	12 s. 30	9½ 10¼	5:54	E	3:20	B	CAP	28
47	16	M.	6:39	D	5:18	B	10 39	2	12 s. 09	10¼ 10¾	6:23	D	4:30	C	CAP	29
48	17	Tu.	6:38	D	5:19	B	10 41	2	11 s. 48	11 11½	6:48	D	5:41	C	CAP	0
49	18	W.	6:36	D	5:20	B	10 44	2	11 s. 27	11¾ —	7:09	D	6:52	D	AQU	1
50	19	Th.	6:35	D	5:22	B	10 47	2	11 s. 05	12¼ 12½	7:30	D	8:03	E	PSC	2
51	20	Fr.	6:33	D	5:23	B	10 50	2	10 s. 44	12¾ 1	7:51	C	9:16	E	PSC	3
52	21	Sa.	6:32	D	5:24	B	10 52	2	10 s. 22	1½ 1¾	8:15	B	10:31	E	PSC	4
53	22	D	6:30	D	5:26	B	10 56	2	10 s. 00	2¼ 2¾	8:41	B	11:49	E	ARI	5
54	23	M.	6:29	D	5:27	B	10 58	3	9 s. 38	3 3½	9:14	B	—	-	ARI	6
55	24	Tu.	6:27	D	5:28	B	11 01	3	9 s. 16	4 4½	9:56	A	1:07	E	TAU	7
56	25	W.	6:26	D	5:29	C	11 03	3	8 s. 54	5 5¾	10:49	A	2:20	E	TAU	8
57	26	Th.	6:24	D	5:30	C	11 06	3	8 s. 31	6 7	11:55	A	3:25	E	AUR	9
58	27	Fr.	6:23	D	5:32	C	11 09	3	8 s. 09	7¼ 8	1:08	B	4:17	E	GEM	10
59	28	Sa.	6:21	D	5:33	C	11 12	3	7 s. 46	8¼ 9	2:25	B	4:58	E	CAN	11

THE SECOND MONTH · 2026 — FEBRUARY — FEBRUARY HATH 28 DAYS

Around, above the world of snow
The light-heeled breezes breathe and blow.
–James Berry Bensel

DAY OF MONTH	DAY OF WEEK	DATES, FEASTS, FASTS, ASPECTS, TIDE HEIGHTS, AND WEATHER
1	D	Septuagesima • FULL SNOW ○ • Painter Thomas Cole born, 1801 — *Groundhogs*
2	M.	Candlemas • Groundhog Day • Groundhog Day gale hit NE U.S. and SE Canada, 1976 — *are*
3	Tu.	☾ AT ☋ • Albert and Walter Spalding opened sporting goods store, 1876 • {11.2 / —} *snowbound,*
4	W.	☾ ON EQ. • ☿ STAT. • Mormon exodus to the American West began, 1846 • {10.2 / 10.8} *no*
5	Th.	St. Agatha • St. Agatha is rich in snow. • Children's writer Brian Jacques died, 2011 • {10.2 / 10.3} *shadows*
6	Fr.	Alan Shepard 1st astronaut to hit golf ball on Moon, 1971 • Tides {10.0 / 9.7} *found.*
7	Sa.	Speed skater Lela Brooks born, 1908 • Actress Dale Evans died, 2001 • Tides {9.7 / 9.1} *Wet*
8	D	Sexagesima • Allende meteorite broke into pieces over large area, northern Mexico, 1969 *and*
9	M.	National Pizza Day (U.S.) • Singer Charles Thomas "Stompin' Tom" Connors born, 1936 — *warming*
10	Tu.	☾ AT APO. • Act of Union proclaimed, merging Upper and Lower Canada, 1841 • {8.8 / 7.6} *now,*
11	W.	Actor Leslie Nielsen born, 1926 • 11–12: 12.5" snow, Dallas/Ft. Worth airport, Tex., 2010 *flowing creeks*
12	Th.	☾ RUNS LOW • U.S. president Abraham Lincoln born, 1809 • Baseball player Joe Garagiola born, 1926 — *make*
13	Fr.	Procaine (now Novocain) patented, 1906 • Opera singer Lily Pons died, 1976 • {9.0 / 7.9} *lovely*
14	Sa.	Sts. Cyril & Methodius • VALENTINE'S DAY • 13–14: In 24 hrs., Dan Meyer created paperclip chain 5340' long, 2004 — *sound.*
15	D	Quinquagesima • NATIONAL FLAG OF CANADA DAY • ♂♄♅ • ♂♇☾ *sound.*
16	M.	PRESIDENTS' DAY • ♂☌☾ • Winter's back breaks. • {10.1 / 9.1} *Presidents' Day*
17	Tu.	Shrove Tuesday • Lunar New Year (China) • Ramadan begins at sundown • NEW ● • ECLIPSE ⊙
18	W.	Ash Wednesday • ☾ AT ☋ • ♂☌☿ • ♂☌♀ • {10.6 / —} *is*
19	Th.	☾ ON EQ. • ♂♄♃ • ♂♀☾ • ☿ GR. ELONG. (18° EAST) • Tides {10.0 / 10.6} *a time*
20	Fr.	*If you command wisely, you'll be obeyed cheerfully.* • {10.3 / 10.5} *to be*
21	Sa.	Skunks mate now. • Lucy Hobbs Taylor became 1st woman in world to graduate from dental school, 1866 *bold—*
22	D	1st S. in Lent • U.S. president George Washington born, 1732 • {10.6 / 9.7} *grab hold*
23	M.	Orthodox Lent begins • ♂♃☾ • Memory is the treasurer of the mind. *of*
24	Tu.	St. Matthias • ☾ AT PERIG. • 4.5 earthquake, eastern Ont./western Que., 2006 *sunrays,*
25	W.	Ember Day • ☾ RIDES HIGH • ♀ STAT. • Tides {10.2 / 8.5} *then*
26	Th.	♂♀♇ • Anti-Slavery Society of Canada formed, 1851 • Tides {10.1 / 8.4} *retreat*
27	Fr.	Ember Day • ♂♃☾ • 22nd U.S. Amendment ratified, 1951 *from the*
28	Sa.	St. Romanus • Ember Day • Alanis Morissette won 4 Grammy Awards, 1996 • Tides {10.4 / 9.1} *cold!*

Q: What two words have the most letters?
A: Post office

Farmer's Calendar
Québécois Tire D'érable

We live on a country road, the asphalt gouged by frost heaves and potholes. In one direction, there's town, with snow heaped in municipal lots. But it's early on a Saturday in sugaring season, so we head outward, where you would have to drive 50 miles to find two parallel roads. Our local sugarman, Holt, who doubles as the town's ax-throwing champ, says that when people think of maple season, it's usually too late. So, he's glad we came early for a full tour of tapping rigs and the brand-spanking-new evaporator. Mmm, the blond-colored sweetness coming off the boil. We do the tour every year. We pretend it's our first time, because, as our 17-year-old jokes, "You have to start from scratch if you want to glimpse the nuances of his sugaring mastery." The kid hasn't forgotten about blueberry cakes stacked neck-high and, wait for it, the *Québécois tire d'érable* that gets him out of bed early this blustery morn. Do you know how proud of him I am? As we sit at the roughhewn tables by the firebox, he pulls out a jar of sour dill pickles from his overcoat and teaches us the correct pairing for something so sweet as maple toffee. That's how proud!

MARCH

SKY WATCH: A total lunar eclipse begins at 4:52 A.M. EST on the 3rd, with totality starting at 6:08 A.M. For observers in the eastern U.S. and Canada, totality begins low in the west in the bright morning twilight and is barely visible. On the 7th and 8th, Venus and Saturn meet low in the west. The conjunction is visible through binoculars at 7:15 P.M., while a small telescope will reveal Saturn's rings to be nearly edgewise. On the 19th at 7:15 P.M., look for Venus to the upper left of the crescent Moon, low in the west. On the 20th, Venus dangles below the Moon. The Moon hovers next to Jupiter on the 25th and 26th, due south at 7:30 P.M., with the conjunction visible for hours. The waxing Moon moves on to meet Leo's main star, Regulus, on the 29th. Spring begins with the vernal equinox on the 20th at 10:46 A.M. EDT.

○ FULL MOON	3rd day	6:38 A.M.	● NEW MOON	18th day	9:23 P.M.
◑ LAST QUARTER	11th day	5:38 A.M.	◐ FIRST QUARTER	25th day	3:18 P.M.

After 2:00 A.M. on March 8, Eastern Daylight Time is given.

GET LOCAL RISE, SET, AND TIDE TIMES VIA ALMANAC.COM/2026.

DAY OF YEAR	DAY OF MONTH	DAY OF WEEK	☼ RISES H. M.	RISE KEY	☼ SETS H. M.	SET KEY	LENGTH OF DAY H. M.	SUN FAST M.	SUN DECLINATION °	'	HIGH TIDE TIMES BOSTON		☾ RISES H. M.	RISE KEY	☾ SETS H. M.	SET KEY	☾ ASTRON. PLACE	☾ AGE
60	1	**D**	6:19	D	**5:34**	C	11 15	4	7 s.	23	9¼	**10**	**3:41**	C	5:30	E	CAN	12
61	2	M.	6:18	D	**5:35**	C	11 17	4	7 s.	00	10¼	**10¾**	**4:54**	C	5:56	E	LEO	13
62	3	Tu.	6:16	D	**5:37**	C	11 21	4	6 s.	37	11	**11½**	**6:04**	D	6:18	D	LEO	14
63	4	W.	6:15	D	**5:38**	C	11 23	4	6 s.	14	11¾	—	**7:12**	D	6:38	C	LEO	15
64	5	Th.	6:13	D	**5:39**	C	11 26	4	5 s.	51	12¼	**12½**	**8:18**	E	6:58	C	VIR	16
65	6	Fr.	6:11	D	**5:40**	C	11 29	5	5 s.	28	12¾	**1¼**	**9:24**	E	7:18	B	VIR	17
66	7	Sa.	6:10	C	**5:41**	C	11 31	5	5 s.	05	1½	**1¾**	**10:30**	E	7:40	B	VIR	18
67	8	**D**	7:08	C	**6:43**	C	11 35	5	4 s.	41	3	**3½**	—	-	9:06	B	LIB	19
68	9	M.	7:06	C	**6:44**	C	11 38	5	4 s.	18	3¾	**4¼**	12:35	E	9:36	A	LIB	20
69	10	Tu.	7:04	C	**6:45**	C	11 41	6	3 s.	54	4½	**5¼**	1:39	E	10:13	A	SCO	21
70	11	W.	7:03	C	**6:46**	C	11 43	6	3 s.	31	5½	**6¼**	2:38	E	10:59	A	OPH	22
71	12	Th.	7:01	C	**6:47**	C	11 46	6	3 s.	07	6¼	**7¼**	3:30	E	11:53	A	SAG	23
72	13	Fr.	6:59	C	**6:48**	C	11 49	7	2 s.	43	7¼	**8¼**	4:15	E	**12:54**	B	SAG	24
73	14	Sa.	6:58	C	**6:50**	C	11 52	7	2 s.	20	8¼	**9**	4:52	E	**2:01**	B	SAG	25
74	15	**D**	6:56	C	**6:51**	C	11 55	7	1 s.	56	9¼	**9¾**	5:23	E	**3:10**	C	CAP	26
75	16	M.	6:54	C	**6:52**	C	11 58	7	1 s.	32	10	**10½**	5:49	E	**4:21**	C	CAP	27
76	17	Tu.	6:53	C	**6:53**	C	12 00	8	1 s.	08	10¾	**11¼**	6:12	D	**5:32**	D	AQU	28
77	18	W.	6:51	C	**6:54**	C	12 03	8	0 s.	45	11½	—	6:33	D	**6:44**	D	AQU	0
78	19	Th.	6:49	C	**6:55**	C	12 06	8	0 s.	21	12	**12¼**	6:55	C	**7:59**	E	PSC	1
79	20	Fr.	6:47	C	**6:57**	C	12 10	8	0 N.	02	12½	**1**	7:18	C	**9:15**	E	PSC	2
80	21	Sa.	6:46	C	**6:58**	C	12 12	9	0 N.	25	1¼	**1¾**	7:44	B	**10:34**	E	PSC	3
81	22	**D**	6:44	C	**6:59**	C	12 15	9	0 N.	49	2	**2½**	8:15	B	**11:54**	E	ARI	4
82	23	M.	6:42	C	**7:00**	C	12 18	9	1 N.	13	2¾	**3½**	8:55	A	—	-	TAU	5
83	24	Tu.	6:40	C	**7:01**	C	12 21	10	1 N.	36	3¾	**4½**	9:45	A	1:11	E	TAU	6
84	25	W.	6:39	C	**7:02**	C	12 23	10	2 N.	00	4¾	**5½**	10:47	A	2:19	E	TAU	7
85	26	Th.	6:37	C	**7:03**	C	12 26	10	2 N.	24	5¾	**6½**	11:58	B	3:15	E	GEM	8
86	27	Fr.	6:35	C	**7:05**	C	12 30	11	2 N.	47	6¾	**7¾**	**1:13**	B	3:58	E	GEM	9
87	28	Sa.	6:33	C	**7:06**	C	12 33	11	3 N.	10	8	**8¾**	**2:28**	C	4:32	E	CAN	10
88	29	**D**	6:32	C	**7:07**	C	12 35	11	3 N.	34	9¼	**9¾**	**3:40**	C	4:59	E	LEO	11
89	30	M.	6:30	C	**7:08**	D	12 38	11	3 N.	57	10	**10½**	**4:50**	D	5:22	D	LEO	12
90	31	Tu.	6:28	C	**7:09**	D	12 41	12	4 N.	20	11	**11¼**	**5:57**	D	5:43	D	LEO	13

 To use this page, see p. 116; for Key Letters, see p. 238. LIGHT = A.M. **BOLD** = P.M.

MARCH

THE THIRD MONTH · 2026 · **MARCH HATH 31 DAYS**

> *I come, I come! ye have called me long,*
> *I come o'er the mountains with light and song.*
> –Felicia Dorothea Hemans, of Spring

DAY OF MONTH	DAY OF WEEK	DATES, FEASTS, FASTS, ASPECTS, TIDE HEIGHTS, AND WEATHER	
1	D	2nd S. in Lent • Peace Corps established, 1961 • Tides {10.6 / 9.6}	Our satellite
2	M.	St. Chad • ☾ AT ☼ • U.S. premiere of film *King Kong*, 1933 • Tides {10.8 / 10.0}	proceeds
3	Tu.	FULL WORM ○ • ECLIPSE ☾ • Australia Act took effect, 1986 • {10.8 / 10.3}	to hide,
4	W.	☾ ON EQ. • Vt. statehood, 1791 • Thomas Jefferson 1st U.S. pres. inaugurated in D.C., 1801	as
5	Th.	St. Piran • Ella and Austin Kurtis created 531.178-lb. Nanaimo bar, setting record, Levack, Ont., 2020	skiers
6	Fr.	Closest approach of *Vega-1* spacecraft to Halley's Comet, 1986 • Tides {10.3 / 10.0}	and
7	Sa.	St. Perpetua • ♂♀Ψ • ♀ IN INF. ☌ • A. G. Bell's phone patented, 1876	sledders
8	D	3rd S. in Lent • DAYLIGHT SAVING TIME BEGINS, 2:00 A.M. • ♂♀♄	take
9	M.	Mattel's Barbie doll debuted, 1959 • Tides {9.5 / 8.4}	one
10	Tu.	☾ AT APO. • ♃ STAT. • Hummingbirds migrate north now. • {9.1 / 7.9}	more
11	W.	☾ RUNS LOW • *A stout heart crushes ill luck.* • Tides {8.8 / 7.6}	ride.
12	Th.	Auto manufacturer Clement Studebaker born, 1831 • {8.7 / 7.5}	If I
13	Fr.	F5 tornado struck Hesston, Kans., and merged with another tornado, 1990 • Tides {8.7 / 7.7}	were
14	Sa.	♂♀☾ • ♂♇☾ • Multi-day storm left 27.2" snow, Iowa City, Iowa, 1951	a bettor,
15	D	4th S. in Lent • Beware the Ides of March. • {9.3 / 8.5}	I'd
16	M.	Comedian Jerry Lewis born, 1926 • Robert Goddard launched 1st liquid-fueled rocket, 1926 • {9.7 / 9.1}	bet
17	Tu.	ST. PATRICK'S DAY • ☾ AT ☼ • ♂♀☾ • ♂♂☾ • Tides {10.1 / 9.7}	we'll
18	W.	NEW ● • ☾ ON EQ. • 1st practical electric razor (Schick) went on sale, 1931 • Tides {10.5 / 10.3}	get
19	Th.	St. Joseph • ♂Ψ☾ • ♂♃☾ • ☿ STAT. • Tides {10.7}	wetter.
20	Fr.	World Frog Day • VERNAL EQUINOX • ♂♀☾ • Tides {10.8 / 10.7}	Spring's
21	Sa.	*All things are easy that are done willingly.* • {11.1 / 10.6}	here
22	D	5th S. in Lent • ☾ AT PERIG. • ♂Ψ☉ • Tides {11.3 / 10.2}	at last,
23	M.	♂♇☾ • *Mir* space station deorbited as planned, falling into the South Pacific Ocean, 2001	it's
24	Tu.	Mickey Mouse animator Ub Iwerks born, 1901 • Fashion designer Tommy Hilfiger born, 1951	warming
25	W.	Annunciation • ☾ RIDES HIGH • ♂♄☉ • Tides {10.5 / 8.8}	up fast,
26	Th.	♂♃☾ • Playwright Tennessee Williams born, 1911 • Super Glue inventor Harry Wesley Coover Jr. died, 2011	but
27	Fr.	Spring blizzard hit Nfld., 2006 • Tides {9.9 / 8.7}	we're still
28	Sa.	1st photos published in Canadian daily newspaper (*The Saturday Globe*), 1891 • Tides {9.9 / 9.0}	wearing
29	D	Palm Sunday • Tennis player Jennifer Capriati born, 1976 • Tides {10.0 / 9.4}	slickers
30	M.	☾ AT ☼ • Chipmunks emerge from hibernation now. • Tides {10.2 / 9.9}	and
31	Tu.	☾ ON EQ. • *As the days grow longer, The storms grow stronger.* • Tides {10.3 / 10.2}	sweaters.

Farmer's Calendar

Spring is an Abstraction

Emperor tulips press their lips into the top of the earth. The coop's border bed is edged by fieldstones we weeded from the garden. The warmth they capture gives the nearest bulbs a jump start. Apart from this, spring is still an abstraction. I get to thinking of my two Uncle Brians. One, an airline worker, long wears the wisdom of traveling in shoulder season. The other, a stonecutter, argues it best to stay put, all times of year. The competing ideals of my Uncle Brians carry on their quiet wars in me in March, a month so named after the Roman god of arms. Should one hit the road to liven the spirits or hunker down until the season improves? My daughter and I inspect the orchard for silver tips on the apple buds. We think over our seasonal restlessness, and we find compromise: Let's brave a hibernal adventure, but without going far! We'll sleep out tonight, the first camp of the year. In the clearing just shy of our farm's cemetery, we build a massive fire and steal some late hours of frosty light. The first few stars dot the night sky with a hush, but we hear them loud and clear. Spring is soon upon us.

APRIL

SKY WATCH: On the 15th and 16th, a grouping of Saturn, Mars, Mercury, and the Moon will be very low in the predawn eastern sky and buried in twilight, making it all but impossible to view even through binoculars. The month does offer intrigue in the west between 7:30 and 8:00 P.M., with Venus low in the sky and Jupiter above. Look for Venus to the left of the crescent Moon on the 18th and Jupiter below the Moon on the 22nd. Another lunar conjunction unfolds 3 nights later, when the Moon almost touches Leo's bright blue star, Regulus. The Moon meets another blue star on the 29th when it's to the right of Virgo's Spica.

○ **FULL MOON** 1st day 10:12 P.M. ● **NEW MOON** 17th day 7:52 A.M.
☽ **LAST QUARTER** 10th day 12:51 A.M. ☾ **FIRST QUARTER** 23rd day 10:32 P.M.

All times are given in Eastern Daylight Time.

GET LOCAL RISE, SET, AND TIDE TIMES VIA ALMANAC.COM/2026.

Day of Year	Day of Month	Day of Week	☼ Rises H.M.	Rise Key	☼ Sets H.M.	Set Key	Length of Day H.M.	Sun Fast M.	Sun Declination ° '	High Tide Times Boston	☾ Rises H.M.	Rise Key	☾ Sets H.M.	Set Key	☾ Astron. Place	☾ Age
91	1	W.	6:27	C	7:10	D	12 43	12	4 N. 44	11¾	—	7:03	E	6:02	C	VIR	14
92	2	Th.	6:25	C	7:11	D	12 46	12	5 N. 07	12	12½	8:09	E	6:22	C	VIR	15
93	3	Fr.	6:23	C	7:12	D	12 49	13	5 N. 30	12¾	1	9:15	E	6:43	B	VIR	16
94	4	Sa.	6:21	C	7:14	D	12 53	13	5 N. 52	1¼	1¾	10:21	E	7:07	B	VIR	17
95	5	D	6:20	C	7:15	D	12 55	13	6 N. 15	1¾	2½	11:25	E	7:36	A	LIB	18
96	6	M.	6:18	C	7:16	D	12 58	13	6 N. 38	2½	3	—	-	8:10	A	SCO	19
97	7	Tu.	6:16	C	7:17	D	13 01	14	7 N. 00	3¼	3¾	12:26	E	8:52	A	OPH	20
98	8	W.	6:15	B	7:18	D	13 03	14	7 N. 23	4	4¾	1:21	E	9:43	A	SAG	21
99	9	Th.	6:13	B	7:19	D	13 06	14	7 N. 45	4¾	5½	2:09	E	10:41	A	SAG	22
100	10	Fr.	6:11	B	7:20	D	13 09	15	8 N. 07	5¾	6½	2:48	E	11:44	B	SAG	23
101	11	Sa.	6:10	B	7:21	D	13 11	15	8 N. 29	6¾	7½	3:21	E	12:51	B	CAP	24
102	12	D	6:08	B	7:23	D	13 15	15	8 N. 51	7¾	8¼	3:49	E	2:00	C	CAP	25
103	13	M.	6:06	B	7:24	D	13 18	15	9 N. 13	8½	9	4:13	D	3:10	C	AQU	26
104	14	Tu.	6:05	B	7:25	D	13 20	16	9 N. 35	9½	9¾	4:35	D	4:21	D	AQU	27
105	15	W.	6:03	B	7:26	D	13 23	16	9 N. 56	10¼	10½	4:56	C	5:34	E	PSC	28
106	16	Th.	6:02	B	7:27	D	13 25	16	10 N. 18	11	11¼	5:18	C	6:50	E	PSC	29
107	17	Fr.	6:00	B	7:28	D	13 28	16	10 N. 39	11¾	—	5:43	B	8:10	E	PSC	0
108	18	Sa.	5:58	B	7:29	D	13 31	16	11 N. 00	12	12¾	6:13	B	9:32	E	ARI	1
109	19	D	5:57	B	7:30	D	13 33	17	11 N. 20	12¾	1½	6:50	B	10:53	E	ARI	2
110	20	M.	5:55	B	7:32	D	13 37	17	11 N. 41	1¾	2¼	7:38	A	—	-	TAU	3
111	21	Tu.	5:54	B	7:33	D	13 39	17	12 N. 01	2½	3¼	8:38	A	12:07	E	TAU	4
112	22	W.	5:52	B	7:34	D	13 42	17	12 N. 22	3½	4¼	9:48	B	1:09	E	GEM	5
113	23	Th.	5:51	B	7:35	D	13 44	17	12 N. 41	4½	5¼	11:03	B	1:58	E	GEM	6
114	24	Fr.	5:49	B	7:36	D	13 47	18	13 N. 01	5½	6¼	12:19	B	2:35	E	CAN	7
115	25	Sa.	5:48	B	7:37	D	13 49	18	13 N. 21	6¾	7½	1:32	C	3:04	E	LEO	8
116	26	D	5:46	B	7:38	D	13 52	18	13 N. 40	7¾	8½	2:41	D	3:28	D	LEO	9
117	27	M.	5:45	B	7:39	D	13 54	18	13 N. 59	8¾	9½	3:48	D	3:48	D	LEO	10
118	28	Tu.	5:43	B	7:41	D	13 58	18	14 N. 18	9¾	10¼	4:54	E	4:08	C	VIR	11
119	29	W.	5:42	B	7:42	D	14 00	18	14 N. 37	10½	10¾	5:58	E	4:27	C	VIR	12
120	30	Th.	5:41	B	7:43	E	14 02	19	14 N. 55	11¼	11½	7:04	E	4:48	B	VIR	13

THE FOURTH MONTH · 2026 — APRIL — APRIL HATH 30 DAYS

The Spring
Is here so good-and-plenty that the old hen has to sing!
–James Whitcomb Riley

DAY OF MONTH	DAY OF WEEK	DATES, FEASTS, FASTS, ASPECTS, TIDE HEIGHTS, AND WEATHER
1	W.	Passover begins at sundown • **All Fools'** • **Full Pink** ○ • Tides {10.2 / —} Spring,
2	Th.	**Maundy Thursday** • Velcro patent expired, 1978 • Tides {10.4 / 10.1} I think,
3	Fr.	**Good Friday** • ☿ Gr. Elong. (28° West) • Rain on Good Friday foreshows a fruitful year. will
4	Sa.	American Rocket Society founded (as American Interplanetary Society), 1930 • {10.4 / 9.6} arrive
5	D	**Easter** • Industrialist/aviator Howard Hughes died, 1976 • Tides {10.2 / 9.2} in a
6	M.	**Easter Monday** • 1st modern Olympic Games opened, Athens, Greece, 1896 • Tides {9.9 / 8.8} blink,
7	Tu.	☾ at Apo. • 7-lb. 0.58-oz. queen triggerfish caught, South Ledge area, Ga., 2024 • {9.6 / 8.4} bring
8	W.	☾ Runs Low • Rare daytime sighting of fireball over northern Maine and N.B., 2023 • {9.3 / 8.1} us
9	Th.	1st free, tax-supported library created at town meeting, Peterborough, N.H., 1833 • Tides {9.0 / 7.9} back
10	Fr.	253-mph wind gust, Barrow Island, Australia, 1996 • {8.8 / 7.9} from
11	Sa.	♂♃☽ • Horticulturist Luther Burbank died, 1926 • Empire State Building completed, N.Y.C., 1931 the
12	D	**2nd S. of Easter** • **Orthodox Easter** • U.S. Civil War began, 1861 brink,
13	M.	☾ at ☊ • ♂♂♀ • U.S. president Thomas Jefferson born, 1743 • {9.3 / 9.1} as our
14	Tu.	National Gardening Day • Teacher Anne Sullivan born, 1866 • {9.7 / 9.2} woodpiles
15	W.	☾ on Eq. • ♂♀☽ • ♂♂☽ • ♂♆☽ • Tides {10.1 / 10.4} shrink.
16	Th.	♂♅♀ • ♂♄☽ • Better spared than ill spent. • Tides {10.4 / 11.0} This
17	Fr.	**New** ● • Storm swept away 1st Minots Ledge Light, near Scituate, Mass., 1851 cold's
18	Sa.	Massive earthquake and resultant fire devastated San Francisco, Calif., 1906 • {11.5 / 10.6} getting
19	D	**3rd S. of Easter** • ☾ at Perig. • ♂♂♂ • ♂♀☽ • ♂☌☽ old,
20	M.	♂♂♄ • ♂♂♃ • Anik-A2 telecommunications satellite launched, 1973 • {11.8 / 10.2} late
21	Tu.	☾ Rides High • U.K.'s Queen Elizabeth II born, 1926 • Actor Tony Danza born, 1951 frosts
22	W.	**Earth Day** • ♂♃☽ • Queen Isabella I of Spain born, 1451 • {11.2 / 9.4} alarming!
23	Th.	**St. George** • Canada issued its 1st postage stamp (3-pence Beaver), 1851 • {10.7 / 9.2} We'd
24	Fr.	♂♂♀ • The Old Farmer's Almanac founder Robert B. Thomas born, 1766 • {10.2 / 9.1} welcome
25	Sa.	**St. Mark** • N.Y. 1st state to require auto license plates, 1901 • Tides {9.9 / 9.2} some
26	D	**4th S. of Easter** • ☾ at ☊ • Quarter-size hail fell, near Ulmer, S.C., 2011 warming;
27	M.	☾ on Eq. • Poplars leaf out about now. • Tides {9.7 / 9.8} it's
28	Tu.	Dennis Tito became world's 1st space tourist, when Soyuz TM-32 launched, 2001 • {9.7 / 10.0} time
29	W.	Confession of a fault makes half amends. • Tides {9.7 / 10.2} to start
30	Th.	29–30: Significant flash flooding in Ala. and Fla., 2014 • Tides {9.6 / 10.3} farming!

Farmer's Calendar
Sowing Before a Night Soak

There's a yellow-beaked light on the edge of afternoon. I'm carving thin rows for snow peas in just-thawed soil, racing before a soak is due at nightfall. I get a call from Holmes, five states to the south. She tells me about the northern flickers that define the route of her walks. It's been 10 years since I've seen her, but the phone rings with excitement whenever she's got a new favorite bird. Today, her enthusiasm is giftwrapped around regional naming conventions, especially attempts to spell out bird calls. She puts her receiver in the direction of what I learn is a pair-forming call. It sounds like she's awfully close to them. The long, rolling rattle lasts a while, say, 7 or 8 seconds. They also squeak a unison vocalization of courtship. For these, her grandma from Michigan used the memory phrase: *wake-up, wake-up*. An old-timer in Virginia tells her it's *wick-a, wick-a*. "Hey Holmes, why are they called flickers?" Oh boy, a can of linguistic worms. By the time she details a debate of theories (the call, the color on the feather shafts, the snap of their wings), nightfall and rain have set in, and I still haven't sowed my peas. If I had a nickel every time a bird laid waste to my goals for the garden!

MAY

SKY WATCH: With the month's later sunsets, dazzling Venus is visible to the lower right of brilliant Jupiter from 8:15 to 8:30 P.M. in the west. On the 1st, the two planets create a perfect triangle with bluish Sirius, also known as the Dog Star. At midmonth, watch Venus and Jupiter, the night's two brightest "stars," move closer together each evening. Look for the Moon to make a stunningly tight conjunction with Venus on the 18th. On the next night, the Moon hovers between Venus and Jupiter, then stands above Jupiter on the 20th. Each meeting will look best between 8:30 and 9:00 P.M. On the 30th, the Moon, rising in the southeast at 10:00 P.M., will stand to the right of the red supergiant star Antares in Scorpius.

○ FULL MOON	1st day	1:23 P.M.
◑ LAST QUARTER	9th day	5:10 P.M.
● NEW MOON	16th day	4:01 P.M.
◐ FIRST QUARTER	23rd day	7:11 A.M.
○ FULL MOON	31st day	4:45 A.M.

All times are given in Eastern Daylight Time.

GET LOCAL RISE, SET, AND TIDE TIMES VIA ALMANAC.COM/2026.

DAY OF YEAR	DAY OF MONTH	DAY OF WEEK	☼ RISES H. M.	RISE KEY	☼ SETS H. M.	SET KEY	LENGTH OF DAY H. M.	SUN FAST M.	SUN DECLINATION °	'	HIGH TIDE TIMES BOSTON		☾ RISES H. M.	RISE KEY	☾ SETS H. M.	SET KEY	☾ ASTRON. PLACE	☾ AGE
121	1	Fr.	5:39	B	**7:44**	E	14 05	19	15 N.	13	**12**	—	**8:09**	E	5:11	B	VIR	14
122	2	Sa.	5:38	B	**7:45**	E	14 07	19	15 N.	31	12¼	**12¾**	**9:14**	E	5:37	B	LIB	15
123	3	**D**	5:37	B	**7:46**	E	14 09	19	15 N.	49	12¾	**1¼**	**10:16**	E	6:10	A	LIB	16
124	4	M.	5:35	B	**7:47**	E	14 12	19	16 N.	06	1¼	**2**	**11:13**	E	6:49	A	SCO	17
125	5	Tu.	5:34	B	**7:48**	E	14 14	19	16 N.	23	2	**2¾**	—	-	7:37	A	OPH	18
126	6	W.	5:33	B	**7:49**	E	14 16	19	16 N.	40	2¾	**3½**	12:04	E	8:32	A	SAG	19
127	7	Th.	5:32	B	**7:51**	E	14 19	19	16 N.	57	3½	**4¼**	12:46	E	9:33	B	SAG	20
128	8	Fr.	5:30	B	**7:52**	E	14 22	19	17 N.	13	4¼	**5**	1:20	E	10:38	B	CAP	21
129	9	Sa.	5:29	B	**7:53**	E	14 24	19	17 N.	29	5	**5¾**	1:49	E	11:45	C	CAP	22
130	10	**D**	5:28	B	**7:54**	E	14 26	19	17 N.	45	6	**6¾**	2:14	E	**12:52**	C	CAP	23
131	11	M.	5:27	B	**7:55**	E	14 28	19	18 N.	00	7	**7½**	2:36	D	**2:00**	D	AQU	24
132	12	Tu.	5:26	B	**7:56**	E	14 30	19	18 N.	15	7¾	**8¼**	2:57	D	**3:10**	D	AQU	25
133	13	W.	5:25	B	**7:57**	E	14 32	19	18 N.	30	8¾	**9¼**	3:18	C	**4:23**	E	PSC	26
134	14	Th.	5:24	A	**7:58**	E	14 34	19	18 N.	44	9¾	**10**	3:41	C	**5:40**	E	PSC	27
135	15	Fr.	5:23	A	**7:59**	E	14 36	19	18 N.	59	10½	**10¾**	4:08	B	**7:01**	E	ARI	28
136	16	Sa.	5:22	A	**8:00**	E	14 38	19	19 N.	12	11½	**11½**	4:42	B	**8:25**	E	ARI	0
137	17	**D**	5:21	A	**8:01**	E	14 40	19	19 N.	26	**12¼**	—	5:25	A	**9:45**	E	TAU	1
138	18	M.	5:20	A	**8:02**	E	14 42	19	19 N.	39	12½	**1¼**	6:21	A	**10:55**	E	TAU	2
139	19	Tu.	5:19	A	**8:03**	E	14 44	19	19 N.	52	1¼	**2**	7:30	B	**11:51**	E	GEM	3
140	20	W.	5:18	A	**8:04**	E	14 46	19	20 N.	05	2¼	**3**	8:47	B	—	-	GEM	4
141	21	Th.	5:17	A	**8:05**	E	14 48	19	20 N.	17	3¼	**4**	10:05	B	12:33	E	CAN	5
142	22	Fr.	5:16	A	**8:06**	E	14 50	19	20 N.	29	4¼	**5**	11:21	C	1:06	E	CAN	6
143	23	Sa.	5:15	A	**8:07**	E	14 52	19	20 N.	40	5¼	**6**	**12:33**	C	1:32	D	LEO	7
144	24	**D**	5:15	A	**8:08**	E	14 53	19	20 N.	51	6¼	**7**	**1:41**	D	1:54	D	LEO	8
145	25	M.	5:14	A	**8:09**	E	14 55	19	21 N.	02	7½	**8**	**2:47**	D	2:14	C	VIR	9
146	26	Tu.	5:13	A	**8:10**	E	14 57	19	21 N.	12	8½	**8¾**	**3:51**	E	2:33	C	VIR	10
147	27	W.	5:13	A	**8:11**	E	14 58	18	21 N.	22	9¼	**9¾**	**4:56**	E	2:53	B	VIR	11
148	28	Th.	5:12	A	**8:11**	E	14 59	18	21 N.	32	10¼	**10¼**	**6:01**	E	3:15	B	VIR	12
149	29	Fr.	5:11	A	**8:12**	E	15 01	18	21 N.	41	11	**11**	**7:05**	E	3:41	B	LIB	13
150	30	Sa.	5:11	A	**8:13**	E	15 02	18	21 N.	50	11¾	**11¾**	**8:08**	E	4:11	A	LIB	14
151	31	**D**	5:10	A	**8:14**	E	15 04	18	21 N.	59	**12¼**	—	**9:07**	E	4:48	A	SCO	15

To use this page, see p. 116; for Key Letters, see p. 238. LIGHT = A.M. **BOLD** = P.M.

THE FIFTH MONTH • 2026 MAY MAY HATH 31 DAYS

Soft purl the streams; the birds renew their notes,
And through the air their mingled music floats.
–**Phillis Wheatley**

DAY OF MONTH	DAY OF WEEK	DATES, FEASTS, FASTS, ASPECTS, TIDE HEIGHTS, AND WEATHER	
1	Fr.	Sts. Philip & James • Vesak • **May Day** • **Full Flower** ○ • Tides {9.5 / —	*A*
2	Sa.	St. Athanasius • 1st illustration sent by radio across Atlantic, 1926 • {10.3 / 9.3	*threatening*
3	D	**5th S. of Easter** • Actress Ann B. Davis born, 1926 • {10.3 / 9.2	*sky*
4	M.	☾ at apo. • Football coach Don Shula died, 2020 • Tides {10.1 / 8.9	*over*
5	Tu.	☾ runs low • Chanel No. 5 fragrance introduced, 1921 • Tides {9.9 / 8.7	*Cinco de*
6	W.	Neurologist Sigmund Freud born, 1856 • Tides {9.7 / 8.5	*Mayo!*
7	Th.	Beaufort Scale Day • *May showers bring milk and meal.* • {9.5 / 8.3	*Rain fills*
8	Fr.	St. Julian of Norwich • ☌♇☾ • ♇ stat. • Naturalist Sir David Attenborough born, 1926	*a vase*
9	Sa.	St. Gregory of Nazianzus • Lt. Cmdr. Richard Byrd/Chief Aviation Pilot Floyd Bennett claimed 1st to fly over North Pole, 1926	
10	D	Rogation Sunday • **Mother's Day** • {9.1 / 8.7	*for Mother's*
11	M.	Three • ☾ at ☊ • Glacier National Park established, Mont., 1910 • {9.1 / 9.1	*Day*
12	Tu.	Chilly • ☾ on Eq. • Singer Perry Como died, 2001 • Tides {9.3 / 9.7	*flowers,*
13	W.	Saints • ☌♄☾ • ☌♆☾ • Cranberries in bud now. • {9.6 / 10.3	*sunshine*
14	Th.	**Ascension** • ☌♂☾ • ☿ in sup. ☌ • Tides {9.9 / 11.0	*gives*
15	Fr.	*Confidence is the companion of success.* • Tides {10.1 / 11.5	*chase*
16	Sa.	**New** ● • ☌☿☾ • U.S. politician William H. Seward born, 1801 • {10.3 / 11.9	*to*
17	D	**1st S. af. Asc.** • ☾ at perig. • ☌☿♅ • ☌♅☾ • {10.4 / —	*scatter*
18	M.	**Victoria Day (Canada)** • ☾ rides high • ☌♀☾ • Tides {12.1 / 10.3	*the*
19	Tu.	St. Dunstan • Parks Canada established, 1911 • Basketball player Kevin Garnett born, 1976	*showers.*
20	W.	☌♃☾ • Levi Strauss and Jacob Davis rec'd patent for riveted pocket openings for pants, 1873	*Storms*
21	Th.	**Orthodox Ascension** • Shavuot begins at sundown • {11.3 / 9.8	*and*
22	Fr.	☌♅☉ • Space Needle foundation poured, Seattle, Wash., 1961 • {10.8 / 9.6	*warm*
23	Sa.	☾ at ☋ • Pirate Capt. William Kidd died, London, 1701 • Tides {10.3 / 9.6	*air*
24	D	**Whit S. • Pentecost** • 116°F, Callville Bay, Nev., 2000 • {9.8 / 9.6	*bring*
25	M.	St. Bede • **Memorial Day, observed** • ☾ on Eq. • Tides {9.5 / 9.7	*new*
26	Tu.	Astronaut Sally Ride born, 1951 • Tides {9.2 / 9.9	*blooms*
27	W.	Ember Day • *In the evening, one may praise the day.* • Tides {9.1 / 10.0	*as fair*
28	Th.	Hubble image of TMR-1C object released, 1998 • {9.0 / 10.1	*as a*
29	Fr.	Ember Day • Standardized sewing pattern inventor Ebenezer Butterick born, 1826 • {9.0 / 10.1	*blue*
30	Sa.	Ember Day • Pure sulfur discovered on Mars, 2024 • Tides {8.9 / 10.1	*Moon*
31	D	**Trinity • Orthodox Pentecost** • **Blue** ○ • {8.9 / —	*is rare.*

Farmer's Calendar

Passing Love Letters

A storybook sunrise begins to form. The 'Kanzan' cherry weeps with heavy-dewed blossoms over the picnic table. My old dog and I listen as a seduction of bees arrive. In my notebook, I twiddle a charm of misty-eyed phrases, trying to sweeten the page. I am transported to an early come-hither with the great love of my life. It was a fair spring, years ago. We stole many hours in an overgrown corner of someone's abandoned farm. A ladybug crawled from my hand to hers. She told me of her favorite childhood activity, "passing love letters." That's what she and her sisters called it when they would blow on the round seed heads of what then became my favorite weed—the dandelion. Am I a sap for sentiment? Yes! But can I also rattle off a dozen permaculture uses for this vivid mark of May? Why, from the nutrient-dense, edible roots to the greenleaf tea you can drench on heavy-feeder vegetables, of course I can! I suppose if there's any advice tucked in these words, maybe it's this: Next time you send the childlike seeds of this wispy puffball to the wind, let the memory of your great loves breeze across your mind.

JUNE

SKY WATCH: Venus and Jupiter draw closer during the first week of June, with their eye-catching conjunction best seen around 9:00 P.M. from the 7th to the 10th, low in the west. In the low predawn eastern sky, orange, medium-bright Mars is now visible beneath the crescent Moon and returning Saturn on the 10th at 4:40 A.M. Jupiter will float between the Moon and Venus on the 16th. Then, the Moon performs two more noteworthy conjunctions: to the upper left of Venus on the 17th; and to the lower left of Virgo's main star, Spica, on the 23rd, best seen from 9:00 to 9:30 P.M. Summer arrives with the solstice on the 21st at 4:24 A.M. EDT.

◐ **LAST QUARTER** 8th day 6:00 A.M.
● **NEW MOON** 14th day 10:54 P.M.
◑ **FIRST QUARTER** 21st day 5:55 P.M.
○ **FULL MOON** 29th day 7:56 P.M.

All times are given in Eastern Daylight Time.

GET LOCAL RISE, SET, AND TIDE TIMES VIA ALMANAC.COM/2026.

DAY OF YEAR	DAY OF MONTH	DAY OF WEEK	☀ RISES H. M.	RISE KEY	☀ SETS H. M.	SET KEY	LENGTH OF DAY H. M.	SUN FAST M.	SUN DECLINATION ° '	HIGH TIDE TIMES BOSTON	☾ RISES H. M.	RISE KEY	☾ SETS H. M.	SET KEY	☾ ASTRON. PLACE	☾ AGE
152	1	M.	5:10	A	8:15	E	15 05	18	22 N. 07	12¼ — 1	9:59	E	5:33	A	OPH	16
153	2	Tu.	5:09	A	8:15	E	15 06	18	22 N. 15	1 — 1¾	10:44	E	6:26	A	SAG	17
154	3	W.	5:09	A	8:16	E	15 07	17	22 N. 22	1¾ — 2¼	11:21	E	7:26	A	SAG	18
155	4	Th.	5:09	A	8:17	E	15 08	17	22 N. 29	2¼ — 3	11:51	E	8:29	B	SAG	19
156	5	Fr.	5:08	A	8:18	E	15 10	17	22 N. 35	3 — 3¾	—	–	9:35	B	CAP	20
157	6	Sa.	5:08	A	8:18	E	15 10	17	22 N. 42	3¾ — 4½	12:16	E	10:41	C	CAP	21
158	7	**D**	5:08	A	8:19	E	15 11	17	22 N. 47	4½ — 5¼	12:39	D	11:47	C	AQU	22
159	8	M.	5:07	A	8:19	E	15 12	17	22 N. 53	5½ — 6	12:59	D	**12:54**	D	AQU	23
160	9	Tu.	5:07	A	8:20	E	15 13	16	22 N. 58	6¼ — 6¾	**1:20**	C	**2:03**	E	PSC	24
161	10	W.	5:07	A	8:21	E	15 14	16	23 N. 02	7¼ — 7¾	**1:41**	C	**3:16**	E	PSC	25
162	11	Th.	5:07	A	8:21	E	15 14	16	23 N. 07	8¼ — 8½	**2:06**	B	**4:33**	E	PSC	26
163	12	Fr.	5:07	A	8:22	E	15 15	16	23 N. 10	9¼ — 9½	**2:35**	B	**5:54**	E	ARI	27
164	13	Sa.	5:07	A	8:22	E	15 15	16	23 N. 14	10¼ — 10¼	**3:13**	B	**7:16**	E	ARI	28
165	14	**D**	5:07	A	8:22	E	15 15	15	23 N. 17	11 — 11¼	**4:02**	A	**8:32**	E	TAU	0
166	15	M.	5:07	A	8:23	E	15 16	15	23 N. 19	12 — —	**5:06**	A	**9:36**	E	TAU	1
167	16	Tu.	5:07	A	8:23	E	15 16	15	23 N. 21	12¼ — 1	**6:21**	B	**10:25**	E	GEM	2
168	17	W.	5:07	A	8:24	E	15 17	15	23 N. 23	1 — 1¾	**7:42**	B	**11:03**	E	GEM	3
169	18	Th.	5:07	A	8:24	E	15 17	14	23 N. 24	2 — 2¾	**9:02**	C	**11:33**	E	CAN	4
170	19	Fr.	5:07	A	8:24	E	15 17	14	23 N. 25	3 — 3¾	**10:18**	C	**11:57**	D	LEO	5
171	20	Sa.	5:07	A	8:24	E	15 17	14	23 N. 26	4 — 4½	**11:29**	D	—	–	LEO	6
172	21	**D**	5:07	A	8:25	E	15 18	14	23 N. 26	5 — 5½	**12:37**	D	**12:18**	D	LEO	7
173	22	M.	5:08	A	8:25	E	15 17	14	23 N. 25	6 — 6½	**1:43**	E	**12:38**	C	VIR	8
174	23	Tu.	5:08	A	8:25	E	15 17	13	23 N. 25	7 — 7¼	**2:48**	E	**12:58**	C	VIR	9
175	24	W.	5:08	A	8:25	E	15 17	13	23 N. 23	8 — 8¼	**3:53**	E	**1:19**	B	VIR	10
176	25	Th.	5:09	A	8:25	E	15 16	13	23 N. 22	8¾ — 9	**4:58**	E	**1:44**	B	LIB	11
177	26	Fr.	5:09	A	8:25	E	15 16	13	23 N. 20	9¾ — 9¾	**6:01**	E	**2:12**	B	LIB	12
178	27	Sa.	5:09	A	8:25	E	15 16	13	23 N. 17	10½ — 10½	**7:01**	E	**2:47**	A	SCO	13
179	28	**D**	5:10	A	8:25	E	15 15	13	23 N. 15	11¼ — 11¼	**7:56**	E	**3:30**	A	OPH	14
180	29	M.	5:10	A	8:25	E	15 15	12	23 N. 11	12 — —	**8:43**	E	**4:21**	A	SAG	15
181	30	Tu.	5:11	A	8:25	E	15 14	12	23 N. 08	12 — 12¾	**9:22**	E	**5:19**	A	SAG	16

To use this page, see p. 116; for Key Letters, see p. 238. LIGHT = A.M. **BOLD = P.M.**

THE SIXTH MONTH • 2026 JUNE JUNE HATH 30 DAYS

The rose just bursting into bloom, / Admired where'er 'tis seen,
Dispenses round a rich perfume, / The garden's pride and queen.
–Susanna Haswell Rowson

DAY OF MONTH	DAY OF WEEK	DATES, FEASTS, FASTS, ASPECTS, TIDE HEIGHTS, AND WEATHER	
1	M.	Visit of Mary[T] • ☾ RUNS LOW • ☾ AT APO. • Actress Marilyn Monroe born, 1926	*Clouds*
2	Tu.	*The forest has ears, the field has eyes.* • Tides {10.1 / 8.8	*and*
3	W.	World Bicycle Day • Geologist James Hutton born, 1726 • {10.0 / 8.7	*mist*
4	Th.	☌♇☾ • Cat "Rayne Beau" lost at Yellowstone, Wyo.; found 2 mos. later in Calif. and reunited w/owners, 2024	*are*
5	Fr.	St. Boniface • Teton dam collapsed, Idaho, 1976 • Tides {9.7 / 8.7	*all about,*
6	Sa.	1st patented drive-in theater in U.S. opened, Pennsauken, N.J., 1933 • D-Day, 1944 • {9.6 / 8.8	*restless*
7	D	Corpus Christi • Orthodox All Saints' • ☾ AT ☊ • {9.4 / 9.0	*students*
8	M.	☾ ON EQ. • *When the bramble blossoms early in June, an early harvest is expected.* • {9.3 / 9.3	*twist*
9	Tu.	☌♀♃ • ☌♆☾ • Writer Charles Dickens died, 1870 • Tides {9.2 / 9.7	*and*
10	W.	☌♄☾ • United States War Dogs Memorial dedicated, Holmdel, N.J., 2006 • {9.3 / 10.2	*shout!*
11	Th.	St. Barnabas • *E.T. the Extra-Terrestrial* movie released, 1982 • Tides {9.4 / 10.8	*School*
12	Fr.	☌♂☾ • Oakland Athletics' Rickey Henderson stole 900th base of career, 1990	*is what*
13	Sa.	☌♅☾ • 111°F, Laredo, Tex., 2023 • Tides {9.7 / 11.7	*they'll*
14	D	3rd S. af. P. • FLAG DAY • NEW ● • ☾ AT PERIG. • {9.9 / 12.0	*soon be*
15	M.	☾ RIDES HIGH • ☿ GR. ELONG. (25° EAST) • Ark. statehood, 1836 • {10.1 / —	*fleein'*
16	Tu.	First of Muharram begins at sundown • ☌☿☾ • Tides {12.1 / 10.2	*from,*
17	W.	OCCN. ♀☾ • ☌♃☾ • Deadly tornado, Windsor, Ont., 1946	*warm and*
18	Th.	*One hour's sleep before midnight is worth two hours after it.* • Tides {11.8 / 10.2	*rainy for*
19	Fr.	JUNETEENTH NATIONAL INDEPENDENCE DAY • ☾ AT ☋ • {11.3 / 10.1	*Juneteenth*
20	Sa.	Home improvement TV host Bob Vila born, 1946 • Tides {10.8 / 10.0	*freedom.*
21	D	4th S. af. P. • FATHER'S DAY • SUMMER SOLSTICE • ☾ ON EQ.	*Dads are*
22	M.	St. Alban • "The Cholmondeley" 17th-century Stradivarius cello sold for $1,217,711 at auction, 1988	*glad on*
23	Tu.	Foot-deep hail, El Dorado, Kans., 1951 • Tides {9.1 / 9.8	*summer's*
24	W.	Nativ. John the Baptist • MIDSUMMER DAY • Pablo Picasso's 1st major art exhibit, Paris, France, 1901	*first*
25	Th.	*25–26:* "Custer's Last Stand," Battle of Little Bighorn, Mont., 1876 • Tides {8.5 / 9.7	*day . . .*
26	Fr.	CN Tower opened, Toronto, Ont., 1976 • Tides {8.5 / 9.8	*Honey-*
27	Sa.	Rain of fish, Tiller's Ferry, S.C., 1901 • Actor Jack Lemmon died, 2001 • {8.5 / 9.9	*do list:*
28	D	5th S. af. P. • ☾ RUNS LOW • ☾ AT APO. • ☿ STAT. • {8.5 / 9.9	*Catch*
29	M.	Sts. Peter & Paul • FULL STRAWBERRY ○ • San Francisco, Calif., founded, 1776	*some*
30	Tu.	Microburst uprooted 300 trees near Belgrade Lakes, Maine, 2021 • Tides {8.7 / —	*rays!*

Farmer's Calendar

Cherry Pie for Cherry Hots

A quick trip to the beach before the noisy crowds arrive in full. Martha Ann and Eddie are year-rounders down the shore. It's our great fortune that they'll have us as often as we'll make the drive. They have the old-world spirit of endless giving, and we do our best to be good guests. They tell us where we can collect deadwood for the chance of a bonfire at dusk, but a wicked sea breeze strikes up a loud chord that shrieks across the empty sheet music of our windbreakers. The sanded gusts bring a snare of salted mist into our faces, as we watch gulls work the edge of a sandbar. When it gets dark, we head back to the house, where we can make good on guest-giving. We leave them with two Montmorency cherry pies—one for the table, one for the freezer. Martha Ann slides us a few jars of Italian cherry hots from last year's garden—you'd be surprised how much they produce from those sandy little raised beds on the side of the house. And Eddie sends us with a couple lengths of homemade soppressata. Like many of their guests, we leave with our arms full.

JULY

SKY WATCH: On the 4th, America's 250th birthday, early risers will see orange, medium-bright Mars closely meet green Uranus low in the east, a conjunction best seen through binoculars at 4:40 A.M. In the evening, Venus continues to brighten but stays low in the west from 9:00 to 9:30 P.M. It meets Leo's Regulus on the 8th and 9th. Look for Venus above the crescent Moon on the 16th and to the right of the Moon on the 17th. The Moon then moves on to dangle below Spica, Virgo's superhot blue star, on the 20th and below orange Antares—one of the galaxy's largest stars—on the 24th.

| ◐ LAST QUARTER | 7th day | 3:29 P.M. | ◑ FIRST QUARTER | 21st day | 7:05 A.M. |
| ● NEW MOON | 14th day | 5:43 A.M. | ○ FULL MOON | 29th day | 10:36 A.M. |

All times are given in Eastern Daylight Time.

GET LOCAL RISE, SET, AND TIDE TIMES VIA ALMANAC.COM/2026.

DAY OF YEAR	DAY OF MONTH	DAY OF WEEK	☀ RISES H. M.	RISE KEY	☀ SETS H. M.	SET KEY	LENGTH OF DAY H. M.	SUN FAST M.	SUN DECLINATION ° '	HIGH TIDE TIMES BOSTON	☽ RISES H. M.	RISE KEY	☽ SETS H. M.	SET KEY	☽ ASTRON. PLACE	☽ AGE
182	1	W.	5:11	A	8:25	E	15 14	12	23 N. 04	12½ / 1¼	9:54	E	6:22	B	SAG	17
183	2	Th.	5:12	A	8:25	E	15 13	12	22 N. 59	1¼ / 2	10:21	E	7:27	B	CAP	18
184	3	Fr.	5:12	A	8:24	E	15 12	11	22 N. 54	2 / 2½	10:44	D	8:33	C	CAP	19
185	4	Sa.	5:13	A	8:24	E	15 11	11	22 N. 49	2½ / 3¼	11:04	D	9:39	C	AQU	20
186	5	**D**	5:13	A	8:24	E	15 11	11	22 N. 44	3¼ / 4	11:24	D	10:45	D	AQU	21
187	6	M.	5:14	A	8:24	E	15 10	11	22 N. 38	4 / 4½	11:45	C	11:52	D	PSC	22
188	7	Tu.	5:15	A	8:23	E	15 08	11	22 N. 31	5 / 5½	—	-	**1:01**	D	PSC	23
189	8	W.	5:15	A	8:23	E	15 08	11	22 N. 24	5¾ / 6¼	12:07	B	**2:14**	E	PSC	24
190	9	Th.	5:16	A	8:22	E	15 06	10	22 N. 17	6¾ / 7	12:33	B	**3:31**	E	ARI	25
191	10	Fr.	5:17	A	8:22	E	15 05	10	22 N. 09	7¾ / 8	**1:06**	B	**4:50**	E	ARI	26
192	11	Sa.	5:18	A	8:22	E	15 04	10	22 N. 01	8¾ / 9	**1:48**	A	**6:07**	E	TAU	27
193	12	**D**	5:18	A	8:21	E	15 03	10	21 N. 53	9¾ / 10	**2:43**	A	**7:17**	E	TAU	28
194	13	M.	5:19	A	8:20	E	15 01	10	21 N. 44	10¾ / 11	**3:53**	A	**8:13**	E	GEM	29
195	14	Tu.	5:20	A	8:20	E	15 00	10	21 N. 35	11¾ / —	**5:12**	B	**8:56**	E	GEM	0
196	15	W.	5:21	A	8:19	E	14 58	10	21 N. 26	12 / 12¾	**6:34**	B	**9:30**	E	CAN	1
197	16	Th.	5:22	A	8:19	E	14 57	10	21 N. 16	12¾ / 1½	**7:54**	C	**9:57**	D	LEO	2
198	17	Fr.	5:22	A	8:18	E	14 56	10	21 N. 06	1¾ / 2½	**9:10**	D	**10:20**	D	LEO	3
199	18	Sa.	5:23	A	8:17	E	14 54	9	20 N. 55	2¾ / 3¼	10:21	D	**10:41**	C	LEO	4
200	19	**D**	5:24	A	8:16	E	14 52	9	20 N. 44	3½ / 4	11:30	E	**11:01**	C	VIR	5
201	20	M.	5:25	A	8:16	E	14 51	9	20 N. 33	4½ / 5	**12:37**	E	**11:23**	B	VIR	6
202	21	Tu.	5:26	A	8:15	E	14 49	9	20 N. 22	5¼ / 5¾	**1:43**	E	**11:46**	B	VIR	7
203	22	W.	5:27	A	8:14	E	14 47	9	20 N. 10	6¼ / 6¾	**2:48**	E	—	-	VIR	8
204	23	Th.	5:28	A	8:13	E	14 45	9	19 N. 57	7¼ / 7½	**3:53**	E	12:13	B	LIB	9
205	24	Fr.	5:29	A	8:12	E	14 43	9	19 N. 45	8¼ / 8½	**4:54**	E	12:46	A	SCO	10
206	25	Sa.	5:30	A	8:11	E	14 41	9	19 N. 32	9¼ / 9¼	**5:51**	E	**1:26**	A	SCO	11
207	26	**D**	5:31	A	8:10	E	14 39	9	19 N. 19	10 / 10	**6:40**	E	**2:15**	A	OPH	12
208	27	M.	5:32	A	8:09	E	14 37	9	19 N. 05	10¾ / 10¾	**7:22**	E	**3:11**	A	SAG	13
209	28	Tu.	5:33	A	8:08	E	14 35	9	18 N. 51	11½ / 11½	**7:56**	E	**4:13**	B	SAG	14
210	29	W.	5:34	B	8:07	E	14 33	9	18 N. 37	12¼ / —	**8:25**	E	**5:18**	B	CAP	15
211	30	Th.	5:35	B	8:06	E	14 31	9	18 N. 22	12¼ / 12¾	**8:49**	E	**6:24**	C	CAP	16
212	31	Fr.	5:36	B	8:05	E	14 29	9	18 N. 08	12¾ / 1½	**9:10**	D	**7:31**	C	CAP	17

JULY

JULY HATH 31 DAYS

From isle to isle the fisher's bark,
Like fairy meteor, seems to glide.
–Susanna Strickland Moodie

DAY OF MONTH	DAY OF WEEK	DATES, FEASTS, FASTS, ASPECTS, TIDE HEIGHTS, AND WEATHER	
1	W.	CANADA DAY • *If the first of July be rainy weather, 'Twill rain more or less for four weeks together.*	*Holiday*
2	Th.	☌♇☾ • Corpse flower bloomed, San Diego Botanic Garden, Encinitas, Calif., 2023	*weekend*
3	Fr.	Dog Days begin. • 1st public drive of Benz Patent Motor Car, Mannheim, Germany, 1886 • {10.0 9.0	*brings*
4	Sa.	INDEPENDENCE DAY • ☾ AT ☊ • ☌♂⛢ • U.S. semiquincentennial (250 yrs.), 2026	*a*
5	**D**	6th S. af. P. • *July:* Deadly heat wave struck parts of U.S. and Canada, 1936 • {9.8 9.4	*scorcher—*
6	M.	☾ ON EQ. • ☌♆☾ • ⊕ AT APHELION • Tides {9.6 9.6	*Sun's*
7	Tu.	☌♄☾ • Dog found and rescued from cave in Narrows, Va., 2024 • Tides {9.4 9.9	*afar*
8	W.	♆ STAT. • 1st public reading of Declaration of Independence, Philadelphia, Pa., 1776	*but still*
9	Th.	Armadillos mate now. • *Puff not against the wind.* • Tides {9.1 10.5	*it tortures!*
10	Fr.	Special Olympics founder Eunice Kennedy Shriver born, 1921 • {9.1 10.8	*Cooling*
11	Sa.	☌♂☾ • ☌⛢☾ • Cornscateous air is everywhere. • Tides {9.2 11.2	*now,*
12	**D**	7th S. af. P. • ☾ RIDES HIGH • ☿ IN INF. ☌ • Tides {9.4 11.5	*bright blue*
13	M.	☾ AT PERIG. • Current U.S. patent numbering system began, 1836 • {9.6 11.8	*days,*
14	Tu.	Bastille Day • NEW ● • ☌☿☾ • ☌♃☾ • {9.9 11.9	*maybe*
15	W.	St. Swithin • After 7 days, Bob Salem summitted Pikes Peak while pushing peanut w/nose, Colo., 2022	*we*
16	Th.	☾ AT ☋ • Religious leader Mary Baker Eddy born, 1821 • Tides {11.8 10.4	*could get*
17	Fr.	☌♀☾ • Spain formally ceded Fla. to U.S., 1821 • Tides {11.6 10.4	*away?*
18	Sa.	☾ ON EQ. • Nadia Comaneci became 1st Olympic gymnast to score perfect 10, 1976	*Trade phones*
19	**D**	8th S. af. P. • Conservationist Mervyn Hugh Cowie died, 1996 • {10.5 10.2	*for ice cream*
20	M.	B.C. joined Can. Confederation, 1871 • Tides {9.9 10.0	*cones even*
21	Tu.	1st known sighting of *Okanagana arctostaphylae* cicada since 1915, Calif., 2020 • {9.2 9.8	*just for*
22	W.	St. Mary Magdalene • Campbell's green bean casserole creator, Dorcas Reilly, born, 1926 • {8.7 9.5	*one day?*
23	Th.	☿ STAT. • Black-eyed Susans in bloom now. • {8.3 9.4	*Hopes*
24	Fr.	National Tell an Old Joke Day (U.S.) • Actress Lynda Carter born, 1951 • {8.1 9.4	*dashed by*
25	Sa.	Sts. James & Christopher • ☾ RUNS LOW • ☾ AT APO. • Tides {8.1 9.5	*lightning*
26	**D**	9th S. af. P. • Apollo 15 launched, 1971 • {8.2 9.6	*flash,*
27	M.	♄ STAT. • ♇ AT ☋ • EF1 tornado hit Dublin, N.H., 2023 • Tides {8.3 9.8	*beach and*
28	Tu.	*Deserve success and you shall command it.* • Tides {8.6 10.0	*garden*
29	W.	St. Martha • FULL BUCK ○ • ☌♃☉ • ☌♇☾ • {8.8 —	*parties*
30	Th.	Seth Barnes Nicholson discovered Jovian moon Carme (Jupiter XI), 1938 • Tides {10.2 9.0	*crashed!*
31	Fr.	St. Ignatius of Loyola • ☾ AT ☊ • 41-lb 1-oz. shortraker rockfish caught, Cross Sound, Elfin Cove, Alaska, 2016	

Farmer's Calendar

The 250th Fourth

My niece has been visiting all week. We're going overboard for the Semiquincentennial cookout on Saturday! "Uncle David, do you think you'll be President when you grow up?" she asks on a drive to town. "Well, I'd have to move from the farm, if that happened," I reply, not quite sure what she's after. "Yeah, I know. That's what I want, 'cuz at the White House, I could have my own big room with bunk beds, and generals would come check on me if anyone picked on me. And plus, I don't like it when Olivia at school touches my hair." "I'm not sure that's what generals are for," I say. She pretends not to hear, "I'd get to eat Fourth of July cake every day." "What's Fourth of July cake," I try to ask, but she's on a tear. "We learned about Kennedy's rose garden in school. And Obama's veggie garden. I'm gonna start an animal farm at the White House—kids get in free. And farmers can get compost for free. And anyone who wants a bunny gets one." It suddenly feels like we're in a Beverly Cleary story. "And no stuffy grownups can stop us kids from making a great big noisy fuss in the garden!"

 Find more facts and fun every day at Almanac.com.

AUGUST

SKY WATCH: During the month's first week, Venus is at its brightest as an evening star, while Mercury appears as a morning star in the east. On the 12th, the year's most spectacular event unfolds when a total solar eclipse passes over typically cloudy Iceland before sweeping across Spain. Also, in the early morning of the 12th, the Perseid meteor shower will dazzle under ideal moonless conditions. In the evening sky at 8:30 P.M., the Moon is just below Venus on the 15th, to the left of Venus and below Spica on the 16th, and next to orange Antares on the 20th. It is near Saturn in the predawn eastern sky on the 30th.

◑ LAST QUARTER 5th day 10:21 P.M. ◐ FIRST QUARTER 19th day 10:46 P.M.
● NEW MOON 12th day 1:37 P.M. ○ FULL MOON 28th day 12:18 A.M.

All times are given in Eastern Daylight Time.

GET LOCAL RISE, SET, AND TIDE TIMES VIA ALMANAC.COM/2026.

Day of Year	Day of Month	Day of Week	☼ Rises H. M.	Rise Key	☼ Sets H. M.	Set Key	Length of Day H. M.	Sun Fast M.	Sun Declination ° '	High Tide Times Boston		☾ Rises H. M.	Rise Key	☾ Sets H. M.	Set Key	☾ Astron. Place	☾ Age
213	1	Sa.	5:37	B	**8:04**	E	14 27	9	17 N. 52	1½	**2**	**9:30**	D	8:37	D	AQU	18
214	2	D	5:38	B	**8:02**	E	14 24	10	17 N. 37	2¼	**2¾**	**9:50**	C	9:44	D	PSC	19
215	3	M.	5:39	B	**8:01**	E	14 22	10	17 N. 21	3	**3¼**	**10:11**	C	10:52	E	PSC	20
216	4	Tu.	5:40	B	**8:00**	E	14 20	10	17 N. 05	3¾	**4**	**10:36**	B	**12:03**	E	PSC	21
217	5	W.	5:41	B	**7:59**	E	14 18	10	16 N. 49	4½	**4¾**	**11:05**	B	**1:17**	E	ARI	22
218	6	Th.	5:42	B	**7:58**	E	14 16	10	16 N. 33	5½	**5¾**	**11:42**	A	**2:33**	E	ARI	23
219	7	Fr.	5:43	B	**7:56**	E	14 13	10	16 N. 16	6½	**6¾**	—	-	**3:50**	E	TAU	24
220	8	Sa.	5:44	B	**7:55**	E	14 11	10	15 N. 59	7½	**7¾**	12:30	A	**5:00**	E	TAU	25
221	9	D	5:45	B	**7:54**	D	14 09	10	15 N. 42	8½	**8¾**	1:32	A	**6:01**	E	TAU	26
222	10	M.	5:46	B	**7:52**	D	14 06	10	15 N. 24	9½	**9¾**	2:45	B	**6:49**	E	GEM	27
223	11	Tu.	5:47	B	**7:51**	D	14 04	11	15 N. 06	10½	**10¾**	4:05	B	**7:26**	E	CAN	28
224	12	W.	5:48	B	**7:49**	D	14 01	11	14 N. 48	11½	**11¾**	5:26	C	**7:56**	E	CAN	0
225	13	Th.	5:49	B	**7:48**	D	13 59	11	14 N. 30	**12¼**	—	6:45	C	**8:21**	D	LEO	1
226	14	Fr.	5:50	B	**7:47**	D	13 57	11	14 N. 11	12½	**1¼**	7:59	D	**8:43**	C	LEO	2
227	15	Sa.	5:51	B	**7:45**	D	13 54	11	13 N. 53	1½	**2**	9:10	E	**9:04**	C	VIR	3
228	16	D	5:52	B	**7:44**	D	13 52	12	13 N. 34	2¼	**2¾**	10:19	E	**9:25**	B	VIR	4
229	17	M.	5:54	B	**7:42**	D	13 48	12	13 N. 15	3	**3½**	11:27	E	**9:48**	B	VIR	5
230	18	Tu.	5:55	B	**7:41**	D	13 46	12	12 N. 55	4	**4¼**	**12:34**	E	**10:14**	B	VIR	6
231	19	W.	5:56	B	**7:39**	D	13 43	12	12 N. 36	4¾	**5**	**1:40**	E	**10:45**	A	LIB	7
232	20	Th.	5:57	B	**7:38**	D	13 41	12	12 N. 16	5¾	**6**	**2:44**	E	**11:22**	A	LIB	8
233	21	Fr.	5:58	B	**7:36**	D	13 38	13	11 N. 56	6½	**6¾**	**3:43**	E	—	-	SCO	9
234	22	Sa.	5:59	B	**7:35**	D	13 36	13	11 N. 36	7½	**7¾**	**4:35**	E	12:08	A	OPH	10
235	23	D	6:00	B	**7:33**	D	13 33	13	11 N. 15	8½	**8¾**	**5:20**	E	1:01	A	SAG	11
236	24	M.	6:01	B	**7:31**	D	13 30	14	10 N. 55	9½	**9½**	**5:57**	E	2:01	B	SAG	12
237	25	Tu.	6:02	B	**7:30**	D	13 28	14	10 N. 34	10¼	**10¼**	**6:27**	E	3:05	B	SAG	13
238	26	W.	6:03	B	**7:28**	D	13 25	14	10 N. 13	11	**11**	**6:53**	E	4:12	B	CAP	14
239	27	Th.	6:04	B	**7:26**	D	13 22	14	9 N. 52	11½	**11¾**	**7:15**	D	5:19	C	CAP	15
240	28	Fr.	6:05	B	**7:25**	D	13 20	15	9 N. 31	**12¼**	—	**7:36**	D	6:26	D	AQU	16
241	29	Sa.	6:06	B	**7:23**	D	13 17	15	9 N. 10	12½	**12¾**	**7:56**	C	7:34	D	PSC	17
242	30	D	6:07	B	**7:21**	D	13 14	15	8 N. 48	1	**1½**	**8:17**	C	8:43	E	PSC	18
243	31	M.	6:08	B	**7:20**	D	13 12	16	8 N. 27	1¾	**2**	**8:41**	B	9:53	E	PSC	19

To use this page, see p. 116; for Key Letters, see p. 238. LIGHT = A.M. BOLD = P.M.

AUGUST

THE EIGHTH MONTH · 2026 · AUGUST HATH 31 DAYS

The butterfly and humble-bee
Come to the pleasant woods with me.
—John Townsend Trowbridge

DAY OF MONTH	DAY OF WEEK	DATES, FEASTS, FASTS, ASPECTS, TIDE HEIGHTS, AND WEATHER	
1	Sa.	Lammas Day • *After Lammas, corn ripens as much by night as by day.* • Colo. statehood, 1876	Warm
2	D	10th S. af. P. • ☾ ON EQ. • ☿ GR. ELONG. (20° WEST) • Tides {10.1 / 9.8}	days and
3	M.	CIVIC HOLIDAY (CANADA) • ♂♄☾ • Singer Tony Bennett born, 1926	thunder—
4	Tu.	♂♄☾ • Musician Louis Armstrong born, 1901 • 114°F, Walla Walla, Wash., 1961	when's
5	W.	Ragweed in bloom. • Historian Mary R. Beard born, 1876 • Tides {9.4 / 10.3}	beach time,
6	Th.	Transfiguration • *Asteroids renamed to honor Space Shuttle Columbia crew killed in Feb. disaster, 2003*	we
7	Fr.	National Lighthouse Day (U.S.) • ♂♄☾ • {8.9 / 10.5}	wonder?
8	Sa.	St. Dominic • ☾ RIDES HIGH • Physicist Ernest Lawrence born, 1901 • {8.8 / 10.7}	Rain
9	D	11th S. af. P. • National Peacekeepers' Day (Canada) • ♂♂☾ • {8.9 / 10.9}	fills
10	M.	St. Lawrence • ☾ AT PERIG. • *Alexander G. Bell tested long-distance call from Brantford to Paris, Ont., 1876*	sky
11	Tu.	St. Clare • Dog Days end. • ♂♂☾ • ♂♃☾ • {9.6 / 11.4}	with
12	W.	NEW ● • ECLIPSE ☉ • *When the Sun shines, nobody minds him; but when he is eclipsed, all consider him.*	
13	Th.	☾ AT ☊ • Gray squirrels have second litters now. • Tides {10.4 / —}	droplets,
14	Fr.	U.S. Social Security Act signed into law, 1935 • {11.5 / 10.6}	will
15	Sa.	Assumption • ☾ ON EQ. • ♂♂♃ • ♀ GR. ELONG. (46° EAST)	someone
16	D	12th S. af. P. • ♂♀☾ • Delaware Memorial Bridge 1st opened, Del./N.J., 1951	kindly
17	M.	Cat Nights commence. • Canada Line rapid rail service opened, Vancouver, B.C., 2009 • {10.1 / 10.3}	turn
18	Tu.	1st radio transmission of weather map, 1926 • {9.5 / 9.9}	off
19	W.	*19–25:* Record heat wave, central U.S., 2023 • {8.9 / 9.6}	the
20	Th.	Astronomer Sir Fred Hoyle died, 2001 • Tides {8.4 / 9.3}	faucet?
21	Fr.	Deadly F3 tornado struck Goderich, Ont., 2011 • {8.0 / 9.1}	Sunshine's
22	Sa.	☾ RUNS LOW • ☾ AT APO. • *Schooner America won what later was America's Cup, 1851*	returning,
23	D	13th S. af. P. • *'Tis not every question that deserves an answer.* • Tides {7.9 / 9.2}	but
24	M.	St. Bartholomew • Hummingbirds migrate south. • Tides {8.1 / 9.5}	cooler—
25	Tu.	♂♇☾ • Spitzer Space Telescope launched, 2003 • Tides {8.4 / 9.8}	a warning:
26	W.	Quincy Market 1st opened, Boston, Mass., 1826 • {8.8 / 10.0}	seasons
27	Th.	☾ AT ☊ • ♀ IN SUP. ♂ • Hurricane Irene made landfall near Cape Lookout, N.C., 2011	are
28	Fr.	St. Augustine of Hippo • FULL STURGEON ○ • ECLIPSE ☾ • {9.6 / —}	turning!
29	Sa.	St. John the Baptist • ☾ ON EQ. • Tides {10.3 / 9.9}	Back-to-schoolers:
30	D	14th S. af. P. • ♂♆☾ • *Fog covered G. Washington's retreat to Manhattan, Battle of Long Isl., 1776*	
31	M.	♂♄☾ • 1st successful U.S. crop dusting demonstration, Troy, Ohio, 1921	Good morning!

Farmer's Calendar

"Everyone's mad at their garden"

A homesteader doesn't take on more than he can handle because he's in it for the ease. Most of the time, I embrace this. But I'm not going to lie, the year has fallen out of whack, and I'm a bit lost on how to make it plumb. I am 2 months behind on the woodpile. There's a rage of debris all over the yard, from a flash 2 inches last month. Our decision to use hand tools to trench a French drain is testing my patience, and I can't seem to find a solid hour to give to the kitchen garden. My wife pauses her repair work on the coop run. She puts a flirtation in her hips and brings over a jar of ice water. She assures me that everyone's mad at their garden this time of year. She's got kind blue eyes that shine with the honeyed glint of her charms. In them, I find echoes of the delphinium, bachelor's button, and globe thistle that bloom in our bouquet bed. She lifts the glasses off the collar of my T and cleans them on the hem of my shirt. "Maybe stop trying to get on top of your chores," she says, sliding the frames back over my eyes, "and instead, get on top of your perspective." Well played, love. Well played.

SEPTEMBER

SKY WATCH: Venus, still near maximum brilliance, is in its final month as an evening star. Sinking lower daily, it's best seen before 8:00 P.M. In the predawn east at 4:30 A.M., the crescent Moon is just above the Pleiades on the 3rd, with dim Uranus just below them; use binoculars for best viewing. The Moon stands to the right of Venus on the 13th, to the left of Venus on the 14th, and above Saturn on the 26th. Neptune, the most distant major planet, comes to opposition on the 25th. It hovers to the upper right of Saturn all night, but at magnitude 7.63, it is best seen through a telescope a few nights later when the nearly full Moon has moved away from the planets. Fall begins with the autumnal equinox on the 22nd at 8:05 P.M. EDT.

☾ **LAST QUARTER** 4th day 3:51 A.M. ● **FIRST QUARTER** 18th day 4:44 P.M.
● **NEW MOON** 10th day 11:27 P.M. ○ **FULL MOON** 26th day 12:49 P.M.

All times are given in Eastern Daylight Time.

GET LOCAL RISE, SET, AND TIDE TIMES VIA ALMANAC.COM/2026.

DAY OF YEAR	DAY OF MONTH	DAY OF WEEK	☀ RISES H. M.	RISE KEY	☀ SETS H. M.	SET KEY	LENGTH OF DAY H. M.	SUN FAST M.	SUN DECLINATION ° '	HIGH TIDE TIMES BOSTON	☾ RISES H. M.	RISE KEY	☾ SETS H. M.	SET KEY	☾ ASTRON. PLACE	☾ AGE
244	1	Tu.	6:09	B	7:18	D	13 09	16	8 N. 05	2½	2¾	9:08	B	11:07	E	PSC	20
245	2	W.	6:10	B	7:16	D	13 06	16	7 N. 43	3¼	3½	9:42	B	12:23	E	ARI	21
246	3	Th.	6:12	B	7:15	D	13 03	17	7 N. 21	4¼	4½	10:26	A	1:39	E	TAU	22
247	4	Fr.	6:13	B	7:13	D	13 00	17	6 N. 59	5	5½	11:22	A	2:50	E	TAU	23
248	5	Sa.	6:14	B	7:11	D	12 57	17	6 N. 37	6¼	6½	—	-	3:53	E	TAU	24
249	6	D	6:15	C	7:10	D	12 55	18	6 N. 14	7¼	7½	12:29	B	4:44	E	GEM	25
250	7	M.	6:16	C	7:08	D	12 52	18	5 N. 52	8¼	8¾	1:45	B	5:24	E	GEM	26
251	8	Tu.	6:17	C	7:06	D	12 49	18	5 N. 29	9½	9¾	3:04	B	5:56	E	CAN	27
252	9	W.	6:18	C	7:04	D	12 46	19	5 N. 07	10¼	10¾	4:22	C	6:22	D	LEO	28
253	10	Th.	6:19	C	7:03	D	12 44	19	4 N. 44	11¼	11½	5:37	D	6:45	D	LEO	0
254	11	Fr.	6:20	C	7:01	D	12 41	19	4 N. 21	12	—	6:49	D	7:06	C	LEO	1
255	12	Sa.	6:21	C	6:59	D	12 38	20	3 N. 58	12¼	12¾	7:59	E	7:27	C	VIR	2
256	13	D	6:22	C	6:57	D	12 35	20	3 N. 35	1	1½	9:08	E	7:49	B	VIR	3
257	14	M.	6:23	C	6:56	C	12 33	20	3 N. 12	1¾	2	10:17	E	8:14	B	VIR	4
258	15	Tu.	6:24	C	6:54	C	12 30	21	2 N. 49	2½	2¾	11:24	E	8:43	B	LIB	5
259	16	W.	6:25	C	6:52	C	12 27	21	2 N. 26	3¼	3½	12:30	E	9:18	A	LIB	6
260	17	Th.	6:26	C	6:50	C	12 24	21	2 N. 03	4¼	4¼	1:32	E	10:01	A	SCO	7
261	18	Fr.	6:27	C	6:48	C	12 21	22	1 N. 40	5	5¼	2:27	E	10:51	A	OPH	8
262	19	Sa.	6:28	C	6:47	C	12 19	22	1 N. 16	6	6¼	3:15	E	11:48	A	SAG	9
263	20	D	6:29	C	6:45	C	12 16	22	0 N. 53	7	7¼	3:54	E	—	-	SAG	10
264	21	M.	6:31	C	6:43	C	12 12	23	0 N. 30	8	8	4:27	E	12:51	B	SAG	11
265	22	Tu.	6:32	C	6:41	C	12 09	23	0 N. 06	8¾	9	4:54	E	1:56	B	CAP	12
266	23	W.	6:33	C	6:40	C	12 07	24	0 S. 16	9½	9¾	5:18	E	3:03	C	CAP	13
267	24	Th.	6:34	C	6:38	C	12 04	24	0 S. 39	10¼	10½	5:40	D	4:10	C	AQU	14
268	25	Fr.	6:35	C	6:36	C	12 01	24	1 S. 03	11	11¼	6:00	D	5:18	D	AQU	15
269	26	Sa.	6:36	C	6:34	C	11 58	25	1 S. 26	11½	—	6:21	C	6:27	E	PSC	16
270	27	D	6:37	C	6:33	C	11 56	25	1 S. 49	12	12¼	6:44	C	7:39	E	PSC	17
271	28	M.	6:38	C	6:31	C	11 53	25	2 S. 13	12¾	1	7:11	B	8:53	E	PSC	18
272	29	Tu.	6:39	C	6:29	C	11 50	26	2 S. 36	1¼	1½	7:43	B	10:10	E	ARI	19
273	30	W.	6:40	C	6:27	C	11 47	26	2 S. 59	2¼	2¼	8:25	A	11:27	E	ARI	20

THE NINTH MONTH · 2026

SEPTEMBER

SEPTEMBER HATH 30 DAYS

Life is made of smallest fragments,
Shade and sunshine, work and play;
So may we, with greatest profit, / Learn a little every day.
–Unknown

DAY OF MONTH	DAY OF WEEK	DATES, FEASTS, FASTS, ASPECTS, TIDE HEIGHTS, AND WEATHER	
1	Tu.	Wreckage of RMS *Titanic* discovered, 1985 • Tides {10.0 / 10.6	*This*
2	W.	Great Fire of London sparked in home of king's baker, 1666	*fall,*
3	Th.	☌♅☾ • Novelist Alison Lurie born, 1926 • Tides {9.4 / 10.5	*let*
4	Fr.	*Be not afraid of going slowly; be afraid only of standing still.* • Tides {9.0 / 10.4	*us*
5	Sa.	☾ RIDES HIGH • Boxer Cassius Clay won Olympic gold medal, 1960 • Tides {8.8 / 10.4	*recall*
6	D	15th S. af. P. • ☾ AT PERIG. • ☌♂☾ • Tides {8.7 / 10.4	*the*
7	M.	**Labor Day** • Singer Buddy Holly born, 1936 • {8.9 / 10.6	*labor*
8	Tu.	International Literacy Day • ☌♃☾ • *Star Trek* TV series debuted, 1966 • {9.3 / 10.8	*of*
9	W.	☾ AT ☋ • Cranberry bog harvest begins, Cape Cod, Mass. • Tides {9.8 / 11.0	*our*
10	Th.	NEW ● • ♅ STAT. • Inventor Elias Howe granted sewing machine patent, 1846	*brethren—*
11	Fr.	Rosh Hashanah begins at sundown • **Patriot Day** • ☾ ON EQ. • 9/11 attacks, 2001	*after*
12	Sa.	☌☿☾ • Lascaux cave art discovered near Montignac, France, 1940 • Tides {10.9 / 10.8	*which*
13	D	16th S. af. P. • Chocolatier Milton Hershey born, 1857 • Tides {10.6 / 10.7	*we'll all*
14	M.	Holy Cross • ☌♀☾ • U.S. president William McKinley died, 1901 • {10.2 / 10.5	*recoil*
15	Tu.	"Queen of Crime" writer Agatha Christie born, 1890 • {9.7 / 10.2	*from*
16	W.	Ember Day • Mass sighting of "Ogopogo" creature, Lake Okanagan, B.C., 1926 • {9.2 / 9.8	*storms*
17	Th.	Harriet Tubman escaped slavery, Md., 1849 • Tides {8.6 / 9.4	*that*
18	Fr.	Ember Day • ☾ RUNS LOW • ☾ AT APO. • Tides {8.2 / 9.1	*we'll be*
19	Sa.	Ember Day • Mummified remains of Ötzi, aka Iceman, discovered, Ötztal Alps, 1991	*weatherin'!*
20	D	17th S. af. P. • Yom Kippur begins at sundown • Tides {7.8 / 8.9	*Football*
21	M.	St. Matthew • ☌♇☾ • Physicist Donald Glaser born, 1926 • {8.0 / 9.1	*fans*
22	Tu.	Harvest Home • **AUTUMNAL EQUINOX** • Am. Rev. War officer Nathan Hale died, 1776 • {8.3 / 9.3	*are*
23	W.	☾ AT ☊ • Woodchucks hibernate now. • Musician John Coltrane born, 1926	*undeterred:*
24	Th.	*August ripens, September gathers in; August bears the burden, September the fruit.* • {9.2 / 10.0	*from*
25	Fr.	Sukkoth begins at sundown • ☾ ON EQ. • ♆ AT ☍ • Tides {9.7 / 10.2	*soggy*
26	Sa.	**FULL HARVEST** ○ • ☌♆☾ • 1st U.S. presidential debate televised, 1960	*stands,*
27	D	18th S. af. P. • ☌♄☾ • *Spring rain damps; Autumn rain soaks.* • {10.6 / —	*their*
28	M.	Hockey player Syd Howe born, 1911 • Tides {10.4 / 11.0	*cheers*
29	Tu.	St. Michael • Goat joined half-marathon and won medal, Conception Bay South, N.L., 2024	*are*
30	W.	St. Gregory the Illuminator • Actor James Dean died, 1955 • Tides {10.1 / 11.1	*heard!*

Farmer's Calendar

Duffy's "Playhouse"

There's a 54-acre whistle-stop on the outskirts of a college town, stewarded by the tenderness of a one-eyed farmer, Duffy (a story for another time). I lived there as a young start. My writing desk faced the '47 Ford rusted in the side pasture, where young cattle would nose through spent grass and weedy burdock. I live a few towns over now, my boots mud-crusted by my own bit of soil. In September, after second-cut hay but before the prize winner pumpkin stand opens, I am sure to pay Duffy a visit. His retriever, Fina, shows off her favorite mud bend in the crick. High above, an earful of cedar waxwings takes flight from the foxy wild grapes that vine the river birch, putting a sweet, jasmine-like scent in the air. We move fence, inching a 500-foot electric line of polywire, to reveal fresh green for the herd. We often retire to the "playhouse," a loft in the old tobacco shed. It's like a roadhouse of antique farm novelties up there, and I never bother to ask how it got its name. The barnwood retains an old char, notes of clove, smoke, and heart of cedar, and a sip of something strong warms the bonds of old friendship.

OCTOBER

SKY WATCH: On the 4th, Saturn comes to opposition at its biggest and brightest appearance of the year. Its rings are now more open when viewed through a telescope. A major astronomical event unfolds in the east after midnight on the 6th, when Jupiter is eclipsed by the Moon in a rare occurrence called an occultation. It can be observed from most of the U.S. and Canada east of the Rockies as soon as the Moon rises. Jupiter emerges from the Moon's dark side just over an hour later. Venus ends its reign as an evening star as it is too low in the sky for visibility. Saturn stands next to the nearly full Moon all night on thc 23rd and 24th. For observers using binoculars, look for the Moon entangled in the Pleiades star cluster on the 27th, with a dim green "star," the planet Uranus, directly beneath them.

◑ LAST QUARTER	3rd day 9:25 A.M.	◐ FIRST QUARTER	18th day 12:12 P.M.
● NEW MOON	10th day 11:50 A.M.	○ FULL MOON	26th day 12:12 A.M.

All times are given in Eastern Daylight Time.

GET LOCAL RISE, SET, AND TIDE TIMES VIA ALMANAC.COM/2026.

Day of Year	Day of Month	Day of Week	☼ Rises H. M.	Rise Key	☼ Sets H. M.	Set Key	Length of Day H. M.	Sun Fast M.	Sun Declination °	'	High Tide Times Boston		☾ Rises H. M.	Rise Key	☾ Sets H. M.	Set Key	☾ Astron. Place	☾ Age
274	1	Th.	6:41	C	**6:26**	C	11 45	26	3 s.	23	3	**3¼**	**9:17**	A	**12:42**	E	TAU	21
275	2	Fr.	6:42	C	**6:24**	C	11 42	27	3 s.	46	4	**4**	**10:21**	A	**1:47**	E	TAU	22
276	3	Sa.	6:43	C	**6:22**	C	11 39	27	4 s.	09	5	**5¼**	**11:34**	B	**2:41**	E	GEM	23
277	4	**D**	6:45	C	**6:20**	C	11 35	27	4 s.	32	6	**6¼**	—	-	**3:24**	E	GEM	24
278	5	M.	6:46	C	**6:19**	C	11 33	27	4 s.	55	7	**7½**	12:50	B	**3:57**	E	CAN	25
279	6	Tu.	6:47	D	**6:17**	C	11 30	28	5 s.	18	8¼	**8½**	2:07	C	**4:24**	E	LEO	26
280	7	W.	6:48	D	**6:15**	C	11 27	28	5 s.	41	9¼	**9½**	3:21	C	**4:48**	D	LEO	27
281	8	Th.	6:49	D	**6:14**	C	11 25	28	6 s.	04	10	**10½**	4:32	D	**5:09**	C	LEO	28
282	9	Fr.	6:50	D	**6:12**	C	11 22	29	6 s.	27	10¾	**11¼**	5:42	D	**5:30**	C	VIR	29
283	10	Sa.	6:51	D	**6:10**	C	11 19	29	6 s.	50	11½	—	6:51	E	**5:52**	B	VIR	0
284	11	**D**	6:52	D	**6:09**	C	11 17	29	7 s.	12	12	**12¼**	7:59	E	**6:16**	B	VIR	1
285	12	M.	6:54	D	**6:07**	C	11 13	29	7 s.	35	12¾	**1**	9:07	E	**6:43**	B	VIR	2
286	13	Tu.	6:55	D	**6:05**	C	11 10	30	7 s.	57	1½	**1½**	10:14	E	**7:16**	A	LIB	3
287	14	W.	6:56	D	**6:04**	B	11 08	30	8 s.	19	2¼	**2¼**	11:18	E	**7:55**	A	SCO	4
288	15	Th.	6:57	D	**6:02**	B	11 05	30	8 s.	42	2¾	**3**	**12:17**	E	**8:43**	A	SCO	5
289	16	Fr.	6:58	D	**6:01**	B	11 03	30	9 s.	04	3¾	**3¾**	**1:07**	E	**9:37**	A	SAG	6
290	17	Sa.	6:59	D	**5:59**	B	11 00	31	9 s.	26	4½	**4½**	**1:50**	E	**10:37**	B	SAG	7
291	18	**D**	7:01	D	**5:57**	B	10 56	31	9 s.	47	5¼	**5½**	**2:25**	E	**11:41**	B	SAG	8
292	19	M.	7:02	D	**5:56**	B	10 54	31	10 s.	09	6¼	**6½**	**2:54**	E	—	-	CAP	9
293	20	Tu.	7:03	D	**5:54**	B	10 51	31	10 s.	31	7¼	**7½**	**3:19**	E	12:46	B	CAP	10
294	21	W.	7:04	D	**5:53**	B	10 49	31	10 s.	52	8	**8¼**	**3:41**	D	1:52	C	CAP	11
295	22	Th.	7:05	D	**5:51**	B	10 46	31	11 s.	13	8¾	**9¼**	**4:02**	D	2:59	D	AQU	12
296	23	Fr.	7:07	D	**5:50**	B	10 43	32	11 s.	34	9½	**10**	**4:23**	C	4:07	D	PSC	13
297	24	Sa.	7:08	D	**5:48**	B	10 40	32	11 s.	55	10¼	**10¾**	**4:45**	C	5:17	E	PSC	14
298	25	**D**	7:09	D	**5:47**	B	10 38	32	12 s.	16	11	**11½**	**5:11**	B	6:31	E	PSC	15
299	26	M.	7:10	D	**5:46**	B	10 36	32	12 s.	36	11¾	—	**5:41**	B	7:48	E	ARI	16
300	27	Tu.	7:11	D	**5:44**	B	10 33	32	12 s.	56	12¼	**12½**	**6:20**	B	9:08	E	ARI	17
301	28	W.	7:13	D	**5:43**	B	10 30	32	13 s.	17	1	**1¼**	**7:10**	A	10:26	E	TAU	18
302	29	Th.	7:14	D	**5:41**	B	10 27	32	13 s.	36	1¾	**2**	**8:12**	A	11:37	E	TAU	19
303	30	Fr.	7:15	D	**5:40**	B	10 25	32	13 s.	56	2¾	**3**	**9:24**	B	**12:37**	E	GEM	20
304	31	Sa.	7:16	D	**5:39**	B	10 23	32	14 s.	16	3¾	**4**	**10:41**	B	**1:23**	E	GEM	21

THE TENTH MONTH • 2026 **OCTOBER** OCTOBER HATH 31 DAYS

Thou glorious orb of light!
Thou chasest hence the gloom of night.
–**John Evans, of the Sun**

DAY OF MONTH	DAY OF WEEK	DATES, FEASTS, FASTS, ASPECTS, TIDE HEIGHTS, AND WEATHER	
1	Th.	☾ at perig. • ☌♅☾ • Walt Disney World opened, Orlando, Fla., 1971 • {9.7 / 11.0	*Players*
2	Fr.	☾ rides high • ♀ stat. • Singer Sting born, 1951 • Tides {9.3 / 10.7	*dive for*
3	Sa.	Watch for banded woolly bear caterpillars. • St. Francis of Assisi died, 1226 • {9.0 / 10.4	*football*
4	**D**	**19th S. af. P.** • ♄ at ☍ • Barbara Walters became co-anchor of *ABC Evening News*, 1976	
5	M.	World Architecture Day • ☌☿♀ • ☌♂☾ • {8.9 / 10.2	*passes,*
6	Tu.	☾ at ☋ • ☌♃☾ • American Library Assoc. founded, 1876 • {9.2 / 10.2	*perfect*
7	W.	*Dread the anger of the dove.* • Tides {9.7 / 10.4	*weather*
8	Th.	☾ on Eq. • Little brown bats hibernate now. • Painter Ozias Leduc born, 1864 • {10.1 / 10.4	*for*
9	Fr.	Collegiate School (later, Yale U.) chartered, Conn., 1701 • Conservationist Roderick Haig-Brown died, 1976	*skipping*
10	Sa.	New ● • Asteroid Cruithne (quasi-satellite of Earth) discovered, 1986 • {10.7 / —	*classes!*
11	**D**	**20th S. af. P.** • ☌♀☾ • Wildlife artist John Ruthven died, 2020	*Rainy*
12	M.	**Columbus Day, observed** • **Indigenous Peoples' Day** • ☌☿☾ • ☿ gr. elong. (25° east)	
13	Tu.	*12–13:* Storm dropped 22.6" snow, Buffalo, N.Y., 2006 • Tides {9.7 / 10.4	*days are*
14	W.	A. A. Milne's *Winnie-the-Pooh* published, 1926 • {9.3 / 10.1	*back,*
15	Th.	☾ runs low • Sugar pine cone measuring 22.9" set record, Cuyahoga Falls, Ohio, 2002 • {8.9 / 9.7	*keeping*
16	Fr.	☾ at apo. • ♇ stat. • Chicago's 1st passenger subway dedicated, Ill., 1943 • {8.5 / 9.4	*students*
17	Sa.	St. Ignatius of Antioch • Actress Margot Kidder born, 1948 • Tides {8.2 / 9.1	*on*
18	**D**	**21st S. af. P.** • St. Luke's little summer. • Inventor Charles Babbage died, 1871	*track.*
19	M.	St. Luke^T • ☌♇☾ • Filmmaker Jason Reitman born, 1977 • Tides {8.0 / 8.8	*Leaves*
20	Tu.	*When the mist creeps up the hill, Fisher, out and try your skill.* • Tides {8.2 / 8.9	*fill*
21	W.	☾ at ☊ • Length of meter redefined, 1983 • {8.6 / 9.2	*gutters,*
22	Th.	FDA approved aspartame sweetener for tabletop use, 1981 • Tides {9.1 / 9.4	*making*
23	Fr.	St. James of Jerusalem • ☾ on Eq. • ☌♆☾ • ♀ in inf. ☌ • {9.7 / 9.8	*homeowners*
24	Sa.	☌♄☾ • ☿ stat. • Eastman Kodak Co. incorporated, N.J., 1901 • {10.3 / 10.0	*mutter.*
25	**D**	**22nd S. af. P.** • 3-lb. 15-oz. brown bullhead caught, Whiteville Lake, Tenn., 2014	*Few*
26	M.	Full Hunter's ○ • 8'-long cannon retrieved from Blackbeard's *Queen Anne's Revenge* wreck near Beaufort, N.C., 2011	
27	Tu.	Timber rattlesnakes move to winter dens. • Tides {10.3 / 11.6	*chilly*
28	W.	Sts. Simon & Jude • ☾ at perig. • ☌♅☾ • Tides {10.2 / 11.7	*nights*
29	Th.	☾ rides high • Racing driver Lance Stroll born, 1998 • Tides {10.0 / 11.5	*to make*
30	Fr.	*We can say nothing of the day 'till the Sun is set.* • {9.8 / 11.3	*us*
31	Sa.	All Hallows' Eve • Reformation Day • Tides {9.5 / 10.9	*shudder.*

Farmer's Calendar

The Great Pumpkin Roll

The fall festival reminds you of a time before event organizers got all worried about getting sued. It's good, cheery, reckless fun—a day filled with activities you or I might come up with in our backyards and not the stiff activities they think up in some creaky committee. Let's see. There's cow patty bingo. The local sugarman leads an ax-throwing demo—everyone gets a turn! In the firefighter's muster, we see which team is first to fill a 55-gallon drum two flights up on scaffolding. This year, the pros go against seniors from the regional vocational school. (The students win by counting the cheer of the crowd, if not by the final score.) And the main event: after a town sing-along, kids line up by grade to roll sugar pumpkins down the main drag, the biggest hill in town. This year, many of the potholes are filled in, which ought to spare a couple twisted ankles! The sheer madness of schoolchildren getting trampled by pumpkins released in heats behind them . . . well, let's just say the first responders set up at the bottom of the hill get to use a couple Band-Aids. All told, some busted up squash, a few scrapes, and smiles for miles.

NOVEMBER

SKY WATCH: The action shifts to the predawn eastern sky, where Mars is now a bright magnitude 1.0. It stands between the Moon and Jupiter on the 1st and is best seen from 5:00 to 6:00 A.M. The Moon will be near Mars on the 2nd. Venus returns and begins its morning star apparition. Look for it to meet the crescent Moon on the 7th with blue-white Spica to the left. On the 16th, an even better grouping has Mars, now at a magnitude 0.6, closely meeting an even brighter Jupiter and Leo's main star, Regulus. In the evening sky, Saturn hangs below the Moon on the 20th, while Uranus comes to opposition on the 25th. The best conjunction happens at 6:00 A.M. on the 30th, in a very tight bunching of the Moon, Jupiter, Regulus, and Mars.

◑ **LAST QUARTER** 1st day 3:28 P.M.	◐ **FIRST QUARTER** 17th day 6:48 A.M.		
● **NEW MOON** 9th day 2:02 A.M.	○ **FULL MOON** 24th day 9:53 A.M.		

After 2:00 A.M. on November 1, Eastern Standard Time is given.

GET LOCAL RISE, SET, AND TIDE TIMES VIA ALMANAC.COM/2026.

DAY OF YEAR	DAY OF MONTH	DAY OF WEEK	☼ RISES H. M.	RISE KEY	☼ SETS H. M.	SET KEY	LENGTH OF DAY H. M.	SUN FAST M.	SUN DECLINATION °	'	HIGH TIDE TIMES BOSTON		☾ RISES H. M.	RISE KEY	☾ SETS H. M.	SET KEY	☾ ASTRON. PLACE	☾ AGE
305	1	D	6:18	D	**4:37**	B	10 19	32	14 s.	35	3¾	**4**	**10:57**	C	**1:00**	E	CAN	22
306	2	M.	6:19	D	**4:36**	B	10 17	32	14 s.	54	4¾	**5**	—	-	**1:28**	E	CAN	23
307	3	Tu.	6:20	D	**4:35**	B	10 15	32	15 s.	12	6	**6¼**	12:11	C	**1:53**	D	LEO	24
308	4	W.	6:21	E	**4:34**	B	10 13	32	15 s.	31	7	**7¼**	1:22	D	**2:14**	D	LEO	25
309	5	Th.	6:23	E	**4:33**	B	10 10	32	15 s.	49	7¾	**8¼**	2:31	D	**2:35**	C	VIR	26
310	6	Fr.	6:24	E	**4:31**	B	10 07	32	16 s.	07	8¾	**9¼**	3:39	E	**2:56**	C	VIR	27
311	7	Sa.	6:25	E	**4:30**	B	10 05	32	16 s.	25	9½	**10**	4:46	E	**3:19**	B	VIR	28
312	8	D	6:26	E	**4:29**	B	10 03	32	16 s.	42	10¼	**10¾**	5:53	E	**3:44**	B	VIR	29
313	9	M.	6:28	E	**4:28**	B	10 00	32	16 s.	59	10¾	**11½**	7:00	E	**4:15**	A	LIB	0
314	10	Tu.	6:29	E	**4:27**	B	9 58	32	17 s.	16	11½	—	8:05	E	**4:52**	A	LIB	1
315	11	W.	6:30	E	**4:26**	B	9 56	32	17 s.	33	12	**12**	9:06	E	**5:37**	A	SCO	2
316	12	Th.	6:31	E	**4:25**	B	9 54	32	17 s.	49	12¾	**12¾**	10:00	E	**6:29**	A	OPH	3
317	13	Fr.	6:33	E	**4:24**	B	9 51	31	18 s.	05	1½	**1½**	10:45	E	**7:27**	A	SAG	4
318	14	Sa.	6:34	E	**4:23**	B	9 49	31	18 s.	21	2¼	**2¼**	11:23	E	**8:29**	B	SAG	5
319	15	D	6:35	E	**4:22**	B	9 47	31	18 s.	36	3	**3**	11:54	E	**9:33**	B	SAG	6
320	16	M.	6:36	E	**4:21**	B	9 45	31	18 s.	51	3¾	**3¾**	**12:20**	E	**10:37**	C	CAP	7
321	17	Tu.	6:38	E	**4:20**	B	9 42	31	19 s.	06	4½	**4¾**	**12:43**	D	**11:42**	C	CAP	8
322	18	W.	6:39	E	**4:20**	B	9 41	31	19 s.	20	5½	**5¾**	**1:03**	D	—	-	AQU	9
323	19	Th.	6:40	E	**4:19**	B	9 39	30	19 s.	34	6¼	**6½**	**1:24**	C	12:47	D	AQU	10
324	20	Fr.	6:41	E	**4:18**	B	9 37	30	19 s.	47	7	**7½**	**1:45**	C	1:54	E	PSC	11
325	21	Sa.	6:42	E	**4:17**	B	9 35	30	20 s.	01	7¾	**8¼**	**2:08**	C	3:05	E	PSC	12
326	22	D	6:44	E	**4:17**	B	9 33	30	20 s.	14	8½	**9¼**	**2:36**	B	4:20	E	PSC	13
327	23	M.	6:45	E	**4:16**	B	9 31	29	20 s.	26	9½	**10**	**3:11**	B	5:39	E	ARI	14
328	24	Tu.	6:46	E	**4:16**	A	9 30	29	20 s.	38	10¼	**10¾**	**3:57**	A	6:59	E	TAU	15
329	25	W.	6:47	E	**4:15**	A	9 28	29	20 s.	50	11	**11¾**	**4:55**	A	8:17	E	TAU	16
330	26	Th.	6:48	E	**4:15**	A	9 27	28	21 s.	01	11¾	—	**6:06**	B	9:24	E	TAU	17
331	27	Fr.	6:49	E	**4:14**	A	9 25	28	21 s.	12	12½	**12¾**	**7:25**	B	10:17	E	GEM	18
332	28	Sa.	6:50	E	**4:14**	A	9 24	28	21 s.	23	1½	**1¾**	**8:44**	C	10:58	E	GEM	19
333	29	D	6:52	E	**4:13**	A	9 21	27	21 s.	33	2½	**2¾**	**10:01**	C	11:30	E	CAN	20
334	30	M.	6:53	E	**4:13**	A	9 20	27	21 s.	43	3½	**3¾**	**11:14**	D	11:57	D	LEO	21

 To use this page, see p. 116; for Key Letters, see p. 238. LIGHT = A.M. **BOLD** = P.M.

NOVEMBER

—THE ELEVENTH MONTH · 2026 — NOVEMBER HATH 30 DAYS—

> Over the river, and through the wood / Old Jowler hears our bells;
> He shakes his pow / With a loud bow wow,
> And thus the news he tells.
> –Lydia Maria Child

DAY OF MONTH	DAY OF WEEK	DATES, FEASTS, FASTS, ASPECTS, TIDE HEIGHTS, AND WEATHER
1	D	All Saints' • **DST ENDS, 2:00 A.M.** • Singer-songwriter Lyle Lovett born, 1957 • Tides {9.2, 10.4} — *Leaf*
2	M.	All Souls' • ☾AT☋ • ♂☌☿ • ☾♃ • Tides {9.2, 10.1} — *pile*
3	Tu.	**ELECTION DAY** • One World Trade Center opened, N.Y.C., 2014 • Tides {9.3, 9.9} — *jumping,*
4	W.	☾ON EQ. • ☿IN INF.☌ • R. Farbiarz's record-setting 35'10"-tall wind chime hung in Eureka Springs, Ark., 2004 — *nice*
5	Th.	Sinclair Lewis 1st American to win Nobel prize for literature, 1930 • Tides {9.9, 9.7} — *fall*
6	Fr.	*Thunder in November indicates a fertile year to come.* • Tides {10.2, 9.7} — *days,*
7	Sa.	Sadie Hawkins Day • ♂♀☾ • Alexander Mackenzie became 2nd Canadian prime minister, 1873 — *brave*
8	D	**24th S. af. P.** • ♂☌☾ • *Sometimes a Great Notion* 1st movie broadcast on HBO, 1972 — *the*
9	M.	**NEW** ● • Bodybuilder Lou Ferrigno born, 1951 • Tides {10.5, 9.4} — *rain*
10	Tu.	S.S. *Edmund Fitzgerald* sank in storm, Lake Superior, 1975 • Tides {10.4, —} — *for*
11	W.	St. Martin of Tours • **VETERANS DAY** • ♀ STAT. • U.S. Highway 66 established, 1926 — *pumpkin*
12	Th.	☾RUNS LOW • *Voyager 1* reached Saturn, 1980 • Tides {8.9, 10.0} — *spice*
13	Fr.	☾AT APO. • ☿ STAT. • Jazz pioneer Bennie Moten born, 1894 • Tides {8.7, 9.7} — *lattes!*
14	Sa.	♂☌♃ • Catch of 2-color, male/female Maine lobster announced, 2023 • Tides {8.4, 9.5} — *Cooling*
15	D	**25th S. af. P.** • ♂♃☾ • Microsoft released Xbox video game system, 2001 — *off,*
16	M.	Sint Eustatius 1st foreign govt. to recognize U.S., 1776 • Tides {8.2, 9.0} — *skies are*
17	Tu.	St. Hugh of Lincoln • ☾AT☋ • Theater director Lee Strasberg born, 1901 • Tides {8.3, 8.9} — *murky,*
18	W.	St. Hilda of Whitby • 7.2 earthquake caused deadly tsunami, Burin Peninsula, Nfld., 1929 • Tides {8.5, 8.8} — *don't*
19	Th.	☾ON EQ. • Astronaut Eileen Collins born, 1956 • Tides {8.9, 8.9} — *forget*
20	Fr.	♂♄☾ • ♂♆☾ • ☿GR. ELONG. (20° WEST) • Tides {9.4, 9.1} — *to defrost*
21	Sa.	*Caution is the parent of safety.* • Tides {10.0, 9.4} — *the turkey.*
22	D	**26th S. af. P.** • Actress Mae West died, 1980 • Tides {10.6, 9.7} — *Into the*
23	M.	St. Clement • 1st issue of *LIFE* magazine debuted, 1936 • Tides {11.2, 9.9} — *oven, or*
24	Tu.	**FULL BEAVER** ○ • ♂☌☾ • 16-lb. black grouper caught, setting junior class record, Key West, Fla., 2013 — *a*
25	W.	☾RIDES HIGH • ☾AT PERIG. • ☌ AT ☋ • Tides {11.9, 10.1} — *fryer,*
26	Th.	**THANKSGIVING DAY** • *After dinner sit awhile; / After supper walk a mile.* — *giving*
27	Fr.	Astronomer Anders Celsius born, 1701 • U.S. Army War College established, 1901 • Tides {10.0, 11.8} — *thanks*
28	Sa.	Albert Grey, later 4th Earl Grey, Canadian governor general, born, 1851 • Tides {9.9, 11.5} — *snowbanks*
29	D	**1st S. of Advent** • ☾AT☋ • Enos 1st chimp to orbit Earth, 1961 — *aren't*
30	M.	St. Andrew • ♂☌☾ • ♂♃☾ • Tides {9.6, 10.4} — *higher!*

Farmer's Calendar

This Thanksgiving's on Fire!

Thanksgiving at Meme and Pepe's: The scene is an ornament of tenderness and care, as if to be photographed for a magazine. Decorative gourds and pumpkin-colored tapers are set on disks of birch. Oliver polished the silver. Emmie and Syl pressed the cloth and laid out the doilies. Meme carved the bird with delicate mastery. The marshmallows on Mommom's yams are caramelized to perfection. Pop and Louisa's famous butter rolls are coming out of the oven, and Pepe is calling for everyone to pour their drinks. Wait! What the heck was that?! An ungodly crash! Baby Norah has climbed onto the tablescape. She's launched a tureen of cranberries onto the floor. Her left hand is a mitten of mashed potatoes, and her right beats on the creamed corn with a lit candlestick. Uncle Mark runs to rescue her, sloshing his wine on the way. Tug, a well-meaning Australian shepherd, has found a chair that leads to the dessert table, three types of pie on his snout. How did gravy get on the window?! And why is the smoke detector going off? Oh, no! The rolls! <End scene>

2026 Find more facts and fun every day at Almanac.com. 145

DECEMBER

SKY WATCH: In the predawn east, dazzling Venus moves higher each morning. On the 1st at 6:00 A.M., look for it to form a large triangle with the Moon below and the blue star Spica above. The year's finest meteor shower, the Geminids, is best seen on the night of the 13th. Medium-slow shooting stars will appear across the sky and are most visible after 8:30 P.M. when the Moon will be absent. Look for the Moon near Saturn on the 17th and close to the Pleiades cluster on the 21st—with Uranus below. All four objects are best seen through binoculars or, in Saturn's case, a small telescope. On the 27th at 10:00 P.M., the Moon hovers below Jupiter and to the right of 0-magnitude Mars. Winter begins with the solstice on the 21st at 3:50 P.M. EST.

◑ LAST QUARTER	1st day	1:08 A.M.	○ FULL MOON	23rd day	8:28 P.M.
● NEW MOON	8th day	7:52 P.M.	◑ LAST QUARTER	30th day	1:59 P.M.
◐ FIRST QUARTER	17th day	12:42 A.M.			

All times are given in Eastern Standard Time.

GET LOCAL RISE, SET, AND TIDE TIMES VIA ALMANAC.COM/2026.

DAY OF YEAR	DAY OF MONTH	DAY OF WEEK	☼ RISES H. M.	RISE KEY	☼ SETS H. M.	SET KEY	LENGTH OF DAY H. M.	SUN FAST M.	SUN DECLINATION °	SUN DECLINATION '	HIGH TIDE TIMES BOSTON		☾ RISES H. M.	RISE KEY	☾ SETS H. M.	SET KEY	☾ ASTRON. PLACE	☾ AGE
335	1	Tu.	6:54	E	**4:13**	A	9 19	27	21	s. 52	4½	**4¾**	—	-	**12:19**	D	LEO	22
336	2	W.	6:55	E	**4:12**	A	9 17	26	22	s. 01	5½	**5¾**	12:24	D	**12:40**	C	LEO	23
337	3	Th.	6:56	E	**4:12**	A	9 16	26	22	s. 09	6½	**7**	1:31	E	**1:01**	C	VIR	24
338	4	Fr.	6:57	E	**4:12**	A	9 15	25	22	s. 17	7½	**8**	2:38	E	**1:23**	B	VIR	25
339	5	Sa.	6:58	E	**4:12**	A	9 14	25	22	s. 25	8¼	**8¾**	3:44	E	**1:48**	B	VIR	26
340	6	**D**	6:59	E	**4:12**	A	9 13	25	22	s. 32	9	**9¾**	4:51	E	**2:16**	B	LIB	27
341	7	M.	7:00	E	**4:11**	A	9 11	24	22	s. 39	9¾	**10½**	5:56	E	**2:51**	A	LIB	28
342	8	Tu.	7:01	E	**4:11**	A	9 10	24	22	s. 45	10½	**11**	6:58	E	**3:33**	A	SCO	0
343	9	W.	7:01	E	**4:11**	A	9 10	23	22	s. 51	11	**11¾**	7:54	E	**4:23**	A	OPH	1
344	10	Th.	7:02	E	**4:11**	A	9 09	23	22	s. 57	11¾	—	8:42	E	**5:19**	A	SAG	2
345	11	Fr.	7:03	E	**4:12**	A	9 09	22	23	s. 02	12½	**12½**	9:22	E	**6:20**	B	SAG	3
346	12	Sa.	7:04	E	**4:12**	A	9 08	22	23	s. 06	1	**1**	9:55	E	**7:23**	B	SAG	4
347	13	**D**	7:05	E	**4:12**	A	9 07	22	23	s. 10	1¾	**1¾**	10:22	E	**8:27**	C	CAP	5
348	14	M.	7:06	E	**4:12**	A	9 06	21	23	s. 14	2½	**2½**	10:46	E	**9:30**	C	CAP	6
349	15	Tu.	7:06	E	**4:12**	A	9 06	21	23	s. 17	3¼	**3¼**	11:06	D	**10:34**	D	AQU	7
350	16	W.	7:07	E	**4:13**	A	9 06	20	23	s. 20	3¾	**4**	11:26	D	**11:38**	D	AQU	8
351	17	Th.	7:08	E	**4:13**	A	9 05	20	23	s. 22	4¾	**5**	11:46	C	—	-	PSC	9
352	18	Fr.	7:08	E	**4:13**	A	9 05	19	23	s. 23	5½	**5¾**	**12:08**	C	12:45	E	PSC	10
353	19	Sa.	7:09	E	**4:14**	A	9 05	19	23	s. 25	6¼	**6¾**	**12:32**	B	1:55	E	PSC	11
354	20	**D**	7:09	E	**4:14**	A	9 05	18	23	s. 25	7¼	**7¾**	**1:03**	B	3:10	E	ARI	12
355	21	M.	7:10	E	**4:14**	A	9 04	18	23	s. 26	8	**8¾**	**1:42**	A	4:28	E	ARI	13
356	22	Tu.	7:11	E	**4:15**	A	9 04	17	23	s. 26	9	**9¾**	**2:33**	A	5:47	E	TAU	14
357	23	W.	7:11	E	**4:16**	A	9 05	17	23	s. 25	9¾	**10½**	**3:39**	A	7:00	E	TAU	15
358	24	Th.	7:11	E	**4:16**	A	9 05	16	23	s. 24	10¾	**11½**	**4:56**	B	8:02	E	GEM	16
359	25	Fr.	7:12	E	**4:17**	A	9 05	16	23	s. 22	11¾	—	**6:19**	B	8:50	E	GEM	17
360	26	Sa.	7:12	E	**4:18**	A	9 06	15	23	s. 20	12¼	**12½**	**7:40**	C	9:28	E	CAN	18
361	27	**D**	7:12	E	**4:18**	A	9 06	15	23	s. 18	1¼	**1½**	**8:58**	C	9:57	E	LEO	19
362	28	M.	7:13	E	**4:19**	A	9 06	14	23	s. 15	2¼	**2½**	**10:11**	D	10:22	D	LEO	20
363	29	Tu.	7:13	E	**4:20**	A	9 07	14	23	s. 11	3	**3¼**	**11:22**	D	10:44	C	LEO	21
364	30	W.	7:13	E	**4:21**	A	9 08	13	23	s. 07	4	**4¼**	—	-	11:05	C	VIR	22
365	31	Th.	7:13	E	**4:21**	A	9 08	13	23	s. 03	5	**5½**	12:30	E	11:27	B	VIR	23

 To use this page, see p. 116; for Key Letters, see p. 238. LIGHT = A.M. BOLD = P.M.

DECEMBER

THE TWELFTH MONTH · 2026 — **DECEMBER HATH 31 DAYS**

Happy the man whose year has been well spent,
Who looks before with hope, back with content.
—John Askham

DAY OF MONTH	DAY OF WEEK	DATES, FEASTS, FASTS, ASPECTS, TIDE HEIGHTS, AND WEATHER	
1	Tu.	Nov. 30–Dec. 1: Ice storm caused power outages, St. Louis, Mo., 2006 • Tides {9.6, 9.9}	Lots of
2	W.	St. Viviana • ☾ON EQ. • Soviet *Mars 3* made 1st unmanned soft landing on Mars, 1971 • {9.6, 9.5}	malls
3	Th.	In 1 hr., Madhvi Chittoor and Jeffco Public Schools (Colo.) collected 441 lbs. 3 ozs. of markers for recycling, 2021	have
4	Fr.	Chanukah begins at sundown • *Be true to your word, your work, and your friend.* • {9.9, 9.0}	lines
5	Sa.	♂♀☾ • Animator Walt Disney born, 1901 • Painter Claude Monet died, 1926 • {10.0, 8.9}	that
6	D	**2nd S. of Advent** • St. Nicholas • Newfoundland officially renamed Newfoundland and Labrador, 2001	
7	M.	St. Ambrose • **NAT'L PEARL HARBOR REMEMBRANCE DAY** • ♂☌☾ • {10.2, 8.9}	form up,
8	Tu.	NEW ● • U.S. entered WWII, 1941 • Tides {10.2, 8.8}	matzo balls
9	W.	☾RUNS LOW • *Wednesday clearing, clear till Sunday.* • Tides {10.1, 8.8}	and
10	Th.	St. Eulalia • Nobel Prizes awarded for 1st time, 1901 • Tides {10.1}	candles
11	Fr.	☾AT APO. • ♄ STAT. • Ind. statehood, 1816 • {8.7, 10.0}	warm up!
12	Sa.	Our Lady of Guadalupe • ♂♀☾ • OSCAR-1 amateur radio satellite launched, transmitting "HI" in Morse code, 1961	
13	D	**3rd S. of Advent** • St. Lucia • ♆ STAT. • ♃ STAT.	Meteors
14	M.	Halcyon Days begin. • ☾AT ☋ • Tilt-a-Whirl trademark registered, 1926 • {8.6, 9.4}	streak
15	Tu.	Beware the Pogonip. • Fire at U.S. Patent Office destroyed thousands of patent documents and models, 1836	and
16	W.	Ember Day • ☾ON EQ. • Beatrix Potter's *The Tale of Peter Rabbit* 1st published, 1901 • {8.7, 8.9}	flakes
17	Th.	♂♆☾ • Wright bros. completed 1st successful flight of self-powered heavier-than-air craft, Kitty Hawk, N.C., 1903	
18	Fr.	Ember Day • ♂♄☾ • Singer Billie Eilish born, 2001 • Tides {9.3, 8.7}	are all
19	Sa.	Ember Day • Canada's 1st telegraph sent, 1846 • {9.7, 8.8}	glistening—
20	D	**4th S. of Advent** • Movie *It's a Wonderful Life* debuted, 1946 • {10.2, 9.0}	goodness
21	M.	St. Thomas • **WINTER SOLSTICE** • ♂☌☾ • Tides {10.7, 9.2}	sakes,
22	Tu.	National Cookie Exchange Day (U.S.) • Beethoven's "Fifth Symphony" premiered, Vienna, Austria, 1808	we
23	W.	**FULL COLD** ○ • ☾RIDES HIGH • 20-lb. 9-oz. southern flounder caught, Nassau Sound, Fla., 1983	are
24	Th.	☾AT PERIG. • Activist Marsha Gomez born, 1951 • Tides {11.9, 10.0}	already
25	Fr.	Christmas • *The greatest things are done by the help of small ones.* • {12.0}	Christmas-ing!
26	Sa.	St. Stephen • **BOXING DAY (CANADA)** • **KWANZAA BEGINS** • {10.2, 11.9}	At New Year's
27	D	**1st S. af. Ch.** • ☾AT ☋ • ♂♃☾ • Tides {10.2, 11.5}	chime,
28	M.	St. John[T] • ♂♂☾ • Iowa statehood, 1846 • Tides {10.2, 11.0}	sing
29	Tu.	Holy Innocents[T] • ☾ON EQ. • Cellist Pablo Casals born, 1876 • Tides {10.1, 10.3}	Auld
30	W.	Coca-Cola Company founder Asa Griggs Candler born, 1851 • Tides {9.9, 9.6}	Lang
31	Th.	St. Sylvester • Actress Betty White died, 2021 • {9.8, 9.0}	Syne!

Farmer's Calendar
My Solstice Cochins

The solstice sun yawns a few lazy rays through the paper birch and hemlock woods. A thin silence surrounds me, save for the old house sound of floorboards aching in the hollow of a long winter's night. From the kitchen, I can see hoarfrost crystals blanketing the holly, the beautyberry, and the red osier dogwood that line the side of the coop. I stir a porridge of spiced oatmeal to bring to the chickens—a pinch each of cinnamon, turmeric, ginger, and black pepper for the health of our aging flock. Easing onto the icy deck in stiff, unlaced boots, each footstep crackles, as the breaking of a crème brûlée. Most of the girls huddle around the feed. Some buff Orpingtons pace with excitement. "It's alright honey, here's some for you, too." It's important to talk to your animals. In the short daylight season, our two white Cochins like to stay in bed, roosting on the highest perch. These fluffy matrons would be happy all day in their bunk. One of the morning chores is to scoot them down. "Go on out, sweet girls," I find myself whispering. "It won't be long before you can tuck back in for another cozy night. I promise."

2026 • Find more facts and fun every day at Almanac.com. • 147

HOLIDAYS AND OBSERVANCES

2026 HOLIDAYS
FEDERAL HOLIDAYS ARE LISTED IN BOLD.

JAN. 1: New Year's Day
JAN. 7: Orthodox Christmas (Julian)
JAN. 19: Martin Luther King Jr.'s Birthday, observed
FEB. 1: Black History Month begins
FEB. 2: Groundhog Day
FEB. 12: Abraham Lincoln's Birthday
FEB. 14: Valentine's Day
FEB. 15: Susan B. Anthony's Birthday *(Fla.)*
FEB. 16: Presidents' Day
FEB. 17: Mardi Gras *(Baldwin & Mobile counties, Ala.; La.)*
FEB. 22: George Washington's Birthday
MAR. 2: Texas Independence Day
MAR. 3: Town Meeting Day *(Vt.)*
MAR. 8: International Women's Day
  Daylight Saving Time begins
MAR. 17: St. Patrick's Day
  Evacuation Day *(Suffolk Co., Mass.)*
MAR. 30: Seward's Day *(Alaska)*
MAR. 31: César Chávez Day
APR. 2: Pascua Florida Day
APR. 13: Holocaust Remembrance Day begins at sundown
APR. 20: Patriots Day *(Maine, Mass.)*
APR. 21: San Jacinto Day *(Tex.)*
APR. 22: Earth Day
APR. 24: National Arbor Day
MAY 1: Asian American, Native Hawaiian, and Pacific Islander Heritage Month begins
MAY 5: Cinco de Mayo
MAY 8: Truman Day *(Mo.)*
MAY 10: Mother's Day
MAY 16: Armed Forces Day
MAY 18: Victoria Day *(Canada)*
MAY 22: National Maritime Day
MAY 25: Memorial Day, observed
JUNE 1: Pride Month begins
JUNE 5: World Environment Day
JUNE 6: D-Day
JUNE 11: King Kamehameha I Day *(Hawaii)*
JUNE 14: Flag Day
JUNE 17: Bunker Hill Day *(Suffolk Co., Mass.)*
JUNE 19: Juneteenth National Independence Day
JUNE 20: West Virginia Day
JUNE 21: Father's Day
JULY 1: Canada Day
JULY 4: Independence Day
JULY 20: International Moon Day
JULY 24: Pioneer Day *(Utah)*
JULY 25: National Day of the Cowboy
AUG. 1: Colorado Day
AUG. 3: Civic Holiday *(parts of Canada)*
AUG. 16: Bennington Battle Day *(Vt.)*
AUG. 19: National Aviation Day
AUG. 26: Women's Equality Day
SEPT. 7: Labor Day
SEPT. 9: Admission Day *(Calif.)*
SEPT. 11: Patriot Day
SEPT. 13: National Grandparents Day
SEPT. 15: National Hispanic/Latinx Heritage Month begins
SEPT. 17: Constitution Day
SEPT. 21: International Day of Peace
SEPT. 30: National Day for Truth and Reconciliation *(Canada)*
OCT. 5: Child Health Day
OCT. 9: Leif Eriksson Day
OCT. 12: Columbus Day, observed
  Indigenous Peoples' Day *(parts of U.S.)*
  National Farmer's Day
  Thanksgiving Day *(Canada)*
OCT. 18: Alaska Day
OCT. 24: United Nations Day
OCT. 30: Nevada Day
OCT. 31: Halloween
NOV. 1: Daylight Saving Time ends

NOV. 3: Election Day
NOV. 4: Will Rogers Day *(Okla.)*
NOV. 11: Veterans Day
 Remembrance Day *(Canada)*
NOV. 19: Discovery of Puerto Rico Day
NOV. 26: Thanksgiving Day
NOV. 27: Acadian Day *(La.)*

DEC. 7: National Pearl Harbor
 Remembrance Day
DEC. 15: Bill of Rights Day
DEC. 17: Wright Brothers Day
DEC. 25: Christmas Day
DEC. 26: Boxing Day *(Canada)*
 Kwanzaa begins

Movable Religious Observances

FEB. 1: Septuagesima Sunday
FEB. 17: Ramadan begins at sundown
 Shrove Tuesday
FEB. 18: Ash Wednesday
FEB. 23: Orthodox Lent begins
MAR. 29: Palm Sunday
APR. 1: Passover begins at sundown
APR. 3: Good Friday
APR. 5: Easter
APR. 12: Orthodox Easter
MAY 10: Rogation Sunday

MAY 14: Ascension Day
MAY 24: Whitsunday–Pentecost
MAY 31: Orthodox Pentecost
 Trinity Sunday
JUNE 7: Corpus Christi
SEPT. 11: Rosh Hashanah begins at
 sundown
SEPT. 20: Yom Kippur begins at sundown
NOV. 29: First Sunday of Advent
DEC. 4: Chanukah begins at sundown

CHRONOLOGICAL CYCLES

Dominical Letter **D**
Epact **11**
Golden Number (Lunar Cycle) **13**
Roman Indiction **4**
Solar Cycle (Julian Calendar) **19**
Year of Julian Period **6739**

ERAS

ERA	YEAR	BEGINS
Byzantine	7535	September 14
Jewish (A.M.)*	5787	September 11
Chinese (Lunar) [Year of the Horse]	4724	February 17
Roman (A.U.C.)	2779	January 14
Nabonassar	2775	April 23
Japanese	2686	January 1
Grecian (Seleucidae)	2338	September 14 (or October 14)
Indian (Saka)	1948	March 22
Diocletian	1743	September 11
Islamic (Hegira)*	1448	June 16
Bahá'í*	183	March 20

*Year begins at sundown.

GLOSSARY OF ALMANAC ODDITIES

Many readers have expressed puzzlement over the rather obscure entries that appear on our **Right-Hand Calendar Pages, 121–147.** These oddities have long been fixtures in this almanac, and we are pleased to provide some definitions. Once explained, they may not seem so odd after all!

EMBER DAYS: These are the Wednesdays, Fridays, and Saturdays that occur in succession following (1) the First Sunday in Lent; (2) Whitsunday–Pentecost; (3) the Feast of the Holy Cross, September 14; and (4) the Feast of St. Lucia, December 13. The word ember is perhaps a corruption of the Old English *ymbrendaeg* (circuit day) or the Latin *quatuor tempora* (four times). The four periods are observed by some Christian denominations for prayer, fasting, and the ordination of clergy.

Folklore has it that the weather on each of the 3 days foretells the weather for the next 3 months; that is, in September, the first Ember Day, Wednesday, forecasts the weather for October; Friday predicts November; and Saturday foretells December.

DISTAFF DAY (JANUARY 7): This was the day after Epiphany, when women were expected to return to their spinning following the Christmas holiday. A distaff is the staff women used for holding the flax or wool in spinning. Hence, the term refers to women's work or the maternal side of the family.

PLOUGH MONDAY (JANUARY): Traditionally, the first Monday after Epiphany was called Plough Monday because it was the day when men returned to their plough, or daily work, following the Christmas holiday. (Every few years, Plough Monday and Distaff Day fall on the same day.) It was customary at this time for farm laborers to draw a plough through the village, soliciting money for a "plough light," which was kept burning in the parish church all year. This traditional verse captures the spirit of it:

Yule is come and Yule is gone,
and we have feasted well;
so Jack must to his flail again
and Jenny to her wheel.

WINTER'S BACK BREAKS (AROUND MID-FEBRUARY): According to weather lore in New England, as well as in England, France, and other parts of Europe, around the middle of February, the severity of winter's cold and storms starts to lessen (the winter's "back," or its strength, is broken). With increasing frequency, there will be periods of warmer temperatures, and storms will tend to be milder, hinting that spring is approaching.

THREE CHILLY SAINTS (MAY): Mamertus, Pancras, and Gervais were three early Christian saints whose feast days, on May 11, 12, and 13, respectively, are traditionally cold; thus, they have come to be known as the Three Chilly Saints. An old French saying translates to "St. Mamertus, St. Pancras, and St. Gervais do not pass without a frost."

MIDSUMMER DAY (JUNE 24): To the farmer, this day is the midpoint of the growing season, halfway between planting and harvest. The Anglican Church considered it a Quarter Day, one of the four major divisions of the liturgical year. It also marks the feast day of St. John the Baptist. (Midsummer Eve is an occasion for festivity and celebrates fertility.)

CORNSCATEOUS AIR (JULY): First used by early almanac makers, this term signifies warm, damp air. Although it signals ideal climatic conditions for growing corn, warm, damp air poses a danger to those affected by asthma and other respiratory problems.

DOG DAYS (JULY 3–AUGUST 11): These 40 days are traditionally the year's hottest and unhealthiest. They once coincided with the year's heliacal (at sunrise) rising of the Dog Star, Sirius. Ancient folks thought that the "combined heat" of Sirius and the Sun caused summer's swelter.

LAMMAS DAY (AUGUST 1): Derived from the Old English *hlaf maesse* (loaf mass), Lammas Day marked the beginning of the harvest. Traditionally, loaves of bread were baked from the first-ripened grain and brought to the churches to be consecrated. In Scotland, Lammastide fairs became famous as the time when trial marriages could be made. These marriages could end after a year with no strings attached.

CAT NIGHTS COMMENCE (AUGUST 17): This term harks back to ancient lore about witches. An Irish legend says that a witch could turn into a cat and regain herself eight times, but on the ninth time (August 17), she couldn't change back and thus began her final life permanently as a cat. Hence the saying "A cat has nine lives."

HARVEST HOME (SEPTEMBER): In Britain and other parts of Europe, this marked the conclusion of the harvest and a period of festivals for feasting and thanksgiving. It was also a time to hold elections, pay workers, and collect rents. These festivals usually took place around the autumnal equinox. Certain groups in the United States, e.g., the Pennsylvania Dutch, have kept the tradition alive.

ST. LUKE'S LITTLE SUMMER (OCTOBER): This is a period of warm weather that occurs on or near St. Luke's feast day (usually October 18).

HALCYON DAYS (DECEMBER): This period of about 2 weeks of calm weather often follows the blustery winds at autumn's end. Ancient Greeks and Romans experienced this weather at about the time of the winter solstice (around December 21), when the halcyon, or kingfisher—having charmed the wind and waves so that waters were especially calm at this time—was thought to brood in a nest floating on the sea.

BEWARE THE POGONIP (DECEMBER): The word *pogonip* refers to frozen fog and was coined by North American indigenous peoples to describe the frozen fogs of fine ice needles that occur in the mountain valleys of the western United States and Canada. According to tradition, breathing the fog is injurious to the lungs. ■

SAVE THE DATES

While it's important to stay in the moment and not look too far ahead, planning for the future is also fun. Here are some events you will want to mark on the calendar in the years (and centuries!) to come.

TOTAL SOLAR ECLIPSE: The next total solar eclipse to be visible from North America will be August 23, 2044. The path of totality is expected to cross over parts of North Dakota, South Dakota, and Montana in the U.S., as well as British Columbia, Alberta, Saskatchewan, Yukon, the Northwest Territories, and Nunavut in Canada. Sky watchers in the U.S. won't have to wait long for the following one: A cross-country eclipse from California to Florida will unfold on August 12, 2045.

TRANSIT OF MERCURY: This occurs when Mercury crosses directly between the Sun and the Earth, where Mercury appears as a tiny black dot moving across the disc of the Sun. The next transit of Mercury will occur in 2032, but viewers in North America will have to wait until May 7, 2049, to see the phenomenon.

BLUE MOON: A second full Moon in a given calendar month is known as a Blue Moon. This occurs every 2 or 3 years. The next one is on May 31, 2026, and after that, December 31, 2028. Every so often, there will be two blue Moons in a calendar year, which takes place in January and March of 2037. Conversely, a second new Moon in a month is called a Black Moon. The next time that occurs is on August 31, 2027.

SOLAR CYCLE: Solar cycle record-keeping began in 1755; the 25th cycle of the Sun started in December 2019 and reached its solar maximum in October 2024. A new cycle starts every 11 years, with Solar Cycle 26 set to begin in 2030.

LEAP YEAR: The year 2028 will include 366 days, as February 29, also known as Leap Day, lands on a Tuesday. The next year that is evenly divisible by four that will *not* be a Leap Year is 2100.

U.S. PRESIDENTIAL ELECTION AND INAUGURATION: On Tuesday, November 7, 2028, the 61st presidential election will be held in the U.S. After the election results are certified in January of 2029, the 48th President of the United States will be sworn in on Saturday, January 20, 2029.

CHRISTMAS/CHANUKAH FIRST NIGHT: In 2024, the first night of Chanukah fell on Christmas for the fifth time since 1900. This will next occur on Tuesday, December 25, 2035. Chanukah will coincide with Christmas Eve in 2027.

EARLIEST/LATEST EASTER DATE: Easter is observed annually on a Sunday between March 22 and April 25, but it is rare for the holiday to land on either of these dates. Easter will not land on March 22 until 2285; it will fall on April 25 in 2038.

200TH CANADIAN CELEBRATION: Canada will mark its bicentennial (200 years) of Confederation in 2067 on the first of July.

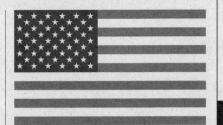

300TH U.S. CELEBRATION: The United States will celebrate its semiquincentennial (250 years) in 2026. America will turn 300 years old (tricentennial) on July 4, 2076.

ALMANAC 250TH: Founded in 1792, *The Old Farmer's Almanac* is the oldest continuously published periodical in North America, with a mission to be "useful . . . with a pleasant degree of humor." In 2042, this almanac will celebrate its 250th edition!

SEQUENTIAL DATES: The last sequential date of the 21st century took place on December 13, 2014 (12/13/14), but you will have to wait until early next century for the dates to align again on January 2, 2103 (01/02/03).

OLYMPICS: The Winter Games are in Italy (Milan and Cortina d'Ampezzo) from February 6–22, 2026; they return to North America in 2034, in Salt Lake City, Utah. The Summer Games will be held on U.S. soil for the first time since 1996 (Atlanta, Georgia) when Los Angeles, California, hosts the 2028 games from July 14–30. ■

WEATHER

Ibyuk Pingo on McKenzie River Delta near Tuktoyaktuk, Northwest Territories, Canada

COOL TRUTHS

MEET THE SHAPE-SHIFTING

In the westernmost reaches of Canada, accessible by boat, helicopter, skis, or skidoo—and sometimes all of the above—the landscape is dotted with pingos, conical ice-cored hills. Unlike mountains that form over millions of years through tectonic plate activity, pingos grow rather rapidly, some within a few hundred years, expanding from the inside out—and up—powered by ice.

When subsurface water seeps into permafrost (perennially frozen ground) and freezes, it expands, pushing the earth above it upward. In other words, a pingo is a frost heave of epic proportions. Some pingos rise to nearly 200 feet, while others measure almost half a mile wide. The Pingo Canadian Landmark in the Northwest Territories' Tuktoyaktuk Peninsula ("Tuk" for short) protects eight of these frosty wonders; the tallest, Ibyuk Pingo, is the second-largest pingo in the world. In the Inuvialuit language, *Ibyuk* means "one that grows."

Photo: Steve McCutcheon/Minden Pictures

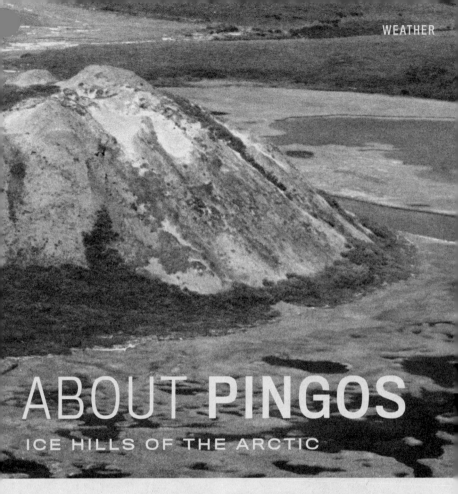

WEATHER

ABOUT PINGOS
ICE HILLS OF THE ARCTIC

What is it like to stand on a pingo? "It felt like I was standing on top of the world, as it is the highest thing around, even though it's not quite 50 meters high," shares Natural Resources Canada research scientist Stephen Wolfe about the summit of Ibyuk. "Imagine that you are being pushed up to the sky by ice."

WHERE IN THE WORLD
These polar pimples define the Arctic tundra in the Northwest Territories and other permafrost sites around the globe, including in Siberia and Alaska. Pingos in the western Arctic typically indicate areas that were once covered by lakes or rivers. The highest known concentration of pingos on Earth is in Tuk, home to 1,350 identified frozen hummocks.

Pingos also pop up under the sea floor. Ice-cored hills known as gas hydrate pingos form in places where methane and water interact beneath the ocean floor. *(continued)*

WHERE IN THE GALAXY

Scientists have spotted pingo-like formations in Mars's polar regions, suggesting that the planet once had (or still has) liquid water underground, which makes pingos of interest in the search for extraterrestrial life. Could Martian microbes be hiding inside a pingo? Stay tuned. Other researchers are studying pingo-like structures on Ceres, the largest satellite of Jupiter.

PINGO LINGO

Pingos are part of the indigenous culture of the western Arctic. In Inuvialuktun, pingo means "conical hill" and is an accepted scientific term. Arctic botanist Alf Erling Porsild first borrowed it from the Inuvialuit in his 1938 paper, "Earth Mounds in Unglaciated Arctic Northwestern America." Porsild Pingo in Tuk is named in his honor.

LIFE CYCLE OF A PINGO

Pingos don't last forever. Like soufflés, they eventually deflate, which can take centuries. This process sometimes reveals layers of earth that have been frozen for thousands of years, offering a peek into ancient climates and ecosys-

KNOW YOUR PINGOS

OPEN-SYSTEM PINGO

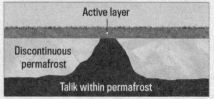
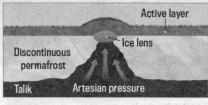
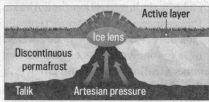

CLOSED-SYSTEM PINGO

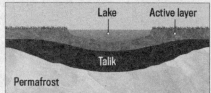
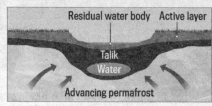
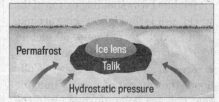

An **OPEN-SYSTEM PINGO** usually has a water source, commonly from a high elevation; the talik (layer of unfrozen ground) in the permafrost acts as a conduit that allows water to flow from higher to lower elevations. When that water is forced toward the surface, it freezes and forms an ice lens, which pushes upward through the soil.

CLOSED-SYSTEM PINGOS form where a talik is surrounded by permafrost on all sides, and the water to create the pingo comes from within that confined area. Most Tuk pingos are closed-system.

Illustration: Rob Schuster, adapted from Encyclopedia Britannica, Inc.

tems. A pingo may become cracked in its center, and as it begins to collapse, the center portion sinks, and the pingo starts to shrink. Eventually, a crater will form in the center, sometimes becoming a basin for a small pond as some or all of the ice beneath it melts.

WHAT'S INSIDE A PINGO?

Frozen soil and ice make up a typical pingo. Many contain pure ice, which appears to have layers—similar to tree rings. The layers are white, which contain lots of bubbles, and blue, which have none. The pattern of bubbles can be used to determine past freezing rates and provide a record of seasonal patterns of warmth and cold.

"I think it would be interesting to compare the composition of the bubbles contained in pingo ice to the composition of bubbles in other types of ice," says Wolfe. "What makes up the air in these bubbles? Do they contain CO_2 and methane? Can we determine the origin of these carbon gases and even determine the age of the gases in these bubbles? This would contribute to understanding the larger carbon cycle of the Arctic."

WHAT'S OUTSIDE A PINGO?

Almost always tundra: herbaceous plants like dryas, grasses, lupines, mosses, and sedges; as well as woody plants like dwarf birch. Sometimes, in protected areas around the pingos, taller willow shrubs may grow where they are sheltered from the wind and can receive sunlight and moisture from melted snow. Large mammals such as grizzly bears and barren-ground caribou will forage and graze around pingos in season, while Arctic foxes, red foxes, and Arctic ground squirrels den in the sandy slopes of pingos.

WHAT GOOD ARE PINGOS?

Rapid changes in ice-saturated permafrost can be identified by observing and characterizing pingos over several years using techniques like radar and other geophysical sensors. "My work has involved mapping and measuring them—and for that, we used mostly satellite imagery and elevation data to see them and determine their sizes," says Wolfe.

Pingos contain masses of pure ice. When that ice melts, the ground retreats and becomes wetter. Although collapsing may be a natural process for some pingos, if many appear to be shrinking at once, it could signal that the status of the permafrost is changing. Vegetation changes on or around pingos, such as increased willow growth or enlarged wetlands, also may indicate that changes to the moisture levels are underway.

The peat top on a pingo is frozen, and that peat stores carbon. If the pingo thaws and collapses, the peat also thaws, and its carbon can eventually decompose, typically within a small thaw lake. When peat decomposes, it releases methane and carbon dioxide into the atmosphere, a process known as permafrost-carbon feedback. As permafrost thaws, more and more of its stored carbon is converted into greenhouse gases. ■

Edited from an interview with **Stephen Wolfe**, who first saw pingos from the air as an undergraduate field assistant with the Geological Survey of Canada.

WEATHER

THE WONDERS
OF WEATHER
A COOL QUIZ TO WARM UP YOUR WISDOM!

1. What's a sun kink?

a. a desert snake with adaptations allowing it to withstand extreme heat

b. a buckle in a railroad track caused by swelling in extreme heat

c. a reduction in signal quality when outdoor ethernet cables get too hot

2. A severe cold snap can *not* cause:

a. car tires to fall off their rims

b. iguanas to enter a form of hibernation and fall out of trees

c. you to become sick

3. When it's really hot and dry, what might a yellow jacket do?

a. become crankier than normal

b. kick out roommates in the communal nest to cool it down

c. host an ice cream social

4. What is a blackberry winter?

a. a brief thaw in late winter that causes blackberries to prematurely leaf out

b. a cold snap in late spring when blackberries bloom

c. warm, humid spring weather that encourages powdery mildew, which turns blackberry leaves white

Illustrations: Nadiinko/Getty Images

WEATHER

5. What's one difference between the Northern Hemisphere's polar jet stream and polar vortex?

a. The jet stream almost always travels east to west, whereas the vortex often shifts its direction of circulation.

b. The jet stream operates largely in the stratosphere, whereas the vortex works mainly in the lower troposphere.

c. The polar jet stream is closer to the equator than the polar vortex.

6. The heat of the Sun is *not* . . .

a. responsible for shifting desert sands.

b. at its surface five times hotter than lightning.

c. measurable using a pyrometer.

7. A town named Cool can be found in:

a. New Jersey

b. Idaho

c. Texas

ANSWERS:

1. b. buckled railway. During heat waves, trains travel more slowly to avoid further stressing tracks.

2. c. sickness. Viruses and other pathogens cause us to become sick, not temperatures. Cold temperatures can weaken our immune systems, increasing our chances of getting sick.

3. a. cranky. As these insects search for water, they may become increasingly aggressive.

4. b. cold snap. This colloquialism refers to a cold snap in April or May.

5. c. The polar jet stream is closer to the equator.

6. b. hotter than lightning. At about 54,000°F, lightning is five times hotter than the Sun's surface (about 10,000°F).

7. c. Texas. California also has a town by this name.

Heidi Stonehill, executive editor of *The Old Farmer's Almanac*, enjoys learning about the many wonders of both wild and welcome weather.

Illustrations: Nadiinko/Getty Images

GARDENING

EAT YOUR SKIRRETS

How (and Why) to Garden Like it's 1776

by Susan Peery

GARDENING

> The kitchen-garden should always be situated on one Side of the House, so as not to appear in Sight; but must be placed near the Stables, for the Conveniency of Dung...
>
> —Philip Miller, English botanist (1691-1771), in *The Gardeners Dictionary*

THE KITCHEN GARDEN AT GEORGE WASHINGTON'S MOUNT VERNON ESTATE IN VIRGINIA

GARDENING

As patriotic fever spiked in the spring of 1776, gardeners in the 13 American Colonies went about their traditional work: cultivating the soil, fertilizing, sowing seeds, and weeding.

Sound familiar? Home gardeners today have gained a few advantages since then—perhaps the most important being the garden hose, providing water at the flick of a faucet. Otherwise, hoes, spading forks, and other garden tools have changed very little, and we are as much at the mercy of the weather as ever.

Although estates and plantations boasted elaborate rose gardens and clipped hedges in the formal English style, even the humblest cottage had a modest kitchen garden, a sunny plot not far from the kitchen door holding the most frequently used herbs, vegetables, and flowers. Kitchen gardens were usually planted, tended, and harvested by women, who were the cooks, pharmacists, herbalists, cleaners, and comforters of the household.

In the New World, settlers re-created their gardens from home in a new way. We know from diaries, letters, early seed catalogs, and other 18th-century sources that kitchen gardens had a simple, functional layout, often an arrangement of rect-

Flowers, vegetables, and herbs were often mixed together.

angular beds divided by paths of marl (a mix of clay and crushed limestone or shells) or pebbles, the whole commonly surrounded with rail fences for protection from livestock. The well was usually nearby, handy for drawing water. Separate plots outside the fence held fruit trees and berry bushes.

It's a compact, utilitarian model familiar to farmers who create urban gardens and edible landscapes today.

Flowers, herbs, and vegetables were often mixed together to maximize the use of space. Spring peas were grown on simple stick fences or tripods tied at the top; pole beans used the same supports later in the spring, typically interplanted with onions and other shorter crops. Certain essential but "vigorous" (invasive) plants like tansy—in those days, strewn on floors to repel insects and neutralize odors—probably grew outside

Photo: Heathglens Farm to Jar

the kitchen garden. Tiny-seeded plants like carrots and radishes were frequently mixed with a handful of sand and sown together in rows; the radishes emerged first and were pulled to be eaten, making space for the slower carrot roots to grow without a lot of thinning.

The larger and more sprawling vegetables, including cucumbers, gourds, pumpkins, squashes, and turnips, grew under and with corn, barley, and other field crops outside the kitchen garden. In the 18th century, turnips were the major root crop for feeding both people and livestock. For most Americans, potatoes were still in the future since they were not widely adopted until the 19th century. Tomatoes, another nightshade, were regarded with a modicum of wariness, even though they were called "love apples."

A plant could have several uses. Parsley, for example, was valued for its culinary use, as a traditional treatment for gout, rheumatism, and kidney stones, and as a breath freshener. Curly or "doubled" parsley was a curiosity; the flat leaf Italian variety was the default in 1776. Horseradish, a deep-rooted perennial, was commonly grown as a condiment and for medicinal purposes; it was dug each fall, with only one division replanted in the kitchen garden.

Now, about what are known as *skirrets*. The skirret *(Sium sisarum)* was described by herbalist John Gerard in *The Herbal* (1597) as "sweet, white, good to be eaten, and most pleasant in taste." Like a short, skinny parsnip, it keeps well and is delicious roasted or cooked in stews. Seeds for this hardy member of the carrot family, often found in the 18th-century kitchen garden, appear in specialized catalogs today in the United States and Canada. Once established, skirrets can be propagated each spring by taking slips from the mother plant.

A GARDEN OF EATING

Lacking a convenient garden center, the 1776 gardener started nearly every annual plant from seed on a schedule determined by both Old World tradition and New World realities. *(continued)*

Skirrets are like short, skinny parsnips.

GARDENING

The 1776 gardener started nearly every annual plant from seed.

Here are some of the kitchen garden staples of 1776, in the words of garden historian Ann Leighton, "for use or for delight."

Sallet For All Palates

Sallet herbs were what we now call salad: anything green and edible—much appreciated after a long winter diet of root vegetables. Favorite spring greens in 1776 included lettuces (planted every 2 weeks for a steady supply), pea shoots, and any other greens available, including beet tops, chard, chives, dandelions, mustard, spinach, various mints, and peppery "Indian cress," known today as nasturtium.

Culinary Cornerstones

Peas were the first crop planted as soon as the ground could be worked. All pea varieties grown in 1776 needed support. When the first crocuses bloomed, gardeners sowed cabbage seed thickly so that the early leaves (called coleworts) could be harvested for salad, making room for cabbage heads to form. Beans—from French (actually a New World bean) or semi-bush snap beans to kidney beans and many varieties of pole and runner beans— were eaten fresh whenever possible or allowed to dry for winter use. They were planted when the pea vines came down and the soil had warmed up.

Roots Aplenty

Nearly everyone grew beets, carrots, horseradish, parsnips, and turnips and often interplanted them with radishes, described by Virginia colonist Richard Bradley in 1718

164

Photos, clockwise from top left: Roter Hahn; ChViroj/Getty Images; Experimental Farm Network; BethAmber/Getty Images; Grahamphoto23/Getty Images; patrickheagney/Getty Images

as "a Root which might be sown promiscuously among other Roots." It was widely believed that radishes had to be pulled by 10 A.M. and kept in a cool cellar until dinner. Some turnips were sown in the kitchen garden for family use (the rest in the field for livestock). The favored carrot of ered essential for their culinary and medicinal value, and in the 18th century, they were generally raised from seeds, not sets. Garlic was rarely used in cooking but was grown for its medicinal uses, as it was believed to cure rabies as well as corns on the feet. Garlic was (and is) planted in the fall.

lemon balm, lemon verbena, marjoram, all of the mints, and native bee balm (also known as Oswego tea).

A New World Flowering

In addition to flowering herbs, kitchen gardeners tucked in spring bulbs, calendula (the pot marigold), feverfew, clove pinks (gillyflowers),

FEVERFEW

SWEET WILLIAM

APOTHECARY'S ROSE

In addition to herbs, kitchen gardeners tucked in spring bulbs and other flowering plants.

1776, the 'Horn', was like our 'Danvers Half Long'. Parsnips (and skirrets!) were favored by those who appreciated their nutty sweetness and hardiness. All modern parsnips are scaled down from their sturdy colonial ancestors, which could attain a length of nearly 3 feet.

An Allium a Day

Leeks and especially onions were consid- Perennial chives were among the first plants to emerge in the spring.

Healing Herbs

Parsley, sage, rosemary, and thyme, just like the song, were revered for their scent, their flavor, and their curative or preventive properties. Other Old World and North American mainstays of 1776 include anise hyssop, chamomile, comfrey, lavender, Sweet William, violets, primroses, and other beloved flowering plants for use and delight—as well as roses (especially Damask and Apothecary's rose) for their beauty and medicinal value. These may have crowded the utilitarian bounds of the kitchen garden, but in a new country perched on the edge of a vast wilderness, they felt like a homecoming. ∎

HISTORY

Sewing Patriotism

HOW FLAG-MAKER MARY PICKERSGILL STITCHED HER WAY INTO U.S. HISTORY

by Joe Bills

As we mark the 250th anniversary of the United States as a nation, thoughts turn to heroes, philosophers, and history makers. For every one of the stories we celebrate, countless others evade the semiquincentennial nod. Such is the case of Mary Pickersgill, who also marks her 250th birthday this year.

Born in Philadelphia on February 12, 1776, Pickersgill learned the art of flag-making from her mother, Rebecca Young (a contemporary of another famous flag-maker, Betsy Ross), who had been making military ensigns and uniforms, blankets, and drum cases since the Revolutionary War.

As a child, Mary moved to Baltimore with her family, and in 1795, she married John Pickersgill. Soon after, they took up residence in Philadelphia. By 1807, she was widowed. Pickersgill returned to Baltimore, renting a house with her mother and young daughter, Caroline. Pickersgill set up shop at home and soon developed a reputation as a quality flag-maker. Her clients included the U.S. Army, the U.S. Navy, and a bevy of merchant ships that frequented the busy harbor. Business was good, allowing her to purchase the house she had been renting. She lived there for the rest of her life.

BROAD STRIPES, BRIGHT STARS

In 1813, Pickersgill was commissioned by Major George Armistead, a commander of Fort McHenry, to create a flag so large that the British could see it from afar. The task was daunting. The colossal flag would be 30×42 feet, far larger than any Pickersgill had ever made before. She gathered 13-year-old Caroline, two teenage nieces, Margaret and Eliza, and an indentured servant named Grace Wisher to assist.

Wisher, an African American teenager, was at the approximate midpoint of her 6 years of servitude. In their book *Mary Young Pickersgill: Flag Maker of the*

166   Painting: Maryland Center for History and Culture

BY MOST ESTIMATES, PICKERSGILL AND HER ASSISTANTS SEWED MORE THAN 350,000 HAND STITCHES.

HISTORY

Star-Spangled Banner, Sally Johnston and Pat Pilling write that Grace's mother received $12 when she delivered the 10-year-old into servitude and another $12 at the conclusion of the 6-year term. In exchange, Pickersgill pledged that Wisher would learn "the art and mystery of Housework and plain sewing."

The flag's 15 2-foot-wide stripes, alternating red and white to represent the 15 states—the original 13 colonies, along with Vermont and Kentucky—in accordance with the Flag Act of 1794, were sewn from two widths of British wool bunting. The 15 cotton stars, measuring 2 feet wide point-to-point, arranged in a blue field, symbolized the states' unity as a nation.

There was not enough room in the Pickersgill house to spread out the flag for the final sewing, so arrangements were made with George Brown, owner of a nearby brewery, to use the floor of one of his malthouses. Composed of some 400 yards of heavy, durable bunting, the flag would weigh about 50 pounds in its final form. The sewing was rigorous work, requiring more than 350,000 hand stitches by most estimates. Cutting, assembling, and sewing the flag took 6 long weeks.

On August 19, 1813, the giant flag was presented to the soldiers at Fort McHenry. For their efforts, the women were paid $405.90 (plus another $168.54 for a smaller 17×25-foot flag)—more than most Baltimoreans of the time earned in a year.

THE PERILOUS FIGHT

For more than a year, the huge flag flew proudly over the fort.

On September 12, 1814, British forces advanced on Baltimore, 5,000 strong and supported by a fleet of 19 ships. By the morning of the 13th, they had battled their way to Fort McHenry. In a heavy rain, the fort was bombarded for 25 hours. The British attack was turned away, the flag continued to fly, and the rest is history.

Francis Scott Key, lawyer and erstwhile poet, was a prisoner aboard a British ship during the Battle of Baltimore and the shelling of Fort McHenry. When the Sun rose, the waving flag assured Key that the fort still stood, and he started composing a poem, "Defence of Fort M'Henry":

 On August 19, 1813, the giant flag was presented to the soldiers at Fort McHenry.

O! say can you see, by the dawn's early light,
What so proudly we hail'd at the twilight's last gleaming,
Whose broad stripes and bright stars through the perilous fight,
O'er the ramparts we watch'd were so gallantly streaming?

Key's poem was set to music borrowed from a song called "To Anacreon in Heaven," composed by John Stafford Smith. "The Star-Spangled Banner" became the national anthem of the United States in 1931.

As it turned out, the banner spangled with stars, as rendered by Pickersgill, would be the only official United States flag to sport 15 stripes. Realizing that adding both stripes and stars for each

FRANCIS SCOTT KEY WAS MOVED TO WRITE "DEFENCE OF FORT M'HENRY" AFTER SEEING THE FLAG FLYING OVER THE FORT.

state admitted to the Union would soon prove unwieldy, Congress passed a law on April 4, 1818, mandating that the U.S. flag be "Thirteen horizontal stripes, alternate red and white; that the union be twenty stars, white in a blue field.... That on the admission of every new state into the Union, one star be added to the union of the flag; and that such addition shall take effect on the fourth day of July then next succeeding such admission."

PROUDLY WE HAIL

Pickersgill's fabled flag remained in Armistead's family for many years. Over time, little pieces and cuttings, including one of the original stars, were given as gifts and mementos. Repair efforts reduced the flag's dimensions to 30×34 feet. In 1912, the flag was donated to the Smithsonian Institution, where it remains on permanent display.

In her later years, Pickersgill gave much of her time to philanthropy. From 1828 to 1851, she served as president of the Impartial Female Humane Society, a charitable organization that helped needy families and aged women.

Today, her legacy is celebrated at The Star-Spangled Banner Flag House (flaghouse.org), which was purchased by the city of Baltimore in 1927 and established as a museum by the Star-Spangled Banner Flag House Association. It is located on the corner of East Pratt and Albemarle streets and was Pickersgill's home from 1807 to 1857. Designated a National Historic Landmark in 1969, its collections preserve the history of Pickersgill and her flag. The house "where inspiration was sewn" also preserves the legacy of the diverse lives of many others who called it home. ■

Joe Bills pledges allegiance to historical accuracy as associate editor of *The Old Farmer's Almanac*.

> **STAY IN THERE AND KEEP SWINGING.**
> –Joe DiMaggio, American baseball player (1914–99)

THE
SWINGINGEST

SPORTS

THINK. DON'T JUST SWING.... THINK.
–Ted Williams,
American baseball
player (1918–2002)

SUMMER OF ALL TIME

HOW THE
1941 BASEBALL
SEASON BECAME
A METAPHOR
FOR TRIUMPHING
OVER THE ODDS

BY MEL ALLEN

Photos: Culver Pictures/SuperStock

SPORTS

"JOE" DI MAGGIO

JOE DIMAGGIO
Centerfielder,
New York Yankees

AGE: 26
GAMES PLAYED: 139
BATTING AVERAGE: .357
HITS: 193
RUNS: 122
HOME RUNS: 30
RUNS BATTED IN: 125*
TOTAL BASES: 348*
WALKS: 76
STRIKEOUTS: 13
ON BASE PERCENTAGE: .440
SLUGGING PERCENTAGE: .643
HIT STREAK: 56 games*
GAMES WITH MULTIPLE HITS: 52
MVP FINISH: 1st
TEAM FINISH: 101-53 (1st in American League, won World Series)

*Led American League

Yankee Stadium, May 15, 1941. A muggy Thursday afternoon. Scarcely 9,000 people in the stands. The New York Yankees and their star centerfielder, Joe DiMaggio, are both in a miserable slump. On this day, the Chicago White Sox thump the Yankees 13 to 1, and DiMaggio's lone first-inning single to centerfield garners no more interest than a passing cloud.

A game that would have long since vanished from memory is always mentioned when historians recall the most unforgettable baseball season of all time. Here began DiMaggio's streak of hitting safely in 56 straight games, a feat called the "greatest individual achievement in baseball history."

That same summer, the lanky Boston Red Sox hitter Ted Williams would also chase a baseball feat: a season with a .400 batting average.

America, meanwhile, was on edge. The day after DiMaggio's then unremarkable base hit brought more foreboding news of Germany's assault on Europe. The summer of 1941 provided daily baseball drama, a relief from war anxiety, as people rushed to newspapers and radios to find out: Did Joe get a hit? How about Ted?

For 5 months, their intensity and passion took hold of an entire country, providing a temporary distraction from mounting fears of war. Eighty-five years later, their singular accomplishments have never been equaled.

JOE AND TED

Joe DiMaggio and Ted Williams were the defining players of their era: DiMaggio played for the perennial champions, the Yankees; Williams for the perennial not-quite-good-enough Red Sox. They had much in common. DiMaggio's parents came from Sicily. Williams' maternal grandparents emigrated from Mexico. As a boy, DiMaggio played for hours on the San Francisco sandlots, using broken oars from his father's fishing boat as bats. Growing up in San Diego, Williams would practice "until the blisters bled." His stated goal in life was to have people say, "There goes the greatest hitter that ever lived."

SPORTS

And yet, they could not have been more different. DiMaggio was even-tempered, unruffled—regardless of circumstances. Williams was brash, tempestuous, and easily rankled. DiMaggio dressed impeccably. Williams hated ties. DiMaggio smoked constantly. Williams loathed the smell. DiMaggio was the most graceful and talented of centerfielders; Williams played left field, it was said, only as a way to quicken his next turn at bat. That summer, DiMaggio was 26, Williams 22 (he would turn 23 on August 30). DiMaggio was known as the most dangerous hitter in baseball, with one possible exception: the tall, skinny Williams.

"TED" WILLIAMS

56 IN A ROW

Consider the odds: A batter faces a pitcher and eight fielders. Most likely, they'll have four at bats in a game. One may be a walk. Talented fielders snatch away possible hits. What supernatural focus is needed to ignore the building pressure of knowing a nation's eyes are waiting for each at bat, wondering, *will he keep the streak alive and get one more hit?*

In 1941, there weren't live radio broadcasts of Yankees' games. Fans tuned in later to station WINS to listen to an announcer recreate the game from a box score, improvising to make the action come alive.

When DiMaggio hit in 10 straight games, few noticed. Early in a season, batters get hot all the time, and Williams was burning up the league. From mid-May to early June, he defined hot streak, batting a scorching .489, though the attention of baseball fans was elsewhere. On May 27, the day DiMaggio's streak reached 12, President Franklin Roosevelt broadcast a fireside chat heard by an estimated 65 million Americans. Baseball games were halted so that fans could listen over loudspeakers about threats posed by Germany. Roosevelt used charged words: "We must not be defeated by the fear of the very danger which we are preparing to resist."

By game 18, sportswriters took note. In mid-June, when game 29 tied a team record, radio news broadcasters spoke about the still-distant war, then added,

TED WILLIAMS

Leftfielder,
Boston Red Sox

AGE: 22

GAMES PLAYED: 143

BATTING AVERAGE: .406*

HITS: 185

RUNS: 135*

HOME RUNS: 37*

RUNS BATTED IN: 120

TOTAL BASES: 335

WALKS: 147*

STRIKEOUTS: 27

ON BASE
PERCENTAGE: .553*

SLUGGING
PERCENTAGE: .735*

HIT STREAK: 23 games

GAMES WITH
MULTIPLE HITS: 50

MVP FINISH: 2nd

TEAM FINISH: 84-70
(2nd in American League,
missed postseason)

*Led American League

On July 16, 1941, DiMaggio went 3-for-4 and extended his hit streak to 56 consecutive games.

"Joe DiMaggio's hitting streak continues." After going hitless in his first two at bats, DiMaggio broke the team record when his ground ball in the seventh hit a pebble and took a last-second hop off the shortstop's shoulder. The official scorer debated: hit or error? He asked a fellow sportswriter: Hit.

So the streak continued, and people cheered no matter where they lived or who they rooted for. The Yankee clubhouse filled with good-luck charms from around the country. Could "Joltin' Joe" overtake George Sisler's 1922 American League record of 41 games? Could he pass "Wee Willie" Keeler's major league record of 44 that had stood since 1897? This was no longer just about baseball. DiMaggio's quest became a national obsession of hope.

Players, too, were caught up in the chase. The left-field scoreboard operator of Fenway Park would shout to Williams as soon as he learned that DiMaggio had again hit safely. Then Williams would relay the news to Dom, DiMaggio's brother, the Red Sox centerfielder. When the *New York Daily News* asked Sisler what his own streak had been like, "You can't imagine the strain," he said. "You try to forget it, but it can't be done."

June 29. A Sunday afternoon doubleheader against the Senators in Washington, D.C. One game away from tying Sisler. DiMaggio was hitless until the sixth inning. Then, a swing, double to left-center. One more hit, one more game, and the American League record would be his. Or would it?

GOING BATTY

Between games, a thief sneaked into the Yankee dugout and made off with "Betsy Ann," DiMaggio's favorite bat. When DiMaggio realized what had happened, he was frantic. He was hit-

Photo: Facebook

SPORTS

less in the second game, down to a final at bat. During the season, he had given a bat to a teammate who now offered it back; he told DiMaggio it held his hit. It did, a solid single.

Keeler's mark was now just ahead. Newspapers appealed for the thief to return Betsy Ann. A package arrived at the stadium.

Game 45. DiMaggio hits a line drive home run at Yankee Stadium. The major league record was his. Now everyone watched and held their breath as he chased time and history, which by July 17, had reached 56 games.

Cleveland's League Park. A rare night game. Over 67,000 fans in attendance. It had rained, and the footing around home plate was soft. Ken Keltner, the Indians stellar third baseman, remembered a game 6 weeks earlier. DiMaggio had scorched a ball down the third base line that deflected off his glove. On this night, he played deeper than ever before, several steps back and closer to the foul line.

DiMaggio's first at bat sent a liner to Keltner's right. He lunged and, from behind third base, threw a laser that caught DiMaggio by half a step. A fourth inning walk. In the seventh, DiMaggio laced another sharp grounder headed for left field. Keltner, still playing abnormally deep, made the out. On his final chance, DiMaggio hit a hard grounder to the shortstop. The crowd quieted. They were witnessing the end of something that transcended sport.

Sportswriters called it one of the most memorable baseball games ever played. Newspapers the next day ran front-page photos of the two Indians pitchers and of Keltner, as if, one writer wrote, "they had assassinated a king." *(continued)*

On September 28, 1941, Williams entered the final day of the 1941 season with a .39955 batting average. He went 6-for-8 in a double-header and finished with a .406 average.

Photo: Yesterday in Baseball/Facebook

SPORTS

DiMaggio once said that the wet dirt at home plate had caused him to lose a half step, and that had made the difference, preventing Americans from being riveted for several more weeks. The next day, he began a new streak of 16 games.

A BATTER HAS GOT TO BE LOOSE

As DiMaggio's streak ended, a second drama was still playing out, another improbable quest—could Williams hit .400?

If DiMaggio was the artist at the plate, Williams studied pitchers with the eye of a scientist. He paid obsessive attention to his bats. Unlike DiMaggio's preference for heavier lumber, Williams wanted his whips light. He would sand them to the bone and then weigh them on delicate scales. "I treated them like babies," he said. A bat company executive once put six bats on a bed, all exactly the same weight except one, which was a half-ounce heavier. With his eyes closed, Williams picked it out. Eddie Collins, Hall of Fame second baseman who was the Boston Red Sox general manager, said about his star player in 1941, "All Ted has ever lived for is his next turn at bat."

For each of the first 23 games of DiMaggio's streak, Williams had a hit, too, as though they had forged a pact of brilliance.

Teammates joked that Williams was rarely without a bat in his hands or talking or thinking about hitting. Once, in a hotel room, he took practice swings, hit a bedpost, collapsed the bed, and knocked his shocked roommate to the floor. What his roommate remembered was not an apology but Williams gushing, "Boy, what power!" Indeed, unlike batters in previous decades who had hit .400, none hit for power; Williams' 37 home runs that season led both leagues. Of his 521 career home runs (despite losing nearly five seasons serving as a Marine pilot in two wars), none captured the country's imagination as the one he hit on July 8, 1941.

The All-Star game was in Detroit. Bottom of the ninth. The American League trailed 5–4. With two outs and two men on base, Williams faced Claude Passeau of the Chicago Cubs. In what has been described as "the biggest hit in All-Star game history," and what Williams called "the most thrilling hit of my life," he launched a home run. As he circled the bases, he was jumping and laughing. DiMaggio waited for him at home plate to join teammates in carrying him off the field.

After the all-star game, Williams struggled and saw his average dip below .400 for the first time since May 24. But it didn't last. By July 26, Williams once again was above .400, and it remained that way through the rest of the season. Fans in all of the stadiums

TALE OF THE TAPE

The 1941 season was one for the ages with Joe DiMaggio's record-setting 56-game hitting streak and Ted Williams's .406 batting average, making him the last player in MLB history to surpass .400. Their quests captivated the country.

While the two enjoyed great success at the plate, neither led the American League in hits that season; that distinction belongs to Cecil Travis of the Washington Nationals, with 218.

IT ALL HAPPENED ONE SUMMER—WHEN AMERICA NEEDED TO BELIEVE IN HEROES.

he played booed their own pitcher if he walked Williams and denied him a chance to hit. But then he started slumping. From .411 on September 14, his average dropped nearly a point a day until the last weekend.

On September 28, the last day of the regular season, Williams' batting average was .39955. Joe Cronin, the Red Sox manager, suggested that if he sat out the doubleheader against the Philadelphia Athletics—games that had no impact since the Yankees had already clinched the pennant—nobody would criticize. The average in the record books would read an even .400. Williams later wrote of the encounter, "I told Cronin I didn't want that. If I couldn't hit .400 all the way I didn't deserve it."

The prior night, he walked the Philadelphia streets for hours, waiting for dawn. On a cold, wet afternoon, he stood at the plate. The A's catcher said, "I wish you all the luck in the world, but we're not giving you a damn thing." The home plate umpire called time, dusted off the plate, and offered a few words: "To hit .400, a batter has got to be loose."

That day, Williams hit four singles, a double, and a home run. By the time game two was in the books, Williams's average stood at .406.

A few months later, war came to America. DiMaggio later served in California and Hawaii. Williams was a combat fighter pilot in the Pacific. It is unlikely their seasons will ever be matched. And it all happened one summer—when America needed to believe in heroes. ■

Mel Allen, retired editor of *Yankee Magazine*, swings for the fences every time he tells a baseball story.

AMUSEMENT

The Fish Scales of Justice

Many a piscine-provoked commotion has reached the U.S. Supreme Court over the years. Controversies involving fish have forced the court to confront fundamental legal issues, such as whether a red grouper counts as a "tangible object."

BY JAY WEXLER • ILLUSTRATIONS BY TIM ROBINSON

A Super Grouper Loophole

The 2015 *Yates v. United States* case posed this fishy question. When commercial fisherman John Yates threw overboard 72 undersized red groupers to avoid being fined for not complying with conservation regulations, the feds charged him with violating the Sarbanes-Oxley Act, which prohibits the cover-up of "any record, document, or tangible object" with the intent to obstruct legal investigation. The law was aimed at accounting fraud and corporate document shredding subsequent to the 2002 Enron scandal.

In the decision authored by Justice Ruth Bader Ginsburg, the court ruled against the government, finding that although a grouper "is no doubt an object that is tangible," it was not a "tangible object" because, well, this was a statute about accountants, not fish. Justice Samuel Alito noted that the phrase "tangible object" should be read as referring only to things similar to other words in the statute and "who wouldn't raise an eyebrow if a neighbor, when asked to identify something similar to a 'record' or 'document,' said 'crocodile'?"

Justice Elena Kagan was unconvinced and, in the dissent, suggested that a more appropriate question to ask a neighbor might be, "Do you think a fish (or, if the concurrence prefers, a crocodile) is a 'tangible object'? As to that query, 'who wouldn't raise an eyebrow' if the neighbor said 'no'?" For Kagan, the fact that a "fish is, of course, a discrete thing that possesses physical form" was sufficient to resolve the case. Her citation for that legal conclusion? "See generally Dr. Seuss, *One Fish Two Fish Red Fish Blue Fish* (1960)."

AMUSEMENT

DISCRIMINATION DECISION

For a weightier fish decision, cast back to 1948 and *Takahashi v. Fish and Game Commission*. Torao Takahashi, born near Tokyo in 1888, immigrated to the West Coast of the United States in 1907. He spent decades as a commercial fisherman before the U.S. Coast Guard arrested him in December of 1941 for being Japanese. The government's reaction to the bombing of Pearl Harbor resulted in the relocation of more than 100,000 people of Japanese descent, and Takahashi was imprisoned at the Manzanar internment camp in California until 1945.

While he was incarcerated, California passed a law (signed by its then-governor, the future Chief Justice Earl Warren) prohibiting those "ineligible to citizenship" from obtaining a fishing license. Federal law made Japanese people ineligible for citizenship, so Takahashi could not renew his license. He sued, claiming that California's law violated the federal Constitution's guarantee of equal protection of the laws.

At the Supreme Court, Dean Acheson (on a brief interlude between stints as President Truman's foreign policy advisor and his Secretary of State) agreed to present Takahashi's case for free. The court held 7–2 for the fisherman, finding that California had violated his equal protection rights and that this violation was not justified as a "fish conservation measure." The majority opinion stopped short of condemning the law for being motivated by racial antagonism.

(continued)

Torao Takahashi

Dean Acheson

AMUSEMENT

DID MAINE TAKE THE BAIT?

What happened in the 1986 *Maine v. Taylor* minnow baitfish case about whether Maine could ban the import of the golden shiner, a popular baitfish? The relevant constitutional provision is the "commerce clause," which gives Congress the authority to regulate interstate commerce. Though the clause is silent on states' powers, the court has always read the "dormant" part of the clause as implicitly restricting the authority of states to interfere with interstate commerce—for example, by discriminating against out-of-state goods to protect local businesses. The idea is that a unified national economy is better than 50 states competing against each other; the latter approach had been tried under the Articles of Confederation and was a disaster. For instance, using the dormant commerce clause, the court struck down an Oklahoma law prohibiting the export of minnows to Texas.

The Maine case, however, came out differently. Maine's justification for banning the import of golden shiners was that out-of-state baitfish could contain parasites, which would threaten Maine's wild fish populations, and there was no way to screen imported baitfish. Under these extraordinary circumstances, the court held that Maine could discriminate against out-of-state baitfish, thus creating what every constitutional law professor calls the "Maine baitfish" exception to the dormant commerce clause. Not everyone thought the result was correct, including Justice John Paul Stevens, whose dissent reasoned that "there is something fishy about this case."

AMUSEMENT

Regulatory Sea Change

The court's 2023–24 term involved perhaps the most far-reaching fish-based case in U.S. history.

Congress routinely uses statutes to authorize agencies to make decisions about everything from airplane safety to food labeling. Sometimes statutes can be ambiguous—in that case, who gets to interpret them, the agency or the courts? In a 1984 case, *Chevron U.S.A. Inc. v. Natural Resources Defense Council, Inc.*, the court said agencies do. Forty years later, the court changed its mind.

Loper Bright Enterprises, Inc. v. Raimondo involved a statute intended to protect fishery resources. One of the statute's provisions said that in some situations, commercial fishing boats must take on objective observers to make sure they aren't overfishing, but it was ambiguous about who would pay for the observer—the boat or the government.

Several herring businesses fishing in the Atlantic Ocean were required by the Commerce Department to pay for their observers under that agency's reading of the statute. The herring fishers sued, arguing that the statute required the government to pay. The agency responded that since the statute was unclear, according to the *Chevron* case, it had the authority to interpret what it meant. The court overruled *Chevron* and held that courts—not agencies—decide what laws mean. The court threw the case back into the judicial ocean for the lower courts to decide who must pay for the observers. The entire federal government will feel the waves of this decision for years to come.

Will more cases involving fish continue to surface at the court? Without a doubt. The court heard a case in the fall of 2024 challenging an agency's approval of a new railway line in Utah despite claims that the project will harm the Colorado pikeminnow, razorback sucker, humpback chub, and bonytail chub in the Colorado River Basin. Stay tuned—and keep your line in the water. ■

Jay Wexler is a professor at Boston University School of Law, a former law clerk for Justice Ruth Bader Ginsburg, and the author of seven books, including *The Odd Clauses: Understanding the Constitution Through Ten of its Most Curious Provisions* (Beacon Press, 2011).

FISHING

GET **KNOTTY**
The right knots reel-y do catch more fish

BY JEFF HELSDON

A knot is the only thing connecting an angler's line to a hook or lure. A good knot will hold as a fish is being reeled in, while an improperly tied knot could let go—and take your catch with it.

Many anglers do not believe monofilament line should be moistened before the final tightening. This is a topic of some debate, but the largest monofilament manufacturer states that wetting the line improves lubrication and ensures a stronger knot when tightened.

One crucial step that should be completed when tying any line is tugging on the line after the knot is tied to ensure it will hold. Do this every time, as it will quickly show any flaws in the knot.

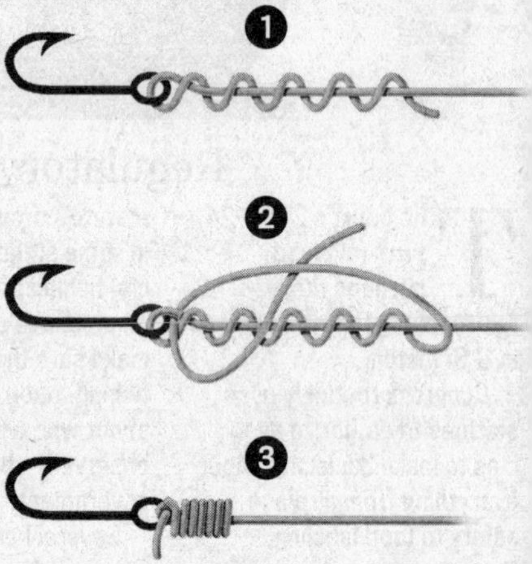

IN A CLINCH

Most anglers know the clinch knot; an extra step makes it the **improved clinch knot.** This is the most commonly used, general-purpose knot for tying a hook, lure, or swivel to a line.

1. Pass the fishing line through the hook or lure eye, leaving 4 to 6 inches of tag line. Wrap the tag end around the main line four or more times. With a thinner diameter line, more twists make a stronger knot.
2. Pass the tag end through the loop formed next to the eye and through the loop created by this step.
3. Moisten, tighten, and cut the tag end.

IMPROVED CLINCH KNOT

WHEN YOU REACH THE END OF YOUR ROPE, TIE A KNOT AND HANG ON.
–Franklin Roosevelt, 32nd U.S. president (1882–1945)

Illustration: Rob Schuster

HOOK, LINE, AND SINKER

The **Palomar knot** is best with braided or monofilament lines and is often used for dropshotting, a live or artificial bait technique where the sinker is at the bottom of the line instead of above it. This knot isn't as useful with large lures as the lure must pass through the loop.

1. Double the line and pass 4 to 6 inches of it through the hook or lure eye. For hooks with small eyes, the line can be passed through once and then back through to create the same result.

2. The tag end on the other side of the eye should be 4 to 6 inches long as well.

3-4. Tie an overhand knot with the loop created while holding onto the tag end so it doesn't slip back through the eye. The hook or lure should now be hanging at the bottom.

5. Pass the hook or lure through the loop at the end of the knot.

6. Tighten while pulling on both the tag end and main line. As the knot tightens, ensure it gathers above the eye. Lubricating the knot at this point helps with monofilament lines. Cut the tag end.

BLOOD KNOT

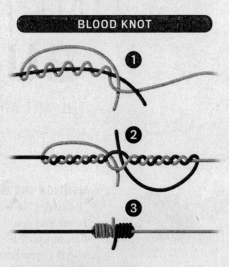

PALOMAR KNOT

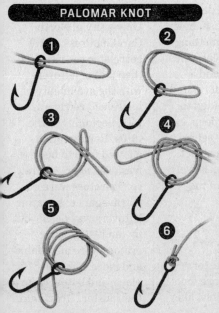

MAKING ENDS MEET

Anglers sometimes need to tie one piece of fishing line to another—to join a leader to a main line or, in an emergency, to cut out a stretch of tangled line and retrieve a lure. A **blood knot** joins two lines.

1. Overlap the two lines to be tied together. Wrap the first line around the second one five times. Then, pass the tag end through the loop in front of where the wrap starts.

2. Wrap the second line around the first one five times and pass the tag end through the same loop.

3. Pull on the tag ends gently, and the knot will tighten on itself. Cut the tag ends. ∎

Jeff Helsdon ties knots at the end of his line while fishing for various species in bodies of water across North America, including Lake Erie.

Illustrations: Rob Schuster

FOOD

UNFINISHED BUSINESS

THE ART AND SCIENCE OF LEFTOVERS

BY SARAH PERREAULT

Leftovers make you feel good twice. First, when you put it away, you feel thrifty and intelligent: "I'm saving food!" Then, a month later, when blue hair is growing out of the ham, and you throw it away, you feel really intelligent: "I'm saving my life!"

—GEORGE CARLIN, AMERICAN COMEDIAN (1937–2008)

MENTION THE WORD "leftovers" in a crowded room and you'll soon find out how people feel about them: how long they're good for, what tastes better a day later than it does fresh, how you know if something is still okay to eat, rules for reheating, and a smorgasbord of related topics. We decided to reach into the deep recesses of the refrigerator to deconstruct the "love 'em or leave 'em" pickings of the food world.

THE LUXURY OF LEFTOVERS

While our ancestors had ways to store food and keep it edible, like drying, salting, and fermenting, the advent of home refrigeration is the origin story of modern leftovers. Helen Zoe Veit, author of *Modern Food, Moral Food* (The University of North Carolina Press, 2013), correlates the rise (and then fall) of leftovers with the availability of household refrigerators, beginning in the 1910s. Refrigeration allowed food to be kept fresher longer. At first, refrigerators were an extravagance, so eating leftovers was posh—but by the 1940s, refrigerators were affordable and more commonplace, and leftovers lost their luster. *(continued)*

Photos: above, Liudmila Chernetska/Getty Images; opposite, halbergman/Getty Images

FOOD

I was planning on taking leftovers home from the party. All my plans were foiled.

—ANONYMOUS

FOOD

The leftovers were in the refrigerator for so long I claimed them as dependents.

—ANONYMOUS

LEFTOVERS

Thanksgiving day
has come and gone,
But remnants of it
still live on.
In turkey pie and
turkey melts,
To cranberry sauce
covering smelts.
I thought the baby
might be spared,
But gravy coats his
hands and hair.
The rolls are now
as hard as bricks,
The yams showed up
served on sticks.
I understand the
turkey wings,
Is potato pudding
really a thing?
My hope is that by
Christmas break,
To not be eating
stuffing cakes.
'Tis no wonder we've
all gone placid,
Off to the store for
more antacid!

—S. P.

During the Great Depression, eating and using leftovers was a necessity. Food rationing and scarcity required cooks to get creative and use whatever wasn't eaten to make more meals. Stale bread could be turned into bread crumbs and muffins repurposed into bread pudding; potatoes were shredded into hash browns, baked into rolls and breads, and used to top savory meat pies; cooked vegetables were perfect for making hash or cream-of-anything soup; leftover meat—beef, chicken, ham—easily became crispy croquettes or meat on toast plus gravy; and almost anything could be combined into a choose-your-own-adventure casserole.

THOSE IN FAVOR

Saving money and reducing food waste are two top reasons people eat leftovers. A MITRE-Gallup survey showed households that throw away leftovers because no one wants to eat them waste approximately 12 cups of food per week. According to Feeding America, we waste more than $408 billion yearly on uneaten food. The average American family of four throws out $1,600 a year in produce alone.

Leftover enthusiasts also mention the genius of convenience—leftovers in the fridge mean not having to spend time preparing another meal or thinking about what to cook. Plus, you are not limited to the reheat-and-eat routine; you can transform leftovers into a different meal, much like clever Depression-era cooks. Add cooked veggies to soups; use meats and cheeses in melty grilled sandwiches; and fill stuffed peppers with leftover rice, or—for the adventurous—turn it into delectable arancini.

Not all grub is meant for leftovers; dressed salads, for instance, or guacamole. Even a leftover staple like pasta has its weaknesses—pair it with a creamy sauce and it just won't hold up.

THOSE OPPOSED

Two words: food poisoning. A common

Photo: Michael Burrell/Getty Images

reason why people dislike leftovers comes down to having gotten sick from consuming them, which certainly qualifies as a legitimate turn-off. It is vital to store and reheat leftovers properly. Food should be stored in the refrigerator or freezer within 2 hours of preparation.

Another cause for throwing shade on leftovers is a dislike of monotony. Some of us cannot fathom eating the same food for more than a day. Adam Wenzel, associate professor of psychology at Saint Anselm College in New Hampshire, explains, "We seem to be 'wired' to want variety in our diets." So those who find leftovers lacking can chalk it up to human biology.

Taste and texture are also cited as grounds for not liking leftovers. The leftover lamenters complain that the food just isn't the same the next day—which is

(continued on page 189)

THE LONG AND SHORT OF LEFTOVERS

For those not willing to take a chance, the USDA provides guidelines for refrigerated leftovers:

- **GOOD FOR 1 TO 2 DAYS:** Cooked chicken breasts, fish and shellfish, lamb chops, and stuffed pork
- **GOOD FOR 3 TO 4 DAYS:** Cooked meat pieces, patties, and nuggets; casseroles; gravy; broth; soups; stews; egg dishes; egg, chicken, tuna, ham, and pasta salads
- **GOOD FOR 7 DAYS:** Cooked whole ham, hard-cooked eggs

TOP SIX EAT AND REPEAT

According to a recent poll, these are the best foods to eat as leftovers.

1. SOUP
2. PIZZA
3. MEAT
4. PASTA
5. RICE
6. VEGETABLES

Photos: Pixabay

TURKEY CROQUETTES

Croquettes are a hodgepodge of leftover ingredients rolled in crumbs of some type. According to the 1877 cookery manual *Kettner's Book of the Table*, "When the croquette is finished differently—that is, when, instead of being dipped in egg and rolled in breadcrumb, it is wrapped in a thin puff paste—it is called a *Rissole*; and when it is wrapped in a thin sheet of veal udder or of bacon fat, it is called a *Kromeski*."

FILLING:
- 2 tablespoons butter
- 2 tablespoons all-purpose flour
- ½ cup milk
- 2 cups leftover finely chopped turkey
- 2 cups leftover mashed potatoes or stuffing
- salt and freshly ground black pepper, to taste

BREADING:
- 1 cup all-purpose flour
- ¼ teaspoon garlic powder
- ¼ teaspoon onion powder
- 2 eggs
- 1 cup bread crumbs or finely crushed cereal such as cornflakes
- ½ cup oil of choice, for frying

- *For filling:* In a saucepan over medium heat, melt butter. Add flour and stir continuously for 1 to 2 minutes, or until mixture bubbles. Do not allow it to brown. Slowly pour in milk, while continuously stirring. When mixture thickens, remove from heat and allow to cool slightly.
- In a bowl, combine turkey, potatoes, salt and pepper, and the cooled white sauce. Place mixture in the refrigerator for at least 1 hour to set.
- Once mixture has set, measure out ¼-cup portions and shape into domes.
- *For breading:* In a bowl, combine flour, garlic powder, and onion powder.
- In a separate bowl, add eggs and whisk with a splash of water.
- In another bowl, add bread crumbs.
- Preheat oven to 350°F.
- In a skillet over medium-high heat, warm oil.
- Dredge turkey mix portions first in flour mixture, then egg, then bread crumbs. Place in skillet, cooking on all sides until lightly browned. Cook in batches; do not overcrowd the skillet. Once browned, place on baking sheets. Bake for 15 to 20 minutes. Allow to cool for 5 minutes on baking sheets, then serve.

Makes 4 servings.

FOOD

true—though there are some foods leftover lovers claim are *always* better the next day, like curries, soups, and stews, to name a few.

TO EAT OR NOT TO EAT

Many of us will use our senses to inspect leftovers to determine if they are fit to cross our palates again. How does it look? If your meatloaf went from brown to gray, trash it. If the cantaloupe has a slimy film, toss it on the compost pile.

If the item passes the look test, the next step is the sniff test. Here's the problem: Many microbes that cause food-borne illnesses have no odor. So even if that 6-day-old turkey leg looks and smells satisfactory, it may not be. When in doubt, throw it out!

Whether you are trying to save money, fear getting sick, or believe some foods taste better a day or two after they're first served, everyone has their stance on leftovers. ■

When it comes to leftovers, **Sarah Perreault**, managing editor of *The Old Farmer's Almanac*, abides by the look-and-sniff test and prefers a bit of age on her curries and Bolognese.

SAVORY SCRAPS OF HISTORY

Stashing your leftovers from dinner is hardly a new concept.

Humans have been storing food for 200,000 to 400,000 years, new research suggests. A bit like how we stow our food in a storage container, early humans stored marrow-rich deer bones for several weeks, extracting the marrow once the bones dried out.

Flatbread estimated to be around 70,000 years old claims the title of world's oldest leftover. The remnants were discovered in a cave about 500 miles north of Baghdad, Iraq.

FOOD

(continued from page 57)

FIRST PRIZE: $300
FRESH TOMATO BACON JAM
Spread on sandwiches, dress up eggs, or add to a charcuterie board.

½ pound bacon
2 cups chopped sweet onions
2 cups peeled and chopped heirloom tomatoes *
3 cups peeled and chopped plum tomatoes
¾ teaspoon smoked paprika
¾ teaspoon sea salt
½ cup brown sugar
⅓ cup maple syrup
3 tablespoons balsamic vinegar

■ Preheat oven to 400°F.

■ Slice bacon in half and arrange on a baking sheet. Bake for 10 to 15 minutes, or until cooked but not crispy.

■ Remove bacon, cut slices in half, and place in a large skillet. Cook for several minutes over medium heat to render fat from bacon. Add onions and continue cooking for 7 minutes, stirring often. Add tomatoes, paprika, salt, brown sugar, and maple syrup. Cook for 25 minutes, stirring frequently. When liquid has reduced, add balsamic vinegar and stir.

■ In a food processor, pulse warm jam several times to chop the bacon.
Makes 4 cups.
–Donna-Marie Ryan, Topsfield, Massachusetts

* *Peeling Tip:* Cut an x into the bottom of a tomato. Submerge it in boiling water for 30 seconds, then immediately submerge it in cold water. Remove from water; the skin will peel away easily.

SECOND PRIZE: $200
GRAMPS' TOMATO TURKEY BURGERS
SEASONING:
1 tablespoon kosher salt
4 teaspoons dried sage
4 teaspoons paprika
2 teaspoons smoked paprika
2 teaspoons freshly ground black pepper
2 teaspoons dried marjoram
1 teaspoon dried thyme

BURGERS:
2 cloves garlic, finely diced
1 ounce cremini (aka baby bella) mushrooms, stemmed and finely diced
1 stalk celery, finely diced
½ onion, finely diced
½ sweet apple, peeled, seeded, and finely diced
2 pounds 85% lean ground turkey
¼ cup sun-dried tomatoes in oil, finely chopped
¼ cup panko bread crumbs
2 tablespoons grated Parmesan cheese
6 slices American cheese
¼ cup ketchup
¼ cup mayonnaise
½ teaspoon Sriracha
6 hamburger buns
tomato slices and bread and butter pickles, for serving

■ Preheat oven to 375°F. Line a baking sheet with parchment paper.

■ *For seasoning:* In a bowl, combine all seasoning ingredients, then divide into two equal parts. Set aside.

■ *For burgers:* In a cast iron or nonstick skillet over medium heat, cook garlic, mushrooms, celery, onions, and apples for 10 minutes, or until onions begin to soften. Remove to a bowl.

■ To the bowl, add ground turkey, sun-dried tomatoes, bread crumbs, Parmesan, and half of the seasoning, and mix thoroughly. Form meat into 6 patties, sprinkle both sides with remaining seasoning, and place on prepared baking sheet. Cook for 15 minutes, or until burgers register an internal temperature of 165°F on a meat thermometer.

■ Remove from oven, add cheese, then return to oven until cheese is melted. Remove from oven and tent with foil for 5 minutes.

■ In a bowl, combine ketchup, mayonnaise, and Sriracha.

■ Place burgers on buns, spread with ketchup mixture, and top with tomatoes and pickles.

Makes 6 servings.

–Paul VanSavage, Binghamton, New York

THIRD PRIZE: $100
ZESTY TOMATO-BASIL ICE CREAM

2 cans (10 ounces each) diced tomatoes with green chilies
¼ cup tomato paste
3 eggs
2 egg yolks
1½ cups sugar
3 cups heavy whipping cream
½ cup milk
1½ tablespoons vanilla extract
2 teaspoons dried basil
½ teaspoon cayenne pepper, or to taste

■ Into a blender, add tomatoes with chilies and tomato paste. Blend well.

■ In a bowl, whisk together eggs and egg yolks. Add sugar and whisk to combine.

■ In a 3-quart saucepan over medium-high heat, bring heavy cream and milk to a boil. Remove from heat. Slowly add 3 tablespoons of hot cream mixture to egg mixture to temper it, whisking to combine. Slowly add the remaining cream mixture, continuing to whisk until blended. Add tomato mixture, vanilla, basil, and cayenne, and mix to thoroughly combine.

■ Cover and place in the refrigerator for 2 hours to chill.

■ Add mixture to an ice cream maker and churn according to manufacturer's directions.

■ Store leftovers in the freezer.

Makes 2 quarts.

–Ronna Farley, Rockville, Maryland

HONORABLE MENTION
TRIPLE TOMATO SALAD WITH CREAMY BALSAMIC DRESSING

SALAD:
1 large green tomato, cored, quartered, and thinly sliced
1 large red tomato, cored, quartered, and thinly sliced
¼ cup finely diced red onion
¼ cup julienned sun-dried tomatoes in oil
¼ cup finely diced English cucumber
2 tablespoons chopped fresh parsley

DRESSING:
3 tablespoons olive oil
2 tablespoons balsamic vinegar
2 tablespoons mayonnaise
2 teaspoons stone-ground brown mustard
1 teaspoon honey
¼ teaspoon kosher salt
¼ teaspoon freshly ground black pepper
¼ teaspoon garlic powder
¼ teaspoon onion powder

■ *For salad:* In a bowl, toss together all salad ingredients. Set aside.

■ *For dressing:* In a bowl, whisk together all dressing ingredients.

■ Drizzle dressing over salad right before serving. Toss lightly to mix.

Makes 4 to 6 servings.

–Aysha Schurman, Ammon, Idaho ■

> I WAS REGALED HERE WITH THE JUICE OF THE MAPLE; THIS IS THE SEASON OF ITS FLOWING. IT IS EXTREMELY DELICIOUS, HAS A MOST PLEASING COOLNESS, AND IS EXCEEDINGLY WHOLESOME.
>
> —Pierre-François-Xavier de Charlevoix, French historian (1682-1781)

SECRETS OF THE SUGAR BUSH

HOW SWEET IT IS TO BE A SUGAR MAPLE TREE

BY KAREN DAVIDSON

Centuries ago, the Anishinaabe peoples marked the new season under the cold glow of a March Sugar Moon, celebrating by night and gathering maple sap by day. These First Nation peoples were the original inhabitants of the hardwood forests straddling southeastern Canada and the northeastern United States, a region comprising parts of Ontario and Quebec in Canada and New Hampshire, Vermont, and parts of Maine, New York, and northern Massachusetts in the U.S. In these forests, believed to be sacred by the Anishinaabe, the sugar maple (*Acer saccharum*) is a keystone species.

A stand of sugar maples tapped for sap is known as a sugar bush. Around the Great Lakes, enterprising Anishinaabe camped in the sugar bush, notching sugar maples in early spring and gathering the clear liquid in birchbark vessels for transfer to moose skin vats. Historians who read the papers of fur trader Alexander Henry noted that in 1763, he described an Anishinaabe

Photo: George Robinson/Getty Images

SPECIAL REPORT

Anishinaabe Peoples

technique of reducing sap into syrup by boiling it over roaring fires, a task accomplished without metal pots or utensils. (Native peoples likely kept evaporating the concentrated sap to a hard sugar since syrup could spoil.)

The Federation of Quebec Maple Syrup Producers (aka *Producteurs et productrices acéricoles du Québec*, or PPAQ) traces the history back even further: Settler André Thévet diarized the distillation of sap by Mi'kmaq in the Atlantic Provinces in 1606. The spring equinox was their cue, as daylight hours warmed above freezing and nighttime temperatures dipped below.

Leaning on indigenous knowledge, the French colonists—indeed all settlers in the region—adapted techniques to include metal vessels in the late 1700s and early 1800s, drilling holes into the trees and affixing wooden spouts to collect the sap, drop by drop, into hollowed-out logs. These vessels were transported by draft horses and stoneboat to a sugar shack where hot rocks boiled down the sap into liquid gold. The crude structures became the gathering points for sugaring-off parties, so focal to the annual social calendar that they became a subject for 19th-century Canadian painter Cornelius Krieghoff. The Quebec sugar camps of the 17th century are still celebrated today as *les cabanes à sucre*.

Over the decades, new techniques were developed, including metal sap spouts in 1860 and metal boilers and taps in 1876. The evaporator was adapted

Photo: Canadian History Ehx

SPECIAL REPORT

André Thévet recorded the distillation of sap by Mi'kmaq people.

Canadian painter Cornelius Krieghoff portrayed maple sugaring in Canada.

Advertisement for a new-and-improved sap spout, circa 1890

in 1889 for maple syrup production in Quebec. While the U.S. adopted clear bottles and plastic jugs, Quebec producers, by the 1950s, preserved their harvest in cans.

The 1950s also saw the first use of plastic tubing for collecting sap.

> **INDUSTRIALIZATION HAS REMOVED SOME OF THE ROMANCE OF MAPLE SYRUP, MAKING IT A COMMODITY NOW EXPORTED WORLDWIDE.**

By the 1970s, plastic tubing had moved more mainstream, and thanks to research and inventive producers, sap yields were increasing. Today, reverse osmosis removes water before boiling. Grading regulations were instituted to ensure high-quality products and differentiated maple syrup based largely on color and flavor. The current system of Grade A pure maple syrup has four classes: Golden Color/Delicate Taste, Amber Color/Rich Taste, Dark Color/Robust Taste, and Very Dark Color/Strong Taste. This era of industrialization has removed some of the romance of maple syrup, making it a commodity now exported worldwide. With its members providing 72 percent of the world's maple syrup, PPAQ oversees a quota system that manages production and supply and keeps prices stable.

SEEING THE FOREST FOR THE TREES
A maple tree must grow 50 to 60 years before it is mature enough to be tapped. Sugar concentrations vary, but assuming 2% sugar content, approximately 43 gallons of sap are required to yield a single gallon of syrup—a ratio that speaks to legendary patience.

The changing climate has exacted a price on what has become a monoculture. In 2021, for example, Vermont and much of Canada experienced a spike of exceptionally warm weather in prime sugaring season, ending sap runs early and capping that year's yield at about 80% of what they'd tapped in 2020.

There are other effects on the ecosystem. Sugar maple seeds are innately equipped to germinate at a lower temperature than other tree species, which could become a

Images, from left: Wikimedia; Wikimedia; Maple Syrup History

drawback in a warming world. If smaller snowpacks persist, the trees lose a critical insulator for their shallow roots. Furthermore, sugar maples need well-draining soil and, as such, don't tolerate flooding, which is becoming more common.

As temperatures rise, insects such as forest tent caterpillars have free range, increasing their detrimental impact. Invasive non-native plants such as buckthorn, bush honeysuckle, and Japanese knotweed can impede the establishment of new maple seedlings.

Under these changing conditions, a sugar bush needs stewardship to be sustainable.

University of Vermont researchers show that biodiversity in the woodlot is the best defender against climate change. In the past, sugar bushes were managed to grow only sugar maples to save on labor. Today, producers are encouraged to introduce red maple (*A. rubrum*) as a companion

SUGAR MAPLES NEED WELL-DRAINING SOILS AND, AS SUCH, DON'T TOLERATE FLOODING, WHICH IS BECOMING MORE COMMON.

species and allow for the development of a stand with a range of tree ages and sizes.

Mark Isselhardt, a maple specialist at the university's extension, explains that "the instance of an old decaying maple falling in the woods and making room for the flush of new, young maple saplings is becoming a rarity."

Sugaring-off has never been predictable, as sap ebbs and flows with the ambient temperature, which has an outsized role in determining if crop totals will meet expectations or fall short. Ideal late winter/early spring conditions for maple sap flow would have cool nights around 20°F (-6.6°C) and warmer days at about 40°F (4.4°C). In recent years, the time period for those ideal conditions has been compressed, starting earlier and ending earlier than in previous decades. Because today's commercial operations can have 50,000 to 100,000 taps, owners may begin collecting as early as December or January to take

Indigenous peoples and French Colonists shared sugar-making responsibilities.

Red maples are a preferred companion to the sugar maple.

Crude sugar shacks became gathering points for sugaring-off parties.

SPECIAL REPORT

Today's commercial operations can have 50,000 to 100,000 taps.

A syrup can showing loggers cutting down the iconic maple forest.

The Global Strategic Maple Syrup Reserve comprises three storage warehouses.

advantage of earlier flows. Isselhardt's team has found that collecting sap in suboptimal temperatures with tubing and pumps can potentially double the volume of sap collected over a season.

TAPPING INTO THE FUTURE

Quebec boasts 2,381,000 acres of sugar bush. Area producers of the PPAQ proclaim: "We are guardians of the forest. We love our maple trees."

Joël Vaudeville, director of communications, says that to meet that pledge, the association's 13,500 members are lobbying the provincial government for less aggressive timbering and more year-round access to public lands to maintain the sugar bush.

"Currently, 18 percent of maple syrup production is done in public forests," Vaudeville explains. "We want this proportion to be 30 percent by 2080 to meet the needs of our sector amidst climate change."

The ever-present supplies of maple syrup mask the long-term health issues of maple forests. Quebec's 2024 harvest was prodigious, gathering 238 million pounds of sap compared to 124 million pounds the year before. To alleviate the ups and downs of annual harvests, Quebec producers maintain a Global Strategic Maple Syrup Reserve. Once pasteurized and put into a barrel, maple syrup can be stored and managed to meet customer demand for Golden, Amber, Dark, and Very Dark grades. Properly stored and sealed, syrup can last almost indefinitely.

The association has devised a public relations campaign using syrup cans that show loggers cutting down the iconic maple forest. The appeal aims to spark Quebeckers' sense of cultural pride and identity and to build public awareness of human-made threats to the sugar bush beyond climate change. ∎

Ontarian **Karen Davidson**, editor of *The Grower*, likes to say *Gimiigwechiwi'in*, meaning "Thank you for all the bounties of the forest," in the native dialect of the Anishinaabe.

Photos, from left: Fertnig/Getty Images; Amazon; PPAQ

SPECIAL REPORT

SAVORING THE PAST

In the countryside, the sugaring-off parties are as popular today as they were centuries ago. No recipe is as revered in Quebec as *pouding chômeur*, roughly translated as "poor man's pudding." In the early 1920s, factory workers concocted this rich dessert with common ingredients such as butter, eggs, flour, and milk topped off with maple syrup. As Anne Fowlie recalls, "This old family recipe from the Eastern Townships was a much-anticipated Christmas treat baked and served by *grand maman*."

POUDING CHÔMEUR (POOR MAN'S PUDDING)

SYRUP:
1½ cups brown sugar
1 tablespoon all-purpose flour
½ cup maple syrup

CAKE:
1 cup sugar
⅓ cup butter
½ cup all-purpose flour
1 teaspoon baking powder
pinch of salt
1 egg
½ cup milk

Preheat oven to 350°F. Grease an 8x8-inch baking dish.

For syrup: In a saucepan, warm syrup ingredients over low heat until brown sugar has melted. Set aside to cool.

For cake: In a bowl, mix sugar and butter until creamy. Add flour, baking powder, and salt and stir to combine. Add egg and milk, and stir to combine.

Pour mixture into prepared pan, then pour syrup over the mixture. Bake for 30 minutes. Serve warm.

Makes 9 servings.

Photo: Caty

ASTROLOGY

The Man of the Signs

Why has this astrological oddity
been a fixture in almanacs for centuries?

by **Theresa Reed**

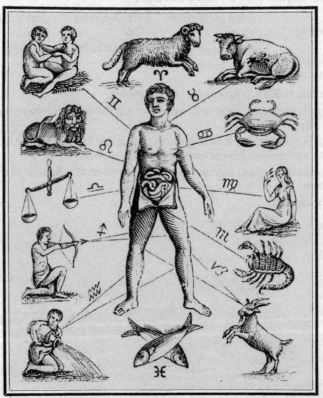

*When viewed against the background of the "mad medicine" of charmed potions,
hell-broths and magical incantations, the prevalent popular medication
of the early and even the later Middle Ages, this astrological medicine
presents an aspect of most precisely coordinated and sound knowledge, founded
upon an accurately determined and predictable order of the heavens.*

–HARRY BOBER, AMERICAN WRITER (1915–88), IN "THE ZODIACAL
MINIATURE OF THE TRÈS RICHES HEURES OF
THE DUKE OF BERRY—ITS SOURCES AND MEANING"

ASTROLOGY

My introduction to astrology came through my uncle, who lived on the farm with my grandmother. He always had a copy of *The Old Farmer's Almanac* tucked amongst his stack of *True Detective* magazines.

After having my fill of hair-raising crime stories, I pored over the *Almanac*. The advice on plants and cooking was intriguing, but what drew me in more was the mysterious *Man of the Signs*, a vintage woodcut of a naked man with astrological symbols assigned to every part of the body. I didn't understand what it meant, but I analyzed it every time I visited.

As I grew up, astrology became a part of my life, but the Man of the Signs remained a mystery. Why was this feature in the *Almanac*? How did astrologers connect the zodiac signs to parts of the body? How was this information used—and is it relevant today?

BODIES OF WORK

The Man of the Signs, also called "Zodiac Man" or "the anatomy," can be traced to the Babylonians, who are credited with developing astrology. Although there is speculation that astrology existed much earlier, the Babylonians created the zodiac wheel, the primary tool used in modern astrology.

As the Babylonians developed the zodiac, they created correspondences between the astrological signs and parts of the body. These correlations were based on the notion of shared characteristics. For example, Aries is associated with the head. Monte Farber, co-author of *Astrology for Wellness: Star Sign Guides for Body, Mind & Spirit and Vitality* (Sterling Ethos, 2019), explains the connection: "Aries, the first sign, is the *head*strong warlike sign that rushes *head*first into battle or to save the day. Aries's symbol is the ram, an animal whose mating ritual involves bashing their horned heads into each other at full speed." It's no surprise to Farber that Aries natives, including a bunch that he knows, "can be prone to headaches."

Other examples are Leo ruling the heart because of the lion-hearted nature of Leos and Gemini presiding over the hands, reflecting the nimbleness of people born under this star sign.

Another method of correlating body parts to the zodiac took the first sign, Aries, and corresponded it to the first body part, the head. Moving down the body, each part was matched with the next zodiac sign, ending with the last sign, Pisces, associated with the feet. While these explanations of the zodiac body assignments differ, both are believed to be valid.

GOOD FOR WHAT AILS YOU

The earliest images of the Zodiac Man date back to the 11th century. Reproductions were frequently featured in textbooks for medical students, calendars and Books of Hours, and almanacs.

Other figures existed, such as the Woman (a rarity), Wound Man, and Vein Man, although none were as popular

ASTROLOGY

as the Man of the Signs.

The Man of the Signs was commonly used in medieval medicine. It was consulted before administering treatment, performing surgeries, or bloodletting. In John Tulley's 1694 almanac, he advises what remedies to take according to the zodiac:

- *With Electuaries, the Moon in Cancer.*
- *With Pills, the Moon in Pisces . . .*
- *Good to take Vomit, the Moon being in Taurus.*
- *To purge the Head by sneezing, the Moon being in Cancer, Leo, or Virgo.*
- *To make Glysters, the Moon being in Aries, Cancer, or Virgo.*
- *To stop Fluxes and Rheums, the Moon being in Taurus, Virgo, or Capricorn.*
- *To Bath when the Moon is in Cancer, Libra, Aquarius, or Pisces.*
- *To cut the Hair of the Head or Beard, when the Moon is in Libra, Sagittarius, Aquarius, or Pisces.*

A contrary belief was to avoid treating an ailment when the Moon was in a sign corresponding to a body part. Using the Aries example, you wouldn't have surgery on your head when the Moon was in Aries.

Despite these contradictions, the Man of the Signs was still used as a reference for medical procedures and was a part of both English and American almanacs.

Another reason the Man of the Signs was in almanacs was an enduring belief in farming according to the Moon's phases, a practice using astronomical and astrological information to determine the best time to tackle agricultural tasks. Rigid rules align with anatomy, such as avoiding castration when the Moon is in Scorpio.

THE MAN AND THE ALMANAC

As scientific discoveries advanced, the Man of the Signs fell out of favor, and the figure was thought to represent nothing more than old superstitions. Some claimed astrology to be "unfashionable" and a "miserable relic" of occult belief that persisted among rural farmers. Sixteenth-century author and theologian Ezra Stiles noted that the occult "subsists among some Almanack Makers and Fortune Tellers." Some impassioned disbelievers of astrology, such as Colonial physician and almanac publisher Nathaniel Ames Sr., began to omit the Man of the Signs

Photo: Library of Congress

ASTROLOGY

from their almanacs, denouncing it as superstition.

Even so, astrology remained popular, and almanacs continued to feature the Man of the Signs. Ben Franklin included the illustration in all but one edition of his *Poor Richard's Almanack* along with directions on how to use it: *"First find the Day of the Month, and against the Day you have the Sign or Place of the Moon in the 5th Column. Then finding the Sign here, it shews the part of the Body it governs."*

Astrology was so vital to almanacs that astrologers were paid a princely sum. Few astrological books were published before the middle of the 19th century, so almanacs played a key role in keeping the information circulating among the public. They can be credited with helping the Man of the Signs survive to today.

Most modern astrologers agree with the traditional pairing of body parts with astrological signs. Current books, such as *Your Body and the Stars: The Zodiac As Your Wellness Guide* (Atria Books/Beyond Words, 2016) by Dr. Stephanie Marango and astrologer Rebecca Gordon, faithfully follow the Man of the Signs from the Aries association with the head to Pisces and the feet.

For example, they write that "the bull's neck is such a prominent region that in medical jargon, *bull neck* is its own term—referring to an individual whose neck is enlarged," and "given the association between the bull and its neck, it may not be surprising that the neck is the body region related to the zodiac's Bull, Taurus." The authors state that fixed Taurus energy can manifest as "neck tension" or "crackling or crunching sensations with movement" and advise neck strengthening and stretching exercises to relieve these issues.

> ## Well-Versed
> Some almanacs used poetry to illustrate the anatomy for their readers. For example, John Foster's 1678 almanac included these verses:
>
> The Head and Face the Ram doth crave,
> The Neck and Throat, the Bull will have,
> The loving Twins do rule the Hands,
> The Breast and Sides in Cancer bands,
> The Heart and Back the Lyon claims,
> Bowels and Belly Virgo gains,
> The Reyns and Loyns are Libra's part,
> The Secrets Scorpio's are by Art,
> Thighs to the Archer do pertain,
> And Capricorn the Knees doth gain,
> Aquarius hath the Legs alone,
> And Pisces must have Feet, or none.

There are some who will continue to dismiss the connection between heavenly bodies and our bodies here on Earth. But when you consider that the Moon rules the tides and women's cycles, is it far-fetched to think that other planets may also play a role? As I typed up this article, my arthritic hands could feel the burn. Is it any surprise to learn that I'm a Gemini? Not if you follow the Man of the Signs. ∎

Theresa Reed (aka "The Tarot Lady") is a tarot expert, astrologer, and author of *The Cards You're Dealt: How To Deal When Life Gets Real* (Weiser Books, 2023) and about a dozen other books.

REGIONAL FORECASTS
HOW WE PREDICT THE WEATHER

We derive our weather forecasts from a secret formula that was devised by the founder of this Almanac, Robert B. Thomas, in 1792. Thomas believed that weather on Earth was influenced by sunspots, which are magnetic storms on the surface of the Sun.

Over the years, we have refined and enhanced this formula with state-of-the-art technology and modern scientific calculations. We employ three scientific disciplines to make our long-range predictions: solar science, the study of sunspots and other solar activity; climatology, the study of prevailing weather patterns; and meteorology, the study of the atmosphere. We predict weather trends and events by comparing solar patterns and historical weather conditions with current solar activity.

Our forecasts emphasize temperature and precipitation deviations from averages, or normals. These are based on 30-year statistical averages prepared by government meteorological agencies and updated every 10 years. Our forecasts are based on the tabulations that span the period 1991 through 2020.

The borders of the 16 weather regions of the contiguous states **(page 205)** are based primarily on climatology and the movement of weather systems. For example, while the average weather in Richmond, Virginia, and Boston, Massachusetts, is very different (although both are in Region 2), both areas tend to be affected by the same storms and high-pressure centers and have weather deviations from normal that are similar.

We believe that nothing in the universe happens haphazardly and that there is a cause-and-effect pattern to all phenomena. However, although neither we nor any other forecasters have as yet gained sufficient insight into the mysteries of the universe to predict the weather with total accuracy, our results are almost always very close to our traditional claim of 80%.

FAIR OR FOUL?

Check the weather with these Almanac *tools:*

- rain gauges that measure up
- thermometers with 0 degrees of difficulty
- a record-breaking Weather Calendar

We're all under the weather—now you can get on top of it!

ORDER TODAY AT ALMANAC.COM/SHOP

ADVERTISEMENT

The Amish "Secret" to Prostate Woes?

The Amish pride themselves on finding more "natural" solutions to a number of health challenges that affect the rest of us...

And prostate woes rank near the top!

Like the rest of us, Amish men struggle with prostate issues like:

- Too many bathroom trips, which disrupt a good nights sleep
- When it can seemingly take forever for our flow to start
- And when our flow does start, it's a weak stream, which causes us to have to stand seemingly forever to go
- When it feels our bladders are not emptying, which makes us very uncomfortable

Saw Palmetto has been kicked around for years as being helpful for prostate issues...

But the Amish have found that while taking some Saw Palmetto can be helpful–There are several other herbs that are just as helpful if not more so, and the Amish take a combination of all of them!

And over the past several years there is one product on the market many Amish men now swear by as being a key to improved prostate health–And that product is Prost-Fix.

30 INGREDIENTS IN ONE SMALL CAPSULE!

Scott Adams, the Product Manager behind Prost-Fix had this to say, "It took a great deal of research and time in order create Prost-Fix. We wanted to create the perfect solution for those looking for help for their prostate –I'm one of those myself and I take the Prost-Fix every day."

And that ingredient list starts with Saw Palmetto, which is considered the "granddaddy" of prostate ingredients. It's been used to help treat prostate issues since the 1800's. And it has been extensively researched over the past four decades...

Many of those studies have shown that Saw Palmetto can help shrink the inner linings of the Prostate which when enlarged can put pressure on the tubes that control urine flow.

But Saw Palmetto is just a small part of what's in Prost-Fix. Here are several of the other ingredients included in each capsule of Prost-Fix:

Zinc: There's more zinc in one's prostate than in any other part of the body. One study supported the premise that zinc is needed for a healthy prostate.

Copper: Copper helps the body maintain healthy blood circulation, which is helpful for the prostate.

Selenium: In several studies Selenium has been shown to help protect the prostate.

Cernitin flower pollen extract: In one study it helped improve prostate symptoms in a majority of men participating.

Quercetin: Helps fight prostate problems within cells.

Pumpkin Seed Extract: Helps maintain a healthy flow.

Nettle Root Extract: Very popular in Europe for prostate issues.

Vitamin B6: Helps boost your immune system.

And that's just a few of the ingredients found within each bottle of Prost-Fix. These ingredients have helped thousands get their prostate issues under control.

"I ordered this product for my father who is healthy and just turned 64. He had issues with frequent bathroom trips. Since taking this product for four weeks, he has noticed a big improvement. We very much appreciated this product!" -James Wilson

If you're looking for help for your prostate issues you need Prost-Fix!

- REDUCE THOSE NIGHTLY INTERRUPTIONS – And get a more restful nights sleep
- INCREASE FLOW RATE – Effective blend of 30 herbs, vitamins & minerals support urinary function
- QUALITY YOU CAN COUNT ON - MADE IN THE USA in a FDA and GMP Certified Facility and tested for purity by a third party
- NO ALLERGENS – NO GMOs, binders, fillers, preservatives, soy, gluten, dairy, shellfish, peanut and eggs
- 60 Veggie caps within each bottle. Each bottle is a 30-day supply

GET A FREE BOTTLE!

One bottle of Prost-Fix is $29.95 and if you order two bottles you'll get a third bottle absolutely FREE! You'll also receive free shipping & handling no matter how many bottles you order. For credit/debit card orders, you can call: **1-888-762-5477** Or go to:

TopValueSupplements.com

Or you can send payment to: MWSB Inc., 834 South Union Street, Olean, NY 14760-3917

Prost-Fix comes with a 30-day money back guarantee.

These statements have not been evaluated by the Food and Drug Administration. This product is not intended to diagnose, cure, or prevent any disease. Results may vary.

REGIONAL FORECASTS
HOW ACCURATE WAS OUR FORECAST LAST WINTER?

Our overall accuracy rate in forecasting the direction of temperature departures from normal for a representative city during meteorological winter (December through February) in each region was 88.9%, as we were correct in 16 of the 18 regions. Our forecast for below-average temperatures was on the mark from the Southeast westward through the Appalachians and the Lower Lakes into the Ohio Valley, where Louisville (Ky.) and Indianapolis (Ind.) had their coldest Januarys since 2014. In Savannah (Ga.), it was the coldest January since 1981 and the ninth-coldest January on record. In the Atlantic Corridor and Heartland regions, many areas ended up colder than we had forecast.

Our forecast for a dry December through February period across much of the eastern and northern U.S. was mostly on target. One exception was in the Ohio Valley, where a wet February helped offset the earlier dryness. Central and southern California and the Desert Southwest ended up being drier for much of the winter as the storm track stayed farther north.

For precipitation, our accuracy rate was 83.3% (correct in 15 of the 18 regions), which makes our total accuracy rate 86.1%—above our traditional average rate of 80%.

A once-in-a-generation storm on January 21 brought 7 to 9 inches of snow from Mobile (Ala.) to Pensacola (Fla.), while New Orleans (La.) received 8 inches. Because of this, our snowy forecast for the Southeast was accurate. Our snowy forecast in the southern Atlantic Corridor also came true, with above-average snowfall in Washington, D.C., and Richmond (Va.). Our forecast for below-average snowfall across much of the northern U.S. also proved to be largely correct.

The table below shows how the actual average temperature differed from our forecast for December through February for one representative city in each region. On average, the actual winter temperature differed from our forecasts by 0.4 degrees F.

REGION/ CITY	PREDICTED	ACTUAL	REGION/ CITY	PREDICTED	ACTUAL
1. Augusta, ME	0.8	0.03	10. St. Louis, MO	1.3	-0.3
2. Washington, DC	0.0	-0.7	11. Houston, TX	1.0	1.2
3. Frederick, MD	-0.7	-1.6	12. Amarillo, TX	-0.3	-0.6
4. Columbia, SC	-0.8	-0.5	13. Reno, NV	1.8	1.2
5. Miami, FL	-1.3	-1.3	14. Las Vegas, NV	1.3	2.3
6. Cleveland, OH	-0.3	-0.2	15. Portland, OR	0.7	0.5
7. Charleston, WV	-1.3	-1.2	16. Fresno, CA	2.7	2.5
8. New Orleans, LA	0.7	0.6	17. Utqiagvik, AK	3.0	3.3
9. Green Bay, WI	0.7	0.6	18. Lihue, HI	0.4	0.9

Get your local forecast via Almanac.com/2026.

REGIONAL FORECASTS
WEATHER REGIONS

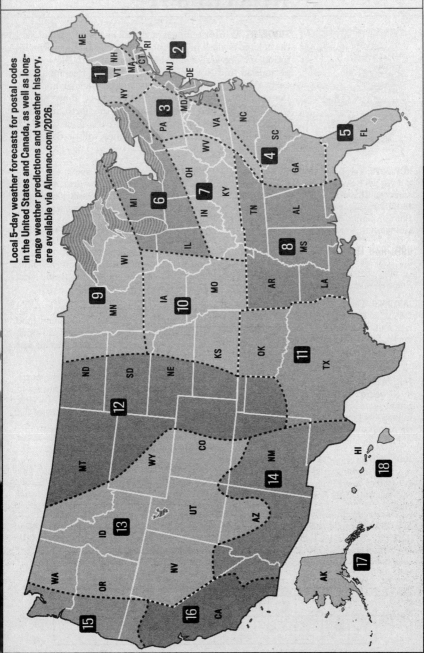

Local 5-day weather forecasts for postal codes in the United States and Canada, as well as long-range weather predictions and weather history, are available via Almanac.com/2026.

REGION 1 FORECAST
NORTHEAST

SUMMARY: Winter temperatures will be above normal, with the coldest periods in December and early January. Precipitation and snowfall will be below normal, with the snowiest periods in mid-November, early and mid-December, and early February. **April** and **May** will be warmer and drier than normal. **Summer** temperatures will be above normal, while rainfall will be above normal in the north and below south. The hottest periods will be in early June and early and late July. **September** and **October** will be cooler and wetter than normal.

NOV. 2025: Temp. 38° (1° below avg.); precip. 3" (avg.). 1–8 Snow showers north; rain, then sunny south; cold. 9–11 Snowstorm, cold. 12–18 Sunny, then rain; turning warmer. 19–26 Showers, mild. 27–30 Snow showers north, sunny south; colder.

DEC. 2025: Temp. 26° (4° below avg.); precip. 2.0" (1.5" below avg.). 1–17 Snowy periods, turning very cold. 18–21 Sunny, cold. 22–31 Snow showers, very cold.

JAN. 2026: Temp. 24° (1° below avg.); precip. 2.5" (1" below avg.). 1–11 Snowy north, flurries south; very cold. 12–17 Sunny, then snow north; flurries south; milder. 18–20 Sunny, mild. 21–26 Flurries, then rainy; cold then turning mild. 27–31 Sunny, cold.

FEB. 2026: Temp. 30° (7° above avg.); precip. 3" (1" below avg. north, 2" above south). 1–2 Snowstorm, chilly. 3–7 Rain, then sunny; mild. 8–14 Showers, very warm. 15–18 Sunny, then rain and snow; mild. 19–22 Showers, mild. 23–28 Snow showers, chilly.

MAR. 2026: Temp. 38° (4° above avg.); precip. 3" (1" above avg. north, 1" below south). 1–9 Snowy north, sunny south; mild. 10–14 Snowy, cold. 15–20 Sunny, mild. 21–31 Rainy, warm.

APR. 2026: Temp. 46° (1° above avg.); precip. 2" (1" below avg.). 1–3 Rainy, warm. 4–15 Isolated showers, chilly. 16–22 Showers; chilly, then mild. 23–30 Sunny, becoming warm.

MAY 2026: Temp. 60° (3° above avg.); precip. 3.5" (avg.). 1–3 Sunny, warm. 4–10 Rain, some heavy; mild. 11–17 Sunny; cool, then warm. 18–31 Scattered t-storms, warm.

JUNE 2026: Temp. 68° (2° above avg.); precip. 3.5" (0.5" below avg.). 1–8 Scattered t-storms, cooler. 9–12 Showers north, sunny south; hot. 13–19 Scattered t-storms, mild. 20–24 Sunny, warm. 25–30 Rain, some heavy; warm.

JULY 2026: Temp. 70° (avg.); precip. 4" (avg.). 1–7 Isolated t-storms, hot. 8–10 Sunny, mild. 11–19 T-storms, then sunny; cool. 20–27 T-storms, then sunny; cool, then turning hot. 28–31 Showers, heavy north; mild.

AUG. 2026: Temp. 67.5° (2° above avg. north, 1° below south); precip. 4" (2" above avg. north, 2" below south). 1–6 Scattered t-storms, warm. 7–10 Heavy rain north, isolated showers south; cool. 11–18 Sunny, then t-storms; mild north, cool south. 19–31 Isolated t-storms, mild.

SEPT. 2026: Temp. 59° (2° below avg.); precip. 5.5" (2" above avg.). 1–7 Showery, cool. 8–11 Sunny, cool. 12–19 Rainy periods, then sunny; cool. 20–30 Showers, cool.

OCT. 2026: Temp. 48° (1° below avg.); precip. 5" (1" above avg.). 1–10 Sunny, cool. 11–21 Rainy periods, some heavy; cool. 22–28 Sunny, milder. 29–31 Rainy, mild.

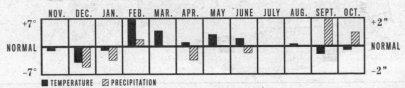

REGION 2 FORECAST
ATLANTIC CORRIDOR

SUMMARY: Winter temperatures will be above normal, while precipitation and snowfall will be below normal. The coldest periods will occur in mid- to late December and early and late January. The snowiest periods will be in late December, early January, and late February. **April** and **May** will end up warmer and drier than usual. **Summer** will be hotter and drier than normal. The hottest periods will be in early June and early and mid-July. Watch for tropical storms in late June and mid-August. **September** and **October** temperatures and precipitation will be below normal.

NOV. 2025: Temp. 46.5° (2° below avg. north, 1° above south); precip. 2.5" (0.5" below avg.). 1–7 Showers, then sunny; chilly. 8–16 Periods of rain, mixed with snow north, then sunny; cold. 17–21 Rainy periods, milder. 22–30 Sunny; mild, then turning cold.

DEC. 2025: Temp. 38° (3° below avg.); precip. 1.5" (2" below avg.). 1–3 Showers, mild. 4–12 Snow showers north, sunny south; turning cold. 13–15 Sunny, cold. 16–29 Rain and snow showers, then sunny; turning very cold. 30–31 Snowy, cold.

JAN. 2026: Temp. 35° (2° below avg.); precip. 1.5" (2" below avg.). 1–7 Flurries north, sunny south; bitter cold. 8–10 Snowy, cold. 11–24 Sunny; cold, then turning mild. 25–26 Rainy, milder. 27–31 Sunny, colder.

FEB. 2026: Temp. 40° (5° above avg.); precip. 4" (2" above avg. north, avg. south). 1–4 Rainy, milder. 5–9 Sunny, colder. 10–16 Rainy, warm. 17–24 Rain, then sunny north; sunny south; mild. 25–28 Snowstorm north, showers south; then sunny; chilly.

MAR. 2026: Temp. 47° (3° above avg.); precip. 2" (2" below avg.). 1–9 Sunny, mild. 10–14 Rain and snow showers, cold. 15–21 Sunny, cool. 22–31 Rainy periods, warm.

APR. 2026: Temp. 55° (2° above avg.); precip. 2.5" (1" below avg.). 1–7 Rainy periods, warm. 8–15 Sunny; warm, then cooler. 16–18 Showers, cool. 19–30 Scattered showers; warm, then turning cool.

MAY 2026: Temp. 65° (3° above avg. north, 1° above south); precip. 3.5" (avg.). 1–2 Sunny, cool. 3–5 Heavy t-storms, mild. 6–20 Scattered t-storms, then sunny; cool, then turning warm. 21–31 Scattered t-storms, warm.

JUNE 2026: Temp. 74° (2° above avg.); precip. 4.5" (0.5" above avg.). 1–9 Scattered t-storms, turning hot. 10–18 T-storms; warm north, hot south. 19–23 Sunny, warm. 24–27 T-storms, tropical storm threat south; mild. 28–30 Sunny, warm.

JULY 2026: Temp. 78° (1° above avg.); precip. 3.5" (0.5" below avg.). 1–14 Isolated t-storms, hot. 15–18 Sunny north, t-storms south; cooler. 19–26 T-storms, then sunny; warm. 27–31 Scattered t-storms, warm.

AUG. 2026: Temp. 75° (avg.); precip. 2" (2" below avg.). 1–14 Scattered t-storms, then sunny; warm. 15–16 Sunny north, tropical storm threat south; warm north, cool south. 17–20 Sunny, warm. 21–31 Sunny north, isolated t-storms south; cooler.

SEPT. 2026: Temp. 68° (1° below avg.); precip. 3" (1" below avg.). 1–12 Scattered t-storms; warm, then turning cool. 13–23 Scattered showers north, sunny south; cool. 24–30 Isolated showers, cool.

OCT. 2026: Temp. 56° (1° below avg.); precip. 3" (1" below avg.). 1–8 Sunny, cool. 9–16 Scattered showers; cool, then turning warm. 17–21 Periods of rain; cool, then turning warm. 22–28 Sunny; cool, then milder. 29–31 Showers, mild.

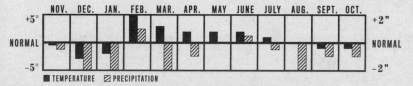

REGION 3 FORECAST
APPALACHIANS

SUMMARY: Winter will be colder than normal, with below-normal precipitation. Snowfall will be below normal in the north and above south. The coldest periods will occur in mid- and late December, early and late January, and early February, while the most snow will arrive in late December, late January, early and late February, and mid-March. **April** and **May** will be warmer than normal, with below-normal rainfall in the north and above-normal south. **Summer** will be cooler than normal in the north and warmer south; rainfall will be below normal. The hottest periods are expected in early June and early July. Watch for a tropical depression in late June. **September** and **October** will be cooler and drier than normal.

NOV. 2025: Temp. 43° (2° below avg. north, avg. south); precip. 3" (1" above avg. north, 1" below south). 1–9 Rain and snow, cold north; sunny, warm south. 10–11 Snowstorm north, rain south; cold. 12–21 Sunny, then rainy; chilly. 22–30 Sunny; chilly north, warm south.

DEC. 2025: Temp. 35° (3° below avg.); precip. 1.5" (2" below avg.). 1–3 Showers, warm. 4–17 Snow showers north, sunny south; colder. 18–20 Sunny, very cold. 21–23 Sunny north, showers south; milder. 24–31 Snowy, very cold.

JAN. 2026: Temp. 29° (2° below avg.); precip. 2" (1.5" below avg.). 1–10 Flurries north, sunny south; very cold. 11–17 Snow showers, milder. 18–22 Sunny, mild. 23–24 Sunny north, snow south; chilly. 25–31 Snowy north, rain south; cold.

FEB. 2026: Temp. 32° (2° above avg.); precip. 4.5" (2" above avg.). 1–9 Snowy north, rain south; then sunny; cold. 10–23 Periods of rain, then sunny; warm. 24–28 Snowy north, showers south; chilly.

MAR. 2026: Temp. 39° (1° below avg.); precip. 2" (1" below avg.). 1–11 Flurries north, sunny south; chilly. 12–16 Snowy periods, heavy south; cold. 17–22 Sunny; cold, then warmer. 23–31 Scattered showers, warm.

APR. 2026: Temp. 52° (1° above avg.); precip. 3" (1" below avg.). 1–7 Rainy periods, warm. 8–15 Sunny north, isolated showers south; warm, then turning colder. 16–22 Scattered showers north, sunny south; cold, then warmer. 23–30 Sunny, then showers; cool.

MAY 2026: Temp. 60.5° (0.5° below avg.); precip. 5" (avg. north, 2" above south). 1–8 Rainy, cool. 9–13 Sunny north, showers south; cool. 14–18 Sunny, warmer. 19–28 Rainy periods, heavy south; mild. 29–31 Sunny north, showers south; warm.

JUNE 2026: Temp. 70° (1° above avg.); precip. 3.5" (1" below avg.). 1–9 Scattered t-storms north, sunny south; hot. 10–24 Isolated t-storms north, sunny south; warm. 25–28 Rainy, tropical depression threat north; cool. 29–30 Sunny, warm.

JULY 2026: Temp. 74° (1° below avg. north, 1° above south); precip. 2.5" (avg. north, 2" below south). 1–7 Sunny, hot. 8–21 Scattered t-storms; warm, then turning cool. 22–31 Sunny, then t-storms north; isolated t-storms south; cool, then warmer.

AUG. 2026: Temp. 71° (1° above avg.); precip. 2.5" (1" below avg.). 1–12 Isolated t-storms, warm. 13–20 Sunny; cool, then warmer. 21–31 Scattered t-storms, mild.

SEPT. 2026: Temp. 63° (2° below avg.); precip. 2" (2" below avg.). 1–6 Sunny, warm. 7–12 Scattered showers, cooler. 13–23 Isolated showers north, sunny south; cool, then warmer. 24–27 Showers, cool. 28–30 Showers north, sunny south; milder.

OCT. 2026: Temp. 53° (1° below avg.); precip. 2.5" (1" below avg.). 1–10 Sunny, cool. 11–21 Rainy periods, cool. 22–28 Sunny, warmer. 29–31 Scattered showers, mild.

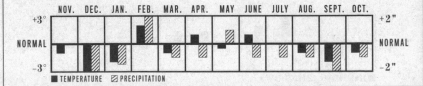

REGION 4 FORECAST
SOUTHEAST

SUMMARY: **Winter** temperatures will be below normal, with the coldest periods in mid- to late December, early and late January, and early February. Precipitation will be below normal, with snowfall above normal in the east and below west. The snowiest periods in the east will be mid-December; in the north, late January. **April** and **May** will be warmer and drier than usual. **Summer** will be warmer than normal, with the hottest periods in early to mid-June and early and late July. Rainfall will be below normal in the north and above south. Watch for a tropical storm in late June and a hurricane in mid-August. **September** and **October** temperatures and precipitation will be below normal.

NOV. 2025: Temp. 55° (1° below avg.); precip. 2.5" (0.5" below avg.). 1–3 Sunny, warm. 4–10 Sunny, then rainy; cool. 11–20 Sunny, then rainy; chilly. 21–30 Sunny; chilly, then turning warm.

DEC. 2025: Temp. 47° (2° below avg.); precip. 2" (2" below avg.). 1–3 Rainy, warm. 4–19 Sunny; mild, then turning cold. 20–21 Snowstorm east, showers west; cold. 22–27 Sunny, milder. 28–31 Sunny, then showers; chilly.

JAN. 2026: Temp. 44° (3° below avg.); precip. 2.5" (2" below avg.). 1–6 Sunny, very cold. 7–14 Sunny, then showers; turning milder. 15–22 Sunny, mild. 23–24 Snowy north, sunny south; cold. 25–29 Rain at times, then sunny; turning very cold. 30–31 Showers, milder.

FEB. 2026: Temp. 51° (4° above avg.); precip. 4.5" (1" above avg. north, avg. south). 1–4 Sunny, then rain, heavy at times; warmer. 5–7 Sunny, much colder. 8–13 Rainy, warmer. 14–21 Sunny, warm. 22–28 Showers, then sunny; turning cooler.

MAR. 2026: Temp. 55° (1° below avg.); precip. 4" (0.5" below avg.). 1–7 Sunny, cool. 8–16 Rainy periods, chilly. 17–22 Sunny, warmer. 23–29 Scattered showers, warm. 30–31 Sunny, cooler.

APR. 2026: Temp. 67° (3° above avg.); precip. 1.5" (2" below avg.). 1–12 Sunny, warm. 13–17 T-storms, cooler. 18–28 Sunny; warm, then turning cool. 29–30 Scattered t-storms, cool.

MAY 2026: Temp. 72° (avg.); precip. 5" (1" above avg.). 1–10 Scattered t-storms, then sunny; cool. 11–14 Rainy, cool. 15–18 Sunny, turning warmer. 19–31 Scattered t-storms; warm north, hot south.

JUNE 2026: Temp. 82° (3° above avg.); precip. 4.5" (avg.). 1–10 Isolated t-storms, then sunny; hot. 11–19 Sunny north, t-storms south; hot. 20–23 Sunny, mild. 24–30 Scattered t-storms, tropical storm threat east; cooler.

JULY 2026: Temp. 86° (3° above avg.); precip. 4.5" (2" below avg. north, 2" above south). 1–10 Sunny, hot. 11–15 Sunny, warm. 16–31 Isolated t-storms north, numerous t-storms south; hot, then turning cooler.

AUG. 2026: Temp. 80° (1° below avg.); precip. 5.5" (1" above avg.). 1–11 Scattered t-storms; warm, then turning cool. 12–14 Isolated t-storms west, hurricane threat east; cool. 15–23 Showers, cool. 24–28 T-storms west, sunny east; mild. 29–31 Scattered t-storms, mild.

SEPT. 2026: Temp. 74° (1° below avg.); precip. 2" (3" below avg.). 1–7 Sunny, mild. 8–18 T-storms, then sunny; cooler. 19–24 Sunny, mild. 25–30 Sunny; cool, then turning warm.

OCT. 2026: Temp. 64° (1° below avg.); precip. 3" (1" above avg. north, 1" below south). 1–14 Periods of rain, then sunny; cool. 15–20 Rain, some heavy north; cool. 21–28 Sunny, milder. 29–31 Showers, then sunny; warm.

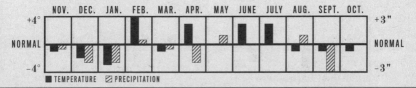

REGION 5 FORECAST

FLORIDA

SUMMARY: Winter will be cooler than normal, with the coldest temperatures in mid- to late December and much of January. Rainfall will be above normal. Watch for a tropical depression in early November. **April** and **May** will be warmer than normal, with rainfall below normal. **Summer** will be warmer and drier than usual. The hottest periods will be in early and mid-June and early July. Watch for a tropical storm in late June and a hurricane in mid-August. **September** and **October** will be cooler than normal, with below-normal precipitation in the north and above-normal south.

NOV. 2025: Temp. 69° (avg.); precip. 3.5" (1" above avg.). 1–8 Sunny north, showers south; mild. 9–11 Tropical depression threat, warm. 12–15 Sunny, cooler. 16–21 Showers, mild. 22–30 Sunny; cool, then turning mild.

DEC. 2025: Temp. 63° (2° below avg.); precip. 1.5" (1" below avg.). 1–10 Sunny, then showers; cool. 11–14 Sunny, mild. 15–17 Showers, mild. 18–30 Sunny, cold. 31 Showers, milder.

JAN. 2026: Temp. 58° (3° below avg.); precip. 1.5" (1" below avg.). 1–12 Sunny, then isolated showers; cold. 13–25 Scattered showers, then sunny; cold, then turning milder. 26–31 Rainy periods, cold.

FEB. 2026: Temp. 62° (avg.); precip. 4.5" (2" above avg.). 1–12 Periods of rain, some heavy; mild. 13–25 Sunny, mild. 26–28 Heavy rain north, sunny south; cooler.

MAR. 2026: Temp. 66° (2° below avg.); precip. 2" (0.5" below avg.). 1–8 Sunny north, isolated showers south; cool. 9–19 Scattered showers, cold. 20–25 Showers north, sunny south; warmer. 26–31 Sunny; warm, then turning cool.

APR. 2026: Temp. 74° (1° above avg.); precip. 1.5" (1" below avg.). 1–13 Sunny, warm. 14–17 Isolated showers north, sunny south; warm. 18–23 Sunny, warm. 24–25 Isolated showers, warm. 26–30 Sunny, then t-storms; turning cooler.

MAY 2026: Temp. 78° (avg.); precip. 4.5" (avg.). 1–12 Sunny north, isolated t-storms south; mild. 13–20 Isolated t-storms, warm. 21–31 Scattered t-storms, more numerous south; hot north, warm south.

JUNE 2026: Temp. 84° (1° above avg.); precip. 6" (1" below avg.). 1–5 Scattered t-storms, some heavy north; warm. 6–11 Sunny, hot. 12–24 Scattered t-storms; hot, then turning cooler. 25–26 Tropical storm threat, warm. 27–30 Sunny, hotter.

JULY 2026: Temp. 85° (1° above avg.); precip. 4.5" (2.5" below avg.). 1–14 Scattered t-storms, hot. 15–21 Sunny north, t-storms south; warm. 22–31 Scattered t-storms, warm.

AUG. 2026: Temp. 83° (avg.); precip. 8" (2" below avg. north, 2" above south). 1–9 Isolated t-storms, warm. 10–12 Hurricane threat, warm. 13–24 T-storms, mild. 25–31 Sunny north, t-storms south; warm.

SEPT. 2026: Temp. 80° (1° below avg.); precip. 7.5" (2" below avg. north, 2" above south). 1–11 Scattered t-storms; warm, then cooler. 12–20 Sunny north, t-storms south; mild. 21–30 Sunny north, isolated t-storms south; mild.

OCT. 2026: Temp. 76.5° (0.5° above avg.); precip. 3.8" (avg. north, 1.5" below south). 1–8 Scattered showers, mild. 9–13 Sunny, cooler. 14–29 Scattered showers, warm. 30–31 Sunny, cooler.

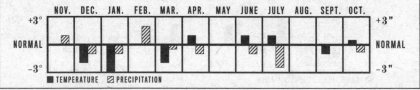

REGION 6 FORECAST
LOWER LAKES

SUMMARY: Winter will be warmer than normal, with the coldest periods in mid- to late December, early and late January, and early February. Precipitation will be below normal, and snowfall will be near to below normal, with the snowiest periods in mid- to late November, much of December, early and late January, early February, and early to mid-March. **April** and **May** temperatures will be above normal, and precipitation will be below normal in the east and above west. **Summer** will be warmer than normal, with the hottest periods in early June and late June into early July. Rainfall will be above normal. **September** and **October** will be cooler and drier than usual.

NOV. 2025: Temp. 41° (avg.); precip. 2" (0.5" below avg.). 1–9 Scattered showers, chilly. 10–15 Periods of snow, then sunny; cold. 16–26 Snowy periods, cold. 27–30 Sunny, turning warm.

DEC. 2025: Temp. 31° (3° below avg.); precip. 2" (1" below avg.). 1–2 Snow, turning colder. 3–13 Lake-effect snow east, flurries west; cold. 14–18 Sunny, then a snowstorm; turning very cold. 19–24 Snowy periods, cold. 25–29 Sunny east, snowy west; very cold. 30–31 Snow, cold.

JAN. 2026: Temp. 26° (2° below avg.); precip. 1.5" (1.5" below avg.). 1–9 Snowy, very cold. 10–21 Flurries east, snowy west; cold, then turning mild. 22–31 Snowy, turning cold.

FEB. 2026: Temp. 32° (5° above avg. east, 3° above west); precip. 2.5" (0.5" above avg.). 1–4 Rain and snow showers, mild east; heavy snow, cold west. 5–8 Sunny, warmer. 9–17 Rainy, warm. 18–28 Rain and snow showers; mild, then turning chilly.

MAR. 2026: Temp. 41° (3° above avg.); precip. 2" (1" below avg.). 1–7 Snowy; chilly, then milder. 8–13 Lake-effect snow east, flurries west; colder. 14–18 Sunny, warmer. 19–28 Showers, turning very warm. 29–31 Sunny, cooler.

APR. 2026: Temp. 50.5° (avg. east, 3° above west); precip. 4" (1" below avg. east, 1" above west). 1–14 Rainy periods; turning cooler east, warm west. 15–24 Showers, mild east; periods of heavy rain, warm west. 25–27 Sunny, mild. 28–30 Rainy, cooler.

MAY 2026: Temp. 59° (1° above avg. east, 1° below west); precip. 4.5" (1" below avg. east, 2" above west). 1–9 Showery; mild east, cool west. 10–19 Sunny east, sunny then rainy west; cool, then milder. 20–31 Scattered t-storms, mild.

JUNE 2026: Temp. 69° (2° above avg.); precip. 4" (avg.). 1–9 Scattered t-storms; mild, then turning hot. 10–18 Sunny, then t-storms; warm. 19–28 Isolated t-storms, warm. 29–30 Sunny, hot.

JULY 2026: Temp. 72° (avg.); precip. 5.5" (2" above avg.). 1–6 Isolated t-storms, hot. 7–11 Sunny, warm. 12–14 T-storms, heavy rain east; warm. 15–22 Sunny, then t-storms, heavy rain west; cooler. 23–31 Isolated t-storms, locally heavy rain; warm.

AUG. 2026: Temp. 70.5° (2° above avg. east, 1° below west); precip. 5" (1" above avg.). 1–16 Scattered t-storms, then sunny; warm, then turning cool. 17–25 Scattered t-storms; cool, then warmer. 26–28 Heavy rain east, sunny west; warm. 29–31 Scattered t-storms, mild.

SEPT. 2026: Temp. 60° (2° below avg.); precip. 3" (avg.). 1–8 Sunny; cool, then warmer. 9–11 Rainy, cooler. 12–16 Periods of rain east, sunny west; cool. 17–30 Showers; cool, then turning mild.

OCT. 2026: Temp. 53° (avg.); precip. 2" (1" below avg.). 1–6 Sunny, cool. 7–16 Scattered showers; mild, then cooler. 17–28 Showers, then sunny; turning warm. 29–31 Showers, mild.

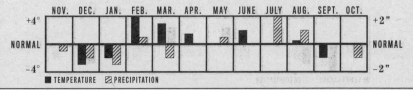

REGION 7 FORECAST
OHIO VALLEY

SUMMARY: Winter will be colder than normal, with the coldest periods in mid- to late December, early January, late January into early February, and mid-March. Precipitation will be below normal, with snowfall near to above normal in the east and below west. The snowiest periods will be in late December, early January, and early and late February. **April** and **May** temperatures will be above normal, while precipitation will be above normal in the east and below west. **Summer** will be warmer than normal, with below-normal rainfall. The hottest periods will be in early June and early and late July. **September** and **October** will average cooler and drier than normal.

NOV. 2025: Temp. 44° (1° below avg.); precip. 2.5" (0.5" below avg.). 1–5 Showers, then sunny east; sunny west; warm, then colder. 6–11 Rain, heavy east; milder, then colder. 12–18 Sunny, then showers; chilly. 19–24 Rain, then sunny; warmer. 25–30 Isolated showers; chilly, then warm.

DEC. 2025: Temp. 36° (3° below avg.); precip. 1.5" (1.5" below avg.). 1–7 Showers, then sunny; turning colder. 8–9 Rain and snow, chilly. 10–18 Sunny, then snow showers; cold. 19–28 Snowy east, sunny west; chilly. 29–31 Snow, much colder.

JAN. 2026: Temp. 32° (2° below avg.); precip. 2.5" (1" below avg.). 1–10 Snowy east, sunny west; very cold. 11–20 Sunny east, isolated showers west; turning warmer. 21–24 Sunny, colder. 25–26 Snow and rain, chilly. 27–31 Sunny east, flurries west; cold.

FEB. 2026: Temp. 37° (2° above avg.); precip. 3.5" (1" above avg. east, 1" below west). 1–5 Heavy snow east, rain to snow west; turning very cold. 6–17 Sunny, then rainy periods; turning very warm. 18–23 Rain at times, mild. 24–28 Snowy east, rainy west; chilly.

MAR. 2026: Temp. 45° (avg.); precip. 3.5" (1" below avg.). 1–8 Isolated showers east, sunny west; cool. 9–15 Snowy east, showers west; cold. 16–26 Scattered showers; cool, then much warmer. 27–31 Rain, heavy west, then sunny; turning cooler.

APR. 2026: Temp. 58° (2° above avg.); precip. 4" (1" above avg. east, 1" below west). 1–11 T-storms, some heavy east; warm. 12–18 Rainy periods, cooler. 19–24 Scattered t-storms, turning warmer. 25–30 Sunny, then isolated showers; cool.

MAY 2026: Temp. 64° (1° above avg. east, 1° below west); precip. 4.5" (0.5" above avg.). 1–2 Sunny, mild. 3–13 Scattered t-storms, cool. 14–18 Sunny, warmer. 19–31 Scattered t-storms, mild.

JUNE 2026: Temp. 74° (3° above avg. east, 1° above west); precip. 4.5" (1" above avg. east, 1" below west). 1–8 Scattered t-storms, then sunny; becoming hot. 9–16 T-storms, warm. 17–18 Heavy rain east, sunny west; warm. 19–30 Sunny, then t-storms; cool, then warmer.

JULY 2026: Temp. 77° (1° above avg.); precip. 3" (1" below avg.). 1–8 Sunny, then t-storms; hot. 9–14 T-storms, heavy west; warm. 15–22 Sunny, then t-storms; turning hot. 23–28 Sunny, warm. 29–31 Sunny east, t-storms west; hot.

AUG. 2026: Temp. 72.5° (1.5° below avg.); precip. 2.5" (1" below avg.). 1–9 Sunny, then t-storms; warm. 10–19 Sunny, mild. 20–28 Scattered t-storms, warm. 29–31 Sunny, mild.

SEPT. 2026: Temp. 66° (2° below avg.); precip. 2" (avg. east, 2" below west). 1–9 Scattered showers; warm, then cooler. 10–20 Sunny; cool, then warmer. 21–30 Scattered showers east, sunny west; cool.

OCT. 2026: Temp. 58° (avg.); precip. 1.5" (1" below avg.). 1–8 Sunny; cool, then warmer. 9–13 Isolated showers, cool. 14–21 Rainy periods; cool, then warmer. 22–31 Sunny, then showers; warm, then cooler.

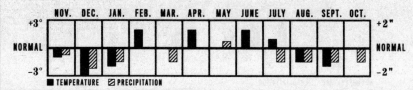

REGION **8** FORECAST

DEEP SOUTH

SUMMARY: Winter will be warmer than normal, with the coldest periods in mid-December, early and late January, and early February. Precipitation and snowfall will be below normal, with the best chances for snow in the north in mid-November, late January, and early February. **April** and **May** will wind up warmer than normal, while precipitation will be above normal in the north and below south. **Summer** will be warmer than normal, with the hottest periods in mid-June and mid-July. Rainfall will be below normal in the north and above south. Watch for tropical storms in early June and late August. **September** and **October** temperatures will average above normal, with rainfall below normal.

NOV. 2025: Temp. 54° (avg.); precip. 3.5" (1" below avg.). 1–6 Sunny; warm, then becoming cool. 7–10 Heavy rain north, scattered showers south; mild. 11–14 Sunny, chilly. 15–20 Rainy periods, mixed with snow north; chilly. 21–30 Sunny, warmer.

DEC. 2025: Temp. 49° (1° below avg.); precip. 3" (2" below avg.). 1–3 Rainy, warm. 4–15 Sunny; mild, then turning chilly. 16–20 Showers, then sunny; cold. 21–31 Sunny, then showers; mild, then turning chilly.

JAN. 2026: Temp. 45° (2° below avg.); precip. 4.5" (1" below avg.). 1–6 Sunny, cold. 7–14 Sunny, then showers; chilly. 15–21 Sunny, warmer. 22–24 Snow showers north, sunny south; colder. 25–28 Rain, then sunny; mild, then colder. 29–31 Showers north, rain south; milder.

FEB. 2026: Temp. 51° (3° above avg.); precip. 5.5" (1" below avg. north, 1" above south). 1–4 Rain and snow north, heavy rain south; turning cold. 5–7 Sunny, cold. 8–11 Showers, warmer. 12–20 Sunny, turning very warm. 21–28 Rainy, then sunny; cooler.

MAR. 2026: Temp. 57.5° (0.5° above avg.); precip. 6" (avg.). 1–8 Sunny, then showers; cool. 9–15 Rainy periods, cool. 16–21 Sunny, warmer. 22–31 Rainy periods, then sunny; warm.

APR. 2026: Temp. 68° (4° above avg.); precip. 4.5" (1" below avg.). 1–8 Sunny, warm. 9–16 Rainy periods north, isolated showers south; warm. 17–30 Sunny, then scattered t-storms; warm.

MAY 2026: Temp. 71° (1° below avg.); precip. 6" (3" above avg. north, 1" below south). 1–12 Scattered t-storms, cool. 13–20 Sunny, then t-storms; mild. 21–31 Numerous t-storms north, isolated t-storms south; warm.

JUNE 2026: Temp. 81° (2° above avg.); precip. 6.5" (1" above avg.). 1–5 Scattered t-storms east, tropical storm threat west; warm. 6–19 Sunny, then t-storms; becoming hot. 20–30 Scattered t-storms, warm.

JULY 2026: Temp. 84° (2° above avg.); precip. 3" (2" below avg.). 1–10 Sunny, warm. 11–22 Scattered t-storms, hot. 23–27 Sunny, cooler. 28–31 Isolated t-storms, warm.

AUG. 2026: Temp. 81° (avg.); precip. 6" (avg. north, 2" above south). 1–13 Scattered t-storms; warm, then cooler. 14–21 Sunny north, t-storms south; mild. 22–24 Scattered t-storms east, tropical storm threat west; warm. 25–31 T-storms, then sunny; mild.

SEPT. 2026: Temp. 76° (1° below avg.); precip. 2.5" (2" below avg.). 1–8 Sunny, then showers; cool, then warmer. 9–14 Sunny, cool. 15–23 Sunny, warm. 24–30 Isolated showers; cool north, mild south.

OCT. 2026: Temp. 68° (2° above avg.); precip. 3" (avg.). 1–11 Scattered showers, warm. 12–19 Sunny, then rainy periods; cooler. 20–31 Sunny, warm.

REGION 9 FORECAST
UPPER MIDWEST

SUMMARY: Winter temperatures will be above normal, with the coldest periods in much of December, early and late January, and early February. Precipitation and snowfall will be below normal. The snowiest periods will occur in late November, late January, and early February. During **April** and **May**, it will be cooler and drier than normal in the east, while the west will be warmer than normal with above-normal precipitation. **Summer** will be cooler and drier than usual. The hottest periods will be in late June and early July. **September** and **October** will be cooler and drier than normal.

NOV. 2025: Temp. 30° (avg.); precip. 1" (1" below avg.). 1–5 Periods of rain and snow, chilly. 6–12 Sunny, cool. 13–16 A few showers, warm. 17–23 Rain and snow showers, then sunny; mild. 24–26 Snowstorm east, flurries west; very cold. 27–30 Flurries, mild.

DEC. 2025: Temp. 15° (4° below avg.); precip. 0.5" (0.5" below avg.). 1–4 Flurries, frigid. 5–10 Isolated snow showers, chilly. 11–19 A few snow showers, bitter cold. 20–25 Scattered snow showers, quite mild. 26–31 Sunny, very cold.

JAN. 2026: Temp. 17° (4° above avg.); precip. 0.5" (0.5" below avg.). 1–4 Flurries, bitter cold. 5–17 Snow showers, turning very mild. 18–28 Snowy periods, then sunny; turning frigid. 29–31 Snowstorm.

FEB. 2026: Temp. 17° (5° above avg.); precip. 1.3" (1" above avg. east, 0.5" below west). 1–6 Snowy periods east, flurries west; very cold. 7–14 Sunny, quite mild. 15–28 Periods of rain and snow east, flurries west; quite mild, then turning chilly.

MAR. 2026: Temp. 34° (6° above avg.); precip. 1.5" (avg.). 1–6 A few snow showers east, sunny west; mild. 7–17 Sunny, mild. 18–26 Showers, warm. 27–31 Rainy east, isolated showers west; cool, then warm.

APR. 2026: Temp. 42° (1° above avg.); precip. 1.5" (0.5" below avg.). 1–6 A few t-storms, warm. 7–10 Sunny; cool, then warm. 11–18 Rainy periods, chilly. 19–25 Showers, cool. 26–30 Rainy, then sunny; turning cool.

MAY 2026: Temp. 53° (2° below avg. east, avg. west); precip. 3.5" (1" below avg. east, 1" above west). 1–11 Showers, then sunny; chilly. 12–14 Sunny, turning warm. 15–19 Scattered showers east, t-storms west; warm, then cool. 20–31 Scattered t-storms, turning warm.

JUNE 2026: Temp. 64° (avg.); precip. 3.5" (1° below avg.). 1–7 Scattered t-storms, some heavy; turning warm. 8–17 Rainy periods, cool. 18–22 Scattered t-storms, warm. 23–30 Sunny, turning hot.

JULY 2026: Temp. 68° (1° below avg.); precip. 2.5" (1" below avg.). 1–3 Sunny, hot. 4–10 Scattered t-storms, turning cool. 11–20 Isolated t-storms, cool. 21–31 Sunny, then scattered t-storms; turning warm.

AUG. 2026: Temp. 66° (avg.); precip. 2.5" (1" below avg.). 1–7 Isolated t-storms, warm. 8–12 Sunny, warm. 13–18 Sunny east, isolated t-storms west; very warm. 19–24 A few t-storms, warm. 25–31 Sunny, then showers; turning cool.

SEPT. 2026: Temp. 57° (2° below avg.); precip. 3.5" (0.5" above avg.). 1–6 Sunny, turning very warm. 7–10 A few showers, chilly. 11–16 Sunny, then showers; cool. 17–30 Rainy periods, cool.

OCT. 2026: Temp. 48° (1° above avg.); precip. 1.5" (1" below avg.). 1–6 Sunny, cool east; showers, mild west. 7–17 Periods of rain and snow, quite chilly. 18–27 Sunny, turning warm. 28–31 Rain and snow showers, mild.

REGION 10 FORECAST
HEARTLAND

SUMMARY: Winter will be warmer than normal, with the coldest periods in mid-December and early and late January. Precipitation will be below normal. Snowfall will be below normal in the north and near normal south, with the snowiest periods in mid-November, late January, and early February. **April** and **May** will be warmer than normal, with below-normal precipitation in the north and above-normal south. **Summer** will be cooler and wetter than usual, with the hottest periods in early and mid-June, early and late July, and early August. **September** and **October** will be warmer than normal in the north and cooler south, with below-normal precipitation.

NOV. 2025: Temp. 44° (1° above avg.); precip. 1" (1" below avg.). 1–5 Sunny, warm. 6–10 Periods of rain and snow, turning cold. 11–14 Sunny, cool. 15–17 A few showers, cool. 18–20 Sunny north, snowstorm south; cold. 21–30 Sunny, then rainy periods; turning quite warm.

DEC. 2025: Temp. 35° (avg.); precip. 0.5" (1" below avg.). 1–2 Rainy, cool. 3–15 Sunny; warm, then turning very cold. 16–19 Flurries, cold. 20–28 Sunny, mild. 29–31 Flurries, chilly.

JAN. 2026: Temp. 31° (1° above avg.); precip. 0.5" (0.5" below avg.). 1–3 Flurries, very cold. 4–11 Sunny, chilly. 12–14 Sunny north, rain and snow showers south; quite mild. 15–20 Sunny, very mild. 21–31 Snowstorm, then sunny; turning frigid.

FEB. 2026: Temp. 36° (4° above avg.); precip. 2" (0.5" above avg. east, 0.5" below west). 1–3 Snowstorm. 4–13 Sunny, quite mild. 14–23 Rainy, then sunny; mild. 24–28 Rain and snow showers, chilly.

MAR. 2026: Temp. 48° (4° above avg.); precip. 1.5" (1" below avg.). 1–7 Sunny, turning warm. 8–11 A few showers, turning chilly. 12–17 Showers, then sunny; turning warm. 18–22 Rainy periods, warm. 23–31 Sunny, then a few t-storms; warm.

APR. 2026: Temp. 60° (5° above avg.); precip. 2.5" (1" below avg.). 1–12 Scattered t-storms, warm. 13–16 A few showers, cool. 17–28 Sunny, then a few t-storms; very warm. 29–30 Sunny, chilly.

MAY 2026: Temp. 63° (1° below avg.); precip. 5" (2" below avg. north, 2" above south). 1–7 Rainy periods, some heavy south; cool. 8–12 Rainy, chilly. 13–19 Sunny, then scattered t-storms; warm. 20–25 Sunny, warm north; showers, cool south. 26–31 Scattered t-storms, very warm.

JUNE 2026: Temp. 74° (1° above avg.); precip. 7" (2" above avg.). 1–7 Scattered t-storms, some heavy; hot. 8–17 Sunny, then t-storms; warm. 18–22 Scattered t-storms, hot. 23–30 A few t-storms, warm.

JULY 2026: Temp. 78° (avg.); precip. 5" (2" above avg. east, avg. west). 1–8 Isolated t-storms, hot. 9–19 Scattered t-storms, warm. 20–22 T-storms, cool. 23–31 Scattered t-storms, turning hot.

AUG. 2026: Temp. 73° (2° below avg.); precip. 4.5" (1" above avg.). 1–7 Scattered t-storms north, sunny south; turning hot. 8–15 Sunny, warm. 16–20 A few t-storms, very warm. 21–29 Isolated t-storms, warm. 30–31 Rainy, cool.

SEPT. 2026: Temp. 68.5° (0.5° above avg.); precip. 1.5" (2" below avg.). 1–5 Sunny, warm. 6–9 A few showers, turning chilly. 10–16 Sunny, turning warm. 17–19 T-storms, warm. 20–23 Sunny, hot. 24–30 Isolated t-storms, turning cool.

OCT. 2026: Temp. 57° (1° above avg. north, 1° below south); precip. 4" (1" above avg.). 1–10 Sunny, then rainy periods; turning warm. 11–15 Sunny north, rainy periods south; chilly. 16–19 Showers, quite chilly. 20–23 Sunny, turning warm. 24–31 Rainy periods, mild.

REGION 11 FORECAST
TEXAS-OKLAHOMA

SUMMARY: Winter will be warmer than normal, with the coldest periods in mid-December, early and late January, and early February. Precipitation and snowfall will be below normal; the best chance for snow is in mid-November. **April** and **May** will be warmer and wetter than usual. Watch for a tropical storm in late May. **Summer** will be hot, with the hottest periods in early and mid-June, mid-July, and late August. Rainfall will be above normal. Watch for a tropical storm in late August. **September** and **October** look to be cooler than normal in the north and warmer south, with above-normal rainfall.

NOV. 2025: Temp. 56° (1° below avg.); precip. 3" (avg.). 1–7 Sunny, very warm. 8–10 Rainy periods, mixed with snow north; turning cold. 11–20 Sunny, then showers; cold. 21–26 Sunny, warm. 27–30 Sunny north, showers south; very warm.

DEC. 2025: Temp. 51° (avg.); precip. 1.5" (1" below avg.). 1–3 Rainy, cold. 4–11 Sunny north, showers south; warm. 12–27 Sunny; cold, then warm. 28–31 A few showers, cool.

JAN. 2026: Temp. 49° (1° below avg.); precip. 2.5" (1" below avg. north, 1" above south). 1–9 Sunny north, showers south; chilly. 10–14 Rainy, cold. 15–19 Sunny, warm. 20–23 Sunny north, showers south; warm. 24–31 A few showers north, rainy periods south; cold.

FEB. 2026: Temp. 54° (3° above avg.); precip. 1.5" (1" above avg. north, 1" below south). 1–6 A few showers, then sunny; turning very cold. 7–13 Sunny, warm. 14–21 Showers, warm. 22–28 Rainy, especially north; chilly.

MAR. 2026: Temp. 60° (avg.); precip. 1.5" (1" below avg.). 1–5 Sunny north, rainy periods south; chilly. 6–9 Rainy, mild OK; sunny, cool TX. 10–18 Sunny, chilly. 19–27 Rainy, then sunny; turning warm. 28–31 Sunny, cool.

APR. 2026: Temp. 72° (5° above avg.); precip. 4" (1" above avg.). 1–7 T-storms north, sunny south; warm. 8–12 Sunny, then t-storms; warm. 13–19 Sunny OK, rainy TX; warm. 20–24 T-storms north, sunny south; very warm. 25–28 Rainy, cool. 29–30 Sunny, cool.

MAY 2026: Temp. 73.5° (2° below avg. north, 1° above south); precip. 8" (3" above avg.). 1–3 T-storms, cool. 4–6 Sunny, warm. 7–11 A few t-storms; cool north, warm south. 12–14 Sunny, cool. 15–21 T-storms, warm. 22–28 Rainy, cool. 29–31 Tropical storm threat.

JUNE 2026: Temp. 81° (1° above avg.); precip. 5.5" (1" above avg. north, 3" above south). 1–3 Sunny, hot. 4–9 T-storms, some heavy; turning cool. 10–16 Sunny, hot. 17–22 Sunny north, a few t-storms south; warm. 23–30 Scattered t-storms, warm.

JULY 2026: Temp. 84° (2° above avg.); precip. 3" (avg.). 1–7 Sunny north, isolated t-storms south; hot. 8–17 Sunny, quite hot. 18–22 T-storms, some heavy; warm. 23–31 Isolated t-storms north, sunny south; hot.

AUG. 2026: Temp. 82.5° (1° below avg. north, 2° above south); precip. 5.5" (3" above avg.). 1–9 Sunny, then a few t-storms; warm north, hot south. 10–12 T-storms, some heavy; warm. 13–22 Sunny, then isolated t-storms; warm. 23–25 Tropical storm threat. 26–31 A few t-storms, warm.

SEPT. 2026: Temp. 78° (1° above avg.); precip. 4.5" (1" above avg.). 1–4 Sunny, warm. 5–9 A few t-storms, hot. 10–19 Sunny; cool, then turning hot. 20–25 Sunny north, isolated t-storms south; hot. 26–30 Rainy periods, some heavy; turning cool.

OCT. 2026: Temp. 67.5° (2° below avg. north, 1° above south); precip. 4.8" (3" above avg. north, 0.5" below south). 1–9 Rainy periods north, a few t-storms south; turning warm. 10–14 Isolated t-storms, turning cool. 15–21 Sunny, then isolated showers; chilly. 22–31 Rainy, then sunny; cool north, warm south.

REGION 12 FORECAST
HIGH PLAINS

SUMMARY: Winter temperatures will be above normal, with the coldest periods in mid-December, late January, and early February. Precipitation and snowfall will be below normal in the north and near normal south. The snowiest periods are expected to be in late February and mid- and late March. **April** and **May** temperatures will be above normal, while rainfall will be below normal across the east and above normal in the west. **Summer** will be hotter and drier than usual, with the hottest periods in late June and early and mid-July. **September** and **October** will have above-normal temperatures and below-normal precipitation.

NOV. 2025: Temp. 39° (1° above avg.); precip. 1" (avg.). 1–4 Sunny, warm. 5–9 Periods of rain and snow, cold. 10–14 Sunny, turning warm. 15–19 Sunny north, rain and snow south; chilly. 20–22 Sunny, warm. 23–25 Rain and snow, cold north; sunny, warm south. 26–30 Sunny, cold.

DEC. 2025: Temp. 36° (7° above avg.); precip. 0.2" (0.3" below avg.). 1–10 Flurries, then sunny; turning very warm. 11–17 Snow showers, cold. 18–31 Sunny, then isolated rain or snow showers; quite warm.

JAN. 2026: Temp. 32° (6° above avg. north, 2° above south); precip. 0.2" (0.3" below avg.). 1–7 Sunny; very warm north, chilly south. 8–20 Isolated rain and snow showers, quite warm. 21–31 A few snow showers, cold.

FEB. 2026: Temp. 32° (5° above avg.); precip. 0.9" (0.3" below avg. north, 1" above south). 1–5 A few snow showers, bitter cold. 6–20 Sunny, then a few rain and snow showers; very warm. 21–23 Sunny, warm. 24–28 Sunny, warm north; snowstorm, cold south.

MAR. 2026: Temp. 43° (4° above avg.); precip. 1" (avg.). 1–9 Sunny north, rainy periods south; warm. 10–13 Snowstorm. 14–19 A few showers, warm. 20–22 Snowstorm. 23–31 Sunny north, a few rain or snow showers south; mild.

APR. 2026: Temp. 54° (5° above avg.); precip. 1" (0.5" below avg.). 1–11 Isolated rain or snow showers, then sunny; turning warm. 12–25 Isolated t-storms, very warm. 26–30 A few showers, turning cool.

MAY 2026: Temp. 58° (avg.); precip. 2.8" (1" below avg. east, 1.5" above west). 1–11 A few showers east, rainy periods west; chilly. 12–17 Sunny, then a few showers; turning warm. 18–31 Scattered t-storms; cool, then warm.

JUNE 2026: Temp. 69.5° (avg. north, 3° above south); precip. 1" (1.5" below avg.). 1–7 A few t-storms; cool north, warm south. 8–14 Isolated t-storms, warm north; sunny, hot south. 15–18 Sunny, warm. 19–25 A few t-storms, warm. 26–30 Sunny, hot.

JULY 2026: Temp. 74° (avg. north, 2° above south); precip. 2" (1" above avg. north, 1" below south). 1–5 Sunny, then a few t-storms; hot. 6–9 A few t-storms, warm north; sunny, hot south. 10–13 Scattered t-storms, warm. 14–18 T-storms north, sunny south; hot. 19–31 A few t-storms; warm north, hot south.

AUG. 2026: Temp. 71° (1° above avg. north, 1° below south); precip. 2.5" (avg. north, 1" above south). 1–5 Sunny, hot north; t-storms, cool south. 6–10 A few t-storms, cool. 11–19 Sunny, then isolated t-storms; warm. 20–23 Scattered t-storms, hot. 24–31 Sunny, then a few t-storms; warm.

SEPT. 2026: Temp. 65° (2° above avg.); precip. 1" (0.5" below avg.). 1–5 Sunny, very warm. 6–14 Sunny north, isolated t-storms south; turning cool. 15–21 A few showers, then sunny; warm. 22–30 Isolated showers, warm.

OCT. 2026: Temp. 50° (1° above avg.); precip. 0.5" (0.5" below avg.). 1–8 A few showers, chilly. 9–18 Sunny, then rain and snow showers; cold. 19–31 Sunny, warm.

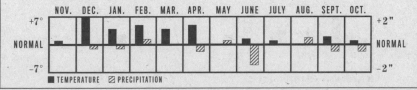

REGION 13 FORECAST
INTERMOUNTAIN

SUMMARY: Winter will be warmer than normal, with the coldest periods in late November, early December, and early February. Precipitation will be slightly above normal, with below-normal snowfall in the north and above-normal south. The snowiest periods will be in late January, early February, and late March. **April** and **May** look cooler and wetter than normal in the north, and warmer and drier south. **Summer** will be cooler and drier than usual in the north, while the south will be hotter and wetter. The hottest periods will be in mid- to late June, mid- to late July, and early to mid-August. **September** and **October** will be cooler than normal in the north but warmer south. Precipitation will be above normal.

NOV. 2025: Temp. 42.5° (3° above avg. east, avg. west); precip. 1.5" (0.5" above avg.). 1–6 Sunny, then a few showers; warm east, turning cold west. 7–13 Sunny, chilly. 14–18 Periods of rain and snow, cool. 19–23 Sunny, turning warm. 24–30 Periods of rain and snow, turning cold.

DEC. 2025: Temp. 39° (6° above avg.); precip. 0.5" (1" below avg.). 1–6 Flurries, very cold. 7–12 Sunny, mild. 13–24 A few showers east, rainy periods west; quite warm. 25–31 A few rain and snow showers east, sunny west; warm.

JAN. 2026: Temp. 37° (3° above avg.); precip. 1" (0.5" below avg.). 1–9 A few rain and snow showers, warm east; sunny, chilly west. 10–15 Sunny, warm. 16–20 A few rain and snow showers, mild. 21–23 Periods of rain and snow, warm north; snowstorm, chilly south. 24–31 Sunny, cold.

FEB. 2026: Temp. 38° (3° above avg.); precip. 2.5" (0.5" above avg.). 1–5 Snowy periods, very cold. 6–12 Rainy periods north, sunny south; warm. 13–16 Sunny, mild. 17–21 Rain and snow showers, mild. 22–28 A few rain and snow showers north, snowy periods south; cold.

MAR. 2026: Temp. 44° (avg.); precip. 2.5" (1" above avg.). 1–7 Sunny north, snowy south; turning mild. 8–12 A few rain and snow showers, chilly. 13–19 Periods of rain and snow, mild. 20–22 Showers, mild north; snowstorm, cold south. 23–31 Periods of rain and snow, cold.

APR. 2026: Temp. 52° (avg. north, 4° above south); precip. 1" (0.5" above avg. north, 0.5" below south). 1–7 A few showers; cold north, warm south. 8–14 Sunny, then rainy periods; turning cool. 15–19 Showers north, sunny south; cool north, warm south. 20–24 Sunny, very warm. 25–30 Rainy periods, cool.

MAY 2026: Temp. 58° (1° below avg. north, 1° above south); precip. 1.3" (0.3" above avg.). 1–6 Showers, then sunny; chilly. 7–15 Rainy periods, cool. 16–23 A few showers, mild. 24–31 Showers; cool north, warm south.

JUNE 2026: Temp. 67.5° (2° below avg. north, 3° above south); precip. 0.5" (avg.). 1–15 Showers, cool north; sunny, warm south. 16–23 Sunny north, a few t-storms south; hot. 24–30 Isolated t-storms, warm north; sunny, hot south.

JULY 2026: Temp. 74° (2° below avg. north, 2° above south); precip. 0.4" (0.1" below avg.). 1–7 Isolated t-storms, warm. 8–20 Sunny, warm north; scattered t-storms, hot south. 21–31 Isolated t-storms, then sunny; turning hot.

AUG. 2026: Temp. 75° (2° above avg.); precip. 1.1" (0.2" below avg. north, 0.3" above south). 1–11 Sunny, hot north; a few t-storms, warm south. 12–15 Sunny, warm. 16–22 Sunny, warm north; isolated t-storms, hot south. 23–31 Isolated t-storms, warm.

SEPT. 2026: Temp. 64.5° (1° below avg. north, 2° above south); precip. 1.5" (0.5" above avg.). 1–8 Sunny north, isolated t-storms south; warm. 9–11 Sunny; hot north, warm south. 12–21 Sunny, then a few showers; cool north, warm south. 22–30 Sunny, then rainy periods; cool north, warm south.

OCT. 2026: Temp. 51° (1° below avg.); precip. 1" (avg.). 1–8 Rainy periods, chilly. 9–19 Sunny, cool. 20–23 Rainy, chilly. 24–31 Sunny, warm.

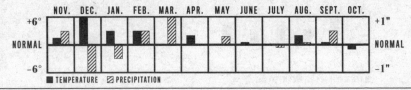

REGION 14 FORECAST
DESERT SOUTHWEST

SUMMARY: Winter will be warmer than normal, with above-normal precipitation in the east and below-normal west. The coldest periods will be in mid-November, early December, and late January. Snowfall will be above normal in the east and near normal west in areas that usually receive snow, with the snowiest periods in early December and early to mid-January. **April** and **May** will be warmer than normal, with above-normal rainfall in the east and below-normal west. **Summer** will be hotter than usual, with the hottest periods in early to mid-June and mid-July. It will be wetter than normal in the east and drier west. **September** and **October** will be warmer and drier than normal.

NOV. 2025: Temp. 57.5° (1° below avg. east, 2° above west); precip. 0.4" (0.1" above avg. east, 0.3" below west). 1–5 Sunny, warm. 6–12 A few showers east, sunny west; chilly. 13–17 A few rain and snow showers east, sunny west; chilly. 18–22 Sunny; chilly east, warm west. 23–30 Isolated showers, warm.

DEC. 2025: Temp. 53° (5° above avg.); precip. 0.2" (0.3" below avg.). 1–3 Snowy periods east, sunny west; cold. 4–6 Isolated showers, mild. 7–15 Sunny; turning cold east, warm west. 16–31 Sunny, then isolated showers; warm.

JAN. 2026: Temp. 49° (1° below avg. east, 1° above west); precip. 0.4" (0.1" below avg.). 1–6 Rainy periods, warm. 7–14 Periods of snow, cold east; sunny, warm west. 15–22 Sunny, then a few showers; chilly. 23–31 Sunny, cold.

FEB. 2026: Temp. 54° (2° above avg.); precip. 1.3" (0.8" above avg.). 1–3 Rain and snow east, rainy west; chilly. 4–17 Sunny, turning warm. 18–28 Rainy periods, turning chilly.

MAR. 2026: Temp. 62° (2° above avg.); precip. 0.3" (avg. east, 0.3" below west). 1–5 A few showers east, sunny west; cool. 6–15 Sunny, then isolated showers; cool. 16–21 Sunny, then a few showers; turning cool. 22–31 Sunny; cool, then warm.

APR. 2026: Temp. 71° (5° above avg.); precip. 0.6" (0.4" above avg. east, 0.2" below west). 1–4 Sunny, warm. 5–10 A few showers east, sunny west; warm. 11–15 Isolated showers, then sunny; cool. 16–18 Showers, cool east; sunny, hot west. 19–23 Sunny, hot. 24–30 A few t-storms east, sunny west; hot, then turning cool.

MAY 2026: Temp. 74° (avg.); precip. 0.5" (avg.). 1–6 Sunny, turning hot. 7–12 Isolated showers, cool. 13–18 Sunny, turning hot. 19–22 Isolated t-storms, cool. 23–31 Isolated t-storms east, sunny west; turning hot.

JUNE 2026: Temp. 88° (3° above avg.); precip. 0.3" (0.2" below avg.). 1–11 Sunny, hot. 12–17 Sunshine, very hot. 18–24 Scattered t-storms, warm east; sunny, hot west. 25–30 Isolated t-storms, hot.

JULY 2026: Temp. 90° (2° above avg.); precip. 2" (1" above avg. east, avg. west). 1–9 Isolated t-storms, warm. 10–19 Sunny, hot. 20–31 Scattered t-storms east, isolated t-storms west; warm.

AUG. 2026: Temp. 87.5° (1° below avg. east, 2° above west); precip. 2" (1" above avg. east, avg. west). 1–5 Scattered t-storms, warm. 6–11 T-storms east, sunny west; warm. 12–23 Sunny; warm east, hot west. 24–31 Isolated t-storms, warm.

SEPT. 2026: Temp. 81° (1° above avg.); precip. 1" (avg.). 1–3 A few t-storms, cool east; sunny, warm west. 4–13 Sunny, warm. 14–22 Isolated t-storms, then sunny; very warm. 23–26 Rainy periods, cool. 27–30 Sunny, cool.

OCT. 2026: Temp. 68.5° (0.5° above avg.); precip. 0.5" (0.5" below avg.). 1–4 A few showers east, sunny west; warm. 5–10 Sunny; warm east, cool west. 11–15 Sunny, then isolated showers; cool east, warm west. 16–31 Sunny; cool, then turning warm.

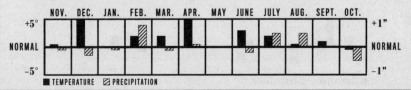

REGION **15** FORECAST

PACIFIC NORTHWEST

SUMMARY: Winter will be warmer than normal, with the coldest periods in late November, early December, and early February. Precipitation and snowfall will be below average, with the snowiest period in early February. **April** and **May** will be cooler than normal in the north and warmer south. Precipitation will be below normal. **Summer** will be cooler and wetter than normal in the north, while southern areas will be hotter and drier than normal. The hottest periods will be in mid- and late July and early and late August. **September** and **October** will be cooler and wetter than usual.

NOV. 2025: Temp. 47° (1° below avg.); precip. 7" (avg. north, 2" above south). 1–6 Rainy, then sunny; cool. 7–13 Showers north, sunny south; turning warm. 14–19 A few showers, mild. 20–30 Rainy periods, some heavy south; turning quite cold.

DEC. 2025: Temp. 49° (5° above avg.); precip. 5.5" (avg. north, 3" below south). 1–9 A few showers north, sunny south; very cold. 10–12 Isolated showers, chilly. 13–20 Rainy periods, some heavy; warm. 21–24 Rainy north, sunny south; mild. 25–31 Sunny, warm.

JAN. 2026: Temp. 45° (1° above avg.); precip. 4" (2" below avg.). 1–9 Sunny, chilly. 10–22 Rainy periods, warm. 23–31 Sunny, then a few showers; cold.

FEB. 2026: Temp. 46° (2° above avg.); precip. 5.5" (1" above avg.). 1–4 Periods of rain and snow north, a few showers south; very cold. 5–12 Rainy periods, warm. 13–19 Sunny, then rainy; turning chilly. 20–23 Sunny, warm. 24–28 Showers, chilly.

MAR. 2026: Temp. 48° (1° above avg.); precip. 2" (2" below avg.). 1–7 Sunny north, a few showers south; warm. 8–19 Rounds of showers, mild. 20–31 Scattered showers, chilly.

APR. 2026: Temp. 51° (avg.); precip. 2.5" (1" below avg.). 1–7 Rainy periods, then sunny; chilly. 8–12 A few showers, warm. 13–21 Scattered showers, turning chilly. 22–30 Sunny, then showers; warm, then chilly.

MAY 2026: Temp. 56° (1° below avg. north, 1° above south); precip. 2.5" (0.5" above avg.). 1–6 Isolated showers, then sunny; cool. 7–13 Rainy periods, cool. 14–18 Sunny, then a few showers; warm. 19–21 Sunny, warm. 22–31 A few showers, cool north; sunny, warm south.

JUNE 2026: Temp. 60° (2° below avg. north, avg. south); precip. 2" (0.5" above avg.). 1–3 Rainy; cool north, warm south. 4–16 Scattered showers; cool north, warm south. 17–23 Sunny, warm. 24–30 Isolated showers, turning cool.

JULY 2026: Temp. 65° (1° below avg.); precip. 0.5" (0.2" above avg. north, 0.2" below south). 1–6 Isolated showers, cool. 7–20 Sunny; warm, then turning hot. 21–31 Isolated t-storms, then sunny; cool, then turning hot.

AUG. 2026: Temp. 69° (2° above avg.); precip. 0.5" (0.5" below avg.). 1–5 Sunny, hot. 6–21 Isolated t-storms, then sunny; warm. 22–25 Scattered showers, cool. 26–31 Sunny, turning hot.

SEPT. 2026: Temp. 61° (1° below avg.); precip. 4.5" (3" above avg.). 1–10 Sunny, very warm. 11–17 Showers, then sunny; cool. 18–30 Rainy periods, chilly.

OCT. 2026: Temp. 54° (1° below avg.); precip. 3" (1.5" below avg. north, 0.5" above south). 1–3 Rainy, chilly. 4–17 Sunny, cool. 18–23 Showers north, rainy periods south; mild. 24–31 Isolated showers, warm.

REGION **16** FORECAST
PACIFIC SOUTHWEST

SUMMARY: Winter will be warmer and drier than normal, with below-normal mountain snows. The coldest temperatures will occur in late January and late February. The stormiest periods will be in late November, mid-January, and late February. **April** and **May** will be warmer than normal with below-normal rainfall. **Summer** will be hotter and drier than normal, with the hottest periods in early and late June and mid- to late August. **September** and **October** will be cooler than normal, with above-normal rainfall in the north and below-normal south.

NOV. 2025: Temp. 60° (1° above avg.); precip. 1" (avg.). 1–4 Sunny, then isolated showers; mild. 5–13 Sunny, cool. 14–16 A few showers, mild north; sunny, cool south. 17–24 Sunny, warm. 25–30 Rainy periods, cool.

DEC. 2025: Temp. 57.5° (1° above avg. north, 4° above south); precip. 0.5" (1.5" below avg.). 1–13 Sunny; cool, then warm. 14–16 A few showers north, sunny south; warm. 17–25 Sunny; mild north, very warm south. 26–31 A few showers, mild.

JAN. 2026: Temp. 58° (2° above avg.); precip. 3" (1° above avg. north, 1" below south). 1–5 Sunny, cool north; a few showers, warm south. 6–14 Showers north, sunny south; warm. 15–18 Rainy, then sunny; turning chilly. 19–23 Rainy periods, some heavy; cool. 24–31 Sunny, cool.

FEB. 2026: Temp. 58° (2° above avg.); precip. 3.5" (1" below avg. north, 2" above south). 1–7 Rainy periods, turning warm. 8–15 Sunny, warm. 16–26 Rainy periods, some heavy south; cool. 27–28 Sunny, cool.

MAR. 2026: Temp. 59° (avg. north, 2° above south); precip. 2.5" (0.5" above avg. north, 0.5" below south). 1–4 Sunny, warm. 5–14 Rainy periods, cool. 15–17 Sunny, mild. 18–22 Rainy periods north, sunny south; cool. 23–31 A few showers, then sunny; cool north, warm south.

APR. 2026: Temp. 62° (1° above avg.); precip. 0.5" (0.5" below avg.). 1–10 Sunny, mild. 11–13 Rainy, cool. 14–18 Sunny, then isolated showers; warm. 19–30 Sunny; very warm, then turning cool.

MAY 2026: Temp. 67° (3° above avg.); precip. 0.2" (0.3" below avg.). 1–9 Sunny; warm, then turning cool. 10–13 Isolated showers, cool. 14–19 Isolated showers, turning warm. 20–31 Sunny, hot inland; A.M. sprinkles, P.M. sun, warm coast.

JUNE 2026: Temp. 74° (5° above avg.); precip. 0" (0.1" below avg.). 1–7 Sunny, warm. 8–15 Sunny, hot. 16–25 Sunny, hot inland; A.M. clouds, P.M. sun, warm coast. 26–30 Sunny, hot.

JULY 2026: Temp. 72.5° (1° below avg. north, 2° above south); precip. 0" (avg.). 1–5 Sunny; cool north, warm south. 6–11 Sunny; very warm, then cooler. 12–17 Sunny; cool north, warm south. 18–31 Sunny, hot inland; A.M. clouds, P.M. sun, warm coast.

AUG. 2026: Temp. 73° (1° above avg.); precip. 0" (avg.). 1–9 Sunny; hot inland, warm coast. 10–17 Isolated sprinkles north, sunny south; warm. 18–21 Sunny, hot. 22–31 Sunny, hot inland; A.M. clouds, P.M. sun, cool coast.

SEPT. 2026: Temp. 72° (avg.); precip. 0.3" (0.2" above avg.). 1–9 Sunny, warm. 10–14 Plenty of sun; cool north, hot south. 15–22 A few showers north, sunny south; cool. 23–30 Isolated showers, cool.

OCT. 2026: Temp. 65° (1° below avg.); precip. 0.6" (0.5" above avg. north, 0.3" below south). 1–9 Isolated showers, then sunny; cool. 10–19 Sunny; warm, then turning cool. 20–22 Rainy, cool. 23–31 Sunny, warm.

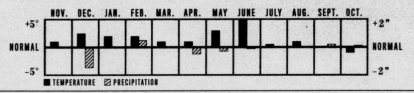

REGION 17 FORECAST
ALASKA

SUMMARY: Winter temperatures will be milder than normal, with the coldest periods occurring in early to mid-December and mid-February. Precipitation and snowfall will be below normal, with the snowiest periods in late November, mid-December, and early February. **April** and **May** will be warmer than normal, with above-normal precipitation in the north and below-normal south. **Summer** will be cooler than normal, with above-normal precipitation. The hottest periods will be in early June and mid-August. **September** and **October** will be drier than normal, with below-normal temperatures in the north, above-normal south.

NOTE: The following abbreviations are used for Alaskan regions: north (N), central (C), south (S), panhandle (P), elsewhere (EW).

NOV. 2025: Temp. 6° N, 39° S (2° above avg.); precip. 0.2" N, 4" S (0.2" below avg. N, 1" below S). 1–3 Periods of rain and snow, chilly. 4–12 Clear, cold N; snow showers, warm C+S. 13–21 Flurries, cold N; periods of rain and snow, warm C+S. 22–28 Snow showers, turning cold. 29–30 Snowstorm P, sunny EW; cold.

DEC. 2025: Temp. -7° N, 30° S (2° below avg.); precip. 0.1" N, 4" S (0.1" below avg. N, 1" below S). 1–8 Snowy periods P, flurries EW; bitter cold. 9–16 Clear; chilly N, frigid C+S. 17–22 Snowstorm P, flurries EW; very cold. 23–31 Rainy periods P, snow showers EW; quite mild.

JAN. 2026: Temp. 0° N, 39° S (10° above avg.); precip. 0.7" N, 5.5" S (0.5" above avg.). 1–13 Flurries N+C, rainy periods S; warm. 14–19 Snow showers N+C, rain and snow S; mild. 20–27 Flurries, quite mild. 28–31 Clear, cold N+P; snowy periods, very mild EW.

FEB. 2026: Temp. -8° N, 34° S (3° above avg.); precip. 0.2" N, 3" S (avg. N, 1" below S). 1–4 Snowstorm C, flurries EW; mild. 5–7 Snowstorm P, clear EW; cold. 8–16 Rainy periods, mild P; flurries, frigid EW. 17–28 Clear, turning cold N; snow showers, mild EW.

MAR. 2026: Temp. -5° N, 40° S (6° above avg.); precip. 0.2" N, 4" S (0.3" below avg. N, 1" below S). 1–13 Flurries N, rainy S; mild. 14–17 Clear, mild. 18–27 Sunny, cold N; periods of rain/snow, mild EW. 28–31 Rain and snow showers, cold.

APR. 2026: Temp. 7° N, 44° S (3° above avg.); precip. 1" N, 2" S (0.3" above avg. N, 1" below S). 1–5 A few rain and snow showers, then sunny; cold. 6–14 Rainy periods P, sunny EW; cold. 15–25 Sunny, then periods of rain and snow; turning warm. 26–30 Sunny, warm.

MAY 2026: Temp. 25.5° N, 50° EW (3° above avg.); precip. 1" N, 3.4" S (0.4" above avg.). 1–7 Flurries N, sunny EW; turning warm. 8–13 A few rain and snow showers N+C, showers S; mild. 14–25 Sunny N, a few showers C+S, rainy periods P; warm C+S, chilly EW. 26–31 A few showers, cool.

JUNE 2026: Temp. 36° N, 55.5° EW (avg.); precip. 1.2" N, 3" S (0.5" above avg. N, 0.5" below S). 1–4 Showers, then sunny; very warm. 5–16 Sunny N, a few showers EW; warm, then turning cool. 17–25 Rainy periods, cool. 26–30 Showers, quite cool.

JULY 2026: Temp. 41.5° N, 56.5° EW (1° below avg.); precip. 2.2" N, 5.5" S (1" above avg.). 1–11 Scattered showers; warm P, cool EW. 12–16 Sunny N+P, showers EW; cool. 17–25 Rainy periods, then cool. 26–31 Sunny, mild N+C; rainy, cool S.

AUG. 2026: Temp. 40.5° N, 56° EW (1° below avg.); precip. 0.5" N, 7.5" S (0.7" below avg. N, 2" above S). 1–15 Showers N+C, rainy periods S; cool. 16–21 Rainy periods P, isolated showers EW; chilly N, very warm EW. 22–31 Rain and snow showers, cold N; sunny, warm C; periods of rain, mild S.

SEPT. 2026: Temp. 32.5° N, 53° EW (2° below avg.); precip. 0.5" N, 5" S (0.6" below avg. N, 2.5" below S). 1–12 Rain and snow showers N, a few showers C, rainy S; turning cool. 13–18 Flurries N, a few showers EW; chilly. 19–30 Periods of rain and snow N+C, a few showers S; cold.

OCT. 2026: Temp. 19° N, 46° S (1° below avg. N, 3° above S); precip. 0.3" N, 7.5" S (0.2" below avg. N, 0.5" above S). 1–3 Sunny, cold. 4–8 Snow showers N+C, rainy S; mild. 9–11 Clear, chilly N+C; rainy, mild S. 12–21 Flurries N, periods of rain and snow C, some rain S; warm. 22–31 Rainy periods, mild P; snowy periods, cold EW.

REGION 18 FORECAST
HAWAII

SUMMARY: **Winter** will be warmer than normal, with the coolest periods in late November, late January into early February, and mid-March. Rainfall will be below normal with the stormiest periods in early and late November, early December, mid-February, and mid- to late March. **April** and **May** will be warmer than normal, with below-normal rainfall in the east and above-normal central and west. **Summer** will be warmer than usual, with the hottest periods in mid- to late June and mid-August. Rainfall will be below normal in the east, above normal central and west. **September** and **October** will be cooler than normal, with the hottest period in early to mid-September. Rainfall will be above normal. Watch for a tropical storm in mid-September.

Key: East (E), Central (C), West (W). Note: Temperature and precipitation are substantially based upon topography. The detailed forecast focuses on the Honolulu–Waikiki area and provides general trends elsewhere.

NOV. 2025: Temp. 77.5° (avg.); precip. 2.2" (1" below avg. E+C, 1" above W). 1–9 Rain E+W, showers C; mild. 10–19 Showers E, sunny C+W; warm. 20–27 Isolated showers, cooler. 28–30 Sunny E; rain, some heavy C+W; mild.

DEC. 2025: Temp. 76.5° (3° above avg. E, avg. W); precip. 2" (6" below avg. E, 1" above C+W). 1–4 Sunny, warm. 5–7 Sunny E, heavy rain C+W; warm. 8–13 Sunny, mild. 14–27 Sunny E; showers, then sunny C+W; warm. 28–31 Isolated showers E, sunny C+W; mild.

JAN. 2026: Temp. 74° (1° above avg.); precip. 0.5" (4" below avg. E, 1" below C+W). 1–5 Isolated showers, warm. 6–17 Sunny E+W, scattered showers C; mild. 18–22 Showers, mild. 23–31 Sunny E; sunny, then showers C+W; warm, then cooler.

FEB. 2026: Temp. 74° (1° above avg.); precip. 1" (1" below avg.). 1–4 Sunny E, showers C+W; cool. 5–10 Sunny, warmer. 11–17 Frequent rains, warm. 18–28 Rainy E+W, isolated showers C; mild.

MAR. 2026: Temp. 75° (avg. E, 2° above W); precip. 1" (1" below avg.). 1–8 Sunny E+C; sunny, then showers W; warm. 9–13 Showers E, sunny C+W; cool. 14–31 Rainy E+W, scattered showers C; warm.

APR. 2026: Temp. 76.5° (avg. E, 2° above W); precip. 0.4" (3" below avg. E, 1" above C+W). 1–9 Sunny, then showers; mild. 10–24 Showers E+W, sunny C; warm. 25–30 Sunny, then showers; cooler.

MAY 2026: Temp. 79° (2° above avg.); precip. 0.3" (0.4" below avg.). 1–9 Showers E+C, sunny W; warm. 10–13 Showers, warm. 14–22 Showers E, sunny C+W; mild. 23–31 Scattered showers, mild.

JUNE 2026: Temp. 80.5° (1° above avg.); precip. 0.2" (0.2" below avg.). 1–12 Showers E+W, sunny C; warm. 13–17 Sunny, warm. 18–30 Scattered showers, warm E+W; sunny, hot C.

JULY 2026: Temp. 81.3° (0.5° below avg. E, 1° above W); precip. 0.8" (1" below avg. E, 1" above C+W). 1–9 Showers, warm. 10–17 Showers E+W, sunny C; warm. 18–20 Sunny E+C, showers W; warm. 21–26 Isolated showers, warm. 27–31 Showers, some heavy; cooler.

AUG. 2026: Temp. 81.5° (1° above avg. E, 1° below W); precip. 0.3" (0.3" below avg.). 1–8 Scattered showers, some heavy E; warm. 9–12 Showers, warm. 13–20 Showers E, sunny C+W; hot. 21–29 Showers, warm. 30–31 Sunny, warm.

SEPT. 2026: Temp. 81° (0.5° above avg.); precip. 1.5" (3" above avg. E, 0.4" below C+W). 1–17 Showers E+W, sunny C; hot. 18–20 Tropical storm threat E, sunny C+W; warm. 21–30 Showers E, sunny C+W; warm.

OCT. 2026: Temp. 79° (1° below avg.); precip. 3" (1" above avg.). 1–8 Showers E+W, sunny C; warm. 9–14 Sunny, cooler. 15–21 Showers, some heavy; cool. 22–31 Rainy, then sunny; mild.

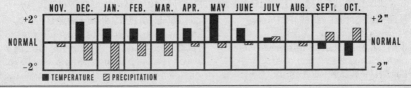

ASTROLOGY
SECRETS OF THE ZODIAC

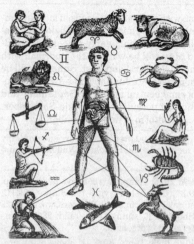

The Man of the Signs

Ancient astrologers believed that each astrological sign influenced a specific part of the body. The first sign of the zodiac—Aries—was attributed to the head, with the rest of the signs moving down the body, ending with Pisces at the feet.

♈ Aries, head	ARI	Mar. 21–Apr. 20
♉ Taurus, neck	TAU	Apr. 21–May 20
♊ Gemini, arms	GEM	May 21–June 20
♋ Cancer, breast	CAN	June 21–July 22
♌ Leo, heart	LEO	July 23–Aug. 22
♍ Virgo, belly	VIR	Aug. 23–Sept. 22
♎ Libra, reins	LIB	Sept. 23–Oct. 22
♏ Scorpio, secrets	SCO	Oct. 23–Nov. 22
♐ Sagittarius, thighs	SAG	Nov. 23–Dec. 21
♑ Capricorn, knees	CAP	Dec. 22–Jan. 19
♒ Aquarius, legs	AQU	Jan. 20–Feb. 19
♓ Pisces, feet	PSC	Feb. 20–Mar. 20

ASTROLOGY VS. ASTRONOMY

Astrology is a tool we use to plan events according to the placements of the Sun, the Moon, and the planets in the 12 signs of the zodiac. In astrology, the planetary movements do not cause events; rather, they explain the path, or "flow," that events tend to follow. *The Moon's astrological place is given on the next page.* **Astronomy** is the study of the actual placement of the known planets and constellations. The Moon's astronomical place is given in the **Left-Hand Calendar Pages, 120–146.** *(The placement of the planets in the signs of the zodiac is not the same astrologically and astronomically.)*

The dates in the **Best Days** table, **pages 226–227,** are based on the astrological passage of the Moon.

WHEN MERCURY IS RETROGRADE

Sometimes the other planets appear to be traveling backward through the zodiac; this is an illusion. We call this illusion *retrograde motion*.

According to astrology, Mercury's retrograde periods can cause our plans to go awry. However, intuition is high during these periods and coincidences can be extraordinary.

When Mercury is retrograde, stay flexible, allow more time for travel, and don't sign contracts. Review projects and plans but wait until Mercury is direct again to make final decisions.

In 2026, Mercury will be retrograde during February 25–March 19, June 28–July 23, and October 24–November 13.

–Celeste Longacre

GARDENING BY THE MOON'S SIGN
USE CHART ON NEXT PAGE TO FIND THE BEST DATES FOR THE FOLLOWING GARDEN TASKS . . .

PLANT, TRANSPLANT, AND GRAFT: Cancer, Scorpio, Pisces, or Taurus
HARVEST: Aries, Leo, Sagittarius, Gemini, or Aquarius
BUILD/FIX FENCES OR GARDEN BEDS: Capricorn

CONTROL INSECT PESTS, PLOW, AND WEED: Aries, Gemini, Leo, Sagittarius, or Aquarius
PRUNE: Aries, Leo, or Sagittarius. During a waxing Moon, pruning encourages growth; during a waning Moon, it discourages it.

SETTING EGGS BY THE MOON'S SIGN

Chicks take about 21 days to hatch. Those born under a waxing Moon in Cancer, Scorpio, or Pisces are healthier and mature faster. To ensure that chicks are born during these times, "set eggs" (place eggs in an incubator or under a hen) 21 days before the desired hatching dates.

EXAMPLE:
The Moon is new on March 18 and full on April 1 (EDT). Between these dates, the Moon is in the sign of Cancer on March 25 and 26. To have chicks born on March 25, count back 21 days; set eggs on March 4.

Below are the best days to set eggs in 2026, using only the fruitful dates between the new and full Moons and counting back 21 days:

JAN.: 1, 9, 10, 27–29	**APR.:** 1, 2, 10, 28, 29	**JULY:** 1, 2, 28, 29	**OCT.:** 1, 2, 19, 28, 29
FEB.: 5, 6, 25	**MAY:** 7, 8, 25, 26	**AUG.:** 7, 24, 25	**NOV.:** 24, 25
MAR.: 4, 5	**JUNE:** 3–5, 23, 30	**SEPT.:** 3, 4, 20–22, 30	**DEC.:** 21–23, 30, 31

The Moon's Astrological Place, 2025–26

	NOV.	DEC.	JAN.	FEB.	MAR.	APR.	MAY	JUNE	JULY	AUG.	SEPT.	OCT.	NOV.	DEC.
1	PSC	ARI	GEM	LEO	LEO	LIB	SCO	SAG	CAP	PSC	TAU	GEM	LEO	VIR
2	ARI	TAU	CAN	LEO	VIR	LIB	SCO	CAP	AQU	PSC	TAU	GEM	LEO	VIR
3	ARI	TAU	CAN	VIR	VIR	SCO	SAG	CAP	AQU	ARI	GEM	CAN	VIR	LIB
4	TAU	GEM	LEO	VIR	VIR	SCO	SAG	AQU	PSC	ARI	GEM	CAN	VIR	LIB
5	TAU	GEM	LEO	LIB	LIB	SCO	SAG	AQU	PSC	TAU	CAN	LEO	LIB	SCO
6	GEM	CAN	LEO	LIB	LIB	SAG	CAP	AQU	ARI	TAU	CAN	LEO	LIB	SCO
7	GEM	CAN	VIR	LIB	SCO	SAG	CAP	PSC	ARI	GEM	LEO	VIR	LIB	SAG
8	CAN	LEO	VIR	SCO	SCO	CAP	AQU	PSC	ARI	GEM	LEO	VIR	SCO	SAG
9	CAN	LEO	LIB	SCO	SAG	CAP	AQU	ARI	TAU	CAN	LEO	LIB	SCO	SAG
10	CAN	VIR	LIB	SAG	SAG	CAP	AQU	ARI	TAU	CAN	VIR	LIB	SAG	CAP
11	LEO	VIR	SCO	SAG	SAG	AQU	PSC	TAU	GEM	LEO	VIR	SCO	SAG	CAP
12	LEO	LIB	SCO	SAG	CAP	AQU	PSC	TAU	GEM	LEO	LIB	SCO	SAG	AQU
13	VIR	LIB	SCO	CAP	CAP	PSC	ARI	GEM	CAN	VIR	LIB	SCO	CAP	AQU
14	VIR	LIB	SAG	CAP	AQU	PSC	ARI	GEM	CAN	VIR	SCO	SAG	CAP	AQU
15	LIB	SCO	SAG	AQU	AQU	ARI	TAU	CAN	LEO	LIB	SCO	SAG	AQU	PSC
16	LIB	SCO	CAP	AQU	AQU	ARI	TAU	CAN	LEO	LIB	SAG	CAP	AQU	PSC
17	LIB	SAG	CAP	PSC	PSC	TAU	GEM	LEO	VIR	LIB	SAG	CAP	AQU	ARI
18	SCO	SAG	CAP	PSC	PSC	TAU	GEM	LEO	VIR	SCO	SAG	CAP	PSC	ARI
19	SCO	SAG	AQU	PSC	ARI	GEM	CAN	VIR	LIB	SCO	CAP	AQU	PSC	ARI
20	SAG	CAP	AQU	ARI	ARI	GEM	CAN	VIR	LIB	SAG	CAP	AQU	ARI	TAU
21	SAG	CAP	PSC	ARI	TAU	GEM	LEO	VIR	SCO	SAG	AQU	PSC	ARI	TAU
22	SAG	AQU	PSC	TAU	TAU	CAN	LEO	LIB	SCO	SAG	AQU	PSC	TAU	GEM
23	CAP	AQU	ARI	TAU	GEM	CAN	VIR	LIB	SCO	CAP	AQU	PSC	TAU	GEM
24	CAP	AQU	ARI	GEM	GEM	LEO	VIR	SCO	SAG	CAP	PSC	ARI	GEM	CAN
25	AQU	PSC	ARI	GEM	CAN	LEO	LIB	SCO	SAG	AQU	PSC	ARI	GEM	CAN
26	AQU	PSC	TAU	CAN	CAN	VIR	LIB	SCO	CAP	AQU	ARI	TAU	CAN	LEO
27	AQU	ARI	TAU	CAN	LEO	VIR	LIB	SAG	CAP	AQU	ARI	TAU	CAN	LEO
28	PSC	ARI	GEM	LEO	LEO	LIB	SCO	SAG	CAP	PSC	TAU	GEM	LEO	VIR
29	PSC	TAU	GEM	—	LEO	LIB	SCO	CAP	AQU	PSC	TAU	GEM	LEO	VIR
30	ARI	TAU	CAN	—	VIR	LIB	SAG	CAP	AQU	ARI	TAU	CAN	VIR	LIB
31	—	GEM	CAN	—	VIR	—	SAG	—	PSC	ARI	—	CAN	—	LIB

ASTROLOGY
BEST DAYS FOR 2026

This chart is based on the Moon's sign and shows the best days each month for certain activities. –*Celeste Longacre*

	JAN.	FEB.	MAR.	APR.	MAY	JUNE	JULY	AUG.	SEPT.	OCT.	NOV.	DEC.
Quit smoking	4, 9, 14	5, 10	6, 9	6, 15	3, 13	9, 13	5, 11	3, 7	3, 7	5, 28	5, 25	3, 7, 30
Bake	2, 3, 30, 31	26, 27	25, 26	22, 23	19, 20	15, 16	13, 14	9, 10	5, 6	3, 4, 30, 31	26, 27	24, 25
Brew	11–13	8, 9	7, 8	3–5	1, 2, 28, 29	24–26	21–23	18, 19	14, 15	11–13	8, 9	5, 6
Dry fruit, vegetables, or meat	4–6	10–12	9–11	6, 7	3–5	9, 10	6–8	3, 4, 30, 31	7–9	5, 6	1, 2, 28, 29	26, 27
Make jams or jellies	21, 22	17–19	17, 18	13, 14	11, 12	7, 8	4, 5, 31	1, 2, 28, 29	24, 25	21–23	18, 19	15, 16
Can, pickle, or make sauerkraut	11–13	8, 9	7, 8	3–5	11, 12	7, 8	4, 5	1, 2, 29	5, 6	3, 4, 30, 31	26, 27	5, 6, 24, 25
Begin diet to lose weight	4, 9, 14	5, 10	6, 9	6, 15	3, 13	9, 13	5, 11	3, 7	3, 7	5, 28	5, 25	3, 7, 30
Begin diet to gain weight	23, 28	20, 24	20, 23	19, 24	17, 21	17, 22	19, 24	15, 20	12, 16	14, 24	10, 21	17, 22
Cut hair to encourage growth	26, 27	22, 23	21, 22	28–30	25–27	22, 23	19, 20	15–17	12, 13	21–23	22, 23	20, 21
Cut hair to discourage growth	9, 10	5–7	5, 6	13, 14	11, 12, 15	11, 12	9, 10	5, 6	1, 2, 28–30	9, 27	5–7	3, 4, 30, 31
Perm hair	19, 20	15, 16	14–16	11, 12	8–10	4–6	2, 3, 29, 30	25–27	21–23	19, 20	15–17	12–14
Color hair	26, 27	22, 23	21, 22	17, 18	15, 16	11, 12	9, 10	5, 6	1, 2, 28–30	26, 27	22, 23	20, 21
Straighten hair	14, 15	10–12	9–11	6, 7	3–5, 30, 31	1, 27, 28	24, 25	20–22	16–18	14, 15	10–12	7–9
Have dental care	7, 8	3, 4	2–4, 30, 31	26, 27	23, 24	19–21	17, 18	13, 14	10, 11	7, 8	3, 4, 30	1, 2, 28, 29
Start projects	19	18	19	18	17	15	15	13	11	11	10	9
End projects	17	16	17	16	15	13	13	11	9	9	8	7
Demolish	11–13	8, 9	7, 8	3–5	1, 2, 28, 29	24–26	21–23	18, 19	14, 15	11–13	8, 9	5, 6
Lay shingles	4–6	1, 2, 28	1, 27–29	24, 25	21, 22	17, 18	15, 16	11, 12	7–9	5, 6	1, 2, 28, 29	26, 27
Paint	9, 10	5–7	5, 6	1, 2, 28–30	25–27	22, 23	19, 20	15–17	12, 13	9, 10	5–7	3, 4, 30, 31
Wash windows	23–25	20, 21	19, 20	15, 16	13, 14	9, 10	6–8	3, 4, 30, 31	26, 27	24, 25	20, 21	17–19
Wash floors	21, 22	17–19	17, 18	13, 14	11, 12	7, 8	4, 5, 31	1, 2, 28, 29	24, 25	21–23	18, 19	15, 16
Go camping	14, 15	10–12	9–11	6, 7	3–5, 30, 31	1, 27, 28	24, 25	20–22	16–18	14, 15	10–12	7–9

See what to do when via Almanac.com/2026.

	JAN.	FEB.	MAR.	APR.	MAY	JUNE	JULY	AUG.	SEPT.	OCT.	NOV.	DEC.
Entertain	4–6	1, 2, 28	1, 27–29	24, 25	21, 22	17, 18	15, 16	11, 12	7–9	5, 6	1, 2, 28, 29	26, 27
Travel for pleasure	4–6	1, 2, 28	1, 27–29	24, 25	21, 22	17, 18	15, 16	11, 12	7–9	5, 6	1, 2, 28, 29	26, 27
Get married	9, 10	5–7	5, 6	1, 2, 28–30	25–27	22, 23	19, 20	15–17	12, 13	9, 10	5–7	3, 4, 30, 31
Ask for a loan	11–13	8, 9	7, 8	3, 4	2, 15	11, 12	9, 10	5, 6	1, 2, 28–30	3, 4, 30, 31	8, 26, 27	5, 6
Buy a home	26, 27	22, 23	21, 22	18, 22, 23	28, 29	24–26	21–23	18, 19	14, 15	11–13	22, 23	20, 21
Move (house/household)	1, 28, 29	24, 25	23, 24	19–21	17, 18	13, 14	11, 12	7, 8	3, 4	1, 2, 28, 29	24, 25	22, 23
Advertise to sell	26, 27	22, 23	21, 22	18, 24, 25	28, 29	24–26	21–23	18, 19	14, 15	11–13	22, 23	20, 21
Mow to promote growth	21, 22	26, 27	25, 26	22, 23	28, 29	24–26	21–23	18, 19	14, 15	11–13	18, 19	15, 16
Mow to slow growth	11–13	8, 9	7, 8	3–5	11, 12	7, 8	4, 5, 31	1, 2, 29	5, 6	3, 4, 30, 31	26, 27	5, 6
Plant aboveground crops	21, 22, 30, 31	26, 27	25, 26	22, 23	28, 29	24–26	21–23	18, 19	14, 15	11–13	18, 19	15, 16
Plant belowground crops	11–13	8, 9	7, 8	3–5	11, 12	7, 8	4, 5, 31	9, 10	5, 6	3, 4, 30, 31	8, 26, 27	5, 6
Destroy pests and weeds	23–25	20, 21	19, 20	15, 16	13, 14	9, 10	6–8	3, 4, 30, 31	26, 27	24, 25	20, 21	17–19
Graft or pollinate	2, 3, 30, 31	26, 27	25, 26	22, 23	19, 20	15, 16	13, 14	9, 10	5, 6	3, 4, 30, 31	26, 27	24, 25
Prune to encourage growth	23–25	20, 21	27–29	24, 25	21, 22	17, 18	24, 25	20–22	16–18	14, 15	20, 21	17–19
Prune to discourage growth	4–6	10–12	9–11	6, 7	3–5	9, 10	6–8	3, 4, 30, 31	7–9	5, 6	1, 2, 28, 29	26, 27
Pick fruit	7, 8	3, 4	2–4, 30, 31	26, 27	23, 24	19–21	17, 18	13, 14	10, 11	7, 8	3, 4, 30	1, 2, 28, 29
Harvest aboveground crops	26, 27	22, 23	30, 31	26, 27	23, 24	19–21	17, 18	13, 14	19, 20	16–18	22, 23	20, 21
Harvest belowground crops	7, 8	3, 4	4, 12, 13	8–10	6, 7	2, 3	9, 10	5, 6	1, 2, 28–30	7, 8	3, 4, 30	1, 2, 28, 29
Cut hay	23–25	20, 21	19, 20	15, 16	13, 14	9, 10	6–8	3, 4, 30, 31	26, 27	24, 25	20, 21	17–19
Begin logging, set posts, pour concrete	16–18	13, 14	12, 13	8–10	6, 7	2, 3, 29, 30	1, 26–28	23, 24	19, 20	16–18	13, 14	10, 11
Purchase animals	2, 3, 30, 31	26, 27	25, 26	22, 23	19, 20	15, 16	13, 14	9, 10	5, 6	3, 4, 30, 31	26, 27	24, 25
Breed animals	11–13	8, 9	7, 8	3–5	1, 2, 28, 29	24–26	21–23	18, 19	14, 15	11–13	8, 9	5, 6
Wean	4, 9, 14	5, 10	6, 9	6, 15	3, 13	9, 13	5, 11	3, 7	3, 7	5, 28	5, 25	3, 7, 30
Castrate animals	19, 20	15, 16	14–16	11, 12	8–10	4–6	2, 3, 29, 30	25–27	21–23	19, 20	15–17	12–14
Slaughter livestock	11–13	8, 9	7, 8	3–5	1, 2, 28, 29	24–26	21–23	18, 19	14, 15	11–13	8, 9	5, 6

FISHING
BEST FISHING DAYS AND TIMES

The best times to fish are when the fish are naturally most active. The Sun, Moon, tides, and weather all influence fish activity. For example, fish tend to feed more at sunrise and sunset, and also during a full Moon (when tides are higher than average). Most of us go fishing simply when we can get the time off, but there are best times, according to fishing lore:

■ One hour before and one hour after high tides, and one hour before and one hour after low tides. The times of high tides for Boston are given on **pages 120–146;** also see **pages 236–237.** (Inland, the times for high tides correspond with the times when the Moon is due south. Low tides are halfway between high tides.)

GET TIDE TIMES AND HEIGHTS NEAREST TO YOUR LOCATION VIA ALMANAC.COM/2026.

■ During the "morning rise" (after sunup for a spell) and the "evening rise" (just before sundown and the hour or so after).

■ During the rise and set of the Moon.

■ Just before the arrival of a storm, although the falling barometric pressure will eventually slow down their feeding. Angling can also be good when the pressure is either steady or on the rise 1 to 2 days after a storm. High pressure accompanying clear weather can bring on sluggishness and reduced activity.

■ When there is a hatch of flies—caddis flies or mayflies, commonly.

■ When the breeze is from a westerly quarter, rather than from the north or east.

■ When the water is still or slightly rippled, rather than during a wind.

THE BEST FISHING DAYS FOR 2026, WHEN THE MOON IS BETWEEN NEW AND FULL

January 1–3, 18–31
February 1, 17–28
March 1–3, 18–31
April 1, 17–30
May 1, 16–31
June 14–29
July 14–29
August 12–28
September 10–26
October 10–26
November 9–24
December 8–23

Dates based on Eastern Time

HOW TO ESTIMATE THE WEIGHT OF A FISH
Measure the fish from the tip of its nose to the tip of its tail. Then measure its girth at the thickest portion of its midsection.

The weight of a fat-bodied fish (bass, salmon) = (length x girth x girth)/800

The weight of a slender fish (trout, northern pike) = (length x girth x girth)/900

EXAMPLE: If a trout is 20 inches long and has a 12-inch girth, its estimated weight is
(20 x 12 x 12)/900 = 2,880/900 = 3.2 pounds

SALMON

TROUT

CATFISH

HUSBANDRY
GESTATION AND MATING TABLES

	PROPER AGE OR WEIGHT FOR FIRST MATING	PERIOD OF FERTILITY (YRS.)	NUMBER OF FEMALES FOR ONE MALE	PERIOD OF GESTATION (DAYS) AVERAGE	RANGE
CATTLE: Cow	15–18 mos.[1]	10–14		283	279–290[2] 262–300[3]
Bull	1 yr., well matured	10–12	50[4] / thousands[5]		
GOAT: Doe	10 mos. or 85–90 lbs.	6		150	145–155
Buck	well matured	5	30		
HORSE: Mare	3 yrs.	10–12		336	310–370
Stallion	3 yrs.	12–15	40–45[4] / record 252[5]		
PIG: Sow	5–6 mos. or 250 lbs.	6		115	110–120
Boar	250–300 lbs.	6	50[6] / 35–40[7]		
RABBIT: Doe	6 mos.	5–6		31	30–32
Buck	6 mos.	5–6	30		
SHEEP: Ewe	1 yr. or 90 lbs.	6		147 / 151[8]	142–154
Ram	12–14 mos., well matured	7	50–75[6] / 35–40[7]		
CAT: Queen	12 mos.	6		63	60–68
Tom	12 mos.	6	6–8		
DOG: Bitch	16–18 mos.	8		63	58–67
Male	12–16 mos.	8	8–10		

[1] Holstein and beef: 750 lbs.; Jersey: 500 lbs. [2] Beef; 8–10 days shorter for Angus. [3] Dairy. [4] Natural. [5] Artificial. [6] Hand-mated. [7] Pasture. [8] For fine wool breeds.

INCUBATION PERIOD OF POULTRY (DAYS)
Chicken	21
Duck	26–32
Goose	30–34
Guinea	26–28
Turkey	28

AVERAGE LIFE SPAN OF ANIMALS IN CAPTIVITY (YEARS)
Cat (domestic)	14	Goose (domestic)	20
Chicken (domestic)	8	Horse	22
Dog (domestic)	13	Pig	12
Duck (domestic)	10	Rabbit	6
Goat (domestic)	14	Turkey (domestic)	10

	ESTRAL/ESTROUS CYCLE (INCLUDING HEAT PERIOD) AVERAGE	RANGE	LENGTH OF ESTRUS (HEAT) AVERAGE	RANGE	USUAL TIME OF OVULATION	WHEN CYCLE RECURS IF NOT BRED
Cow	21 days	18–24 days	18 hours	10–24 hours	10–12 hours after end of estrus	21 days
Doe goat	21 days	18–24 days	2–3 days	1–4 days	Near end of estrus	21 days
Mare	21 days	10–37 days	5–6 days	2–11 days	24–48 hours before end of estrus	21 days
Sow	21 days	18–24 days	2–3 days	1–5 days	30–36 hours after start of estrus	21 days
Ewe	16½ days	14–19 days	30 hours	24–32 hours	12–24 hours before end of estrus	16½ days
Queen cat		15–21 days	3–4 days, if mated	9–10 days, in absence of male	24–56 hours after coitus	Pseudo-pregnancy
Bitch	24 days	16–30 days	7 days	5–9 days	1–3 days after first acceptance	Pseudo-pregnancy

GARDENING
PLANTING BY THE MOON'S PHASE

ACCORDING TO THIS AGE-OLD PRACTICE, CYCLES OF THE MOON AFFECT PLANT GROWTH.

Plant annual flowers and vegetables that bear crops above ground during the light, or waxing, of the Moon: from the day the Moon is new to the day it is full.

Plant flowering bulbs, biennial and perennial flowers, and vegetables that bear crops below ground during the dark, or waning, of the Moon: from the day after it is full to the day before it is new again.

The Planting Dates columns give the safe periods for planting in areas that receive frost. (See **page 232** for frost dates in your area.) The Moon Favorable columns give the best planting days within the Planting Dates based on the Moon's phases for 2026. (See **pages 120–146** for the exact days of the new and full Moons.)

The dates listed in this table are meant as general guidelines only. For planting dates based on frost dates in your local area, go to Almanac.com/2026.

Aboveground crops are marked *.
(E) means early; (L) means late.

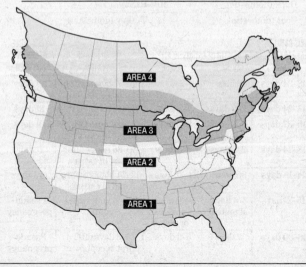

*Barley	
*Beans	(E)
	(L)
Beets	(E)
	(L)
*Broccoli plants	(E)
	(L)
*Brussels sprouts	
*Cabbage plants	
Carrots	(E)
	(L)
*Cauliflower plants	(E)
	(L)
*Celery plants	(E)
	(L)
*Collards	(E)
	(L)
*Corn, sweet	(E)
	(L)
*Cucumbers	
*Eggplant plants	
*Endive	(E)
	(L)
*Kale	(E)
	(L)
Leek plants	
*Lettuce	
*Muskmelons	
*Okra	
Onion sets	
*Parsley	
Parsnips	
*Peas	(E)
	(L)
*Pepper plants	
Potatoes	
*Pumpkins	
Radishes	(E)
	(L)
*Spinach	(E)
	(L)
*Squashes	
Sweet potatoes	
*Swiss chard	
*Tomato plants	
Turnips	(E)
	(L)
*Watermelons	
*Wheat, spring	
*Wheat, winter	

AREA 1		AREA 2		AREA 3		AREA 4	
PLANTING DATES	MOON FAVORABLE	PLANTING DATES	MOON FAVORABLE	PLANTING DATES	MOON FAVORABLE	PLANTING DATES	MOON FAVORABLE
2/15-3/7	2/17-3/3	3/15-4/7	3/18-4/1	5/15-6/21	5/16-31, 6/14-21	6/1-30	6/14-29
3/15-4/7	3/18-4/1	4/15-30	4/17-30	5/7-6/21	5/16-31, 6/14-21	5/30-6/15	5/30-31, 6/14-15
3/7-31	8/12-28	7/1-21	7/14-21	6/15-7/15	6/15-29, 7/14-15	–	–
2/7-28	2/7-16	3/15-4/3	3/15-17, 4/2-3	4/25-5/15	5/2-15	5/25-6/10	6/1-10
3/1-30	9/1-9, 9/27-30	8/15-31	8/29-31	7/15-8/15	7/30-8/11	6/15-7/8	6/30-7/8
2/15-3/15	2/17-3/3	3/7-31	3/18-31	5/15-31	5/16-31	6/1-25	6/14-25
3/7-30	9/10-26	8/1-20	8/12-20	6/15-7/7	6/15-29	–	–
2/11-3/20	2/17-3/3, 3/18-20	3/7-4/15	3/18-4/1	5/15-31	5/16-31	6/1-25	6/14-25
2/11-3/20	2/17-3/3, 3/18-20	3/7-4/15	3/18-4/1	5/15-31	5/16-31	6/1-25	6/14-25
2/15-3/7	2/15-16, 3/4-7	3/7-31	3/7-17	5/15-31	5/15	5/25-6/10	6/1-10
3/1-9/7	8/1-11, 8/29-9/7	7/7-31	7/7-13, 7/30-31	6/15-7/21	6/30-7/13	6/15-7/8	6/30-7/8
2/15-3/7	2/17-3/3	3/15-4/7	3/18-4/1	5/15-31	5/16-31	6/1-25	6/14-25
3/7-31	8/12-28	7/1-8/7	7/14-29	6/15-7/21	6/15-29, 7/14-21	–	–
2/15-28	2/17-28	3/7-31	3/18-31	5/15-6/30	5/16-31, 6/14-29	6/1-30	6/14-29
3/15-30	9/15-26	8/15-9/7	8/15-28	7/15-8/15	7/15-29, 8/12-15	–	–
2/11-3/20	2/17-3/3, 3/18-20	3/7-4/7	3/18-4/1	5/15-31	5/16-31	6/1-25	6/14-25
3/7-30	9/10-26	8/15-31	8/15-28	7/1-8/7	7/14-29	–	–
3/15-31	3/18-31	4/1-17	4/1, 4/17	5/10-6/15	5/16-31, 6/14-15	5/30-6/20	5/30-31, 6/14-20
3/7-31	8/12-28	7/7-21	7/14-21	6/15-30	6/15-29	–	–
3/7-4/15	3/18-4/1	4/7-5/15	4/17-5/1	5/7-6/20	5/16-31, 6/14-20	5/30-6/15	5/30-31, 6/14-15
3/7-4/15	3/18-4/1	4/7-5/15	4/17-5/1	6/1-30	6/14-29	6/15-30	6/15-29
2/15-3/20	2/17-3/3, 3/18-20	4/7-5/15	4/17-5/1	5/15-31	5/16-31	6/1-25	6/14-25
3/15-9/7	8/15-28	7/15-8/15	7/15-29, 8/12-15	6/7-30	6/14-29	–	–
2/11-3/20	2/17-3/3, 3/18-20	3/7-4/7	3/18-4/1	5/15-31	5/16-31	6/1-15	6/14-15
3/7-30	9/10-26	8/15-31	8/15-28	7/1-8/7	7/14-29	6/25-7/15	6/25-29, 7/14-15
2/15-4/15	2/15-16, 3/4-17, 4/2-15	3/7-4/7	3/7-17, 4/2-7	5/15-31	5/15	6/1-25	6/1-13
2/15-3/7	2/17-3/3	3/1-31	3/1-3, 3/18-31	5/15-6/30	5/16-31, 6/14-29	6/1-30	6/14-29
3/15-4/7	3/18-4/1	4/15-5/7	4/17-5/1	5/15-6/30	5/16-31, 6/14-29	6/1-30	6/14-29
4/15-6/1	4/17-5/1, 5/16-31	5/25-6/15	5/25-31, 6/14-15	6/15-7/10	6/15-29	6/15-7/7	6/15-29
2/1-28	2/2-16	3/1-31	3/4-17	5/15-6/7	5/15, 6/1-7	6/1-25	6/1-13
2/20-3/15	2/20-3/3	3/1-31	3/1-3, 3/18-31	5/15-31	5/16-31	6/1-15	6/14-15
4/15-2/4	1/15-17, 2/2-4	3/7-31	3/7-17	4/1-30	4/2-16	5/10-31	5/10-15
1/15-2/4	1/18-2/1	3/7-31	3/18-31	4/15-5/7	4/17-5/1	5/26-31	5/26-31
3/15-30	9/15-26	8/7-31	8/12-28	7/15-31	7/15-29	7/10-25	7/14-25
3/1-20	3/1-3, 3/18-20	4/1-30	4/1, 4/17-30	5/15-6/30	5/16-31, 6/14-29	6/1-30	6/14-29
2/10-28	2/10-16	4/1-30	4/2-16	5/1-31	5/2-15	6/1-25	6/1-13
3/7-20	3/18-20	4/23-5/15	4/23-5/1	5/15-31	5/16-31	6/1-30	6/14-29
1/21-3/1	2/2-16	3/7-31	3/7-17	4/15-30	4/15-16	5/15-6/5	5/15, 6/1-5
10/1-21	10/1-9	9/7-30	9/7-9, 9/27-30	8/15-31	8/29-31	7/10-31	7/10-13, 7/30-31
2/7-3/15	2/17-3/3	3/15-4/20	3/18-4/1, 4/17-20	5/15-31	5/16-31	6/1-25	6/14-25
10/1-21	10/10-21	8/1-9/15	8/12-28, 9/10-15	7/17-9/7	7/17-29, 8/12-28	7/20-8/5	7/20-29
3/15-4/15	3/18-4/1	4/15-30	4/17-30	5/15-6/15	5/16-31, 6/14-15	6/1-30	6/14-29
3/23-4/7	4/2-7	4/21-5/9	5/2-9	5/15-6/15	5/15, 6/1-13	6/1-30	6/1-13, 6/30
2/7-3/15	2/17-3/3	3/15-4/15	3/18-4/1	5/1-31	5/1, 5/16-31	5/15-31	5/16-31
3/7-21	3/18-21	4/7-30	4/17-30	5/15-31	5/16-31	6/1-15	6/14-15
1/20-2/15	2/2-15	3/15-31	3/15-17	4/7-30	4/7-16	5/10-31	5/10-15
3/1-10/15	9/1-9, 9/27-10/9	8/1-20	8/1-11	7/1-8/15	7/1-13, 7/30-8/11	–	–
3/15-4/7	3/18-4/1	4/15-5/7	4/17-5/1	5/15-6/30	5/16-31, 6/14-29	6/1-30	6/14-29
2/15-28	2/17-28	3/1-20	3/1-3, 3/18-20	4/7-30	4/17-30	5/15-6/10	5/16-31
10/15-12/7	10/15-26, 11/9-24	9/15-10/20	9/15-26, 10/10-20	8/11-9/15	8/12-28, 9/10-15	8/5-30	8/12-28

GARDENING
FROSTS AND GROWING SEASONS

Dates given are normal averages (from 1991–2020) for a light freeze; local weather and topography may cause variations. The possibility of frost occurring after the spring dates and before the fall dates is 30 percent. The classification of freeze temperatures is usually based on their effect on plants. **Light freeze:** 29° to 32°F—tender plants killed. **Moderate freeze:** 25° to 28°F—widely destructive to most plants. **Severe freeze:** 24°F and colder—heavy damage to most plants.

–dates courtesy of National Centers for Environmental Information

STATE	CITY	GROWING SEASON (DAYS)	LAST SPRING FROST	FIRST FALL FROST	STATE	CITY	GROWING SEASON (DAYS)	LAST SPRING FROST	FIRST FALL FROST
AK	Juneau	171	Apr. 26	Oct. 15	NC	Fayetteville	212	Apr. 5	Nov. 4
AL	Mobile	269	Mar. 3	Nov. 28	ND	Bismarck	126	May 19	Sept. 23
AR	Pine Bluff	230	Mar. 22	Nov. 8	NE	Omaha	174	Apr. 23	Oct. 15
AZ	Phoenix	354*	Jan. 9	Dec. 30	NE	North Platte	131	May 16	Sept. 25
AZ	Tucson	309*	Feb. 2	Dec. 9	NH	Concord	136	May 15	Sept. 29
CA	Eureka	268	Mar. 4	Nov. 28	NJ	Newark	211	Apr. 6	Nov. 4
CA	Sacramento	281*	Feb. 17	Nov. 26	NM	Carlsbad	223	Mar. 27	Nov. 6
CO	Denver	154	May 4	Oct. 6	NM	Los Alamos	149	May 9	Oct. 6
CO	Grand Junction	159	May 3	Oct. 10	NV	Las Vegas	292*	Feb. 11	Dec. 1
CT	Hartford	165	Apr. 27	Oct. 10	NY	Albany	159	May 2	Oct. 9
DE	Wilmington	199	Apr. 13	Oct. 30	NY	Syracuse	158	May 5	Oct. 11
FL	Orlando	337*	Jan. 30	Jan. 3**	OH	Akron	174	Apr. 30	Oct. 22
FL	Tallahassee	238	Mar. 19	Nov. 13	OH	Cincinnati	179	Apr. 23	Oct. 20
GA	Athens	217	Mar. 31	Nov. 4	OK	Lawton	206	Apr. 7	Oct. 31
GA	Savannah	253	Mar. 12	Nov. 21	OK	Tulsa	207	Apr. 5	Oct. 30
IA	Atlantic	142	May 6	Sept. 26	OR	Pendleton	155	Apr. 30	Oct. 3
IA	Cedar Rapids	155	May 4	Oct. 7	OR	Portland	260	Mar. 6	Nov. 22
ID	Boise	166	Apr. 30	Oct. 14	PA	Franklin	160	May 9	Oct. 17
IL	Chicago	193	Apr. 17	Oct. 28	PA	Williamsport	167	May 1	Oct. 16
IL	Springfield	177	Apr. 20	Oct. 15	RI	Kingston	148	May 8	Oct. 4
IN	Indianapolis	172	Apr. 26	Oct. 16	SC	Charleston	305*	Feb. 17	Dec. 20
IN	South Bend	159	May 7	Oct. 14	SC	Columbia	235	Mar. 21	Nov. 12
KS	Topeka	182	Apr. 19	Oct. 19	SD	Rapid City	144	May 9	Oct. 1
KY	Lexington	185	Apr. 20	Oct. 23	TN	Memphis	229	Mar. 24	Nov. 9
LA	Monroe	238	Mar. 14	Nov. 8	TN	Nashville	206	Apr. 6	Oct. 30
LA	New Orleans	311*	Feb. 8	Dec. 17	TX	Amarillo	184	Apr. 20	Oct. 22
MA	Boston	208	Apr. 8	Nov. 3	TX	Denton	235	Mar. 21	Nov. 12
MA	Worcester	167	Apr. 29	Oct. 14	TX	San Antonio	267	Mar. 2	Nov. 25
MD	Baltimore	192	Apr. 16	Oct. 26	UT	Cedar City	119	May 31	Sept. 28
ME	Portland	160	May 1	Oct. 9	UT	Spanish Fork	162	May 2	Oct. 12
MI	Lansing	151	May 7	Oct. 6	VA	Norfolk	239	Mar. 23	Nov. 18
MI	Marquette	152	May 15	Oct. 15	VA	Richmond	204	Apr. 9	Oct. 31
MN	Duluth	129	May 19	Sept. 26	VT	Burlington	158	May 3	Oct. 9
MN	Willmar	149	May 4	Oct. 1	WA	Seattle	246	Mar. 12	Nov. 14
MO	Jefferson City	193	Apr. 14	Oct. 25	WA	Spokane	158	May 1	Oct. 7
MS	Columbia	243	Mar. 13	Nov. 12	WI	Green Bay	148	May 7	Oct. 3
MS	Tupelo	218	Mar. 30	Nov. 4	WI	Sparta	133	May 15	Sept. 26
MT	Fort Peck	135	May 13	Sept. 26	WV	Parkersburg	186	Apr. 20	Oct. 24
MT	Helena	132	May 15	Sept. 25	WY	Casper	105	June 1	Sept. 15

*In leap years, add 1 day **In following year

GARDENING
PHENOLOGY: NATURE'S CALENDAR

Study nature, love nature, stay close to nature. It will never fail you.
–FRANK LLOYD WRIGHT, AMERICAN ARCHITECT (1867–1959)

For centuries, farmers and gardeners have looked to events in nature to tell them when to plant vegetables and flowers and when to expect insects. Making such observations is called "phenology," the study of phenomena. Specifically, this refers to the life cycles of plants and animals as they correlate to weather and temperature, or nature's calendar.

VEGETABLES
- Plant peas when forsythias bloom.
- Plant potatoes when the first dandelion blooms.
- Plant beets, carrots, cole crops (broccoli, brussels sprouts, collards), lettuce, and spinach when lilacs are in first leaf or dandelions are in full bloom.
- Plant corn when oak leaves are the size of a squirrel's ear (about ½ inch in diameter). Or, plant corn when apple blossoms fade and fall.
- Plant bean, cucumber, and squash seeds when lilacs are in full bloom.
- Plant tomatoes when lilies-of-the-valley are in full bloom.
- Transplant eggplants and peppers when bearded irises bloom.
- Plant onions when red maples bloom.

FLOWERS
- Plant morning glories when maple trees have full-size leaves.
- Plant zinnias and marigolds when black locusts are in full bloom.
- Plant pansies, snapdragons, and other hardy annuals when aspens and chokecherries have leafed out.

INSECTS
- When purple lilacs bloom, grasshopper eggs hatch.
- When chicory blooms, beware of squash vine borers.
- When Canada thistles bloom, protect susceptible fruit; apple maggot flies are at peak.
- When foxglove flowers open, expect Mexican beetle larvae.
- When crabapple trees are in bud, eastern tent caterpillars are hatching.
- When morning glory vines begin to climb, Japanese beetles appear.
- When wild rocket blooms, cabbage root maggots appear.

If the signal plants are not growing in your area, notice other coincident events; record them and watch for them in ensuing seasons.

MISCELLANY
TABLE OF MEASURES

LINEAR
1 hand = 4 inches
1 foot = 12 inches
1 yard = 3 feet
1 rod = 5½ yards
1 mile = 320 rods = 1,760 yards = 5,280 feet
1 international nautical mile = 6,076.1155 feet
1 knot = 1 nautical mile per hour
1 fathom = 2 yards = 6 feet
1 furlong = ⅛ mile = 660 feet = 220 yards
1 league = 3 miles = 24 furlongs

SQUARE
1 square foot = 144 square inches
1 square yard = 9 square feet
1 square rod = 272¼ square feet
1 acre = 160 square rods = 43,560 square feet
1 square mile = 640 acres = 102,400 square rods

CUBIC
1 cubic foot = 1,728 cubic inches
1 cubic yard = 27 cubic feet
1 cord = 128 cubic feet
1 U.S. liquid gallon = 4 quarts = 231 cubic inches
1 imperial gallon = 1.20 U.S. gallons = 0.16 cubic foot
1 board foot = 144 cubic inches

DRY
2 pints = 1 quart
4 quarts = 1 gallon
2 gallons = 1 peck
4 pecks = 1 bushel

LIQUID
4 gills = 1 pint
63 gallons = 1 hogshead
2 hogsheads = 1 pipe or butt
2 pipes = 1 tun

KITCHEN
3 teaspoons = 1 tablespoon
16 tablespoons = 1 cup
1 cup = 8 ounces
2 cups = 1 pint
2 pints = 1 quart
4 quarts = 1 gallon

WEIGHT: AVOIRDUPOIS
(for general use)
1 ounce = 16 drams
1 pound = 16 ounces
1 short hundredweight = 100 pounds
1 short ton = 2,000 pounds
1 long ton = 2,240 pounds

METRIC CONVERSIONS

LINEAR
1 inch = 2.54 centimeters
1 centimeter = 0.39 inch
1 foot = 30.48 centimeters
1 yard = 0.914 meter
1 meter = 39.37 inches
1 mile = 1.61 kilometers
1 kilometer = 0.62 mile

SQUARE
1 square inch = 6.45 square centimeters
1 square foot = 0.09 square meter
1 square yard = 0.84 square meter
1 square meter = 10.76 square feet
1 square mile = 2.59 square kilometers
1 square kilometer = 0.386 square mile
1 acre = 0.40 hectare
1 hectare = 2.47 acres

CUBIC
1 cubic yard = 0.76 cubic meter
1 cubic meter = 1.31 cubic yards

WEIGHT
1 gram = 0.035 ounce
1 ounce = 28.349 grams
1 kilogram = 2.2 pounds
1 pound = 0.45 kilogram
1 short ton = 0.091 metric ton
1 metric ton = 1.10 short tons

KITCHEN
½ teaspoon = 2.46 mL
1 teaspoon = 4.93 mL
1 tablespoon = 14.79 mL
¼ cup = 59.15 mL
⅓ cup = 78.86 mL
½ cup = 118.29 mL
¾ cup = 177.44 mL
1 cup = 236.59 mL
1 U.S. fluid ounce = 30.0 mL
1 milliliter (mL) = 0.034 U.S. fluid ounce
1 U.S. liquid pint = 0.47 liter
1 U.S. liquid quart = 0.946 liter
1 liter = 2.1 U.S. liquid pints = 1.057 U.S. liquid quarts
1 U.S. liquid gallon = 3.78 liters

TO CONVERT CELSIUS AND FAHRENHEIT: °C = (°F − 32)/1.8; °F = (°C × 1.8) + 32

CALENDAR
TIDAL GLOSSARY

APOGEAN TIDE: A monthly tide of decreased range that occurs when the Moon is at apogee (farthest from Earth).

CURRENT: Generally, a horizontal movement of water. Currents may be classified as tidal and nontidal. Tidal currents are caused by gravitational interactions between the Sun, Moon, and Earth and are part of the same general movement of the sea that is manifested in the vertical rise and fall, called tide. Nontidal currents include the permanent currents in the general circulatory systems of the sea as well as temporary currents arising from more pronounced meteorological variability.

DIURNAL TIDE: A tide with one high water and one low water in a tidal day of approximately 24 hours.

MEAN LOWER LOW WATER: The arithmetic mean of the lesser of a daily pair of low waters, observed over a specific 19-year cycle called the National Tidal Datum Epoch.

NEAP TIDE: A tide of decreased range that occurs twice a month, when the Moon is in quadrature (during its first and last quarters, when the Sun and the Moon are at right angles to each other relative to Earth).

PERIGEAN TIDE: A monthly tide of increased range that occurs when the Moon is at perigee (closest to Earth).

RED TIDE: Toxic algal blooms caused by several genera of dinoflagellates that usually turn the sea red or brown. These pose a serious threat to marine life and may be harmful to humans.

RIP CURRENT: A potentially dangerous, narrow, intense, surf-zone current flowing outward from shore.

SEMIDIURNAL TIDE: A tide with one high water and one low water every half-day. East Coast tides, for example, are semidiurnal, with two highs and two lows during a tidal day of approximately 24 hours.

SLACK WATER (SLACK): The state of a tidal current when its speed is near zero, especially the moment when a reversing current changes direction and its speed is zero.

SPRING TIDE: A tide of increased range that occurs at times of syzygy each month. Named not for the season of spring but from the German *springen* ("to leap up"), a spring tide also brings a lower low water.

STORM SURGE: The local change in the elevation of the ocean along a shore due to a storm, measured by subtracting the astronomic tidal elevation from the total elevation. It typically has a duration of a few hours and is potentially catastrophic, especially on low-lying coasts with gently sloping offshore topography.

SYZYGY: The nearly straight-line configuration that occurs twice a month, when the Sun and the Moon are in conjunction (on the same side of Earth, at the new Moon) and when they are in opposition (on opposite sides of Earth, at the full Moon). In both cases, the gravitational effects of the Sun and the Moon reinforce each other, and tidal range is increased.

TIDAL BORE: A tide-induced wave that propagates up a relatively shallow and sloping estuary or river with a steep wave front.

TSUNAMI: Sometimes mistakenly called a "tidal wave," a tsunami is a series of long-period waves caused by an underwater earthquake or volcanic eruption. In open ocean, the waves are small and travel at high speed; as they near shore, some may build to more than 30 feet high, becoming a threat to life and property.

VANISHING TIDE: A mixed tide of considerable inequality in the two highs and two lows, so that the lower high (or higher low) may appear to vanish. ■

CALENDAR
TIDE CORRECTIONS

Many factors affect tides, including the shoreline, time of the Moon's southing (crossing of the meridian), and the Moon's phase. The High Tide Times column on the **Left-Hand Calendar Pages, 120–146,** lists the times of high tide at Commonwealth Pier in Boston (MA) Harbor. The heights of some of these tides, reckoned from Mean Lower Low Water, are given on the **Right-Hand Calendar Pages, 121–147.** Use the table below to calculate the approximate times and heights of high tide at the places shown. Apply the time difference to the times of high tide at Boston and the height difference to the heights at Boston. A more detailed and accurate tide calculator for the United States and Canada can be found via **Almanac.com/2026.**

EXAMPLE:
The conversion of the times and heights of the tides at Boston to those at Cape Fear, North Carolina, is given below:

High tide at Boston	11:45 A.M.
Correction for Cape Fear	– 3 55
High tide at Cape Fear	7:50 A.M.
Tide height at Boston	11.6 ft.
Correction for Cape Fear	– 5.0 ft.
Tide height at Cape Fear	6.6 ft.

Estimations derived from this table are *not* meant to be used for navigation. *The Old Farmer's Almanac* accepts no responsibility for errors or any consequences ensuing from the use of this table.

TIDAL SITE	TIME (H. M.)	HEIGHT (FT.)	TIDAL SITE	TIME (H. M.)	HEIGHT (FT.)
CANADA			Cape Cod Canal		
Alberton, PE	*–5 45	–7.5	East Entrance	–0 01	–0.8
Charlottetown, PE	*–0 45	–3.5	West Entrance	–2 16	–5.9
Halifax, NS	–3 23	–4.5	Chatham Outer Coast	+0 30	–2.8
North Sydney, NS	–3 15	–6.5	Inside	+1 54	**0.4
Saint John, NB	+0 30	+15.0	Cohasset	+0 02	–0.07
St. John's, NL	–4 00	–6.5	Cotuit Highlands	+1 15	**0.3
Yarmouth, NS	–0 40	+3.0	Dennis Port	+1 01	**0.4
MAINE			Duxbury–Gurnet Point	+0 02	–0.3
Bar Harbor	–0 34	+0.9	Fall River	–3 03	–5.0
Belfast	–0 20	+0.4	Gloucester	–0 03	–0.8
Boothbay Harbor	–0 18	–0.8	Hingham	+0 07	0.0
Chebeague Island	–0 16	–0.6	Hull	+0 03	–0.2
Eastport	–0 28	+8.4	Hyannis Port	+1 01	**0.3
Kennebunkport	+0 04	–1.0	Magnolia–Manchester	–0 02	–0.7
Machias	–0 28	+2.8	Marblehead	–0 02	–0.4
Monhegan Island	–0 25	–0.8	Marion	–3 22	–5.4
Old Orchard Beach	0 00	–0.8	Monument Beach	–3 08	–5.4
Portland	–0 12	–0.6	Nahant	–0 01	–0.5
Rockland	–0 28	+0.1	Nantasket Beach	+0 04	–0.1
Stonington	–0 30	+0.1	Nantucket	+0 56	**0.3
York	–0 09	–1.0	Nauset Beach	+0 30	**0.6
NEW HAMPSHIRE			New Bedford	–3 24	–5.7
Hampton	+0 02	–1.3	Newburyport	+0 19	–1.8
Portsmouth	+0 11	–1.5	Oak Bluffs	+0 30	**0.2
Rye Beach	–0 09	–0.9	Onset–R.R. Bridge	–2 16	–5.9
MASSACHUSETTS			Plymouth	+0 05	0.0
Annisquam	–0 02	–1.1	Provincetown	+0 14	–0.4
Beverly Farms	0 00	–0.5	Revere Beach	–0 01	–0.3

TIDAL SITE	TIME (H. M.)	HEIGHT (FT.)	TIDAL SITE	TIME (H. M.)	HEIGHT (FT.)
Rockport	−0 08	−1.0	**PENNSYLVANIA**		
Salem	0 00	−0.5	Philadelphia	+2 40	−3.5
Scituate	−0 05	−0.7	**DELAWARE**		
Wareham	−3 09	−5.3	Cape Henlopen	−2 48	−5.3
Wellfleet	+0 12	+0.5	Rehoboth Beach	−3 37	−5.7
West Falmouth	−3 10	−5.4	Wilmington	+1 56	−3.8
Westport Harbor	−3 22	−6.4	**MARYLAND**		
Woods Hole			Annapolis	+6 23	−8.5
Little Harbor	−2 50	**0.2	Baltimore	+7 59	−8.3
Oceanographic			Cambridge	+5 05	−7.8
Institute	−3 07	**0.2	Havre de Grace	+11 21	−7.7
RHODE ISLAND			Point No Point	+2 28	−8.1
Bristol	−3 24	−5.3	Prince Frederick–		
Narragansett Pier	−3 42	−6.2	Plum Point	+4 25	−8.5
Newport	−3 34	−5.9	**VIRGINIA**		
Point Judith	−3 41	−6.3	Cape Charles	−2 20	−7.0
Providence	−3 20	−4.8	Hampton Roads	−2 02	−6.9
Sakonnet	−3 44	−5.6	Norfolk	−2 06	−6.6
Watch Hill	−2 50	−6.8	Virginia Beach	−4 00	−6.0
CONNECTICUT			Yorktown	−2 13	−7.0
Bridgeport	+0 01	−2.6	**NORTH CAROLINA**		
Madison	−0 22	−2.3	Cape Fear	−3 55	−5.0
New Haven	−0 11	−3.2	Cape Lookout	−4 28	−5.7
New London	−1 54	−6.7	Currituck	−4 10	−5.8
Norwalk	+0 01	−2.2	Hatteras		
Old Lyme–			Inlet	−4 03	−7.4
Highway Bridge	−0 30	−6.2	Kitty Hawk	−4 14	−6.2
Stamford	+0 01	−2.2	Ocean	−4 26	−6.0
Stonington	−2 27	−6.6	**SOUTH CAROLINA**		
NEW YORK			Charleston	−3 22	−4.3
Coney Island	−3 33	−4.9	Georgetown	−1 48	**0.36
Fire Island Light	−2 43	**0.1	Hilton Head	−3 22	−2.9
Long Beach	−3 11	−5.7	Myrtle Beach	−3 49	−4.4
Montauk Harbor	−2 19	−7.4	St. Helena–		
New York City–Battery	−2 43	−5.0	Harbor Entrance	−3 15	−3.4
Oyster Bay	+0 04	−1.8	**GEORGIA**		
Port Chester	−0 09	−2.2	Jekyll Island	−3 46	−2.9
Port Washington	−0 01	−2.1	St. Simon's Island	−2 50	−2.9
Sag Harbor	−0 55	−6.8	Savannah Beach		
Southampton–			River Entrance	−3 14	−5.5
Shinnecock Inlet	−4 20	**0.2	Tybee Light	−3 22	−2.7
Willets Point	0 00	−2.3	**FLORIDA**		
NEW JERSEY			Cape Canaveral	−3 59	−6.0
Asbury Park	−4 04	−5.3	Daytona Beach	−3 28	−5.3
Atlantic City	−3 56	−5.5	Fort Lauderdale	−2 50	−7.2
Bay Head–Sea Girt	−4 04	−5.3	Fort Pierce Inlet	−3 32	−6.9
Beach Haven	−1 43	**0.24	Jacksonville–		
Cape May	−3 28	−5.3	Railroad Bridge	−6 55	**0.1
Ocean City	−3 06	−5.9	Miami Harbor Entrance	−3 18	−7.0
Sandy Hook	−3 30	−5.0	St. Augustine	−2 55	−4.9
Seaside Park	−4 03	−5.4			

*VARIES WIDELY; ACCURATE ONLY TO WITHIN 1½ HOURS. CONSULT LOCAL TIDE TABLES FOR PRECISE TIMES AND HEIGHTS.
**WHERE THE DIFFERENCE IN THE HEIGHT COLUMN IS SO MARKED, THE HEIGHT AT BOSTON SHOULD BE MULTIPLIED BY THIS RATIO.

CALENDAR
TIME CORRECTIONS

Astronomical data for Boston (42°22' N, 71°3' W) is given on **pages 104, 106, 108–109, and 120–146**. Use the Key Letters shown on those pages with this table to find the number of minutes you must add to or subtract from Boston time to get the correct time for your city. (Times are approximate.) For more information on the use of Key Letters, see **How to Use This Almanac, page 116**.

GET TIMES SIMPLY AND SPECIFICALLY: Find astronomical times calculated for your area via **Almanac.com/2026**.

TIME ZONES CODES represent standard time. Atlantic is –1, Eastern is 0, Central is 1, Mountain is 2, Pacific is 3, Alaska is 4, and Hawaii-Aleutian is 5.

STATE	CITY	NORTH LATITUDE °	'	WEST LONGITUDE °	'	TIME ZONE CODE	A	B	C	D	E
AK	Anchorage	61	10	149	59	4	–46	+27	+71	+122	+171
AK	Cordova	60	33	145	45	4	–55	+13	+55	+103	+149
AK	Fairbanks	64	48	147	51	4	–127	+2	+61	+131	+205
AK	Juneau	58	18	134	25	4	–76	–23	+10	+49	+86
AK	Ketchikan	55	21	131	39	4	–62	–25	0	+29	+56
AK	Kodiak	57	47	152	24	4	0	+49	+82	+120	+154
AL	Birmingham	33	31	86	49	1	+30	+15	+3	–10	–20
AL	Decatur	34	36	86	59	1	+27	+14	+4	–7	–17
AL	Mobile	30	42	88	3	1	+42	+23	+8	–8	–22
AL	Montgomery	32	23	86	19	1	+31	+14	+1	–13	–25
AR	Fort Smith	35	23	94	25	1	+55	+43	+33	+22	+14
AR	Little Rock	34	45	92	17	1	+48	+35	+25	+13	+4
AR	Texarkana	33	26	94	3	1	+59	+44	+32	+18	+8
AZ	Flagstaff	35	12	111	39	2	+64	+52	+42	+31	+22
AZ	Phoenix	33	27	112	4	2	+71	+56	+44	+30	+20
AZ	Tucson	32	13	110	58	2	+70	+53	+40	+24	+12
AZ	Yuma	32	43	114	37	2	+83	+67	+54	+40	+28
CA	Bakersfield	35	23	119	1	3	+33	+21	+12	+1	–7
CA	Barstow	34	54	117	1	3	+27	+14	+4	–7	–16
CA	Fresno	36	44	119	47	3	+32	+22	+15	+6	0
CA	Los Angeles-Pasadena-Santa Monica	34	3	118	14	3	+34	+20	+9	–3	–13
CA	Palm Springs	33	49	116	32	3	+28	+13	+1	–12	–22
CA	Redding	40	35	122	24	3	+31	+27	+25	+22	+19
CA	Sacramento	38	35	121	30	3	+34	+27	+21	+15	+10
CA	San Diego	32	43	117	9	3	+33	+17	+4	–9	–21
CA	San Francisco-Oakland-San Jose	37	47	122	25	3	+40	+31	+25	+18	+12
CO	Craig	40	31	107	33	2	+32	+28	+25	+22	+20
CO	Denver-Boulder	39	44	104	59	2	+24	+19	+15	+11	+7
CO	Grand Junction	39	4	108	33	2	+40	+34	+29	+24	+20
CO	Pueblo	38	16	104	37	2	+27	+20	+14	+7	+2
CO	Trinidad	37	10	104	31	2	+30	+21	+13	+5	0
CT	Bridgeport	41	11	73	11	0	+12	+10	+8	+6	+4
CT	Hartford-New Britain	41	46	72	41	0	+8	+7	+6	+5	+4
CT	New Haven	41	18	72	56	0	+11	+8	+7	+5	+4
CT	New London	41	22	72	6	0	+7	+5	+4	+2	+1
CT	Norwalk-Stamford	41	7	73	22	0	+13	+10	+9	+7	+5
CT	Waterbury-Meriden	41	33	73	3	0	+10	+9	+7	+6	+5
DC	Washington	38	54	77	1	0	+35	+28	+23	+18	+13
DE	Wilmington	39	45	75	33	0	+26	+21	+18	+13	+10

238   Get local rise, set, and tide times via Almanac.com/2026.   2026

STATE	CITY	NORTH LATITUDE °	NORTH LATITUDE '	WEST LONGITUDE °	WEST LONGITUDE '	TIME ZONE CODE	A	B	C	D	E
FL	Fort Myers	26	38	81	52	0	+87	+63	+44	+21	+4
FL	Jacksonville	30	20	81	40	0	+77	+58	+43	+25	+11
FL	Miami	25	47	80	12	0	+88	+57	+37	+14	−3
FL	Orlando	28	32	81	22	0	+80	+59	+42	+22	+6
FL	Pensacola	30	25	87	13	1	+39	+20	+5	−12	−26
FL	St. Petersburg	27	46	82	39	0	+87	+65	+47	+26	+10
FL	Tallahassee	30	27	84	17	0	+87	+68	+53	+35	+22
FL	Tampa	27	57	82	27	0	+86	+64	+46	+25	+9
FL	West Palm Beach	26	43	80	3	0	+79	+55	+36	+14	−2
GA	Atlanta	33	45	84	24	0	+79	+65	+53	+40	+30
GA	Augusta	33	28	81	58	0	+70	+55	+44	+30	+19
GA	Macon	32	50	83	38	0	+79	+63	+50	+36	+24
GA	Savannah	32	5	81	6	0	+70	+54	+40	+25	+13
HI	Hilo	19	44	155	5	5	+94	+62	+37	+7	−15
HI	Honolulu	21	18	157	52	5	+102	+72	+48	+19	−1
HI	Lanai City	20	50	156	55	5	+99	+69	+44	+15	−6
HI	Lihue	21	59	159	23	5	+107	+77	+54	+26	+5
IA	Davenport	41	32	90	35	1	+20	+19	+17	+16	+15
IA	Des Moines	41	35	93	37	1	+32	+31	+30	+28	+27
IA	Dubuque	42	30	90	41	1	+17	+18	+18	+18	+18
IA	Waterloo	42	30	92	20	1	+24	+24	+24	+25	+25
ID	Boise	43	37	116	12	2	+55	+58	+60	+62	+64
ID	Lewiston	46	25	117	1	3	−12	−3	+2	+10	+17
ID	Pocatello	42	52	112	27	2	+43	+44	+45	+46	+46
IL	Cairo	37	0	89	11	1	+29	+20	+12	+4	−2
IL	Chicago-Oak Park	41	52	87	38	1	+7	+6	+6	+5	+4
IL	Danville	40	8	87	37	1	+13	+9	+6	+2	0
IL	Decatur	39	51	88	57	1	+19	+15	+11	+7	+4
IL	Peoria	40	42	89	36	1	+19	+16	+14	+11	+9
IL	Springfield	39	48	89	39	1	+22	+18	+14	+10	+6
IN	Fort Wayne	41	4	85	9	0	+60	+58	+56	+54	+52
IN	Gary	41	36	87	20	1	+7	+6	+4	+3	+2
IN	Indianapolis	39	46	86	10	0	+69	+64	+60	+56	+52
IN	Muncie	40	12	85	23	0	+64	+60	+57	+53	+50
IN	South Bend	41	41	86	15	0	+62	+61	+60	+59	+58
IN	Terre Haute	39	28	87	24	0	+74	+69	+65	+60	+56
KS	Fort Scott	37	50	94	42	1	+49	+41	+34	+27	+21
KS	Liberal	37	3	100	55	1	+76	+66	+59	+51	+44
KS	Oakley	39	8	100	51	1	+69	+63	+59	+53	+49
KS	Salina	38	50	97	37	1	+57	+51	+46	+40	+35
KS	Topeka	39	3	95	40	1	+49	+43	+38	+32	+28
KS	Wichita	37	42	97	20	1	+60	+51	+45	+37	+31
KY	Lexington-Frankfort	38	3	84	30	0	+67	+59	+53	+46	+41
KY	Louisville	38	15	85	46	0	+72	+64	+58	+52	+46
LA	Alexandria	31	18	92	27	1	+58	+40	+26	+9	−3
LA	Baton Rouge	30	27	91	11	1	+55	+36	+21	+3	−10
LA	Lake Charles	30	14	93	13	1	+64	+44	+29	+11	−2
LA	Monroe	32	30	92	7	1	+53	+37	+24	+9	−1
LA	New Orleans	29	57	90	4	1	+52	+32	+16	−1	−15
LA	Shreveport	32	31	93	45	1	+60	+44	+31	+16	+4
MA	Brockton	42	5	71	1	0	0	0	0	0	−1
MA	Fall River-New Bedford	41	42	71	9	0	+2	+1	0	0	−1
MA	Lawrence-Lowell	42	42	71	10	0	0	0	0	0	+1
MA	Pittsfield	42	27	73	15	0	+8	+8	+8	+8	+8
MA	Springfield-Holyoke	42	6	72	36	0	+6	+6	+6	+5	+5
MA	Worcester	42	16	71	48	0	+3	+2	+2	+2	+2

TIME CORRECTIONS

STATE	CITY	NORTH LATITUDE °	'	WEST LONGITUDE °	'	TIME ZONE CODE	KEY LETTERS (MINUTES) A	B	C	D	E
MD	Baltimore	39	17	76	37	0	+32	+26	+22	+17	+13
MD	Hagerstown	39	39	77	43	0	+35	+30	+26	+22	+18
MD	Salisbury	38	22	75	36	0	+31	+23	+18	+11	+6
ME	Augusta	44	19	69	46	0	−12	−8	−5	−1	0
ME	Bangor	44	48	68	46	0	−18	−13	−9	−5	−1
ME	Eastport	44	54	67	0	0	−26	−20	−16	−11	−8
ME	Ellsworth	44	33	68	25	0	−18	−14	−10	−6	−3
ME	Portland	43	40	70	15	0	−8	−5	−3	−1	0
ME	Presque Isle	46	41	68	1	0	−29	−19	−12	−4	+2
MI	Cheboygan	45	39	84	29	0	+40	+47	+53	+59	+64
MI	Detroit-Dearborn	42	20	83	3	0	+47	+47	+47	+47	+47
MI	Flint	43	1	83	41	0	+47	+49	+50	+51	+52
MI	Ironwood	46	27	90	9	1	0	+9	+15	+23	+29
MI	Jackson	42	15	84	24	0	+53	+53	+53	+52	+52
MI	Kalamazoo	42	17	85	35	0	+58	+57	+57	+57	+57
MI	Lansing	42	44	84	33	0	+52	+53	+53	+54	+54
MI	St. Joseph	42	5	86	26	0	+61	+61	+60	+60	+59
MI	Traverse City	44	46	85	38	0	+49	+54	+57	+62	+65
MN	Albert Lea	43	39	93	22	1	+24	+26	+28	+31	+33
MN	Bemidji	47	28	94	53	1	+14	+26	+34	+44	+52
MN	Duluth	46	47	92	6	1	+6	+16	+23	+31	+38
MN	Minneapolis-St. Paul	44	59	93	16	1	+18	+24	+28	+33	+37
MN	Ortonville	45	19	96	27	1	+30	+36	+40	+46	+51
MO	Jefferson City	38	34	92	10	1	+36	+29	+24	+18	+13
MO	Joplin	37	6	94	30	1	+50	+41	+33	+25	+18
MO	Kansas City	39	1	94	20	1	+44	+37	+33	+27	+23
MO	Poplar Bluff	36	46	90	24	1	+35	+25	+17	+8	+1
MO	St. Joseph	39	46	94	50	1	+43	+38	+35	+30	+27
MO	St. Louis	38	37	90	12	1	+28	+21	+16	+10	+5
MO	Springfield	37	13	93	18	1	+45	+36	+29	+20	+14
MS	Biloxi	30	24	88	53	1	+46	+27	+11	−5	−19
MS	Jackson	32	18	90	11	1	+46	+30	+17	+1	−10
MS	Meridian	32	22	88	42	1	+40	+24	+11	−4	−15
MS	Tupelo	34	16	88	34	1	+35	+21	+10	−2	−11
MT	Billings	45	47	108	30	2	+16	+23	+29	+35	+40
MT	Butte	46	1	112	32	2	+31	+39	+45	+52	+57
MT	Glasgow	48	12	106	38	2	−1	+11	+21	+32	+42
MT	Great Falls	47	30	111	17	2	+20	+31	+39	+49	+58
MT	Helena	46	36	112	2	2	+27	+36	+43	+51	+57
MT	Miles City	46	25	105	51	2	+3	+11	+18	+26	+32
NC	Asheville	35	36	82	33	0	+67	+55	+46	+35	+27
NC	Charlotte	35	14	80	51	0	+61	+49	+39	+28	+19
NC	Durham	36	0	78	55	0	+51	+40	+31	+21	+13
NC	Greensboro	36	4	79	47	0	+54	+43	+35	+25	+17
NC	Raleigh	35	47	78	38	0	+51	+39	+30	+20	+12
NC	Wilmington	34	14	77	55	0	+52	+38	+27	+15	+5
ND	Bismarck	46	48	100	47	1	+41	+50	+58	+66	+73
ND	Fargo	46	53	96	47	1	+24	+34	+42	+50	+57
ND	Grand Forks	47	55	97	3	1	+21	+33	+43	+53	+62
ND	Minot	48	14	101	18	1	+36	+50	+59	+71	+81
ND	Williston	48	9	103	37	1	+46	+59	+69	+80	+90
NE	Grand Island	40	55	98	21	1	+53	+51	+49	+46	+44
NE	Lincoln	40	49	96	41	1	+47	+44	+42	+39	+37
NE	North Platte	41	8	100	46	1	+62	+60	+58	+56	+54
NE	Omaha	41	16	95	56	1	+43	+40	+39	+37	+36
NH	Berlin	44	28	71	11	0	−7	−3	0	+3	+7
NH	Keene	42	56	72	17	0	+2	+3	+4	+5	+6

Get local rise, set, and tide times via Almanac.com/2026.

TIME CORRECTIONS

STATE	CITY	NORTH LATITUDE °	'	WEST LONGITUDE °	'	TIME ZONE CODE	KEY LETTERS (MINUTES) A	B	C	D	E
NH	Manchester-Concord	42	59	71	28	0	0	0	+1	+2	+3
NH	Portsmouth	43	5	70	45	0	−4	−2	−1	0	0
NJ	Atlantic City	39	22	74	26	0	+23	+17	+13	+8	+4
NJ	Camden	39	57	75	7	0	+24	+19	+16	+12	+9
NJ	Cape May	38	56	74	56	0	+26	+20	+15	+9	+5
NJ	Newark-East Orange	40	44	74	10	0	+17	+14	+12	+9	+7
NJ	Paterson	40	55	74	10	0	+17	+14	+12	+9	+7
NJ	Trenton	40	13	74	46	0	+21	+17	+14	+11	+8
NM	Albuquerque	35	5	106	39	2	+45	+32	+22	+11	+2
NM	Gallup	35	32	108	45	2	+52	+40	+31	+20	+11
NM	Las Cruces	32	19	106	47	2	+53	+36	+23	+8	−3
NM	Roswell	33	24	104	32	2	+41	+26	+14	0	−10
NM	Santa Fe	35	41	105	56	2	+40	+28	+19	+9	0
NV	Carson City-Reno	39	10	119	46	3	+25	+19	+14	+9	+5
NV	Elko	40	50	115	46	3	+3	0	−1	−3	−5
NV	Las Vegas	36	10	115	9	3	+16	+4	−3	−13	−20
NY	Albany	42	39	73	45	0	+9	+10	+10	+11	+11
NY	Binghamton	42	6	75	55	0	+20	+19	+19	+18	+18
NY	Buffalo	42	53	78	52	0	+29	+30	+30	+31	+32
NY	New York	40	45	74	0	0	+17	+14	+11	+9	+6
NY	Ogdensburg	44	42	75	30	0	+8	+13	+17	+21	+25
NY	Syracuse	43	3	76	9	0	+17	+19	+20	+21	+22
OH	Akron	41	5	81	31	0	+46	+43	+41	+39	+37
OH	Canton	40	48	81	23	0	+46	+43	+41	+38	+36
OH	Cincinnati-Hamilton	39	6	84	31	0	+64	+58	+53	+48	+44
OH	Cleveland-Lakewood	41	30	81	42	0	+45	+43	+42	+40	+39
OH	Columbus	39	57	83	1	0	+55	+51	+47	+43	+40
OH	Dayton	39	45	84	10	0	+61	+56	+52	+48	+44
OH	Toledo	41	39	83	33	0	+52	+50	+49	+48	+47
OH	Youngstown	41	6	80	39	0	+42	+40	+38	+36	+34
OK	Oklahoma City	35	28	97	31	1	+67	+55	+46	+35	+26
OK	Tulsa	36	9	95	60	1	+59	+48	+40	+30	+22
OR	Eugene	44	3	123	6	3	+21	+24	+27	+30	+33
OR	Pendleton	45	40	118	47	3	−1	+4	+10	+16	+21
OR	Portland	45	31	122	41	3	+14	+20	+25	+31	+36
OR	Salem	44	57	123	1	3	+17	+23	+27	+31	+35
PA	Allentown-Bethlehem	40	36	75	28	0	+23	+20	+17	+14	+12
PA	Erie	42	7	80	5	0	+36	+36	+35	+35	+35
PA	Harrisburg	40	16	76	53	0	+30	+26	+23	+19	+16
PA	Lancaster	40	2	76	18	0	+28	+24	+20	+17	+13
PA	Philadelphia-Chester	39	57	75	9	0	+24	+19	+16	+12	+9
PA	Pittsburgh-McKeesport	40	26	80	0	0	+42	+38	+35	+32	+29
PA	Reading	40	20	75	56	0	+26	+22	+19	+16	+13
PA	Scranton-Wilkes-Barre	41	25	75	40	0	+21	+19	+18	+16	+15
PA	York	39	58	76	43	0	+30	+26	+22	+18	+15
RI	Providence	41	50	71	25	0	+3	+2	+1	0	0
SC	Charleston	32	47	79	56	0	+64	+48	+36	+21	+10
SC	Columbia	34	0	81	2	0	+65	+51	+40	+27	+17
SC	Spartanburg	34	56	81	57	0	+66	+53	+43	+32	+23
SD	Aberdeen	45	28	98	29	1	+37	+44	+49	+54	+59
SD	Pierre	44	22	100	21	1	+49	+53	+56	+60	+63
SD	Rapid City	44	5	103	14	2	+2	+5	+8	+11	+13
SD	Sioux Falls	43	33	96	44	1	+38	+40	+42	+44	+46
TN	Chattanooga	35	3	85	19	0	+79	+67	+57	+45	+36
TN	Knoxville	35	58	83	55	0	+71	+60	+51	+41	+33
TN	Memphis	35	9	90	3	1	+38	+26	+16	+5	−3
TN	Nashville	36	10	86	47	1	+22	+11	+3	−6	−14

TIME CORRECTIONS

STATE/PROVINCE	CITY	NORTH LATITUDE °	'	WEST LONGITUDE °	'	TIME ZONE CODE	KEY LETTERS (MINUTES) A	B	C	D	E
TX	Amarillo	35	12	101	50	1	+85	+73	+63	+52	+43
TX	Austin	30	16	97	45	1	+82	+62	+47	+29	+15
TX	Beaumont	30	5	94	6	1	+67	+48	+32	+14	0
TX	Brownsville	25	54	97	30	1	+91	+66	+46	+23	+5
TX	Corpus Christi	27	48	97	24	1	+86	+64	+46	+25	+9
TX	Dallas-Fort Worth	32	47	96	48	1	+71	+55	+43	+28	+17
TX	El Paso	31	45	106	29	2	+53	+35	+22	+6	−6
TX	Galveston	29	18	94	48	1	+72	+52	+35	+16	+1
TX	Houston	29	45	95	22	1	+73	+53	+37	+19	+5
TX	McAllen	26	12	98	14	1	+93	+69	+49	+26	+9
TX	San Antonio	29	25	98	30	1	+87	+66	+50	+31	+16
UT	Kanab	37	3	112	32	2	+62	+53	+46	+37	+30
UT	Moab	38	35	109	33	2	+46	+39	+33	+27	+22
UT	Ogden	41	13	111	58	2	+47	+45	+43	+41	+40
UT	Salt Lake City	40	45	111	53	2	+48	+45	+43	+40	+38
UT	Vernal	40	27	109	32	2	+40	+36	+33	+30	+28
VA	Charlottesville	38	2	78	30	0	+43	+35	+29	+22	+17
VA	Danville	36	36	79	23	0	+51	+41	+33	+24	+17
VA	Norfolk	36	51	76	17	0	+38	+28	+21	+12	+5
VA	Richmond	37	32	77	26	0	+41	+32	+25	+17	+11
VA	Roanoke	37	16	79	57	0	+51	+42	+35	+27	+21
VA	Winchester	39	11	78	10	0	+38	+33	+28	+23	+19
VT	Brattleboro	42	51	72	34	0	+4	+5	+5	+6	+7
VT	Burlington	44	29	73	13	0	0	+4	+8	+12	+15
VT	Rutland	43	37	72	58	0	+2	+5	+7	+9	+11
VT	St. Johnsbury	44	25	72	1	0	−4	0	+3	+7	+10
WA	Bellingham	48	45	122	29	3	0	+13	+24	+37	+47
WA	Seattle-Tacoma-Olympia	47	37	122	20	3	+3	+15	+24	+34	+42
WA	Spokane	47	40	117	24	3	−16	−4	+4	+14	+23
WA	Walla Walla	46	4	118	20	3	−5	+2	+8	+15	+21
WI	Eau Claire	44	49	91	30	1	+12	+17	+21	+25	+29
WI	Green Bay	44	31	88	0	1	0	+3	+7	+11	+14
WI	La Crosse	43	48	91	15	1	+15	+18	+20	+22	+25
WI	Madison	43	4	89	23	1	+10	+11	+12	+14	+15
WI	Milwaukee	43	2	87	54	1	+4	+6	+7	+8	+9
WI	Oshkosh	44	1	88	33	1	+3	+6	+9	+12	+15
WI	Wausau	44	58	89	38	1	+4	+9	+13	+18	+22
WV	Charleston	38	21	81	38	0	+55	+48	+42	+35	+30
WV	Parkersburg	39	16	81	34	0	+52	+46	+42	+36	+32
WY	Casper	42	51	106	19	2	+19	+19	+20	+21	+22
WY	Cheyenne	41	8	104	49	2	+19	+16	+14	+12	+11
WY	Sheridan	44	48	106	58	2	+14	+19	+23	+27	+31
CANADA											
AB	Calgary	51	5	114	5	2	+13	+35	+50	+68	+84
AB	Edmonton	53	34	113	25	2	−3	+26	+47	+72	+93
BC	Vancouver	49	13	123	6	3	0	+15	+26	+40	+52
MB	Winnipeg	49	53	97	10	1	+12	+30	+43	+58	+71
NB	Saint John	45	16	66	3	−1	+28	+34	+39	+44	+49
NS	Halifax	44	38	63	35	−1	+21	+26	+29	+33	+37
NS	Sydney	46	10	60	10	−1	+1	+9	+15	+23	+28
ON	Ottawa	45	25	75	43	0	+6	+13	+18	+23	+28
ON	Peterborough	44	18	78	19	0	+21	+25	+28	+32	+35
ON	Thunder Bay	48	27	89	12	0	+47	+61	+71	+83	+93
ON	Toronto	43	39	79	23	0	+28	+30	+32	+35	+37
QC	Montreal	45	28	73	39	0	−1	+4	+9	+15	+20
SK	Saskatoon	52	10	106	40	1	+37	+63	+80	+101	+119

Get local rise, set, and tide times via Almanac.com/2026.

CALENDAR
GLOSSARY OF TIME

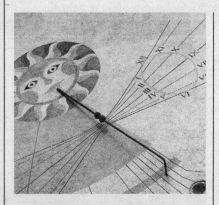

ATOMIC TIME (TA) SCALE: A time scale based on atomic or molecular resonance phenomena. Elapsed time is measured by counting cycles of a frequency locked to an atomic or molecular transition.

DATE: A unique instant defined in a specified time scale. NOTE: The date can be conventionally expressed in years, months, days, hours, minutes and seconds, and fractions thereof.

GREENWICH MEAN TIME (GMT): A 24-hour system based on mean solar time plus 12 hours at Greenwich, England. Greenwich Mean Time can be considered approximately equivalent to Coordinated Universal Time (UTC), which is broadcast from all standard time-and-frequency radio stations. However, GMT is now obsolete and has been replaced by UTC.

INTERNATIONAL ATOMIC TIME (TAI): An atomic time scale based on data from a worldwide set of atomic clocks. It is the internationally agreed-upon time reference conforming to the definition of the second, the fundamental unit of atomic time in the International System of Units (SI).

LEAP SECOND: A second used to adjust UTC to be within 0.9 sec of UT1 (a time scale based on Earth's varying rotation rate). An inserted "positive" second or omitted "negative" second may be applied at the end of June or December of each year.

MEAN SOLAR TIME: Apparent solar time corrected for the effects of orbital eccentricity and the tilt of Earth's axis relative to the ecliptic plane; in other words, corrected by the equation of time, which is defined as the hour angle of the true Sun minus the hour angle of the mean Sun.

SECOND: The basic unit of time or time interval in the International System of Units (SI), which is equal to 9,192,631,770 periods of radiation corresponding to the transition between the two hyperfine levels of the ground state of cesium-133 as defined at the 1967 Conférence Générale des Poids et Mesures.

SIDEREAL TIME: The measure of time defined by the apparent diurnal motion of the vernal equinox; hence, a measure of the rotation of Earth with respect to the reference frame that is related to the stars rather than the Sun. A mean solar day is about 4 minutes longer than a sidereal day.

–(U.S.) National Institute of Standards and Technology (NIST)

GENERAL STORE CLASSIFIEDS

For advertising information and rates, go to Almanac.com/Advertising or call RJ Media at 212-986-0016. The 2027 edition closes on April 30, 2026.

ASTROLOGY

SOPHIA GREEN Don't tell me, I'll tell you! Helps all problems—Reunites lovers. Guaranteed! **Call: 956-878-7053.**

Free Reading - Psychic Grace Spellcaster
Gifted Spiritualist
Chakra Healing - Love Cleansing - Love Spells
Solves Problems: Love, Finance, Career, Happiness, Luck. Reunites Lovers.
Fast Results.
786-514-8062

FREE READING
PSYCHIC SPIRITUALIST ROSELLA
Solves ALL problems. I don't judge.
Specializing: Divorce, Fear, Court Cases.
Spiritual Soul Cleansing.
Don't worry about tomorrow!
Call! 586-215-3838

Free 5-Minute Tarot Reading
World-Renowned & Trusted Psychic Hope
Call today! Gain clarity!
Specializing: Love, Marriage, Breakups, Career, Finance, Life Path.
Get Help!
Call Today! 316-391-3224

ATTENTION: SISTER LIGHT
Spartanburg, South Carolina
One FREE READING when you call.
I will help you with all problems.
Call: 864-576-9397

Reverend Evette
Need Help Desperately?
CALL IMMEDIATELY!
Does what others claim! 100% Guaranteed!
Voted #1 Psychic Reader
Answers ALL questions!
Solves life's problems.
Specializing: Love, Marriage, Breakups, Divorce, Family Issues, Financial Matters, Spirituality, Life Direction, LGBTQ+ Issues.
Reunites Lovers!
Removes bad luck, negativity, evil influences.
9 Pisgah Avenue, Chattanooga, TN 37411
Call: 423-894-6699
Visit: https://psychicreadingsbyevette.com

ASTROLOGY (CONT.)

FREE READING!
Problems? Unhappy? Separated from lover?
Bring them back! Control his/her mind.
Call enemies' names. Removes sickness & bad luck! Immediate Solutions!
(Psychic Lisa) 407-300-3357

DOCTOR JOMBO, African Voodoo Doctor
Relationships, Uncrossing, Permanent Protection. Finances, MegaMillions, Powerball. Powerful Results! **310-809-5370**

BUSINESS OPPORTUNITIES

$800 WEEKLY POTENTIAL! Process HUD/FHA refunds from home. Free information available. **Call 860-357-1599**

CATALOGS & BOOKS

Catalog, $4.00
Armadillo Astronomy Theory.
Field Philosophy Famous Cartoons $14.00.
Faire of literature Lyra exploration $14.00
3 Eastern Lane, West Gardiner, Maine 04345
www.DorranceBookstore.com
800-788-7654 – Philosophy Arrow

HEALTH

MACULAR DEGENERATION?

Restore Lost Vision!

No need to travel.

Call for free booklet:
888-838-3937

Also helps RP, Stargardt, and Diabetic Retinopathy

OrganicMD.com and BetterEyeHealth.com

JEWELRY

W W W . A Z U R E G R E E N . N E T
Jewelry, Amulets, Incense, Oils, Statuary, Gifts, Herbs, Candles, Gemstones. 8,000 Items. Wholesale inquiries welcome.

CLASSIFIEDS

PERSONALS

ASIAN WOMEN! Overseas Penpals. Romance! Free brochure (send SASE). P.I.C., Box 4601-OFA, Thousand Oaks, CA 91359. Call today: **805-492-8040. www.pacisl.com**

PSYCHIC READINGS

Free Reading
7th-Generation Psychic Healer Sarah
Energy Specialist
50 Years' Experience
One phone reading will amaze & convince you!
Call: 732-242-2821
Visit: www.psychicclairvoyantguide.com

PSYCHIC ELLA, Love Specialist Reunites Lovers! Solves ALL problems. Love, Career, Family. Never Fails! **817-766-0843**

**ANGEL PSYCHIC
MEDIUM CLAIRVOYANT**
Spiritual - Positive Energy
*Accurate *Honest *Healing
Call: 323-466-3684
www.TruePsychicReader.com

PSYCHIC SPIRITUALISTS

ALANA, Psychic Spiritualist Solves Problems: Love, Business, Family. Reunites Lovers, Twin Flames! Free Question. **469-585-5000.**

**Supernatural Healer - God Gifted
45 years' experience.
Succeeds where others failed!**
FREE CONSULTATION
Feeling overwhelmed by spiritual disturbances? Specializing: Breaking spells, removing curses. Spiritual Cleansing, energy protection. Paranormal investigations, ghost removals. Clearing bad luck, generational curses. Unlocking financial blessings, crop abundance. Restoring balance & happiness. Guarantees immediate solutions!
Call: 202-830-6783
https://www.bringbacklover.com

Reverend Abigail – Gifted Spiritual Healer
Powerful Spiritual Cleansing!
Reveals Past, Present, Future.
Restores Love, Relationships,
Financial Blessings.
Removes Negative Energy, Black Magic.
Never fails! **423-553-5199**

PSYCHIC SPIRITUALISTS (CONT.)

Need Help Fast! Spiritualist Leza Specializing: Reuniting Love, Money, Health, Lucky Charms, Protection. **Call: 229-630-5386**

Ruth Ann, Psychic Spiritualist
Spiritual Indian Cleansings. 55 years' exp.
Removes: Worries, Problems, Sickness.
Reunites Lovers. Solves ALL problems.
Available 24/7.
Call: 512-454-1295
709 Blackson Avenue, Austin, TX 78752

SARAH DAVIS
Helps in ALL problems.
Removes Curses, Evil, Voodoo, Bad Luck.
Returns Lover, Marriage, Business, Health, Money. Call for Lucky Numbers.
512-586-3696

**Tired of Suffering?
FREE READING**
Sister Margaret, Gifted Healer
Restores love, luck, health & happiness.
Stop worrying! Start living!
Regain your faith!
Call Now! 209-200-3679

PSYCHICS

Psychic Hannah
New York Psychic
30 years' experience. Calls out your enemies.
Image Candles-Lucky Charms.
One Free Question!
Call: 347-448-6189

**REV. BLACK, VOODOO HEALER
FREE READING!**
Helps All Problems!
Love, Marriage, Money.
Removes evil influences, bad luck, sickness that doctors can't cure.
Call: 252-366-4078

Psychic Tilly – Spiritualist
Voice Vibration Readings!
Crystal Spiritual Channeling
Solves problems - Reunites lovers!
Removes 3rd-party interference & obstacles
Tells past, present, future. Fast Results!
832-892-3298

(continued)

CLASSIFIEDS

PSYCHICS (CONT.)

Psychic Jolene – Spiritually Gifted
"Believing is the first step to improve your life." Resolves All Problems! Love, Money, Curses. Offering: Powerful Spiritual Items.
800-770-8161
www.psychictarotpalmreader.com

Spiritual Healer Lynn
Clears all negative energy!
Worried? Suffering?
Solves ALL problems!
Specializes: Love, Health, Finances.
Call today! 800-849-9064

ITALIA – Spiritual Advisor
My divine gift helps overcome life's greatest obstacles. Specializing: love, health, finances, depression, or spiritual challenges. Find Clarity!
Call 248-227-8765
www.lovepsychichelp.com

Free Psychic Reading
Psychic Agnes – Rated #1 in America!
Reunites Lovers. Powerful Love Spells.
Relationship Repair. Spiritual Cleansings.
Tarot Readings. Amazing Results!
Happiness Awaits! Call 888-868-5646

SELF HELP

W.I.M.C – Prayer Meeting Host: Prophet Davis Wednesdays @ 8 p.m. CST **Call 667-770-1523** Pin Code #103602 ProphetDavis.com

SPIRITUALISTS

ANN, GOD'S MESSENGER Religious Holy Worker. Reunites lovers forever. Clears stumbling blocks. Stops rootwork! Solves problems. Never fails! 51 years' exp. Fayetteville, N.C. **Call: 910-864-3981.**

VOODOO HEALER

REV. JACKSON, VOODOO HEALER Guaranteed to remove Cross Conditions, Bad Luck, Sickness, Roots, Pain. **252-469-6420.**

Advertisements and statements contained herein are the sole responsibility of the persons or entities that post the advertisement, and *The Old Farmer's Almanac* does not make any warranty as to the accuracy, completeness, truthfulness, or reliability of such advertisements. *The Old Farmer's Almanac* has no liability whatsoever for any third-party claims arising in connection with such advertisements or any products or services mentioned therein.

THE OLD FARMER'S GENERAL STORE
FEATURING UNIQUE MAIL-ORDER PRODUCTS FOR OUR READERS WHO SHOP BY MAIL

Steel Mobile Home Roofover

Built for Strength. Designed for Life
CALL NOW!
PERMA-ROOF OFFERS
- Lifetime Warranty
- Saves on Utilities
- Expert Installation
- Eliminates Leaks & Roof Rumble
- Maintenance-Free

(800) 633-8969 www.roofover.com

Proclaimed by qualified design engineers to be the simplest, quietest, and most practical grain mills and meat grinders in the world. Send $5.00 for flour sample and a color catalog of grain mills and other related items to:

Since 1963 **Retsel Corporation**
1567 E. Hwy 30, McCammon, Idaho 83250
www.RETSEL.com
Grains at Wholesale Prices

Stop Rodent Damage NOW!
Spray for rats, mice, squirrels, rabbits, skunks, raccoons, & more

▶ **Non-Toxic *Rataway Fragrance*** – safe around children, pets & personnel
▶ **Protects wiring** – everything: cars, trucks, machinery, homes, businesses
▶ **Saved buyers over $$$20 million since 1999**
▶ **$25 makes a gallon** – enough to spray an engine 50 times or once a week for a year
▶ **Save TIME, $$$, WIRING** – *FREE shipping within USA!*

 Order now at rataway.com, call or send check to:
**Rataway.com · 2114 S. Rice Rd.,
Ojai, CA 93023 · 805-646-2177**

✤ www.LuckShop.com ✤

CASINO JACKPOT
NECKLACE • POCKET PIECE

Helps You WIN! WIN! WIN!

Helps give the Lottery player or Casino gambler that special "hot-streaky" luck in a hurry—so you can hit the jackpot!

Order Now for LUCK IN A HURRY! HIT the JACKPOT!
60 Day Money Back Guarantee
No. J4270... Only $16.95 (2 for $30.00)

TRIPLE POWER
LUCKY MILLIONAIRE'S
NECKLACE • POCKET PIECE

Just Carry or Wear to Draw Lots of Money to You, Fast! Overcome All Money Problems. Bust thru Any Block on Your Money: Credit Cards, Housing, Welfare, Gambling, Court Case, Pay Raise, Taxes or Overdue Bills, or People that Owe You Money. Try this Lucky Millionaire's Piece, Now! It has 3 Super Luck Symbols for Triple Power.

Order Now for your chance at a Money Miracle!
60 Day Money Back Guarantee
No. J7000... Only $16.95 (2 for $30.00)

STOP EVIL
SPRINKLING SALTS & YARD DRESSING

No. A1240   Only $6.95 (3 for $15.00)
No. A1241 $16.95 for 1lb. bag

Triple Action Salt works to move out all evil, enemies, and jinx on you and your home & family. Use Inside, Outside, or both. Instructions Included. Makes the devil run and Satan be gone. For DOUBLE Protection, Sprinkle inside and outside your home.

LUCKY GAMBLERS MOJO BAGS

M1001	Extra Strong	$12.95
M2002	Double Power	$25.00
M3003	Triple Strength	$50.00

All bags are packed with secret power and super strong mojo roots to give you FAST LUCK when playing any numbers game — Bingo, Lottery, Races, or Casinos. Hit that jackpot and be a WINNER, today!

FREE!!! Extra Strong "Money Drawing" Brand Perfume

LUCKY BRACELET
No. B4095   Only $11.95

All Purpose/Luck in a Hurry – Gemstone Bracelet brings luck in everything—Success, Health & Wealth.

LUCKY RABBIT'S FOOT
– PERFUMED OIL –
No. P5100 $8.95 each (2 for $15.00)

Use for FAST LUCK in everything: money, love, family or work problems.
Sweet-smelling oil comes with a LUCKY RABBIT'S FOOT attached.
Put some oil on you and your rabbit's foot and be RICHER, HAPPIER, LUCKIER than ever before.

"LAS VEGAS" GAMBLER'S PURSE

No. M7000 Only $9.95
Get on a roll and feel that hot streak. You have all the power with this "LUCKY" Purse.

FAST CASH MONEY OIL

No. X1814 Only $9.95
A money growing oil, to bring money miracles. Multiply your cash, now! 1 oz. bottle.

FREE GIFT & CATALOG WITH EVERY ORDER!

CALL 312-332-1634
to place Credit/Debit Card orders

- Credit/Debit Card orders are shipped out the same day or next day.
- PREPAID CASH OR MONEY ORDER ACCEPTED
- NO C.O.D. ORDERS
- PREPAID CHECK – please include STREET ADDRESS & PHONE NUMBER on check or order will be delayed.
* ADD $4.95 for POSTAGE & HANDLING
* ADD $4.00 Extra ($8.95 Total) for RUSH SERVICE

CHURCH GOODS CO. ® DEPT. F-26
P.O. Box 718 • Glenview, Illinois 60025
www.LuckShop.com

For online orders, please enter code "F-26" to get above discounted Postage & Handling Rates

MONEY GROW WALLET
No. M7002 $15.95

Helps you Increase & Hold your money. Lucky for Gambling. Comes with oil & gift.

LUCKY HAND ROOT

Free Green Flannel Bag

No. H0566 Only $7.98
The best and luckiest gambling root for lottery or any casino game.

WE MAKE NO SUPERNATURAL CLAIMS. ALL ITEMS SOLD AS CURIOS ONLY. FULL SATISFACTION IS GUARANTEED OR YOUR MONEY BACK.

AMUSEMENT

2025 ESSAY CONTEST WINNERS
"The Best Gift I Ever Gave"

Thank you to all who submitted touching anecdotes and amusing stories!

First Prize: $300

Growing up in Silver Springs, Florida, our house faced a sandy dirt road, where you could see folks traveling from a grocery store down the way that sold a little bit of everything. Down the road from us lived Aunt Sally with her 12 children. Two of them walked barefoot to the store every day to get a block of ice for their ice box. They would call out a hello on their way to the store, and we would wave. Coming back, they were in a big hurry so that the ice wouldn't melt. They would pick it up with their fingers and run as far as they could before dropping it in the sand and waiting for their fingers to warm up. One morning, Dad took me and my brother, Tommy, into town to the local hardware store to look at little red wagons. We bought the shiniest one. After supper, we walked to Aunt Sally's house to deliver the wagon. All the little kids gathered round and took turns being pulled in it. The next afternoon, as they walked to the store, they were grinning and singing. Coming home, they were pulling the little red wagon with a block of ice.

–Susan S. Brownewell, Palmetto, Florida

Second Prize: $200

Waking up one stormy Christmas Eve morning in my Brazos River dwelling, hearing a loud mournful sound, I went outside into the drizzle and climbed over the levee, discovering a terrified heifer treading water, trapped in debris. The exhausted cow had been too close to a collapsing riverbank. What to do? Call 911 regarding a drowning cow? Having no rope, I improvised with neckties plus extension cords. Wading out and lassoing her was easy. I got her ashore, and once her hooves were on firmer turf, she bolted up the levee. After a bit of a chase, she stopped as I tried to calm her. A pickup in the distance, driving down the levee road, suddenly stopped. A woman was running toward us, crying, "Sheba!" The cow, mooing loudly, ran toward the voice. Happy reunion. The next morning, a knock at my door: the woman, carrying still-warm kolaches as thanks for rescuing her prize cow, plus announcing that Sheba had given birth in the night after her ordeal. I never realized! My heart swelled with joy on that Christmas morning—another kind of birth in a barn. A memorable gift for sure.

–Rex Poland, Dallas, Texas

AMUSEMENT

Third Prize: $100

My wife and I were struggling to make ends meet when our car broke down. We couldn't afford a used car, let alone a new one. A neighbor knew of our plight. He had a second car he wasn't using and offered it to me. "What do you want for it?" I said. He looked me over, then said, "What's it worth, d'you think." At least $5,000, I thought, but I couldn't say that. "Three thousand?" He nodded. "No money down. Pay in installments when you can." We shook on it. We scrambled that summer for the first $200. When I brought it over, he shook his head. "Don't need it at the moment," he smiled. "Whyn't you hold onto it, 'case a need comes up." I almost cried. That was the cushion that kept our heads above water. Slowly, steadily, finally far enough ahead of the wolf at the door, we gathered $1,000 for our first payment. He had his wife meet me at the door. "It wasn't a loan, he said for me to tell you. There's no need to pay it back." I never forgot their generosity. When we could pay it forward, we did. First was helping a friend with rent. Next, a Christmas for a struggling family. Sometimes, an envelope with $50 was slipped into someone's mailbox. The ones I like best are in the checkout line behind someone who comes up short. I offer to get the missed items. If they get embarrassed, I give them a short version of my neighbor's car story, and that smooths everything over.

–James Marino,
Sun City Center, Florida

Honorable Mention

She was a senior Buff Orpington chicken—a breed I was fond of for their gentle demeanor, their golden feathers, and the bounty of big brown eggs. This hen wanted to be a mother, and her desire played out in sadness every time I'd gather her eggs. I finally let her sit a nest last autumn. Long past the hatch time, she grew sadder and sadder. Me, too. I headed out for a distant feed store that had Lavender Orpington chicks, not Buffs. Before dusk, the about-to-be surrogate mama seemed to understand that we were trading eggs for babies. A miracle unfolded as an exhausted, grief-stricken hen turned into the most joyful mother I have ever seen. Contentedly snuggling under her, the chicks—and the hen and I—shared the best gift, ever.

–Linda Whiteley,
Huachuca City, Arizona ■

ANNOUNCING THE 2026 ESSAY CONTEST TOPIC:
MY MOST EMBARRASSING MOMENT—THAT *STILL* MAKES ME LAUGH
See contest rules on page 251.

AMUSEMENT
MADDENING MIND-MANGLERS

A. ALL ABOUT THREE
1. Name the traditional gift for a third wedding anniversary:
a. fruit or flowers
b. wood
c. leather

2. Which is Morse code for the number three?
a. 3 dots, 2 dashes
b. 3 dots
c. 2 dots, 3 dashes

3. Who was the third child of their family?
a. Benjamin Franklin
b. Martha Washington
c. Wilbur Wright

B. RIDDLE ME THIS
How could the letter G surprise a farmer?

C. COMBO CONUNDRUM
Change these words into a single word:
No more stars

D. PERPLEXING PAIR
What word fits the first clue, but when rearranged fits the second?

*Everyone keeps me on hand,
I've ever to labor bent;
But twist me about and then
I'm only an ornament.*

E. BY ANY OTHER NAME
Match each less-used plant name to its more familiar label:

____ **1.** nose tweaker   **a.** caladium *(Caladium bicolor)*

____ **2.** old man's pepper **b.** Johnny-jump-up *(Viola tricolor)*

____ **3.** sea tomato   **c.** nasturtium *(Tropaeolum majus)*

____ **4.** stoplight   **d.** rugosa rose *(Rosa rugosa)*

____ **5.** tickle-my-fancy   **e.** common yarrow *(Achillea millefolium)*

____ **6.** youth-and-old-age **f.** zinnia *(Zinnia)*

F. MATH FUN

The product of two numbers is six times their sum, and the sum of their squares is 325.

What are the numbers?

ANSWERS

A. 1. c. leather (modern=crystal or glass); 2. a (b=s, c=2); 3. c (a=15 of 17 of father, who remarried; b=1 of 8). **B.** by changing oats into goats. **C.** astronomers. **D.** finger, fringe. **E.** 1. c; 2. e; 3. d; 4. a; 5. b; 6. f. **F.** 10 and 15.

Do you have a favorite puzzler for "Maddening Mind-Manglers" that you'd like to share? Send it to us at Mind-Manglers, The Old Farmer's Almanac, P.O. Box 520, Dublin, NH 03444, or via Almanac.com/Contact, Subject: Mind-Manglers.

POETRY CORNER

Happy Lives

*Not on life's crowded highways
Do they the journey make,
But in the quiet byways
Enchanted paths they take,
With comrades ever near them
To share their happiness—
With birds and flowers to cheer them,
And books to balm and bless.*

–Frank Dempster Sherman,
in *The Old Farmer's Almanac*, 1927

ESSAY AND RECIPE CONTEST RULES

Cash prizes (first, $300; second, $200; third, $100) will be awarded for the best essays in 200 or fewer words on the subject "My Most Embarrassing Moment—That *Still* Makes Me Laugh" and the best "Berries" recipes. Entries must be yours, original, and unpublished. Amateur cooks only, please. One recipe per person. All entries become the property of Yankee Publishing, which reserves all rights to the material. The deadline for entries is January 31, 2026. Enter at Almanac.com/EssayContest or at Almanac.com/RecipeContest or label "Essay Contest" or "Recipe Contest" and mail to The Old Farmer's Almanac, P.O. Box 520, Dublin, NH 03444. Include your name, mailing address, and email address. Winners will appear in *The 2027 Old Farmer's Almanac* and on Almanac.com. ■

AMUSEMENT

ANECDOTES & PLEASANTRIES

A sampling from the thousands of letters, clippings, articles, and emails sent to us by our Almanac *family in the United States and Canada.*

ILLUSTRATIONS BY TIM ROBINSON

Oh, and By the Way . . .

Nearing the end of a long life, a fellow named Henry fell and broke his hip. The operation to insert a pin into his joint would be routine, but still, at his age, well, who knew what might happen?

While his prognosis was good if all went as planned, he and his wife of many years were understandably concerned about all of the possibilities. As they talked in his hospital room before the operation, Henry paused and looked into his wife's eyes.

"One thing," he said, ". . . and it's important. . . ."

His wife swallowed hard. "Yes?"

"If I don't make it, whatever you do, don't sell my woodworking tools for what I told you I paid for them."

–*courtesy of R. S., Middleton, New Hampshire*

Truly Relatable

A Texas farmer set out to visit Ireland. After landing in Dublin and driving an hour outside of the city, he stopped at a pub to grab a pint. He struck up a conversation with the local sitting next to him only to learn that he was also a farmer.

The Irishman inquired, "Tell me, what's it like farming in Texas?"

The Texan said, "Farming in Texas has been quite rewarding for me. If I started out in the morning and drove west, I could drive all day before I reached the end of my property. Same thing east, north, or south. I could drive any direction all day and wouldn't reach the end of my farmland."

"Ahh, I know what you mean," said the Irishman, "I've got a tractor like that as well."

–courtesy of J. B., Fairmount, Indiana

TALK ABOUT BAGGAGE

The most recent *Unclaimed Baggage Found Report* gave us a peek inside some of the interesting (and downright weird) items left behind by travelers. Here are 10 of the most fascinating things discovered:

- freeze-dried chicken foot
- Turkish ceremonial wedding headdress
- teeth bedazzling kit
- medieval larping (live action role-playing) suit of armor

- letter signed by Eleanor Roosevelt, dated 1944
- preserved rattlesnake in a jar of whiskey
- antique French book on performing exorcisms
- authentic box of Prada crayons
- toilet brush shaped like a cherry
- old-fashioned mustache curler

–courtesy of M. A., Denver, Colorado, from UnclaimedBaggage.com

(continued)

AMUSEMENT

THIS YEAR'S CRINGERS
(Feel free to leave the room.)

- Just so everyone's clear, I'm going to put my glasses on.
- I once worked at a pizza shop to get by. I kneaded the dough.
- My friends and I have named our band "Duvet." It's a cover band.
- What did the surgeon say to the patient who insisted on closing up their own incision? Suture self.
- I'm trying to organize a hide-and-seek tournament, but good players are really hard to find.
- I've started telling everyone about the benefit of eating dried grapes. It's all about raisin' awareness.
- "Dad, are we pyromaniacs?" "Yes, we arson."
- Writing my name in cursive is my signature move.

–courtesy of D. D., Calgary, Alberta

For Good Measure

- Time it takes to temporarily sail 220 yards at 1 nautical mile per hour: knotfurlong
- One-millionth of a mouthwash: microscope
- Time between slipping on a peel and hitting the pavement: bananosecond
- One million aches: megahurtz
- Basic unit of laryngitis: hoarsepower
- Eight nickels: two paradigms

–courtesy of C. B., Concord, North Carolina

JUST CURIOUS

Did the coiner of "one-hit wonder" have any other ideas?

At a Loss For Words

Over the last 20 years, humans have been speaking 3,000 fewer words a day. Research from the American Psychological Association shows the average number of daily spoken words dropped from 16,000 to around 13,000. This decline is being attributed to, what else, texting and social media. And for those who have always believed that women talk more than men—it's true, but not by much. Women speak about 13,349 words per day versus men at 11,950 words per day. So, what have we really learned? We couldn't say.

–courtesy of F. T., Waltham, Massachusetts

YES, THAT MIGHT WORK

Many years ago, I was in the office of our Director of Promotions, packing boxes for a national meeting in Portland, Oregon. The director was busy talking on the telephone. I wasn't paying much attention to the conversation until I suddenly heard her say, "Well, why don't you try circumcision? I think that might work."

When she saw me suddenly look up with a rather startled expression, she quickly explained, "I'm helping my son with a crossword puzzle."

–courtesy of Rev. R. W., Apopka, Florida

(continued)

AMUSEMENT

How To Live To Be 100 Years Old . . . Or More!

*We could all learn a thing or two from "Andy"
Anderson of Benicia, California, who lived to the age of 106!
He shared this wisdom on his 100th birthday:*

- Always maintain a good sense of humor.
- Never be too good to start at the bottom.
- Exercise every single day, even when you don't feel like it.
- Don't spend more money than you make.
- Eat around the mold; don't go wasting food.
- Your family is the most precious thing you will ever have in life.
- Don't ever be afraid to be your true self.
- Education is important but not necessary. Life can be an education in itself.
- You must be able to forgive, even if it's difficult to do.
- Love is not always easy; sometimes you have to work at it.
- Try not to take yourself so seriously.
- My full name is William Bradford James Anderson, and my initials always remind me to ask myself, "Why be just anybody?"

–courtesy of M. W., Madison, Wisconsin, from PopSugar.com

CHEW ON THIS

In the "who volunteered for that study?" department, a connection was found between chewing on sticks and brain health. The research showed that simply chewing on wood, as opposed to something soft such as gum, stimulates an increase in a key antioxidant in the brain, which in turn improves memory. And you thought subbing cottage cheese for potato chips was good for you.

–courtesy of A. W., Sandy, Utah ■

Send your contributions for *The 2027 Old Farmer's Almanac* by January 31, 2026, to "A & P," The Old Farmer's Almanac, P.O. Box 520, Dublin, NH 03444, or via Almanac.com/Contact.

THE OLD FARMER'S ALMANAC

Reference Compendium

CALENDAR
Phases of the Moon............... 258
When Will the Moon Rise? 258
Full Moon Names 258
The Origin of Full Moon Names... 259
Meanings of Full Moon Names.... 259
The Origin of Month Names...... 260
Easter Dates (2026–29) 260
Friggatriskaidekaphobia Trivia... 260
The Origin of Day Names 261
How to Find the Day of the Week
  for Any Given Date 261
Animal Signs of the Chinese
  Zodiac 262

WEATHER
A Table Foretelling the Weather
  Through All the Lunations of Each
  Year, or Forever 263
Safe Ice Thickness 263
Heat Index Table................ 264
The UV Index for Measuring
  Ultraviolet Radiation Risk 264
What Are Cooling/Heating
  Degree Days? 265
How to Stay Cool................ 265
Weather Lore for the Year 266
How to Measure Hurricane
  Strength 267
Atlantic Tropical (and Subtropical)
  Storm Names for 2026......... 267
Eastern North-Pacific Tropical
  (and Subtropical) Storm Names
  for 2026...................... 267
Retired Atlantic Hurricane Names . 267
How To Measure Tornadoes 268
Wind/Barometer Table.......... 268
Windchill Table................. 269
How to Measure Earthquakes.... 269

IN THE GARDEN
A Gardener's Worst Phobias 270
Plants for Lawns................ 270
Lawn-Growing Tips 270
Flowers and Herbs That Attract
  Butterflies.................... 271
Flowers That Attract
  Hummingbirds 271
pH Preferences of Trees, Shrubs,
  Flowers, and Vegetables 272
How to Rotate Crops 273
Sowing Vegetable Seeds......... 274
A Beginner's Vegetable Garden .. 274
Soil Fixes...................... 274
When to Fertilize and Water 275
A Guide to Harvesting and
  Storing Vegetables............ 276
How to Grow Bulbs.............. 278

AROUND THE HOUSE
Substitutions for Common
  Ingredients................... 280
Freezer Tips.................... 282
Freezer Storage Times 282
When to Replace, Clean, Renew .. 283
Plastics 284
Practical Uses for Household
  Ingredients................... 285
Planning for the Unexpected 286

WORDS OF WISDOM
Founding Fodder 288

CALENDAR

PHASES OF THE MOON

- New
- Waxing Crescent
- First Quarter
- Waxing Gibbous
- Full
- Waning Gibbous
- Last Quarter
- Waning Crescent
- New

(WAXING / WANING)

WHEN WILL THE MOON RISE?

Use the following saying to remember the time of moonrise on a day when a Moon phase occurs. Keep in mind that the phase itself may happen earlier or later that day, depending on location.

The new Moon always rises near sunrise;

The first quarter, near noon;

The full Moon always rises near sunset;

The last quarter, near midnight.

Moonrise occurs about 50 minutes later each day.

FULL MOON NAMES

NAME	MONTH	VARIATIONS
Full Wolf Moon	JANUARY	Full Greetings Moon
Full Snow Moon	FEBRUARY	Full Hungry Moon
Full Worm Moon	MARCH	Full Eagle Moon Full Sore Eye Moon Full Sugar Moon Full Wind Strong Moon
Full Pink Moon	APRIL	Full Budding Moon Moon When the Geese Lay Eggs
Full Flower Moon	MAY	Full Frog Moon Full Planting Moon
Full Strawberry Moon	JUNE	Full Hoer Moon Full Hot Moon
Full Buck Moon	JULY	Full Raspberry Moon Full Salmon Moon
Full Sturgeon Moon	AUGUST	Full Black Cherries Moon Full Flying Up Moon
Full Harvest Moon*	SEPTEMBER	Full Corn Moon Full Yellow Leaf Moon
Full Hunter's Moon	OCTOBER	Full Falling Leaves Moon Full Migrating Moon
Full Beaver Moon	NOVEMBER	Full Frost Moon
Full Cold Moon	DECEMBER	Full Long Night Moon

*The Harvest Moon is always the full Moon closest to the autumnal equinox. If the Harvest Moon occurs in October, the September full Moon is usually called the Corn Moon.

Learn more about Full Moon names via Almanac.com/2026.

CALENDAR

THE ORIGIN OF FULL MOON NAMES

Historically, some Native Americans who lived in the area that is now the United States kept track of the seasons by giving a distinctive name to each recurring full Moon. (This name was applied to the entire lunar month in which it occurred.) The names were used by various tribes and/or by colonial Americans, who also brought their own traditions.

Meanings of Full Moon Names

JANUARY'S full Moon was called the **Wolf Moon** because wolves were more often heard at this time.

FEBRUARY'S full Moon was called the **Snow Moon** because it was a time of heavy snow. It was also called the **Hungry Moon** because hunting was difficult and hunger often resulted.

MARCH'S full Moon was called the **Worm Moon** because, as the weather warmed, wormlike insect larvae emerged from winter homes, such as the bark of trees.

APRIL'S full Moon was called the **Pink Moon** because it heralded the appearance of the moss pink, or wild ground phlox—one of the first spring flowers.

MAY'S full Moon was called the **Flower Moon** because blossoms were abundant everywhere at this time.

JUNE'S full Moon was called the **Strawberry Moon** because it appeared when the strawberry harvest took place.

JULY'S full Moon was called the **Buck Moon**; it arrived when a male deer's antlers were in full growth mode.

AUGUST'S full Moon was called the **Sturgeon Moon** because this large fish, found in the Great Lakes and Lake Champlain, was caught easily at this time.

SEPTEMBER'S full Moon was called the **Corn Moon** because this was the time to harvest corn.

The **Harvest Moon** is the full Moon that occurs closest to the autumnal equinox. It can occur in either September or October. Around this time, the Moon rises only about 30 minutes later each night, providing extra light after sunset for harvesting.

OCTOBER'S full Moon was called the **Hunter's Moon** because this was the time to hunt in preparation for winter.

NOVEMBER'S full Moon was called the **Beaver Moon** because it was the time when beavers finished preparations for winter and retreated to their lodges.

DECEMBER'S full Moon was called the **Cold Moon**. It was also called the **Long Night Moon** because nights at this time of year were the longest.

CALENDAR

THE ORIGIN OF MONTH NAMES

JANUARY. For the Roman god Janus, protector of gates and doorways. Janus is depicted with two faces, one looking into the past, the other into the future.

FEBRUARY. From the Latin *februa,* "to cleanse." The Roman Februalia was a festival of purification and atonement that took place during this time of year.

MARCH. For the Roman god of war, Mars. This was the time of year to resume military campaigns that had been interrupted by winter.

APRIL. From the Latin *aperio,* "to open (bud)," because plants begin to grow now.

MAY. For the Roman goddess Maia, who oversaw the growth of plants. Also from the Latin *maiores,* "elders," who were celebrated now.

JUNE. For the Roman goddess Juno, patroness of marriage and the well-being of women. Also from the Latin *juvenis,* "young people."

JULY. To honor Roman dictator Julius Caesar (100 B.C.–44 B.C.). In 46 B.C., with the help of Sosigenes, he developed the Julian calendar.

AUGUST. To honor the first Roman emperor (and grandnephew of Julius Caesar), Augustus Caesar (63 B.C.–A.D. 14).

SEPTEMBER. From the Latin *septem,* "seven," because this was the seventh month of the early Roman calendar.

OCTOBER. From the Latin *octo,* "eight," because this was the eighth month of the early Roman calendar.

NOVEMBER. From the Latin *novem,* "nine," because this was the ninth month of the early Roman calendar.

DECEMBER. From the Latin *decem,* "ten," because this was the tenth month of the early Roman calendar.

Easter Dates (2026–29)

Christian churches that follow the Gregorian calendar celebrate Easter on the first Sunday after the paschal full Moon on or just after the vernal equinox.

YEAR	EASTER
2026	April 5
2027	March 28
2028	April 16
2029	April 1

The Julian calendar is used by some churches, including many Eastern Orthodox. The dates below are Julian calendar dates for Easter converted to Gregorian dates.

YEAR	EASTER
2026	April 12
2027	May 2
2028	April 16
2029	April 8

FRIGGATRISKAIDEKAPHOBIA TRIVIA

Here are a few facts about Friday the 13th:

In the 14 possible configurations for the annual calendar (see any perpetual calendar), the occurrence of Friday the 13th is this:

6 of 14 years have one Friday the 13th.
6 of 14 years have two Fridays the 13th.
2 of 14 years have three Fridays the 13th.

No year is without one Friday the 13th, and no year has more than three.

Months that have a Friday the 13th begin on a Sunday.

2026 has a Friday the 13th in February, March, and November.

CALENDAR

THE ORIGIN OF DAY NAMES

The days of the week were named by ancient Romans with the Latin words for the Sun, the Moon, and the five known planets. These names have survived in European languages, but English names also reflect Anglo-Saxon and Norse influences.

ENGLISH	LATIN	FRENCH	ITALIAN	SPANISH	ANGLO-SAXON AND NORSE
SUNDAY	dies Solis (Sol's day)	dimanche	domenica	domingo	Sunnandaeg (Sun's day)
		from the Latin for "Lord's day"			
MONDAY	dies Lunae (Luna's day)	lundi	lunedì	lunes	Monandaeg (Moon's day)
TUESDAY	dies Martis (Mars's day)	mardi	martedì	martes	Tiwesdaeg (Tiw's day)
WEDNESDAY	dies Mercurii (Mercury's day)	mercredi	mercoledì	miércoles	Wodnesdaeg (Woden's day)
THURSDAY	dies Jovis (Jupiter's day)	jeudi	giovedì	jueves	Thursdaeg (Thor's day)
FRIDAY	dies Veneris (Venus's day)	vendredi	venerdì	viernes	Frigedaeg (Frigga's day)
SATURDAY	dies Saturni (Saturn's day)	samedi	sabato	sábado	Saeterndaeg (Saturn's day)
		from the Latin for "Sabbath"			

How to Find the Day of the Week for Any Given Date

To compute the day of the week for any given date as far back as the mid-18th century, proceed as follows:

Add the last two digits of the year to one-quarter of the last two digits (discard any remainder), the day of the month, and the month key from the key box below. Divide the sum by 7; the remainder is the day of the week (1 is Sunday, 2 is Monday, and so on). If there is no remainder, the day is Saturday. If you're searching for a weekday prior to 1900, add 2 to the sum before dividing; prior to 1800, add 4. The formula doesn't work for days prior to 1753. From 2000 through 2099, subtract 1 from the sum before dividing.

Example:
THE DAYTON FLOOD WAS ON MARCH 25, 1913.

Last two digits of year:	13
One-quarter of these two digits:	3
Given day of month:	25
Key number for March:	4
Sum:	45

45 ÷ 7 = 6, with a remainder of 3. The flood took place on Tuesday, the third day of the week.

KEY

JANUARY	1
LEAP YEAR	0
FEBRUARY	4
LEAP YEAR	3
MARCH	4
APRIL	0
MAY	2
JUNE	5
JULY	0
AUGUST	3
SEPTEMBER	6
OCTOBER	1
NOVEMBER	4
DECEMBER	6

CALENDAR

ANIMAL SIGNS OF THE CHINESE ZODIAC

The animal designations of the Chinese zodiac follow a 12-year cycle and are always used in the same sequence. The Chinese year of 354 days begins 3 to 7 weeks into the western 365-day year, so the animal designation changes at that time, rather than on January 1. This year, the Lunar New Year in China starts on February 17.

RAT

Ambitious and sincere, you can be generous with your money. Compatible with the dragon and the monkey. Your opposite is the horse.

1936	1948	1960
1972	1984	1996
2008	2020	2032

OX OR BUFFALO

A leader, you are bright, patient, and cheerful. Compatible with the snake and the rooster. Your opposite is the sheep.

1937	1949	1961
1973	1985	1997
2009	2021	2033

TIGER

Forthright and sensitive, you possess great courage. Compatible with the horse and the dog. Your opposite is the monkey.

1938	1950	1962
1974	1986	1998
2010	2022	2034

RABBIT OR HARE

Talented and affectionate, you are a seeker of tranquility. Compatible with the sheep and the pig. Your opposite is the rooster.

1939	1951	1963
1975	1987	1999
2011	2023	2035

DRAGON

Robust and passionate, your life is filled with complexity. Compatible with the monkey and the rat. Your opposite is the dog.

1940	1952	1964
1976	1988	2000
2012	2024	2036

SNAKE

Strong-willed and intense, you display great wisdom. Compatible with the rooster and the ox. Your opposite is the pig.

1941	1953	1965
1977	1989	2001
2013	2025	2037

HORSE

Physically attractive and popular, you like the company of others. Compatible with the tiger and the dog. Your opposite is the rat.

1930	1942	1954
1966	1978	1990
2002	2014	2026

GOAT OR SHEEP

Aesthetic and stylish, you enjoy being a private person. Compatible with the pig and the rabbit. Your opposite is the ox.

1931	1943	1955
1967	1979	1991
2003	2015	2027

MONKEY

Persuasive, skillful, and intelligent, you strive to excel. Compatible with the dragon and the rat. Your opposite is the tiger.

1932	1944	1956
1968	1980	1992
2004	2016	2028

ROOSTER OR COCK

Seeking wisdom and truth, you have a pioneering spirit. Compatible with the snake and the ox. Your opposite is the rabbit.

1933	1945	1957
1969	1981	1993
2005	2017	2029

DOG

Generous and loyal, you have the ability to work well with others. Compatible with the horse and the tiger. Your opposite is the dragon.

1934	1946	1958
1970	1982	1994
2006	2018	2030

PIG OR BOAR

Gallant and noble, your friends will remain at your side. Compatible with the rabbit and the sheep. Your opposite is the snake.

1935	1947	1959
1971	1983	1995
2007	2019	2031

Love calendar lore? Find more via Almanac.com/2026.

WEATHER

A Table Foretelling the Weather Through All the Lunations of Each Year, or Forever

This table is the result of many years of actual observation and shows what sort of weather will probably follow the Moon's entrance into any of its quarters. For example, the table shows that the week following January 10, 2026, will be cold with high winds because the Moon enters the last quarter at 10:48 A.M. EST. (See the **Left-Hand Calendar Pages, 120–146,** for Moon phases.)

EDITOR'S NOTE: Although the data in this table is taken into consideration in the year-long process of compiling the annual long-range weather forecasts for *The Old Farmer's Almanac,* we rely far more on our projections of solar activity.

TIME OF CHANGE	SUMMER	WINTER
Midnight to 2 A.M.	Fair	Hard frost, unless wind is south or west
2 A.M. to 4 A.M.	Cold, with frequent showers	Snow and stormy
4 A.M. to 6 A.M.	Rain	Rain
6 A.M. to 8 A.M.	Wind and rain	Stormy
8 A.M. to 10 A.M.	Changeable	Cold rain if wind is west; snow, if east
10 A.M. to noon	Frequent showers	Cold with high winds
Noon to 2 P.M.	Very rainy	Snow or rain
2 P.M. to 4 P.M.	Changeable	Fair and mild
4 P.M. to 6 P.M.	Fair	Fair
6 P.M. to 10 P.M.	Fair if wind is northwest; rain if wind is south or southwest	Fair and frosty if wind is north or northeast; rain or snow if wind is south or southwest
10 P.M. to midnight	Fair	Fair and frosty

This table was created more than 190 years ago by Dr. Herschell for the Boston Courier; *it first appeared in* The Old Farmer's Almanac *in 1834.*

SAFE ICE THICKNESS*

ICE THICKNESS	PERMISSIBLE LOAD
4 inches	Single person on foot
5 inches	Small group skating
5–7 inches	Snowmobile, small ATV
7–8 inches	Multi-rider ATV, UTV
8–10 inches	Passenger car, small SUV
10–12 inches	Light truck, compact SUV
12–15 inches	Medium truck, midsize SUV
16 inches	Heavy truck, full-size SUV

Ice is never 100 percent safe. It forms on lakes and ponds unevenly, so while it may be 4 inches thick in one area, it could be much thinner a few feet away. Avoid ice that is cracked or near inlets or moving water.

***Solid, clear, blue/black pond and lake ice**

The strength value of river ice is 15 percent less. Slush ice has only half the strength of blue ice.

WEATHER

HEAT INDEX TABLE

TEMP. °F (°C)	\	\	\	RELATIVE HUMIDITY (%)	\	\	\	\	\
	40	45	50	55	60	65	70	75	80
100 (38)	109 (43)	114 (46)	118 (48)	124 (51)	129 (54)	136 (58)			
98 (37)	105 (41)	109 (43)	113 (45)	117 (47)	123 (51)	128 (53)	134 (57)		
96 (36)	101 (38)	104 (40)	108 (42)	112 (44)	116 (47)	121 (49)	126 (52)	132 (56)	
94 (34)	97 (36)	100 (38)	103 (39)	106 (41)	110 (43)	114 (46)	119 (48)	124 (51)	129 (54)
92 (33)	94 (34)	96 (36)	99 (37)	101 (38)	105 (41)	108 (42)	112 (44)	116 (47)	121 (49)
90 (32)	91 (33)	93 (34)	95 (35)	97 (36)	100 (38)	103 (39)	105 (41)	109 (43)	113 (45)
88 (31)	88 (31)	89 (32)	91 (33)	93 (34)	95 (35)	98 (37)	100 (38)	103 (39)	106 (41)
86 (30)	85 (29)	87 (31)	88 (31)	89 (32)	91 (33)	93 (34)	95 (35)	97 (36)	100 (38)
84 (29)	83 (28)	84 (29)	85 (29)	86 (30)	88 (31)	89 (32)	90 (32)	92 (33)	94 (34)
82 (28)	81 (27)	82 (28)	83 (28)	84 (29)	84 (29)	85 (29)	86 (30)	88 (31)	89 (32)
80 (27)	80 (27)	80 (27)	81 (27)	81 (27)	82 (28)	82 (28)	83 (28)	84 (29)	84 (29)

RISK LEVEL FOR HEAT DISORDERS: ▨ CAUTION ▨ EXTREME CAUTION ▨ DANGER

EXAMPLE: *When the temperature is 88°F (31°C) and the relative humidity is 60 percent, the heat index, or how hot it feels, is 95°F (35°C).*

THE UV INDEX FOR MEASURING ULTRAVIOLET RADIATION RISK

The U.S. National Weather Service's daily forecasts of ultraviolet levels use these numbers for various exposure levels:

UV INDEX NUMBER	EXPOSURE LEVEL	ACTIONS TO TAKE
0, 1, 2	Low	Wear UV-blocking sunglasses on bright days. In winter, reflection off snow can nearly double UV strength. If you burn easily, cover up and apply SPF 30+ sunscreen.
3, 4, 5	Moderate	Apply SPF 30+ sunscreen; wear a hat and sunglasses. Stay in shade when sun is strongest.
6, 7	High	Apply SPF 30+ sunscreen; wear a hat, sunglasses, and protective clothing; limit midday exposure.
8, 9, 10	Very High	Apply SPF 30+ sunscreen; wear a hat, sunglasses, and protective clothing; limit midday exposure. Seek shade. Unprotected skin will be damaged and can burn quickly.
11 or higher	Extreme	Apply SPF 30+ sunscreen; wear a hat, sunglasses, and protective clothing; avoid midday exposure; seek shade. Unprotected skin can burn in minutes.

Get your local forecast via Almanac.com/2026.

85	90	95	100
135 (57)			
126 (52)	131 (55)		
117 (47)	122 (50)	127 (53)	132 (56)
110 (43)	113 (45)	117 (47)	121 (49)
102 (39)	105 (41)	108 (42)	112 (44)
96 (36)	98 (37)	100 (38)	103 (39)
90 (32)	91 (33)	93 (34)	95 (35)
85 (29)	86 (30)	86 (30)	87 (31)

What Are Cooling/Heating Degree Days?

In an attempt to measure the need for air-conditioning, each degree of a day's mean temperature that is above a base temperature, such as 65°F (U.S.) or 18°C (Canada), is considered one cooling degree day. If the daily mean temperature is 75°F, for example, that's 10 cooling degree days.

Similarly, to measure the need for heating fuel consumption, each degree of a day's mean temperature that is below 65°F (18°C) is considered one heating degree. For example, a day with a high of 60°F and low of 40°F results in a mean of 50°, or 15 degrees less than 65°. Hence, that day had 15 heating degree days.

HOW TO STAY COOL

When temperatures rise, try these useful tips to help you to beat the heat and stay cool—even if you don't have air conditioning:

TAKE CARE OF YOUR BODY
- Drink 1 cup of water every 15 to 20 minutes (24 to 32 ounces per hour).
- Minimize sun exposure during the warmest time of the day (typically between 11 A.M. and 3 P.M.).
- To help with hydration, eat foods with water content greater than 90 percent, such as cucumbers, strawberries, tomatoes, and watermelon.
- Rub ice cubes on pulse points—temples, wrists, neck, inside of elbows and knees—for a cooling effect.
- Eat a popsicle instead of ice cream. A popsicle's high water content will help cool you down more efficiently than ice cream.
- Wear loose, lightweight cotton or linen clothing to create airflow.
- Take a cold shower or go for a swim.
- Place a wet shirt or towel in the freezer until it is cold but not frozen stiff, and then wear it around your neck.

KEEP YOUR AREA COOL
- Place bottles of frozen, salted water (3 tablespoons of salt per 1 liter of water) in front of fans to cool the surrounding air.
- Keep windows closed during the day when outdoor temperatures are higher than indoors. Conversely, open windows at night to allow ventilation when outdoor air is cooler.
- Cover windows in rooms that face the Sun.
- Use ceiling fans—when they are an option—to help distribute airflow.
- Limit use of heat-producing appliances, such as an oven.

CREATE A RESTFUL NIGHT
- Wear pajamas and use a thin sheet. The combination allows your body to maintain a controlled temperature around your skin.
- Fill a water bottle half full and freeze it. Place under the sheets to help keep you cool during the night.
- Place your sheets in a plastic bag and freeze them before bed to start the night on the cool side.

WEATHER

WEATHER LORE FOR THE YEAR

According to weather lore, specific precipitation and temperatures at certain times of the year are believed to lead to foretold outcomes in the ensuing months. Below is a collection of monthly lore from yesteryear to help you forecast the weather yet to come.

JANUARY
- In January if the Sun appear, March and April pay full dear.
- A summerish January, a winterish spring.
- A warm January, a cold May.

FEBRUARY
- There is always one fine week in February.
- Fogs in February mean frosts in May.
- When it rains in February, all the year suffers.

MARCH
- When March has April weather, April will have March weather.
- March damp and warm Will do farmer much harm.
- In March much snow, To plants and trees much woe.

APRIL
- If it thunders on All Fools' Day It brings good crops of corn and hay.
- April weather Rain and sunshine, both together.
- After a wet April, a dry June.

MAY
- In the middle of May comes the tail of winter.
- The more thunder in May, the less in August and September.
- A leaking May and a warm June Bring on the harvest very soon.

JUNE
- A cold and wet June spoils the rest of the year.
- When it is hottest in June, it will be coldest in the corresponding days of the next February.
- A good leak in June / Sets all in tune.

JULY
- As July, so the next January.
- Whatever July and August do not boil, September cannot fry.
- If it rains on July 10th, it will rain for seven weeks.

AUGUST
- When the dew is heavy in August, the weather generally remains fair.
- If the first week in August is unusually warm, the winter will be white and long.
- A fog in August indicates a severe winter and plenty of snow.

SEPTEMBER
- Heavy September rains bring drought.
- If the storms in September clear off warm, all the storms of the following winter will be warm.
- Fair on September 1st, fair for the month.

OCTOBER
- There are always nineteen fine days in October.
- Much rain in October, much wind in December.
- Full Moon in October without frost, no frost till full Moon in November.

NOVEMBER
- As November, so the following March.
- When in November the water rises, it will show itself the whole winter.
- A heavy November snow will last till April.

DECEMBER
- Thunder in December presages fine weather.
- So far as the Sun shines on Christmas Day, / So far will the snow blow in May.

–Source: Weather Lore by Richard Inwards

WEATHER

How to Measure Hurricane Strength

The **SAFFIR-SIMPSON HURRICANE WIND SCALE** assigns a rating from 1 to 5 based on a hurricane's intensity. It is used to estimate the potential property damage from a hurricane landfall. Wind speed is the determining factor in the scale, as storm surge values are highly dependent on the slope of the continental shelf in the landfall region. Wind speeds are measured at a height of 33 feet (10 meters) using a 1-minute average.

CATEGORY ONE. Average wind: 74–95 mph. Significant damage to mobile homes. Some damage to roofing and siding of well-built frame homes. Large tree branches snap and shallow-rooted trees may topple. Power outages may last a few to several days.

CATEGORY TWO. Average wind: 96–110 mph. Mobile homes may be destroyed. Major roof and siding damage to frame homes. Many shallow-rooted trees snap or topple, blocking roads. Widespread power outages could last from several days to weeks. Potable water may be scarce.

CATEGORY THREE. Average wind: 111–129 mph. Most mobile homes destroyed. Frame homes may sustain major roof damage. Many trees snap or topple, blocking numerous roads. Electricity and water may be unavailable for several days to weeks.

CATEGORY FOUR. Average wind: 130–156 mph. Mobile homes destroyed. Frame homes severely damaged or destroyed. Windborne debris may penetrate protected windows. Most trees snap or topple. Residential areas isolated by fallen trees and power poles. Most of the area uninhabitable for weeks to months.

CATEGORY FIVE. Average wind: 157+ mph. Most homes destroyed. Nearly all windows blown out of high-rises. Most of the area uninhabitable for weeks to months.

ATLANTIC TROPICAL (AND SUBTROPICAL) STORM NAMES FOR 2026

Arthur	Hanna	Omar
Bertha	Isaias	Paulette
Cristobal	Josephine	Rene
Dolly	Kyle	Sally
Edouard	Leah	Teddy
Fay	Marco	Vicky
Gonzalo	Nana	Wilfred

EASTERN NORTH PACIFIC TROPICAL (AND SUBTROPICAL) STORM NAMES FOR 2026

Amanda	Iselle	Rachel
Boris	Julio	Simon
Cristina	Karina	Trudy
Douglas	Lowell	Vance
Elida	Marie	Winnie
Fausto	Norbert	Xavier
Genevieve	Odalys	Yolanda
Hernan	Polo	Zeke

The lists above are used in rotation and recycled every 6 years, e.g., the 2026 list will be used again in 2032.

RETIRED ATLANTIC HURRICANE NAMES

These storms have been some of the most destructive and costly.

NAME	YEAR	NAME	YEAR	NAME	YEAR	NAME	YEAR
Igor	2010	Harvey	2017	Laura	2020	Fiona	2022
Irene	2011	Irma	2017	Eta	2020	Ian	2022
Sandy	2012	Florence	2018	Iota	2020	Helene	2024
Matthew	2016	Dorian	2019	Ida	2021	Milton	2024

WEATHER

HOW TO MEASURE TORNADOES

The original **FUJITA SCALE** (or F Scale) was developed by Dr. Theodore Fujita to classify tornadoes based on wind damage. All tornadoes, and other severe local windstorms, were assigned a number according to the most intense damage caused by the storm. An enhanced F (EF) scale was implemented in the United States on February 1, 2007. The EF scale uses 3-second gust estimates based on a more detailed system for assessing damage, taking into account different building materials.

F SCALE		EF SCALE (U.S.)
F0 · 40–72 mph (64–116 km/h)	LIGHT DAMAGE	EF0 · 65–85 mph (105–137 km/h)
F1 · 73–112 mph (117–180 km/h)	MODERATE DAMAGE	EF1 · 86–110 mph (138–178 km/h)
F2 · 113–157 mph (181–253 km/h)	CONSIDERABLE DAMAGE	EF2 · 111–135 mph (179–218 km/h)
F3 · 158–207 mph (254–332 km/h)	SEVERE DAMAGE	EF3 · 136–165 mph (219–266 km/h)
F4 · 208–260 mph (333–419 km/h)	DEVASTATING DAMAGE	EF4 · 166–200 mph (267–322 km/h)
F5 · 261–318 mph (420–512 km/h)	INCREDIBLE DAMAGE	EF5 · over 200 mph (over 322 km/h)

Wind/Barometer Table

BAROMETER (REDUCED TO SEA LEVEL)	WIND DIRECTION	CHARACTER OF WEATHER INDICATED
30.00 to 30.20, and steady	WESTERLY	Fair, with slight changes in temperature, for 1 to 2 days
30.00 to 30.20, and rising rapidly	WESTERLY	Fair, followed within 2 days by warmer and rain
30.00 to 30.20, and falling rapidly	SOUTH TO EAST	Warmer, and rain within 24 hours
30.20 or above, and falling rapidly	SOUTH TO EAST	Warmer, and rain within 36 hours
30.20 or above, and falling rapidly	WEST TO NORTH	Cold and clear, quickly followed by warmer and rain
30.20 or above, and steady	VARIABLE	No early change
30.00 or below, and falling slowly	SOUTH TO EAST	Rain within 18 hours that will continue a day or two
30.00 or below, and falling rapidly	SOUTHEAST TO NORTHEAST	Rain, with high wind, followed within 2 days by clearing, colder
30.00 or below, and rising	SOUTH TO WEST	Clearing and colder within 12 hours
29.80 or below, and falling rapidly	SOUTH TO EAST	Severe storm of wind and rain imminent; in winter, snow or cold wave within 24 hours
29.80 or below, and falling rapidly	EAST TO NORTH	Severe northeast gales and heavy rain or snow, followed in winter by cold wave
29.80 or below, and rising rapidly	GOING TO WEST	Clearing and colder

NOTE: *A barometer should be adjusted to show equivalent sea-level pressure for the altitude at which it is to be used. A change of 100 feet in elevation will cause a decrease of 1/10 inch in the reading.*

WEATHER

WINDCHILL TABLE

As wind speed increases, your body loses heat more rapidly, making the air feel colder than it really is. The combination of cold temperature and high wind can create a cooling effect so severe that exposed flesh can freeze.

WIND SPEED (mph) \ TEMPERATURE (°F)	35	30	25	20	15	10	5	0	-5	-10	-15	-20	-25	-30	-35
Calm															
5	31	25	19	13	7	1	-5	-11	-16	-22	-28	-34	-40	-46	-52
10	27	21	15	9	3	-4	-10	-16	-22	-28	-35	-41	-47	-53	-59
15	25	19	13	6	0	-7	-13	-19	-26	-32	-39	-45	-51	-58	-64
20	24	17	11	4	-2	-9	-15	-22	-29	-35	-42	-48	-55	-61	-68
25	23	16	9	3	-4	-11	-17	-24	-31	-37	-44	-51	-58	-64	-71
30	22	15	8	1	-5	-12	-19	-26	-33	-39	-46	-53	-60	-67	-73
35	21	14	7	0	-7	-14	-21	-27	-34	-41	-48	-55	-62	-69	-76
40	20	13	6	-1	-8	-15	-22	-29	-36	-43	-50	-57	-64	-71	-78
45	19	12	5	-2	-9	-16	-23	-30	-37	-44	-51	-58	-65	-72	-79
50	19	12	4	-3	-10	-17	-24	-31	-38	-45	-52	-60	-67	-74	-81
55	18	11	4	-3	-11	-18	-25	-32	-39	-46	-54	-61	-68	-75	-82
60	17	10	3	-4	-11	-19	-26	-33	-40	-48	-55	-62	-69	-76	-84

FROSTBITE OCCURS IN 30 MINUTES   10 MINUTES   5 MINUTES

EXAMPLE: *When the temperature is 15°F and the wind speed is 30 miles per hour, the windchill, or how cold it feels, is –5°F. See a Celsius version of this table via Almanac.com/2026.*
–courtesy of National Weather Service

HOW TO MEASURE EARTHQUAKES

In 1979, seismologists developed a measurement of earthquake size called **MOMENT MAGNITUDE**. It is more accurate than the previously used Richter scale, which is precise only for earthquakes of a certain size and at a certain distance from a seismometer. All earthquakes can now be compared on the same magnitude scale.

MAGNITUDE	DESCRIPTION	EFFECT
LESS THAN 3	MICRO	GENERALLY NOT FELT
3–3.9	MINOR	OFTEN FELT, LITTLE DAMAGE
4–4.9	LIGHT	SHAKING, SOME DAMAGE
5–5.9	MODERATE	SLIGHT TO MAJOR DAMAGE
6–6.9	STRONG	DESTRUCTIVE
7–7.9	MAJOR	SERIOUS DAMAGE
8 OR MORE	GREAT	SEVERE DAMAGE

IN THE GARDEN

A GARDENER'S WORST PHOBIAS

NAME OF FEAR	OBJECT FEARED
Alliumphobia	Garlic
Anthophobia	Flowers
Apiphobia	Bees
Arachnophobia	Spiders
Botanophobia	Plants
Bufonophobia	Toads
Dendrophobia	Trees
Entomophobia	Insects
Lachanophobia	Vegetables
Mottephobia	Moths
Myrmecophobia	Ants
Ophidiophobia	Snakes
Ornithophobia	Birds
Ranidaphobia	Frogs
Rupophobia	Dirt
Scoleciphobia	Worms
Spheksophobia	Wasps

PLANTS FOR LAWNS

Choose varieties that suit your soil and your climate. All of these can withstand mowing and considerable foot traffic.

Ajuga or bugleweed (*Ajuga reptans*)
Corsican mint (*Mentha requienii*)
Dwarf cinquefoil (*Potentilla tabernaemontani*)
English pennyroyal (*Mentha pulegium*)
Green Irish moss (*Sagina subulata*)
Pearly everlasting (*Anaphalis margaritacea*)
Roman chamomile (*Chamaemelum nobile*)
Rupturewort (*Herniaria glabra*)
Speedwell (*Veronica officinalis*)
Stonecrop (*Sedum ternatum*)
Sweet violets (*Viola odorata* or *V. tricolor*)
Thyme (*Thymus serpyllum*)
White clover (*Trifolium repens*)
Wild strawberries (*Fragaria virginiana*)
Wintergreen or partridgeberry (*Mitchella repens*)

Lawn-Growing Tips

■ Test your soil: The pH balance should be 6.2 to 6.7; less than 6.0 puts your lawn at risk for fungal diseases. If the pH is too low, correct it with liming, best done in the fall.

■ The best time to apply fertilizer is just before a light rain.

■ If you put lime and fertilizer on your lawn, spread half of it as you walk north to south, the other half as you walk east to west to cut down on missed areas.

■ Any feeding of lawns in the fall should be done with a low-nitrogen, slow-acting fertilizer.

■ In areas of your lawn where tree roots compete with the grass, apply some extra fertilizer to benefit both.

■ Moss and sorrel in lawns usually means poor soil, poor aeration or drainage, or excessive acidity.

■ Control weeds by promoting healthy lawn growth with natural fertilizers in spring and early fall.

■ Raise the level of your lawn mower blades during the hot summer days. Taller grass resists drought better than short.

■ You can reduce mowing time by redesigning your lawn, reducing sharp corners, and adding sweeping curves.

■ During a drought, let the grass grow longer between mowings and reduce fertilizer.

■ Water your lawn early in the morning or in the evening.

Get growing via Almanac.com/2026.

IN THE GARDEN

Flowers and Herbs That Attract Butterflies

Allium	*Allium*
Aster	*Aster, Symphyotrichum*
Bee balm	*Monarda*
Butterfly bush	*Buddleia*
Catmint	*Nepeta*
Clove pink	*Dianthus*
Coreopsis	*Coreopsis*
Cornflower	*Centaurea*
Creeping thyme	*Thymus serpyllum*
Daylily	*Hemerocallis*
Dill	*Anethum graveolens*
False indigo	*Baptisia*
Fleabane	*Erigeron*
Floss flower	*Ageratum*
Globe thistle	*Echinops*
Goldenrod	*Solidago*
Helen's flower	*Helenium*
Hollyhock	*Alcea*
Honeysuckle	*Lonicera*
Lavender	*Lavandula*
Lilac	*Syringa*
Lupine	*Lupinus*
Lychnis	*Lychnis*
Mallow	*Malva*
Mealycup sage	*Salvia farinacea*
Milkweed	*Asclepias*
Mint	*Mentha*
Oregano	*Origanum vulgare*
Pansy	*Viola*
Parsley	*Petroselinum crispum*
Phlox	*Phlox*
Privet	*Ligustrum*
Purple coneflower	*Echinacea purpurea*
Rock cress	*Arabis*
Sea holly	*Eryngium*
Shasta daisy	*Leucanthemum*
Snapdragon	*Antirrhinum*
Stonecrop	*Hylotelephium, Sedum*
Sweet alyssum	*Lobularia*
Sweet marjoram	*Origanum majorana*
Sweet rocket	*Hesperis*
Verbena	*Verbena*
Zinnia	*Zinnia*

FLOWERS* THAT ATTRACT HUMMINGBIRDS

Beard tongue	*Penstemon*
Bee balm	*Monarda*
Butterfly bush	*Buddleia*
Catmint	*Nepeta*
Clove pink	*Dianthus*
Columbine	*Aquilegia*
Coral bells	*Heuchera*
Daylily	*Hemerocallis*
Desert candle	*Yucca*
Flag iris	*Iris*
Flowering tobacco	*Nicotiana alata*
Foxglove	*Digitalis*
Larkspur	*Delphinium*
Lily	*Lilium*
Lupine	*Lupinus*
Petunia	*Petunia*
Pincushion flower	*Scabiosa*
Red-hot poker	*Kniphofia*
Scarlet sage	*Salvia splendens*
Soapwort	*Saponaria*
Summer phlox	*Phlox paniculata*
Trumpet honeysuckle	*Lonicera sempervirens*
Verbena	*Verbena*
Weigela	*Weigela*

*NOTE: *Choose varieties in red and orange shades, if available.*

IN THE GARDEN

pH PREFERENCES OF TREES, SHRUBS, FLOWERS, AND VEGETABLES

An accurate soil test will indicate your soil pH and will specify the amount of lime or sulfur that is needed to bring it up or down to the appropriate level. A pH of 6.5 is just about right for most home gardens, since most plants thrive in the 6.0 to 7.0 (slightly acidic to neutral) range. Some plants (azaleas, blueberries) prefer more strongly acidic soil in the 4.0 to 6.0 range, while a few (asparagus, plums) do best in soil that is neutral to slightly alkaline. Acidic, or sour, soil (below 7.0) is counteracted by applying finely ground limestone, and alkaline, or sweet, soil (above 7.0) is treated with ground sulfur.

COMMON NAME	OPTIMUM pH RANGE	COMMON NAME	OPTIMUM pH RANGE	COMMON NAME	OPTIMUM pH RANGE
TREES AND SHRUBS		Bee balm	6.0–7.5	Snapdragon	5.5–7.0
Apple	5.0–6.5	Begonia	5.5–7.0	Sunflower	6.0–7.5
Azalea	4.5–6.0	Black-eyed Susan	5.5–7.0	Tulip	6.0–7.0
Beautybush	6.0–7.5	Bleeding heart	6.0–7.5	Zinnia	5.5–7.0
Birch	5.0–6.5	Canna	6.0–8.0		
Blackberry	5.0–6.0	Carnation	6.0–7.0	**VEGETABLES**	
Blueberry	4.0–5.0	Chrysanthemum	6.0–7.5	Asparagus	6.0–8.0
Boxwood	6.0–7.5	Clematis	5.5–7.0	Bean	6.0–7.5
Cherry, sour	6.0–7.0	Coleus	6.0–7.0	Beet	6.0–7.5
Crab apple	6.0–7.5	Coneflower, purple	5.0–7.5	Broccoli	6.0–7.0
Dogwood	5.0–7.0	Cosmos	5.0–8.0	Brussels sprout	6.0–7.5
Fir, balsam	5.0–6.0	Crocus	6.0–8.0	Cabbage	6.0–7.5
Hemlock	5.0–6.0	Daffodil	6.0–6.5	Carrot	5.5–7.0
Hydrangea, blue-flowered	4.5–5.5	Dahlia	6.0–7.5	Cauliflower	5.5–7.5
Hydrangea, pink-flowered	6.0–7.0	Daisy, Shasta	6.0–8.0	Celery	5.8–7.0
Juniper	5.0–6.0	Daylily	6.0–8.0	Chive	6.0–7.0
Laurel, mountain	4.5–6.0	Delphinium	6.0–7.5	Collard	6.5–7.5
Lemon	6.0–7.5	Foxglove	6.0–7.5	Corn	5.5–7.0
Lilac	6.0–7.0	Geranium	5.5–6.5	Cucumber	5.5–7.0
Maple, sugar	6.0–7.5	Gladiolus	5.0–7.0	Eggplant	6.0–7.0
Oak, white	5.0–6.5	Hibiscus	6.0–8.0	Garlic	5.5–8.0
Orange	6.0–7.5	Hollyhock	6.0–8.0	Kale	6.0–7.5
Peach	6.0–7.0	Hyacinth	6.5–7.5	Leek	6.0–8.0
Pear	6.0–7.5	Iris, blue flag	5.0–7.5	Lettuce	6.0–7.0
Pecan	6.4–8.0	Lily-of-the-valley	4.5–6.0	Okra	6.0–7.0
Plum	6.0–8.0	Lupine	5.0–6.5	Onion	6.0–7.0
Raspberry, red	5.5–7.0	Marigold	5.5–7.5	Pea	6.0–7.5
Rhododendron	4.5–6.0	Morning glory	6.0–7.5	Pepper, sweet	5.5–7.0
Willow	6.0–8.0	Narcissus, trumpet	5.5–6.5	Potato	4.8–6.5
		Nasturtium	5.5–7.5	Pumpkin	5.5–7.5
FLOWERS		Pansy	5.5–6.5	Radish	6.0–7.0
Alyssum	6.0–7.5	Peony	6.0–7.5	Spinach	6.0–7.5
Aster, New England	6.0–8.0	Petunia	6.0–7.5	Squash, crookneck	6.0–7.5
Baby's breath	6.0–7.0	Phlox, summer	6.0–8.0	Squash, Hubbard	5.5–7.0
Bachelor's button	6.0–7.5	Poppy, oriental	6.0–7.5	Swiss chard	6.0–7.0
		Rose, hybrid tea	5.5–7.0	Tomato	5.5–7.5
		Rose, rugosa	6.0–7.0	Watermelon	5.5–6.5

Get growing via Almanac.com/2026.

IN THE GARDEN

How to Rotate Crops

Crop rotation is the practice of planting annual vegetables with their botanical families. Each vegetable family rotates together; it is not necessary to grow every family or every plant in each family. The benefits of rotating crops include fewer pests and soilborne diseases, improved soil nutrition, and better soil structure. Failure to rotate vegetable crops eventually results in plants that fail to thrive and decreased harvest.

Here's how crop rotation works: In a single-crop plot, legumes (pea family) are planted in year 1, nightshade plants (tomatoes, etc.) in year 2, and gourds in year 3. In year 4, the cycle begins again. Alternatively, these three crops could be planted in three separate plots in year 1 and moved to the next plot in ensuing years. Additional families can be added. A simple plot plan keeps track of what goes where.

PLANT FAMILIES AND MEMBERS

Plants in the same family are genetically related and thus share similar characteristics (e.g., leaf appearance, tendrils for climbing).

CARROT, aka **PARSLEY** (Apiaceae, aka Umbelliferae): caraway, carrot*, celeriac, celery, chervil, coriander, dill, fennel, lovage, parsley, parsnip

GOOSEFOOT, aka **CHARD** (Chenopodiaceae): beet*, orache, quinoa, spinach, Swiss chard

GOURD, aka **SQUASH** (Cucurbitaceae): cucumber, gourd, melon, pumpkin, squash (summer and winter), watermelon

GRASS (Poaceae, aka Gramineae): sweet corn

MALLOW (Malvaceae): okra

MINT (Lamiaceae, aka Labiatae): basil, Chinese artichoke, oregano, rosemary, sage, summer savory, sweet marjoram

MORNING GLORY (Convolvulaceae): sweet potato

MUSTARD (Brassicaceae, aka Cruciferae): arugula, bok choy, broccoli, brussels sprouts, cabbage, cauliflower, collard, kale, kohlrabi, komatsuna, mizuna, mustard greens, radish*, rutabaga, turnip

NIGHTSHADE (Solanaceae): eggplant, pepper, potato, tomatillo, tomato

ONION (Amaryllidaceae*): chives, garlic, leek, onion, shallot

PEA (Fabaceae, aka Leguminosae): bush, kidney, lima, pole, and soy beans; lentil; pea; peanut

SUNFLOWER (Asteraceae, aka Compositae): artichoke (globe and Jerusalem), calendula, chamomile, endive, escarole, lettuce, radicchio, salsify, sunflower, tarragon

*These can be planted among any family.

IN THE GARDEN

SOWING VEGETABLE SEEDS

SOW OR PLANT IN COOL WEATHER	Beets, broccoli, brussels sprouts, cabbage, lettuce, onions, parsley, peas, radishes, spinach, Swiss chard, turnips
SOW OR PLANT IN WARM WEATHER	Beans, carrots, corn, cucumbers, eggplant, melons, okra, peppers, squashes, tomatoes
SOW OR PLANT FOR ONE CROP PER SEASON	Corn, eggplant, leeks, melons, peppers, potatoes, spinach (New Zealand), squashes, tomatoes
RESOW FOR ADDITIONAL CROPS	Beans, beets, cabbage, carrots, kohlrabi, lettuce, radishes, rutabagas, spinach, turnips

A Beginner's Vegetable Garden

The vegetables suggested below are common, easy-to-grow crops. Make 11 rows, 10 feet long, with at least 18 inches between them. Ideally, the rows should run north and south to take full advantage of the sun. This garden, planted as suggested, can feed a family of four for one summer, with a little extra for canning and freezing or giving away.

ROW
1. Zucchini (4 plants)
2. Tomatoes (5 plants, staked)
3. Peppers (6 plants)
4. Cabbage

ROW
5. Bush beans
6. Lettuce
7. Beets
8. Carrots
9. Swiss chard
10. Radishes
11. Marigolds (to discourage rabbits!)

SOIL FIXES

If you have **sandy** soil, amend with compost; humus; aged manure; sawdust with extra nitrogen; heavy, clay-rich soil.

If your soil contains a lot of **silt**, amend with coarse sand (not beach sand) or gravel and compost, or aged horse manure mixed with fresh straw.

If your soil is dense with **clay**, amend with coarse sand (not beach sand) and compost.

TO IMPROVE YOUR SOIL, ADD THE PROPER AMENDMENT(S) . . .

bark, ground: made from various tree barks; improves soil structure

compost: an excellent conditioner

leaf mold: decomposed leaves, which add nutrients and structure to soil

lime: raises the pH of acidic soil and helps to loosen clay soil

manure: best if composted; never add fresh ("hot") manure; is a good conditioner

coarse sand (not beach sand): improves drainage in clay soil

topsoil: usually used with another amendment; replaces existing soil

Get growing via Almanac.com/2026.

IN THE GARDEN

IMPORTANT TIMES TO . . .

	. . . FERTILIZE:	. . . WATER:
BEANS	After heavy bloom and set of pods	When flowers form and during pod-forming and picking
BEETS	At time of planting	Before soil gets bone-dry
BROCCOLI	3 weeks after transplanting	Continuously for 4 weeks after transplanting
BRUSSELS SPROUTS	3 weeks after transplanting	Continuously for 4 weeks after transplanting
CABBAGE	2 weeks after transplanting	Frequently in dry weather
CARROTS	5 to 6 weeks after sowing	Before soil gets bone-dry
CAULIFLOWER	3 to 4 weeks after transplanting	Frequently
CELERY	At time of transplanting, and after 2 months	Frequently
CORN	When 8 to 10 inches tall, and when first silk appears	When tassels form and when cobs swell
CUCUMBERS	1 week after bloom, and every 3 weeks thereafter	Frequently
LETTUCE	3 weeks after transplanting	Frequently
MELONS	1 week after bloom, and again 3 weeks later	Once a week
ONION SETS	At time of planting, and then every 2 weeks until bulbing begins	In early stage to get plants going
PARSNIPS	1 year before planting	Before soil gets bone-dry
PEAS	After heavy bloom and set of pods	When flowers form and during pod-forming and picking
PEPPERS	At time of planting, and after first fruit set	Need a steady supply
POTATO TUBERS	At bloom time or time of second hilling	When the size of marbles
PUMPKINS	Just before vines start to run, when plants are about 1 foot tall	1 inch of water per week; water deeply, especially during fruit set
RADISHES	Before spring planting	Need plentiful, consistent moisture
SPINACH	When plants are one-third grown	Frequently
SQUASHES, SUMMER & WINTER	When first blooms appear	Frequently
TOMATOES	When fruit are 1 inch in diameter, and then every 2 weeks	For 3 to 4 weeks after transplanting and when flowers and fruit form

IN THE GARDEN

A GUIDE TO HARVESTING AND STORING VEGETABLES

After a season of nurturing, your plants are finally producing harvestable vegetables. How do you know when your produce is ready to pick? What are the best ways to store your bounty? Here are your harvesting and storing tips.

VEGETABLE	HARVESTING	STORING
GREEN BEANS	Snap or snip when pods are tender and seeds are not fully developed	Place in a plastic bag or airtight container and refrigerate for 4 to 7 days; blanch, then freeze for up to 8 months
BEETS	Dig to remove when roots are 1 to 2 inches in diameter; cut to remove all but ½ inch of green tops; greens can also be cut and eaten	Refrigerate for 5 to 7 days; remove soil and bury in sand or sawdust in a cool, humid location for 3 to 6 months
BROCCOLI	Cut stem at 6 inches when green head buds are firm and tight	Refrigerate for 5 to 10 days; blanch, then freeze for up to 1 year
BRUSSELS SPROUTS	Cut from bottom of plant when sprouts are 1 inch in diameter	Place in a plastic bag and refrigerate for up to 1 week; blanch, then freeze for up to 6 months
CARROTS	Dig to remove at any desired size, up to 1 inch in diameter at top after first frost; cut to remove all but ½ inch of green tops	Place in a plastic bag and refrigerate for up to 1 month; store in sand or sawdust in a cool, humid location for 6 months
CUCUMBERS	Cut when green and firm and 6 to 8 inches in length	Place in a plastic bag and refrigerate or store in a cool location for 7 to 10 days

Get growing via Almanac.com/2026.

VEGETABLE	HARVESTING	STORING
EGGPLANT	Pick when skin is shiny and uniform in color and thumbnail creates indentation; cut to remove all but 1 inch of stem	Refrigerate for up to 1 week
GARLIC	Dig to remove when foliage yellows and falls over, but is not completely dry	Cure bulbs in a single layer in a dry location for 2 weeks; brush off dirt, remove tops and roots, and store in a cool, dry area for up to 6 months
ONIONS	Pull when tops are brown and fallen over; remove roots and cut tops to remove all but 1 to 2 inches	Cure in a dry location for 1 to 3 weeks; store in mesh bags or storage boxes in a cool, ventilated area for up to 4 months
PARSNIPS	Dig to remove following a few frosts but before ground freezes; cut leaves to remove all but 2 to 3 inches	Refrigerate in a plastic bag for at least 2 weeks; store in sand or sawdust in a cold, humid location for 4 to 6 months
PEAS	Pick when pods are still tender	Peak flavor is immediately after harvest, but can be refrigerated for 5 to 7 days; blanch, then freeze for up to 8 months
PEPPERS	Cut when fruit reaches desired size and color, removing all but 1 inch of stem	Place in a plastic bag and refrigerate or store in a cool location for 1 to 2 weeks; seed, cut, and freeze for up to 8 months
POTATOES	Dig to remove after most of foliage has died; handle carefully to avoid damage	Cure in a dry, humid location for up to 2 weeks; store in a cool, dark location for up to 6 months
RADISHES	Pull when 1 inch in diameter; cut off tops and tails	Wash and dry thoroughly; place in a plastic bag and refrigerate for up to 2 weeks
SUMMER SQUASHES	Collect when fruit is tender and 4 to 8 inches long; cut to remove all but 1 inch of stem	Place in a plastic bag and refrigerate for 7 to 10 days
TOMATOES	Pick when fruit is firm and the proper color (red, orange, yellow, etc.); ripen in a loosely sealed paper bag	Store in a cool, dry location for 5 to 7 days; do not refrigerate; freeze whole and cored (with or without peels), or sliced for up to 8 months
WINTER SQUASHES	Cut when vines are brown and stems drying, while rind is deep in color and hard; remove all but 1 inch of stem	Wash and then process in a diluted bleach solution; allow to thoroughly dry and then cure in warm, humid conditions for up to 10 days; store in a cool, dry location for 2 to 6 months, depending on variety

IN THE GARDEN

HOW TO GROW BULBS

SPRING-PLANTED BULBS

COMMON NAME	LATIN NAME	HARDINESS ZONE	SOIL	LIGHT*	SPACING (INCHES)
ALLIUM	*Allium*	3–10	Well-draining/moist	○	12
BEGONIA, TUBEROUS	*Begonia*	10–11	Well-draining/moist	◐●	12–15
BLAZING STAR/ GAYFEATHER	*Liatris*	7–10	Well-draining	○	6
CALADIUM	*Caladium*	10–11	Well-draining/moist	◐●	8–12
CALLA LILY	*Zantedeschia*	8–10	Well-draining/moist	○◐	8–24
CANNA	*Canna*	8–11	Well-draining/moist	○	12–24
CYCLAMEN	*Cyclamen*	7–9	Well-draining/moist	◐	4
DAHLIA	*Dahlia*	9–11	Well-draining/fertile	○	12–36
DAYLILY	*Hemerocallis*	3–10	Adaptable to most soils	○◐	12–24
FREESIA	*Freesia*	9–11	Well-draining/moist/sandy	○◐	2–4
GARDEN GLOXINIA	*Incarvillea*	4–8	Well-draining/moist	○	12
GLADIOLUS	*Gladiolus*	4–11	Well-draining/fertile	○◐	4–9
IRIS	*Iris*	3–10	Well-draining/sandy	○	3–6
LILY, ASIATIC/ORIENTAL	*Lilium*	3–8	Well-draining	○◐	8–12
PEACOCK FLOWER	*Tigridia*	8–10	Well-draining	○	5–6
SHAMROCK/SORREL	*Oxalis*	5–9	Well-draining	○◐	4–6
WINDFLOWER	*Anemone*	3–9	Well-draining/moist	○◐	3–6

FALL-PLANTED BULBS

COMMON NAME	LATIN NAME	HARDINESS ZONE	SOIL	LIGHT*	SPACING (INCHES)
BLUEBELL	*Hyacinthoides*	4–9	Well-draining/fertile	○◐	4
CHRISTMAS ROSE/ HELLEBORE	*Helleborus*	4–8	Neutral–alkaline	○◐	18
CROCUS	*Crocus*	3–8	Well-draining/moist/fertile	○◐	4
DAFFODIL	*Narcissus*	3–10	Well-draining/moist/fertile	○◐	6
FRITILLARY	*Fritillaria*	3–9	Well-draining/sandy	○◐	3
GLORY OF THE SNOW	*Chionodoxa*	3–9	Well-draining/moist	○◐	3
GRAPE HYACINTH	*Muscari*	4–10	Well-draining/moist/fertile	○◐	3–4
IRIS, BEARDED	*Iris*	3–9	Well-draining	○◐	4
IRIS, SIBERIAN	*Iris*	4–9	Well-draining	○◐	4
ORNAMENTAL ONION	*Allium*	3–10	Well-draining/moist/fertile	○	12
SNOWDROP	*Galanthus*	3–9	Well-draining/moist/fertile	○◐	3
SNOWFLAKE	*Leucojum*	5–9	Well-draining/moist/sandy	○◐	4
SPRING STARFLOWER	*Ipheion uniflorum*	6–9	Well-draining loam	○◐	3–6
STAR OF BETHLEHEM	*Ornithogalum*	5–10	Well-draining/moist	○◐	2–5
STRIPED SQUILL	*Puschkinia scilloides*	3–9	Well-draining	○◐	6
TULIP	*Tulipa*	4–8	Well-draining/fertile	○◐	3–6
WINTER ACONITE	*Eranthis*	4–9	Well-draining/moist/fertile	○◐	3

* ○ **FULL SUN**   ◐ **PARTIAL SHADE**   ● **FULL SHADE**

DEPTH (INCHES)	BLOOMING SEASON	HEIGHT (INCHES)	NOTES
3–4	Spring to summer	6–60	Usually pest-free; a great cut flower
1–2	Summer to fall	8–18	North of Zone 10, lift in fall
4	Summer to fall	8–20	An excellent flower for drying; north of Zone 7, lift in fall
2	Summer	8–24	North of Zone 10, lift in fall
1–4	Summer	24–36	Fragrant; north of Zone 8, lift in fall
Level	Summer	18–60	North of Zone 8, lift in fall
1–2	Spring to fall	3–12	Naturalizes well in warm areas; north of Zone 7, lift in fall
4–6	Late summer	12–60	North of Zone 9, lift in fall
2	Summer	12–36	Mulch in winter in Zones 3 to 6
2	Summer	12–24	Fragrant; can be grown outdoors in warm climates
3–4	Summer	6–20	Does well in woodland settings
3–6	Early summer to early fall	12–80	North of Zone 10, lift in fall
4	Spring to late summer	3–72	Divide and replant rhizomes every 2 to 5 years
4–6	Early summer	36	Fragrant; self-sows; requires excellent drainage
4	Summer	18–24	North of Zone 8, lift in fall
2	Summer	2–12	Plant in confined area to control
2	Early summer	3–18	North of Zone 6, lift in fall
3–4	Spring	8–20	Excellent for borders, rock gardens, and naturalizing
1–2	Spring	12	Hardy, but requires shelter from strong, cold winds
3	Early spring	5	Naturalizes well in grass
6	Early spring	14–24	Plant under shrubs or in a border
3	Midspring	6–30	Different species can be planted in rock gardens, woodland gardens, or borders
3	Spring	4–10	Self-sows easily; plant in rock gardens, raised beds, or under shrubs
2–3	Late winter to spring	6–12	Use as a border plant or in wildflower and rock gardens; self-sows easily
4	Early spring to early summer	3–48	Naturalizes well; a good cut flower
4	Early spring to midsummer	18–48	An excellent cut flower
3–4	Late spring to early summer	6–60	Usually pest-free; a great cut flower
3	Spring	6–12	Best when clustered and planted in an area that will not dry out in summer
4	Spring	6–18	Naturalizes well
3	Spring	4–6	Fragrant; naturalizes easily
4	Spring to summer	6–24	North of Zone 5, plant in spring, lift in fall
3	Spring	4–6	Naturalizes easily; makes an attractive edging
4–6	Early to late spring	8–30	Excellent for borders, rock gardens, and naturalizing
2–3	Late winter to spring	2–4	Self-sows and naturalizes easily

AROUND THE HOUSE

Substitutions for Common Ingredients

ITEM	QUANTITY	SUBSTITUTION
BAKING POWDER	1 teaspoon	¼ teaspoon baking soda plus ¼ teaspoon cornstarch plus ½ teaspoon cream of tartar
BUTTERMILK	1 cup	1 tablespoon lemon juice or vinegar plus milk to equal 1 cup; or 1 cup plain yogurt
CHOCOLATE, UNSWEETENED	1 ounce	3 tablespoons cocoa powder plus 1 tablespoon unsalted butter, shortening, or vegetable oil
CRACKER CRUMBS	¾ cup	1 cup dry bread crumbs; or 1 tablespoon quick-cooking oats (for thickening)
CREAM, HEAVY	1 cup	¾ cup milk plus ⅓ cup melted, unsalted butter (this will not whip)
CREAM, LIGHT	1 cup	⅞ cup milk plus 3 tablespoons melted, unsalted butter
CREAM, SOUR	1 cup	⅞ cup buttermilk or plain yogurt plus 3 tablespoons melted, unsalted butter
CREAM, WHIPPING	1 cup	⅔ cup well-chilled evaporated milk, whipped; or 1 cup nonfat dry milk powder whipped with 1 cup ice water
EGG	1 whole	2 yolks plus 1 tablespoon cold water; or 3 tablespoons vegetable oil plus 1 tablespoon water (for baking); or 2 to 3 tablespoons mayonnaise (for cakes)
EGG WHITE	1 white	2 teaspoons meringue powder plus 3 tablespoons water, combined
FLOUR, ALL-PURPOSE	1 cup	1 cup plus 3 tablespoons cake flour (not advised for cookies or quick breads); or 1 cup self-rising flour (omit baking powder and salt from recipe)
FLOUR, CAKE	1 cup	1 cup minus 3 tablespoons sifted all-purpose flour plus 3 tablespoons cornstarch
FLOUR, SELF-RISING	1 cup	1 cup all-purpose flour plus 1½ teaspoons baking powder plus ¼ teaspoon salt
HERBS, DRIED	1 teaspoon	1 tablespoon fresh, minced and packed
HONEY	1 cup	1¼ cups sugar plus ½ cup liquid called for in recipe (such as water or oil); or 1 cup pure maple syrup
KETCHUP	1 cup	1 cup tomato sauce plus ¼ cup sugar plus 3 tablespoons apple-cider vinegar plus ½ teaspoon salt plus pinch of ground cloves combined; or 1 cup chili sauce
LEMON JUICE	1 teaspoon	½ teaspoon vinegar
MAYONNAISE	1 cup	1 cup sour cream or plain yogurt; or 1 cup cottage cheese (puréed)
MILK, SKIM	1 cup	⅓ cup instant nonfat dry milk plus ¾ cup water

Get more home tips at Almanac.com.

ITEM	QUANTITY	SUBSTITUTION
MILK, TO SOUR	1 cup	1 tablespoon vinegar or lemon juice plus milk to equal 1 cup. Stir and let stand 5 minutes.
MILK, WHOLE	1 cup	½ cup evaporated whole milk plus ½ cup water; or ¾ cup 2 percent milk plus ¼ cup half-and-half
MOLASSES	1 cup	1 cup honey or dark corn syrup
MUSTARD, DRY	1 teaspoon	1 tablespoon prepared mustard less 1 teaspoon liquid from recipe
OAT BRAN	1 cup	1 cup wheat bran or rice bran or wheat germ
OATS, OLD-FASHIONED	1 cup	1 cup steel-cut Irish or Scotch oats
QUINOA	1 cup	1 cup millet or couscous (whole wheat cooks faster) or bulgur
SUGAR, DARK-BROWN	1 cup	1 cup brown sugar, packed; or 1 cup sugar plus 2 to 3 tablespoons molasses
SUGAR, GRANULATED	1 cup	1 cup firmly packed brown sugar; or 1¾ cups confectioners' sugar (makes baked goods less crisp); or 1 cup superfine sugar
SUGAR, LIGHT-BROWN	1 cup	1 cup sugar plus 1 to 2 tablespoons molasses; or ½ cup dark-brown sugar plus ½ cup sugar
SWEETENED CONDENSED MILK	1 can (14 ounces)	1 cup evaporated milk plus 1¼ cups sugar. Combine and heat until sugar dissolves.
VANILLA BEAN	1-inch bean	1 teaspoon vanilla extract
VINEGAR, APPLE-CIDER	—	malt, white-wine, or rice vinegar
VINEGAR, BALSAMIC	1 tablespoon	1 tablespoon red- or white-wine vinegar plus ½ teaspoon sugar
VINEGAR, RED-WINE	—	white-wine, sherry, champagne, or balsamic vinegar
VINEGAR, RICE	—	apple-cider, champagne, or white-wine vinegar
VINEGAR, WHITE-WINE	—	apple-cider, champagne, fruit (raspberry), rice, or red-wine vinegar
YEAST	1 cake (⅗ ounce)	1 package (¼ ounce) or 1 scant tablespoon active dried yeast
YOGURT, PLAIN	1 cup	1 cup sour cream (thicker; less tart) or buttermilk (thinner; use in baking, dressings, sauces)

AROUND THE HOUSE

Freezer Tips

Got extra veggies from your summer harvest? What about that ground beef you won't use before the sell-by date? You can freeze almost any food, but just remember that not all foods freeze well, and those frozen at peak quality will taste better when thawed. Here are a few freezing techniques to help get you started.

- Cool all cooked food thoroughly in the refrigerator before freezing.
- Use resealable plastic containers (not glass) or freezer bags.
- To prevent sticking, place items in a single layer on a baking sheet lined with parchment paper and freeze until solid. Then, place in plastic bags or resealable containers and freeze.
- Label containers or plastic bags with the name of the food, serving size, and date of freezing.
- Freeze in one or two portions so you thaw only what you need and avoid waste.
- Remove as much air as possible to cut down on the amount of freezer burn.
- To freeze items more quickly, place them directly against the side of the freezer.
- Allow extra space for liquids or foods with liquid to expand.

FREEZER STORAGE TIMES
(freezer temperature 0°F or colder)

PRODUCT	MONTHS IN FREEZER
FRESH MEAT	
Beef	6 to 12
Lamb	6 to 9
Veal	6 to 9
Pork	4 to 6
Ground beef, veal, lamb, pork	3 to 4
Frankfurters	1 to 2
Sausage, fresh pork	1 to 2
Cold cuts	Not recommended
FRESH POULTRY	
Chicken, turkey (whole)	12
Chicken, turkey (pieces)	6 to 9
Cornish game hen, game birds	6 to 9
Giblets	3 to 4
COOKED POULTRY	
Breaded, fried	4
Pieces, plain	4
Pieces covered with broth, gravy	6
FRESH FISH AND SEAFOOD	
Clams, mussels, oysters, scallops, shrimp	3 to 6
Fatty fish (bluefish, mackerel, perch, salmon)	2 to 3
Lean fish (flounder, haddock, sole)	6
FRESH FRUIT (PREPARED FOR FREEZING)	
All except those listed next	10 to 12
Avocados, bananas, plantains	3
Lemons, limes, oranges	4 to 6
FRESH VEGETABLES (PREPARED FOR FREEZING)	
Beans, beets, bok choy, broccoli, brussels sprouts, cabbage, carrots, cauliflower, celery, corn, greens, kohlrabi, leeks, mushrooms, okra, onions, peas, peppers, soybeans, spinach, summer squashes	10 to 12
Asparagus, rutabagas, turnips	8 to 10
Artichokes, eggplant	6 to 8
Tomatoes (overripe or sliced)	2
Bamboo shoots, cucumbers, endive, lettuce, radishes, watercress	Not recommended
CHEESE (except those listed below)	6
Cottage cheese, cream cheese, feta, goat, fresh mozzarella, Neufchâtel, Parmesan, processed cheese (opened)	Not recommended
DAIRY PRODUCTS	
Margarine (not diet)	12
Butter	6 to 9
Cream, half-and-half	4
Milk	3
Ice cream	1 to 2

Get more home tips at Almanac.com

AROUND THE HOUSE

WHEN TO REPLACE/CLEAN/RENEW COMMON HOUSEHOLD ITEMS

How long do everyday food products stay viable or safe after opening or using them? What are the recommended time frames for replacing or cleaning things inside and outside the home? Here are some guidelines for items found around the house.

ITEM	STATUS	STORAGE	DURATION	TIPS
Baking soda	Open	Pantry, cupboard	6 months	Put a little in bowl, add lemon juice or vinegar. If it fizzes, it's still suitable for baking.
Butter	Open / Open	Counter / Refrigerator	1 to 2 days / 1 to 2 months	Can turn rancid; refrigeration will extend life.
Jelly/jam	Open	Refrigerator	6 to 12 months	Replace if smell or color changes; mold may occur.
Mayonnaise	Open	Refrigerator	2 months	Throw away if discoloration or odor occurs.
Nut oils	Open	Pantry, cupboard	3 to 8 months	Store in a cool, dry place; refrigeration may extend life.
Olive/vegetable oil	Open	Pantry, cupboard	3 to 5 months	Store in a cool, dry place; refrigeration may extend life.
Peanut butter	Open / Open	Pantry, cupboard / Refrigerator	2 to 3 months / 6 to 9 months	Replace if rancid taste or smell occurs.
Red/white wine	Open	Refrigerator	2 to 5 days	Use a stopper for a tight seal.

ITEM	USE	STORAGE	REPLACE	TIPS
20-lb. propane tank	As needed	Outside	10 to 12 years	Cannot be refilled past date on tank; recertified tanks good for additional 5 years.
Bleach	As needed	Laundry area	6 to 12 months	Will begin to break down after 6 months.
Fire extinguisher	As needed	Kitchen, other	12 years	Check gauge monthly to ensure factory-recommended pressure level.
Gasoline for equipment	As needed	Shed, detached garage	3 to 6 months	Store in tightly closed container, away from heat sources and light.
Smoke alarms	Ongoing	Bedrooms, hallways	10 years	Test monthly to ensure proper function.
Sponges	Daily	Kitchen	1 to 2 weeks	To clean between replacements, soak in 1:10 bleach/warm water solution for 1 minute, microwave damp (if nonmetallic) for 1 minute, or run through dishwasher cycle.
Toothbrushes	Daily	Bathroom	3 to 4 months	Replace more often if bristles fray or when user(s) have been sick.

ITEM	USE	LOCATION	CLEAN	TIPS
Bird feeders	Daily	Outdoors	Twice a month	To avoid bacteria buildup, wash with soap and boiling water or diluted bleach solution; rinse and dry completely.
Chimney	Heating season	Furnace, fireplace	Once a year	Professional inspection will show if chimney sweep or maintenance is needed.
Dryer vent hose	Daily, weekly	Dryer to outdoor vent	Once a year	Clean lint trap after each use; if clothes do not dry properly, check/clean vent hose.
Gutters	During storms	Roofline	Twice a year	Leaves will be more prevalent during fall, so clean out more often.

AROUND THE HOUSE

PLASTICS

In your quest to go green, use this guide to use and sort plastic. The number, usually found with a triangle symbol on a container, indicates the type of resin used to produce the plastic. Visit **EARTH911.COM** for recycling information in your state.

NUMBER 1 • *PETE or PET (polyethylene terephthalate)*
IS USED IN . . . . microwavable food trays; salad dressing, soft drink, water, and juice bottles
STATUS . . . . hard to clean; absorbs bacteria and flavors; avoid reusing
IS RECYCLED TO MAKE . . . carpet, furniture, new containers, Polar fleece

NUMBER 2 • *HDPE (high-density polyethylene)*
IS USED IN . . . . household cleaner and shampoo bottles, milk jugs, cutting boards
STATUS . . . . transmits no known chemicals into food
IS RECYCLED TO MAKE . . . detergent bottles, fencing, floor tiles, pens

NUMBER 3 • *V or PVC (vinyl)*
IS USED IN . . . . clear food packaging, window frames, blister packs for medicine and retail packaging
STATUS . . . . is believed to contain phthalates that interfere with hormonal development; avoid reusing
IS RECYCLED TO MAKE . . . cables, mud flaps, paneling, roadway gutters

NUMBER 4 • *LDPE (low-density polyethylene)*
IS USED IN . . . . bread and shopping bags, carpet, clothing, furniture
STATUS . . . . transmits no known chemicals into food
IS RECYCLED TO MAKE . . . envelopes, floor tiles, lumber, trash can liners

NUMBER 5 • *PP (polypropylene)*
IS USED IN . . . . food storage containers, medicine and syrup bottles, drinking straws, yogurt tubs
STATUS . . . . transmits no known chemicals into food
IS RECYCLED TO MAKE . . . battery cables, brooms, ice scrapers, rakes

NUMBER 6 • *PS (polystyrene)*
IS USED IN . . . . disposable cups and plates, egg cartons, take-out containers
STATUS . . . . is believed to leach styrene, a possible human carcinogen, into food; avoid reusing
IS RECYCLED TO MAKE . . . foam packaging, insulation, light switch plates, rulers

NUMBER 7 • *Other (miscellaneous)*
IS USED IN . . . . 3- and 5-gallon water jugs, nylon, some food containers
STATUS . . . . contains bisphenol A, which has been linked to heart disease and obesity; avoid reusing
IS RECYCLED TO MAKE . . . . custom-made products

AROUND THE HOUSE

PRACTICAL USES FOR HOUSEHOLD INGREDIENTS

Baking soda, lemon juice, salt, and vinegar are kitchen staples. Did you know that there are other uses for these common ingredients? Keep these items stocked to help with housekeeping and to reduce your need for multiple costly cleaners.

BAKING SODA

- To soothe an insect bite/sting, apply a paste of baking soda and water.
- Clean toothbrushes by soaking them in a mixture of 2 tablespoons of baking soda and 1 cup of warm water for 15 minutes and then allowing them to air-dry.
- Remove gas and oil odors from clothing by allowing it to sit in a trash bag with baking soda for at least 24 hours prior to washing.
- Remove coffee stains from mugs and tomato sauce stains from plastic containers by wiping them with a damp sponge dipped in baking soda paste.
- To remove pesticides and/or dirt, wash fresh fruit and vegetables in a mixture of 2 teaspoons of baking soda and 2 cups of water.

LEMON

- To keep insects away while painting outdoors, add a few drops of lemon juice to house paint.
- Clean discolored kitchen utensils with a cloth dipped in lemon juice. Rinse with warm water.
- Freshen the air in your house by simmering a pot of sliced lemons and water on the stovetop.
- Dry out a poison ivy rash by applying lemon juice for about 15 minutes before rinsing off with cool water. Repeat as necessary.
- Lighten hair color by rinsing with a mixture of 1 part lemon juice and 2 parts water.

SALT

- Kill weeds in driveway cracks and between bricks and stones by pouring boiling salted water over them.
- To relieve a sore throat, gargle with warm saltwater (¼ teaspoon salt to 1 cup water).
- Sprinkle salt on carpets to dry muddy footprints. Allow it to sit for 15 minutes, then vacuum.
- Rub a paste of salt and olive oil over watermarks on wood with a sponge until removed.
- Revive kitchen sponges by soaking them in a saltwater solution (¼ cup salt per liter of water) overnight.

VINEGAR

- To loosen a bumper sticker, cover it for up to 5 minutes with a paper towel saturated in white vinegar. Slowly peel the sticker off and remove any bumper residue with a clean cloth wet with white vinegar.
- Run white vinegar through a brewing cycle to clean drip coffeemakers. Rinse thoroughly by running two brewing cycles with water before using.
- Apply white vinegar to disinfect wooden cutting boards.
- Clean tile grout by spraying it with diluted white vinegar. Leave for 10 minutes and then scrub.
- To deter ants, spray a solution of equal parts white vinegar and water on kitchen surfaces.

AROUND THE HOUSE

Planning for the Unexpected

Preparation is vital to safely navigating power outages, natural disasters, and weather-related situations. Gathering supplies and making a plan ahead of time will help your household to be ready for these or other unexpected emergencies.

- Can opener
- Duct tape
- Garbage bags
- Plastic tarp for a temporary shelter
- Blankets and/or sleeping bags
- Extra set of clothing for each person
- Towels
- Face masks
- Over-the-counter medications
- Extra keys for car and home
- Whistle

BUILD A KIT

Every home should have an emergency supply kit packed in lightweight, plastic storage containers located in an accessible area. Check kits every 6 months and replace supplies as needed.

Emergency kits should include:
- 1 gallon of water per person per day for at least 3 days
- Enough nonperishable foods to last at least 3 days, such as canned goods, peanut butter, granola bars, etc.
- One flashlight with fresh batteries for each person
- Battery-powered radio
- New, extra batteries of different sizes for items in your kit that require them
- A new first aid kit
- Personal hygiene items, such as toothbrushes and toothpaste, shampoo, and bodywash
- Hand soap and sanitizer
- Multi-purpose tool, scissors, and knife
- Matches and grill lighter

MAKE A PLAN

In the event of an emergency or evacuation, make sure to have a plan that everyone in the household knows. Discussing the plan two to three times a year is important so each household member knows what to do. Be sure to include these steps:
- Create a map that outlines the closest exit for each room.
- Choose two places to meet in case you get separated—one outside at a safe distance from your home in the event of a fire and another beyond your neighborhood if an evacuation is required.
- Practice your evacuation plan twice a year.
- Assign one household member to collect the emergency kit.
- Make an emergency contact card for each member of the household. Choose an out-of-area contact person that each member knows how to reach.
- If pets are in the home, decide how they will be cared for and who is responsible for their safety.

BE READY FOR OUTAGES

When the power goes out, many of life's necessities (and luxuries) will go away, so preparing for an outage that could last a few hours to a few days will help your household navigate the situation. In addition to readying your emergency supply kit, follow these tips during a power outage:

- Keep freezers and refrigerators closed. A refrigerator will keep food cold for about 4 hours. A full freezer will keep the temperature for about 48 hours. Use coolers with ice if necessary. Monitor temperatures with a thermometer. Throw out food if the temperature in the cooler is 40°F or higher.
- Have ice packs frozen in advance for use in coolers.
- Stockpile extra batteries and alternative power sources, such as a portable charger or power bank.
- Supply flashlights or lanterns with new batteries for every household member.
- Install carbon monoxide detectors with battery backup in central locations on every level of your home.
- Locate emergency heating and cooling centers near you.
- During winter, choose a south-facing room where all household members and pets can spend time together. Open shades during the day to allow heat from the Sun to warm up the room.

PREP YOUR RIDE

In the event you run out of gas, get stuck in a snowstorm, or are in an accident, you should always have these supplies in your car:

- Spare tire
- Jumper cables
- Tool kit
- Flashlight with extra batteries
- Reflective vest and reflective triangles
- Road flares
- A new first aid kit
- Nonperishable food items, such as nuts, granola bars, dried fruit
- Drinking water
- Fire extinguisher
- Duct tape
- Shovel
- Snow brush/ice scraper
- Extra clothing and jacket
- Blankets
- Sand and/or salt

MORE TIPS

- Sign up for emergency alerts in your area.
- Have cash on hand or in your emergency kit for times when credit/debit cards cannot be used.
- Make a plan for pets, including extra food, water dish, leash, collar, etc.
- For children, stockpile games, books, and a deck of cards.
- Regularly inspect gutters, roof, and overhanging tree branches to ensure they will hold up in a weather emergency.
- Keep important documents, such as birth certificates, social security cards, passports, insurance policies, etc., in one place where they will be easy to collect.

WORDS OF WISDOM

FOUNDING FODDER

For your reading pleasure in this 250th anniversary year of our Nation's founding, we glimpse into previous editions of our almanac published during U.S. anniversaries. The entries reproduced here are as they originally appeared.

200 YEARS AGO

APRIL 1826: To raise asparagus, the soil should be the best in your garden, moderately light and yielding. Open a trench three feet wide and 12 inches deep. The warmer the place the better. Fill the trench half full of good dung; sprinkle over the rich earth making it level, and then place roots upon it 8 or 9 inches apart. If you have not roots, then take seed and place them half that distance, and cover with rich earth. Roots will produce shoots fit to cut the 2d year, but seeds will require another year.

150 YEARS AGO

TO PATRONS 1876: 'Tis *a hundred years* this year since our fathers founded the Nation. Long live the Republic! And that she may live long, let her sons cherish *public and private* virtue. Put *good men* in office, and *keep them there during good behavior.*

JANUARY 1876: When the chores are all done, and the day's work is through, there will still be time to read and study some, and we might as well make up the mind to learn more, to do more, and to be more this year than we ever did or ever were before.

100 YEARS AGO

APRIL 1926: A ton of manure is actually worth just the value of the increased crop which it produces, minus the cost of handling; but as this value must vary with different crops, seasons, and soils there can be no set value for all conditions, yet an approximate value can be reached which will serve all practical purposes.

AUGUST 1926: Take the auto and part of the family (send the others later) to see what other farmers have done. . . . Some fields will look good and other fields will not appeal to you. Make the acquaintance of some of the owners. They will tell you what they did, perhaps what they ought to have done, and what they hope to do. The actual first hand experience of others, added to your own, produce education—the ability to solve both your problems and the problems of others.

50 YEARS AGO

MAY 1976: In this changing country world we may well find a profit from our forests. But this again depends on the knowledge and energy of the forest owner. For those of us who live in the country it must seem that with scrubby fields and scrubby half-grown forests, we have the worst of two worlds. Wildlife—particularly woodcock, grouse, and rabbits are increasingly scarce. Our problems and nature's are compounded.

NOVEMBER 1976: The old farmer may have confined his reading to the Bible, his State History, farm journals, and his Almanac. Today we have the compulsion to read everything. With so much to read, we have forgotten how to read selectively. We buy, or subscribe to, more magazines, more newsprint, more books than we can read—let alone enjoy. But of course, we don't *have* to read everything. . . . I wonder if the speed reader can ever again enjoy the quiet page.